The Guide to t
American Rev
In New Jersey

The Guide to the American Revolutionary War In New Jersey

Battles, Raids, and Skirmishes

Norman Desmarais

Busca, Inc.
Ithaca, New York

Busca, Inc.
P.O. Box 854
Ithaca, NY 14851
Ph: 607-546-4247
Fax: 607-546-4248
E-mail: info@buscainc.com
www.buscainc.com

BUSCA = SEARCH

First Edition

Printed in the United States of America

ISBN: 978-1-934934-04-3

Publisher's Cataloging-In-Publication Data
(Prepared by The Donohue Group, Inc.)

Desmarais, Norman.
    The guide to the American Revolutionary War in New Jersey : battles, raids and skirmishes / Norman Desmarais. -- 1st ed.

        p. : ill., maps ; cm. -- (Battlegrounds of freedom ; [4])

    Includes index.

    1. United States--History--Revolution, 1775-1783--Campaigns--New Jersey. 2. United States--History--Revolution, 1775-1783--Battlefields--New Jersey. 3. New Jersey--History, Military--18th century. I. Title. II. Series: Battlegrounds of freedom ; [4].

E230.5.N2 D47 2011
973.3/3

All state maps Copyright © 2011 DeLorme (www.delorme.com) Street Atlas USA®.
Reprinted with permission.

Photography: author unless otherwise noted

Composition: P.S. We Type ◆ Set ◆ Edit

This volume is part of the BATTLEGROUNDS OF FREEDOM series.

To the men and women of our armed forces who go in harm's way to preserve the freedoms our ancestors have secured for us.

CONTENTS

Please see the Busca website **www.buscainc.com** for more Resources on the volumes by Norman Desmarais including complete chronological and alphabetical lists of battles, raids, and skirmishes; a complete Bibliography for all sources used and cited in the creation of these volumes; and photos.

LIST OF ILLUSTRATIONS

ACKNOWLEDGMENTS

I would like to express my gratitude to Jack Montgomery, acquisitions librarian at the University of Western Kentucky, Bowling Green, for igniting the spark to write this book, for his encouragement through the project, and for introducing me to Connie Mills, the Kentucky Library Coordinator at the Kentucky Library and Museum who provided valuable assistance in locating primary sources for the Kentucky chapter. Michael Cooper, my publisher fanned the flame, nurtured the idea, and brought it to fruition.

I also wish to thank Providence College, my employer, for providing research and faculty development funds as well as time to pursue research. That research began with one sabbatical and extended beyond another. The staffs at the Phillips Memorial Library of Providence College and the other academic libraries in Rhode Island were very helpful in obtaining and providing much material. Amy Goggin, interlibrary loan librarian at Providence College, deserves special mention for her diligent efforts to obtain many obscure items which normally don't circulate, such as microforms.

Edward Ayres, Historian for the Jamestown-Yorktown Foundation, based at the Yorktown Victory Center in Yorktown, Virginia provided valuable assistance in locating Revolutionary War era maps. Michael Cobb, curator of the Hampton History Museum in Hampton, Virginia, graciously guided me through his museum collection—both the public display and the storage area and helped me locate sites in southern Virginia. Peggy Haile-McPhillips, City Historian at the Norfolk (Virginia) Public Library, helped greatly in identifying and locating places in the Norfolk area that had changed names and had long ago disappeared.

David Loiterstein, Marketing Manager at Readex, also deserves my gratitude. He arranged for me to review the Early American Imprints Series I: Evans, 1639–1800 and the Early American Newspapers Series I, 1690–1876 and Series II, 1758–1900. The review periods coincided with important stages in my research. This undoubtedly made for better, more thorough, reviews; and it provided me with access to a wealth of primary sources that opened new avenues of research.

The members of the Brigade of the American Revolution (B.A.R.), the Continental Line, and the British Brigade generously give of themselves to help re-create the era of the American War for Independence. Some of these people work at musea or at historical sites. Some are members of their town historical societies or even historians for their city or town. Many are amateur historians who know a great deal about the Revolutionary War in their area. They provided enormous insight into events and the location of sites. Special thanks go to Bob Winowitch and David Clemens who guided me around Long Island to ensure that I visited all the relevant sites there. They also provided historical material and referred me to important sources for further information.

Other B.A.R. members, including Reinhard Batcher III, Todd Braisted, Todd Harburn, Thomas F. Kehr, Lawrence McDonald, Alan Morrison, Thaddeus J. Weaver, and Vivian Leigh Stevens read portions of the manuscript, suggested corrections and/or identified sources of additional information.

Many of the photographs were taken at various re-enactments. Without the efforts of the members of the B.A.R., these photos would not have been possible. Marshall Sloat,

Scott Dermond, Daniel O'Connell, Todd Harburn, Paul Bazin, and Deborah Mulligan deserve credit for providing additional photographs.

There's a certain serendipity to research. During the 225th anniversary re-enactment of the march to Yorktown, Virginia, as the troops crossed the Hudson River in whale boats, I overheard B.A.R. member Daniel Hess talking about an engagement in which one of his ancestors had fought. I had been trying to locate documentation for that event; so I asked him about it after disembarking. He later sent me a copy of his ancestor's pension application which not only described the event which I had been trying to document but also identified two other events unknown to me.

DeLorme's Street Atlas USA software was very valuable in creating and annotating all the maps. GPS devices are useful for locating known places with addresses. They are not so useful for getting to a general location such as a particular hill or field. Maps are more useful for this purpose; but it takes a specially trained eye to identify changes in terrain that may cover earthworks or fortifications. Marshall Sloat has such an eye and I am grateful to him for accompanying me on some research trips, both as a companion and navigator. He helped me locate landmarks, monuments, and other physical features that would elude the common person. He also helped document the visits with photographs.

I wish to extend special thanks to my wife, Barbara, for her patience and support during the long periods of research and writing. She also accompanied me on many research trips and read maps and gave me directions as we drove to sites. She visited more forts and battlefields than she cares to remember.

Mark Hurwitz proofread the entire text and provided valuable feedback and suggestions. He also wrote the foreword. June Fritchman kindly offered some help with corrections and revisions of prior manuscripts in this series.

FOREWORD

by
Mark Hurwitz
Commander
Brigade of the American Revolution

To paraphrase Historian Geoffrey C. Ward, "the American War for Independence was fought from the walls of Quebec to the swamps of Florida, from Boston, to the Mississippi River." Now, if a shot was fired in anger, Norman Desmarais has documented it in this landmark study and guide, *The Guide to the American Revolutionary War.* It is a worthy successor to his *Battlegrounds of Freedom* (2005).

This comprehensive guide to the famous and unknown sites is groundbreaking. Beyond Lexington, Concord, Trenton, Brandywine, Saratoga, Monmouth, and Yorktown, Norman has fretted out the smaller actions and skirmishes which make up the eight year conflict, 1775–1783. Amazingly, Norman has found sites where settlers were scalped on the frontier to ships exchanging cannon fire on the high seas.

Norman Desmarais's passion for history comes as no surprise to me. After corresponding with Mr. Desmarais on an earlier multimedia CD-ROM project (*The American Revolution.*—American Journey: History in Your Hands series.—Woodbridge, CT: Primary Source Media, 1996), I finally got to meet him in November, 1995, when he attended a Brigade of the American Revolution (B.A.R.) event at Fort Lee Historic Park, Fort Lee, NJ. At that time, I had the opportunity to introduce him to Carl Becker, Commander of the 2nd Rhode Island Regiment, from his native state. Carl recruited him on the spot, and Norman, the academic historian, began his career as a re-enactor.

Becoming a "living historian" allows one to have laboratory to work in, wearing the uniforms, feeling the sweat, handling the weapons, experiencing the linear tactics, hearing the field music, smelling the smoke, which gives real perspective to the study of this period of history. This experience even goes beyond the "Staff Rides" of historic battlefields that the U.S. Army conducts with its officers.

The B.A.R. and the 2nd R.I. Regiment gave Norman the opportunity to visit many of the historic battle sites and get to see them "from the inside" and with the eye of a common soldier. This travel fueled his love for research and launched his encyclopedic study of Revolutionary War battle sites covering all of North America.

As a re-enactor, I have been studying the American War of Independence for nearly 35 years. Reading Desmarais's manuscript, I made discoveries both near and far.

- ◆ Being brought up and currently residing in my hometown of Springfield, NJ, I knew of the famous Battle of Springfield, June 23rd, 1780. Norman's research uncovered the following precursor, among many other actions there: "The militia killed and wounded 8 or 10 Waldeckers near Springfield on Sunday morning, January 19, 1777. They captured the rest of the party, 39 or 40, including 2 officers without suffering any casualties." (*The Pennsylvania Evening Post,* January 23, 1777)
- ◆ Meanwhile he found, west of the Mississippi: "St. Louis, Missouri—A small marker at 4th & Walnut Streets in downtown St. Louis which commemorates

the action that occurred on May 26, 1780." Desmarais's detailed entry then illuminates this unique action.

♦ Then at the end of the War for Independence, Savage Point, GA (Savage Point is located at a bend in the Ogeechee River at Richmond Hill State Park.): "Gen. Wayne suffered 5 men and horses killed and 8 wounded. He captured a British standard, 127 horses, and a number of packs." (*The Pennsylvania Packet or the General Advertiser.* 11:924 (August 15, 1782) p. 3)

I hope that readers can use this guide to find for themselves that history truly "happened here" as they travel the breadth of America and Canada.

PREFACE

The Guide to the American Revolutionary War in New Jersey: Battles, Raids, and Skirmishes is the third volume of a multi-volume geographic history of the American War for Independence. The idea for the project came at a re-enactment of a 225th anniversary event when I overheard some of my fellow interpreters commenting about the several events on the calendar that summer that they knew nothing about. There had been no guidebooks published about the Revolutionary War since the nation's bicentennial in 1975. Moreover, those guidebooks and most of the history textbooks only cover the major, better known battles such as Lexington and Concord, Bunker Hill, Trenton and Princeton, Saratoga, Camden, Guilford Courthouse, and Yorktown.

Battlegrounds of Freedom: A Historical Guide to the Battlefields of the War of American Independence[1] served the purpose of an overview. It covered all the major battles and several of the minor ones, along with the winter encampments at Morristown and Valley Forge. It also included a chapter on re-enacting to make it distinctive from other guidebooks. The success of that volume encouraged me to continue the project.

This continuation of the *Battlegrounds of Freedom* series covers the battles and, much more specifically, the raids and skirmishes of the Revolutionary War, many of which do not get covered even in the most detailed history books. The series intends to provide comprehensive, if not exhaustive, coverage of the military engagements of the American War for Independence. It also aims to serve as a guide to the sites and the military engagements. It does not intend to cover specifically naval battles; but it does include naval actions in which one of the parties was land-based. British ships fired frequently on shore installations, ship-building industries, towns, houses, or troops on land. Such actions usually provoked a hostile response, even if a weak one. These minor clashes also illustrate the dangers faced by coastal residents and by troops moving within sight of enemy ships. Actions on inland lakes or bays are considered along with land actions as are attacks on enemy watering parties or other landing parties.

The work also covers engagements between French or Spanish troops and Crown forces as well as raids by Native Americans instigated or led either by British officers and agents or by Congressional forces. It does not attempt to cover raids on the cabins of western settlers that would have occurred regardless of the war, even though the residents retaliated.

Francis B. Heitman's *Historical Register of Officers of the Continental Army during the War of the Revolution, April 1775 to December 1783*[2] provides an alphabetical list of 420 engagements. This list seems to have been adopted as the U.S. Army's official list of battles and actions. Howard Henry Peckham's *The Toll of Independence: Engagements & Battle Casualties of the American Revolution*[3] expands this list to 1,330 military engagements and 220 naval engagements. He gives a brief description of the actions arranged chronologically, but his concern is primarily to tally the casualties. My research started with Peckham's work for the list of engagements, as his is comparatively the most extensive.

The multiple *Guide to the American Revolutionary War* volumes more than double the number of engagements (more than 3,000) found in Peckham. They correct some of the entries and provide documentary references. The lack of primary source materials makes some actions very difficult to discover and document. The problem is most evident in "neutral territory," such as Elizabethtown, New Jersey, and Staten Island, New York, where conflict pretty much became part of everyday life. Sometimes, military actions occurred in several places during the same expedition or as part of a multi-pronged effort. Rather than repeat a narrative in several different places, we refer the reader to the main or a related account through *See* and *See also* references. However, each volume of the series is intended to be self-contained as much as possible with respect to the others.

Mark Mayo Boatner's *Encyclopedia of the American Revolution*[4] and his *Landmarks of the American Revolution: A Guide to Locating and Knowing What Happened at the Sites of Independence*[5] have long been considered the Bible for Revolutionary War aficionados and re-enactors. These works appeared in a new edition in 2007.[6] This is an excellent source to begin research on the Revolutionary War together with *The Encyclopedia of the American Revolutionary War: A Political, Social, and Military History.*[7]

Each volume in the *Battlegrounds of Freedom* series covers its respective states affected by the war and each location where an engagement occurred. It follows a hybrid geographical/chronological approach to accommodate various audiences: readers interested in American history, re-enactors, tourists, and visitors. The states are arranged from north to south and east to west. Within each state, the engagements appear chronologically. Locations with multiple engagements also appear chronologically so readers can follow the text as a historical sequence or "story" of a site before proceeding to the next one. For example, the treatment of the events at Fort Lee covers engagements dating from October 1776 through May 1781 before proceeding to the events at Leonia and Englewood (English Neighborhood) from October 1776 through March 1783. Cross references have been added as necessary.

The text identifies the location of the sites as best as can be determined, provides the historical background to understand what happened there, indicates what the visitor can expect to see there, and identifies any interpretive aids. It is not meant to replace the guides produced for specific sites and available at visitor centers. These guides usually provide more details about the features of a particular site. Also, monographs devoted to specific engagements or campaigns will be more detailed than what we can present here.

Strategic Objectives

The presence of large numbers of troops in an area gave residents cause for concern. The soldiers were always short of food and constantly searching for provisions. It took a lot of food to feed an army. While troops were allotted daily rations, they rarely received their full allocation.

A soldier's typical weekly ration would consist of:
+ 7 pounds of beef or 4 pounds of pork
+ 7 pounds of bread or flour sufficient to bake it
+ 3 pints of peas or beans
+ ½ pound of rice
+ ¼ pound of butter[8]

This would translate to the following weekly rations for an army of 1,000 men:
+ 3½ tons of beef or 2 tons of pork
+ 3½ tons of bread or flour sufficient to bake it
+ 94 bushels of peas or beans
+ 1¾ tons of rice
+ 250 pounds of butter

The threat of a foraging expedition caused residents to hide their cattle and the expedition usually elicited an attack from the enemy. As one side tried to obtain food and supplies, the other tried to prevent them from doing so or to re-capture the stolen goods along with the enemy's baggage and supplies. While most of these actions were militarily insignificant, they often had the effect of reducing both forces. Crown forces were harder to replace because they usually had to come from overseas.

Military objectives not only included the capture of enemy forts, strongholds, and armies but also the control of important crossroads, rivers, and ferries. The rivers were the 18th-century highways and made travel and transportation much quicker than the unpaved roads. Controlling these strategic points either facilitated or blocked troop movements and supply lines.

Nomenclature

The two sides in the American War for Independence are generally referred to as the British and the Americans. However, this is a gross oversimplification. While it is a convenient way to refer to both sides, it is often inaccurate, particularly when discussing engagements in the South where most of the actions were between militia units or armed mobs with very few, if any, regular soldiers. For example, Major Patrick Ferguson was the only British soldier at the Battle of Kings Mountain (South Carolina). Many actions in the South seem to have been occasions for people to settle grudges with their neighbors in feuds that resemble that between the Hatfields and the McCoys. In a sense, the war in the South was very much a civil war. In other areas, it took on the nature of a world war.

Moreover, the provincials were British citizens—at least until they declared their independence on July 4, 1776. Prior to that date, the provincials believed their grievances were with Parliament and not the King. Most of the citizens did not favor independence but rather hoped for redress of their grievances and the re-establishment of relations with Parliament. However, when King George III sided with Parliament and declared the colonies in rebellion on August 23, 1775, the provincials realized that their hopes were dashed. After the news reached the colonies on October 31, 1775, they began to see independence as their only recourse.

The Declaration of Independence made a definite break between England and her American colonies; but it took a while for those ideas to become widely accepted. In fact, it took 18 months after the outbreak of the war to enunciate that objective; and it took eight years to win the war that secured the independence of the United States of America. Even though England officially recognized the new country with the signing of the Treaty of Paris in 1783, it often continued to act as though it still controlled the colonies. This was one of the factors that led to the War of 1812.

While the provincials called themselves Americans, to refer only to those who favored independence as Americans is too broad, as they were less than a majority of the population. Although all the provincials were British citizens until the signing of Declaration of Independence and their effective independence at the end of the war, to refer to them as Americans confuses a political position with hegemony. That would be comparable to referring to Republicans or Democrats as Americans, implying that the other party is not American. Similarly, to refer to them as Patriots implies that those who remained loyal to the King were less patriotic when they fought to maintain life as they knew it.

Consequently, we refer to the supporters of independence as Rebels, Whigs, or Congressional troops. We also distinguish between the local militias and the regular soldiers of the Continental Army ("Continentals") as narratives allow further distinction. We also refer to Allied forces to designate joint efforts by Congressional forces and their foreign allies, primarily French and Spanish.

Similarly, the "British" armies were more complex than just English troops. They certainly consisted of Irish, Scot, and Welsh troops. We sometimes refer to them by regiment, e.g. 71st Highlanders, Black Watch, Royal Welch Fusiliers, when individual regiments are prominent in an engagement. They are also referred to generically as Regulars or Redcoats. (Some derogatory references call them lobsterbacks or bloodybacks because of the flesh wounds from whipping—a common form of punishment at the time.)

While British troops are often called Redcoats, not all wore red coats. The artillerymen wore dark blue coats. While some of the dragoons wore red, others such as Tarleton's Legion, wore green coats. There are instances where the two sides confused each other because of the similarity of the coats. For example, Major General Henry "Light-Horse Harry" Lee (1756–1818) and his legion tried to surprise Lieutenant Colonel Banastre Tarleton (1744–1833) on the morning of February 25, 1781. The front of Lee's Legion encountered two mounted Loyalists who mistook them for Tarleton's Legion. The Loyalists were taken to General Lee who took advantage of their mistake by posing as Tarleton. He learned that Colonel John Pyle had recruited about 400 Loyalists and that they were on their way to join Tarleton. Lee and his men continued the ruse, surrounded the Loyalists, and captured them all, depriving General Charles Cornwallis of badly needed troops at Yorktown.

Loyalist troops were issued both red and green uniforms with a wide variety of facings. Those who wore the green coats were sometimes referred to as Green Coats or simply as the Greens. Some authors refer to the Loyalists as Tories, a term which has taken on derogatory significance.

Moreover, King George III, who was of German origin, arranged to reinforce his armies with large numbers of German troops. They wore coats of various shades of blue, as well as green with red facings. Many of these soldiers came from the provinces of Hesse Hanau and Hesse Kassel and became known as Hessians. Other regiments were known by their provinces of origin (e.g., Braunschweiger or Brunswick and Waldeck) or by the name of their commander (von Lossberg, von Donop, etc.).

We use the terms Crown forces, King's troops, Royal Navy to refer to these combined forces or the regiment name, commanding officer, or group designation (e.g. Hessians, Loyalists) to be more specific.

People of color fought on both sides. We use the currently politically correct terminology of African Americans, even though not all of them came from Africa, and Native Americans as the generic terms. We also use the specific tribal name, if known: Iroquois, Mohawk, Oneida, Cherokee, etc. Mulattoes referred to people of mixed race. Quotations retain the terminology used by the original writer.

The Native American tribes tended to support the Crown because they realized that the settlers coveted their land and presented a greater threat than the British Army. Great Britain had fewer troops in the West (west of the Appalachians) than in the East (along the East Coast and east of the Appalachians), so it needed their support. More than 1,200 Delawares, Shawnees, and Mingoes lived in the Ohio valley. North of them, 300 Wyandots, Hurons, and 600 Ottawas and thousands of Chippewas inhabited southern Michigan and the shores of Lake Erie. Several hundred Potawatomis extended toward the southern end of Lake Michigan. The area north and east of Fort Pitt was occupied by the Senecas, and several hundred Miamis lived along the Maumeee and upper Wabash rivers. The Weas, Piankeshaws, Kickapoos, and other tribes settled on the Wabash and west toward the Mississippi, while an unknown number of Foxes, Sauks, and Mascoutens lived beyond the Great Lakes.

The Native American tribes were unreliable and not great assets as combatants. Sometimes, they were even a liability. For example, the murder of Jane McCrea by her Native American escorts during the Saratoga campaign brought new recruits to the Congressional forces and deterred Loyalists from actively supporting the Crown troops. British commanders often found it impossible to determine whether the Native Americans would fight and for how long. When they did fight, they usually did so in small groups and for limited periods. They were also often divided by rivalries among themselves, easily frightened by any show of strength, and usually unwilling to leave their families for long campaigns. Without the support of the Native Americans, however, Crown forces had no hope of controlling the West. The Crown forces provided the tribes with gifts every year to insure their continued support. These gifts included a large supply of ammunition and clothing as well as gifts for the chief warriors.[9]

Nobody knows how many provincials remained loyal to King George III during the American War for Independence. Many history books credit John Adams with estimating that one-third of the population favored the Revolution, one-third were against it, and another third leaned to whichever side happened to control the area. The quotation reads:

> I should say that full one-third were averse to the revolution. These, retaining that overweening fondness, in which they had been educated, for the English, could not cordially like the French; indeed, they most heartily detested them. An opposite third conceived a hatred of the English, and gave themselves up to an enthusiastic gratitude to France. The middle third, composed principally of the yeomanry, the soundest part of the nation, and always averse to war, were rather lukewarm both to England and France.[10]

On another occasion, Mr. Adams noted that the colonies had been nearly "unanimous" in their opposition to the Stamp Act in 1765 but, by 1775, the British had "seduced and deluded nearly one third of the people of the colonies."[11]

In the first quotation, Ray Raphael[12] notes that Adams was writing about the political sentiments of Americans toward the conflict between England and France in 1797; but the two quotations somehow blended together in popular historiography to refer to the American War for Independence. So Adams has become the definitive contemporary source on the political allegiance of the period.

Conventions and Parts of This Book

Cognizant that one may begin a tour anywhere, the first occurrence of a person's name in a section identifies him or her as completely as possible with the full form of the name with birth and death dates, if known. Some readers will probably find this awkward or cumbersome as they read several sections. We hope that those who consult a specific section will find this helpful.

Most chapters begin with a map of the sites in that state to facilitate orientation, and additional maps face the beginning of their respective sections. Some chapters with many actions are subdivided north to south and east to west, and these divisions are reflected with references to their respective maps. These maps have pointers to engagement locations and are printed on regular paper like the photos.

Engagements are then listed chronologically within their subdivisions along with the corresponding map. Locations with multiple engagements group those events in chronological order under the same heading to provide a historical sequence or "story" of a site before proceeding to the next one. Cross references have been added as necessary.

Each site begins with the name of the city or town (or the most commonly known name of the engagement), and the name (and alternate names) of the battle or action. The location names are followed by the dates, in parentheses, of significant actions discussed in the text. Specially formatted text identifies the location of the site, indicates what the visitor can expect to see, and identifies any interpretive aids. Historical background to understand what happened at a site follows. In any case, this book does not mean to replace more-detailed tourist guides for specific sites that are available at visitor centers.

Events are marked with a bullet character (★) for easy identification and to dispel confusion.

Travelers should take care to map their route for most efficient travel as many sites are not along main roads. Sometimes, one must backtrack to visit a place thoroughly. Travelers should also be aware that some locations in a particular state may be farther than other locations in a neighboring state. Consulting maps allows the visitor to proceed from one location to another with the least amount of backtracking. It also offers options for side trips as desired. Consult the maps and the appendices at the publisher's web site (**www.buscainc.com**) to see how battle sites are grouped and keyed to major cities or locations.

One of the appendices gives a chronological list of battles, actions, and skirmishes. History books often present events in purely chronological order. However, that is not a good approach for a guidebook to follow, as events can occur simultaneously great distances apart. For example, the powder alarm in Williamsburg, Virginia occurred on the same day as the battles of Lexington and Concord in Massachusetts. The web site also features a comprehensive state-by-state alphabetical list of locations where actions (battles, raids, or skirmishes) took place.

Other books take a thematic approach, covering campaigns or specific themes like the war on the frontier. This technique, while more focused, often ignores information relevant to a site that properly belongs to another theme. For example, a theme covering Major General John Burgoyne's (1722–1792) campaign of 1777 may not cover the capture of Fort Ticonderoga in 1775 or its role in the Seven Years War (also known as the French and Indian War).

The many photographs, with descriptive captions and keyed to the text, are important for identifying details of historic buildings, monuments, battlefields, and equipment. Many of the photos are of battle and event re-enactments. All photos, except otherwise identified, are by the author. Full-color photos of some of the images in this and other volumes are on the publisher's web site (**www.buscainc.com**).

Another feature that modern readers and visitors will find useful are URLs for web sites of various parks and tourist organizations. These URLs are correlated with various battle sites and sometimes events. Visitors may want to consult these web sites ahead of time for important, updated information on special events, hours, fees, etc. These URLs were active and accurate at the time this book went to press.

The Glossary provides definitions for some 18th-century military and historical terms. There are also scholarly reference Notes for sources used in this book and an

Index. The full Bibliography of the sources consulted for the *Battlegrounds of Freedom* series is on the publisher's web site (**www.buscainc.com**).

Most of the sites described in this book are reconstructions or restorations. Many buildings were damaged during the War for Independence or fell into disrepair over the years. They were refurbished, for the most part, for the nation's bicentennial in 1975–1976. Battlefield fortifications were sometimes destroyed after a battle so they could not be re-used by the enemy at a later time. For example, the hornworks and siege trenches at Yorktown, Virginia were destroyed after the surrender of General Charles Cornwallis so the Crown forces could not re-use them for a subsequent assault. They were, however, rebuilt and used again during the War of Rebellion (Civil War). There are many houses and structures still standing that demonstrate what life was like in the 18th century. Only those related to the battles are covered.

Many of the sites have been obliterated by urban development and have nothing to see or visit. Houses and other construction have supplanted them. One battlefield is covered by a shopping mall; another has been submerged under a man-made lake; others were destroyed by high-rise apartment or office buildings. Many are remembered only with a roadside marker. Some don't even have that.

Many sites have little importance to the outcome of the war. Some actions were mere skirmishes or raids lasting only a few minutes. For example, some actions consisted of a single volley. After one of the forces fired, it fled. Yet, some important events, such as the capture of Fort Kaskaskia by George Rogers Clark in Illinois and the capture of Fort Ticonderoga by Benedict Arnold, Ethan Allen, and the Green Mountain Boys were effected without firing a single shot. The battle at Black Mingo Creek, South Carolina lasted only 15 minutes. Other engagements, particularly those involving Lieutenant Colonel Francis Marion, known as the Swamp Fox, were fought in the swamps of South Carolina and are hard to find.

Some sites remain undeveloped and virtually ignored. This is not necessarily bad. While erosion, neglect, and plant or tree growth slowly undermine earthworks, they do significantly less damage than the rapid deterioration resulting from bikers and walkers.

One cannot easily cover all the sites of the American War for Independence. However, one can visit all the sites and events that affected the outcome of the war. One can also visit enough locally significant spots to get an understanding of what the war was like for the people of that region. This book tries to cover the extant battle sites and hopes to serve as a companion on the voyage of discovery.

Norman Desmarais
normd@providence.edu

Introduction

Colonial New Jersey was a rural society in the 18th century. The many farms and fertile fields provided excellent opportunities for forage for the four armies (Continental, British, German, and Loyalist) operating in the colony during the American War for Independence. They made severe demands on the land and the people. The proximity of two or more of these armies for extended periods of time, such as winter encampments, compounded the situation. There are still many farms operating in the state today.

New Jersey had the largest and most active Loyalist population of all the thirteen colonies. Many Loyalists tried to convince their fellow countrymen to remain loyal to the King, despite the severe taxes and restrictions on colonial trade. Whigs, on the other hand, thought that independence from Great Britain was the only way to secure their political and religious freedoms.

A group of Whigs imitated their counterparts in Boston, Massachusetts in protesting the tax on tea in 1774. They dressed as Native Americans and burned a supply of British tea stored aboard a ship at Greenwich, near Salem. The event was called the Greenwich Tea Burning.

Southern New Jersey, generally known as West Jersey saw an increase in local hatred between Whigs, Loyalists and neutrals while the British occupied Philadelphia, Pennsylvania in 1777–1778. Bandits of various types, most notably the "Pine-Banditti" so-called because they lived in caves in the pines, controlled a large tract of eastern New Jersey, called the neutral zone. Both British and Congressional generals led regular military incursions against each other from time to time into this no-man's land.

Despite its large and active Loyalist population, New Jersey contributed a total of 15,174 men to the Congressional war effort—4,448 militia and 10,726 Continental Army. Situated between New York and Philadelphia, two important Revolutionary cities, New Jersey experienced much tension and saw a lot of fighting during the American War for Independence.

The New Jersey Historical Commission is located at 225 West State Street, Trenton, NJ 08625; (website: **www.newjerseyhistory.org,** phone: 609-292-6062). The New Jersey Historical Society operates a museum and a library at 52 Park Place (website: **www.jerseyhistory.org;** phone: 973-596-8500) in the middle of Newark's art district. There is no published guide to historical markers and no official tourist information centers; but historians and popular writers have compensated for the government's tourism shortcomings. A couple of helpful books include Alfred Hoyt Bill's *New Jersey and the Revolutionary War* (Rutgers University Press, 1992), Adrian Coulter Leiby's *The Revolutionary War in the Hackensack Valley; the Jersey Dutch and the Neutral Ground, 1775–1783* (Rutgers University Press, 1962) and Mark Di Ionno's *A Guide to New Jersey's Revolutionary War Trail: For Families and History Buffs* (Rutgers University Press, 2000).

1
Northern New Jersey

See the map of Northern New Jersey.

Passaic

Acquackanonk (Nov. 21, 1776; Jan. 17, 1777; Sept. 27, 1778; Apr. 21, 1779)

Second River (Jan. 17, 1777; Sept. 12, 1777; June 1, 1779; Apr. 15, 1782)

Slotterdam (May 12, 1777; Sept. 12, 1777)

Schuyler's Ferry (Sept. 11, 12, 13, 1777)

Brown's Ferry, Passaic River (Oct. 6, 1780)

> Acquackanonk, located about 8 miles west of Fort Lee and 9 miles north of Newark, is now known as Passaic. Slotterdam was on the east bank of the Passaic River.

General George Washington (1732–1799) retreated from Fort Lee through Hackensack to Acquackanonk on Thursday, November 21, 1776. His troops crossed the Passaic River on the 21st and 22nd, destroying the bridge after they had crossed to prevent the Crown forces from gaining on them. The Crown forces probably reached the Passaic River, at Acquackanonk, on November 25th. Finding the bridge destroyed, they probably did not cross until November 26th. They forded the river and proceeded as far as Third River, plundering the inhabitants all along the route of the march.[1]

★ A band of Whigs plundered Captain Drummond's store at Acquackanonk Bridge around Friday, January 17, 1777. They took property valued at more than 1,000 livres and took it to Newark Mountains, sold it at public auction, and divided the amount among those who seized it. About the same time, they or another party, robbed the house of Loyalist Captain John Richards (d. 1778) of Second River and took seven young slaves, with his sheep, oxen, cows, and horses.[2]

★ While Colonel Joseph Barton attacked a picket under Peter Fell at Paramus Church on a foggy Monday morning, May 12, 1777 (see Paramus), a smaller detachment of less than 300 men under Colonel Edward Vaughan Dongan (1748–1777), marched from Bergen Town on Monday afternoon, May 12, 1777 to attack General Nathaniel Heard (1730–1792), who lay at Pompton, Slotterdam, on the east bank of the Passaic, with 350 New Jersey militiamen.

The Loyalists were unable to reach their destination by the intended time due to the morasses and other impediments. Colonel Dongan arrived at Saddle River at dawn, attacked and captured the Point. He took prisoners two Congressional officers (Captain David Marinus (1751–1778) and Lieutenant David Van Busson) and three enlisted men (John Van Busson, Andrew Cadmus, and another). He also captured a small cask of powder, some musket and cannon balls, eight or nine stand of arms, a drum, and some other articles.

General Nathaniel Heard (1730–1792) claimed that Barton's men inflicted more casualties on themselves in their confusion than on Peter Fell's detachment. Captain Hardnut or Hudnut was wounded in the groin by a bayonet, but not mortally. Captain Marinus and Lieutenant Van Busson were taken to the Sugar House prison from which

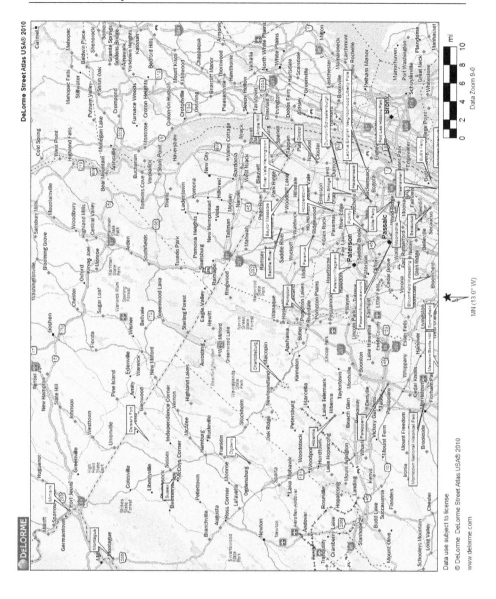

Northern New Jersey: Map for The Guide to the American Revolutionary War in New Jersey © *2011 DeLorme (www.delorme.com) Street Atlas USA®*

they escaped a year later. Marinus died from cold and exposure within two weeks after getting back to Slotterdam, and Van Busson was promoted to captain of Marinus's company.[3]

★ Schuyler's Ferry (September 11, 12, 13, 1777) see **Elizabethtown** and **New Bridge.**

★ About 1,500 Crown troops landed in Bergen County on Friday, September 12, 1777, while another party landed at Elizabethtown and proceeded to Second River to destroy stores at Morristown, Pompton, and the Clove (Ramapo Valley). The militia assembled immediately and harassed them as they proceeded between Slotterdam and the New Bridge until Sunday the 14th, when the Crown forces received intelligence that General Rufus Putnam (1738–1824) was on the way to cut off their retreat between Hackensack and the North River. The next day, they plundered the inhabitants, taking all their livestock and some inhabitants. However, they retreated so quickly that they left part of their livestock behind.

See **Slotterdam** and **New Bridge.**

See also **Elizabethtown.**

★ A flotilla of 11 or 12 brigs, sloops and galleys, and their flat-bottomed boats carrying a large body of Crown troops was spotted off Elizabethtown Point, at 10:30 AM on Sunday, September 27, 1778. They were headed for Crane's Ferry. Brigadier General William Winds (1727–1789), unable to see their rear due to the haze, thought they were coming in force and ordered the alarm guns and signals fired. He marched his militiamen down to meet them; but they changed course and went up to Newark Bay and then up the Hackensack River to join nearly 100 small vessels, such as sloops, shallops, row-galleys, and flat-bottomed boats, to bring off their plunder.

General Winds then marched from Acquackanonk to Hackensack with more than 1,000 militiamen and more on the way. He made an unsuccessful attempt to engage the enemy in battle. However, during the night of the 28th, their vessels at De Hart's Point, near Elizabethtown, began a smart firing with small cannon or large swivels (see Photo NJ-1) upon the militia sentries and wounded one. The militiamen returned a brisk fire and probably wounded some men.[4]

Photo NJ-1. Whaleboat with swivel gun

★ Lieutenant Colonel Abraham Van Buskirk (1750–1783) sent Captain Joseph Ryerson (1760–1854), Lieutenant Jacob Van Buskirk, and Ensign Earle with a detachment of 42 men of the 4th Battalion of New Jersey Volunteers on Wednesday, April 21, 1779. They fell in with a party of Congressional troops at Acquackanonk about daybreak. They charged immediately and put the Congressional troops to the rout. As they pursued the retreating troops, the Loyalists killed and wounded many of the stragglers whom they passed on the field, begging for mercy.

When 100 Carolina troops and 60 militiamen arrived to reinforce the retreating Congressional troops, Captain Ryerson's party, much fatigued, withdrew to rising ground. The Congressional troops, now so much superior in number, continued to retreat instead of attacking. Captain Ryerson lost one man missing and two wounded.[5]

★ A man named Lawrence was at Second River enlisting men for the British service on Tuesday, June 1, 1779. While some Whigs were trying to save the papers which his wife threw in the fire, Mr. Lawrence escaped. The Whigs saved his enlisting roll and captured 13 inhabitants who had enlisted and imprisoned them in the Morristown jail.[6]

★ Loyalists under Captain Frederick Hauser were rowing guard near Brown's Ferry on the Passaic River on Friday night, October 6, 1780 when they met a detachment of Continental troops in five boats. Captain Hauser called to them and received no answer, so he began to fire at them. Two of the boats surrendered. Captain Hauser captured four Continental light infantrymen. The others on board had jumped ashore and escaped. One other boat was sunk with one man killed and two wounded left on board. Some Continental dragoons captured and bound three Loyalists who had landed some time before the five boats were spotted.[7]

★ Sir James Jay (1732–1815), brother of John Jay, Esq. (1745–1829), had frequented Elizabethtown but eluded capture. A Loyalist learned that he was to lodge somewhere in the neighborhood of Second River for a few nights. The Loyalist watched Sir James Jay's movements and helped Lieutenant John Buskirk and a small party from the Flagstaff Fort on Staten Island capture Mr. Jay at the house of Colonel Arent Schuyler De Peyster (1736–1832) during the night of Monday, April 15, 1782. Lieutenant Buskirk returned with his prisoner the next morning.[8]

Fort Lee (Oct. 9, 1776; Oct. 18, 1776; Oct. 27, 1776; Oct. 28, 1776; Nov. 7, 1776; Nov. 16, 1776; Nov. 20, 1776; Feb. 22, 1777; May 14, 1781; May 15, 1781; May 18, 1781)

Fort Lee Historic Park (**www.fieldtrip.com/nj/14611776.htm**) is on Hudson Terrace south of the George Washington Bridge (on its New Jersey side) in Palisades Interstate Park.

Fort Lee Historic Park is the site of the northern redoubt of Fort Lee, about 0.5 miles northeast of the main fort. The reconstructed fort has a cannon battery overlooking the Hudson River and the Manhattan skyline. The battery has parapets with embrasures (see Photo-NJ-2, NJ-3) and firing steps. The visitor center shows a 12-minute film every hour; and lighted displays depict the campaign. Exhibits include models, miniature scenes, and pictures accompanied by descriptive text.

Fort Lee, called Fort Constitution in 1776, was built 300 feet above the Hudson River in September 1776, by Continental troops as a link in the fortifications defending New York and the Hudson River against British warships. It was across the Hudson from Fort Washington. (See also Fort Washington, New York.)

Photo NJ-2. Fort Lee, New Jersey. This view of the reconstructed northern redoubt of Fort Lee shows a façade of the fort protected by fascines with embrasures for two gun emplacements.

Photo NJ-3. Embrasures with earthen façade. Part of the Grand French Battery, Yorktown, Virginia.

The guns of Fort Constitution fired on Captain Hyde Parker, Jr.'s (1739–1807) *HMS Phoenix*, Captain Andrew Snape Hamond's (1738–1828) *Roebuck* and two other ships on October 9, 1776. They inflicted 27 casualties.

★ On October 18, 1776, a body of Crown forces landed at Bourdit's Ferry, planning to take Fort Constitution. Major General Nathanael Greene (1742–1786) arranged two brigades of militia and the flying camp in such a way that he repulsed three successive attacks. He lost only one man and inflicted considerable casualties.

At the same time, three or four men-of-war came up to pass Fort Washington. Colonel Robert Magaw (1738–1790), commander of the fort, had 60 shots fired from an 18-pounder. Forty-four hit their target, forcing the Crown forces to retire. One of the ships had four feet of water in her hold, her rigging badly damaged, and a number of her men killed.[9]

★ About 7 AM on October 27, 1776, two British frigates moved up the Hudson River and anchored directly between Fort Washington and Fort Lee. The ships were soon driven away by cannon fire. Another British ship moved up the river early in the morning the following day and began a brisk cannonade (see Photo NJ-4, NJ-5) upon the shore. Colonel Magaw had an 18-pounder fire 60 rounds at her with 26 shots going through her. The gun was mostly loaded with two balls. The ship also came under fire from two 18-pounders from the shore, causing great confusion and distress and the loss of a great number of men. Other ships came to the ship's assistance and four boats towed her away. Had the tide continued half an hour longer, the guns would have sunk her.

As the ships began to fire, the Crown forces brought up their field pieces and prepared to attack the lines. However, Colonel Magaw had arranged his men to prevent such a move. A cannonade and small arms fire continued almost all day, with very little

Photo NJ-4. Shell, also called a bomb, is hollow metal ball to be filled with gunpowder. The fuse is wedged in the hole with wooden shims.

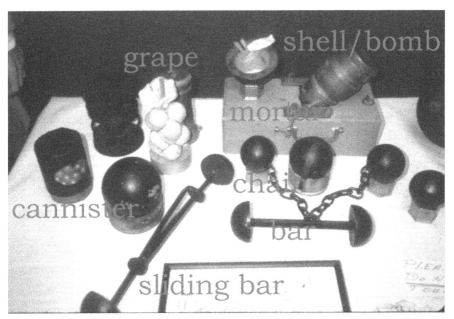

Photo NJ-5. Artillery shots

intermission. Magaw lost only one man and killed several of the enemy. The firing ceased in the evening and did not resume the following morning.[10]

★ During the evening of Thursday, November 7, 1776, Colonel Benjamin Tupper (1743–1778) with the pettiaugers (see Photo NJ-6) loaded with flour attempted to pass

Photo NJ-6. Pettiauger Mercury *(replica). Courtesy of Gene Tozzi, Sailing Master, Pettiauger* Mercury.

the British ships near Fort Lee. The British sent several barges, two tenders and a row galley to attack them. The crews ran the pettiaugers ashore and landed the men. The Crown forces attempted to land several times but were repulsed. The skirmish lasted about an hour and a half before the British withdrew. Colonel Tupper lost one man mortally wounded.[11]

★ General Charles Cornwallis (1738–1805) led 4,500 men [two battalions of Hessian grenadiers (see Photo NJ-7), two companies of jaegers (see Photo NJ-8), and eight battalions of British reserves] across the Hudson River 5 miles north of Fort Lee, where Major General Nathanael Greene (1742–1786) was in command, on Saturday, November 16, 1776. They assembled on the east shore opposite Closter Landing (Lower Landing, also known as Huyler's Landing which is six or seven miles above Fort Lee) and moved south to attack Fort Lee so quickly that the Continentals barely had time to escape. When the British entered the fort, they found only 12 men, all of them drunk. They took about 150 other prisoners captured in the vicinity. In their hurried retreat from Fort Lee, the Continentals left tents unfolded and pots boiling on camp fires. Tables were prepared for the officers' dinner and loaded guns were abandoned.[12]

★ General Charles Cornwallis (1738–1805) and a body of about 5,000 Crown troops broke camp quietly about 10 PM Wednesday night, November 20, 1776. They were ferried across the Hudson River on large flatboats at dawn the following morning. They left New York from two points and landed below Dobbs Ferry about 6 miles from Fort Lee and marched on the fort. General George Washington (1732–1799), at Hackensack, received intelligence of the landing at 10 AM and delegated command to Major General Israel Putnam (1718–1790) and departed when he received news of the advancing Crown troops. General Putnam handed the command over to his senior colonel, probably Colonel David Brearley (1745–1790) of the New Jersey militia, half an hour later and fled with all his men a short while later, without firing a single shot. They headed over the west side of the Hackensack River, leaving behind seven mortars (see Photo NJ-9), 32 cannon, 432 tents, 400,000 rounds of ammunition, provisions for three months for 5,000 men, and 73 invalids. They retreated through New Jersey during the last weeks of 1776. The Crown forces pursued the Continentals, "always keeping a day's march out of reach." Cornwallis and General William Howe (1732–1786) joined forces on December 6 and continued advancing together as the Continental Army seemed to disintegrate. General Henry Clinton (1730–1795) occupied Rhode Island, using it as a base to harass American shipping. The British seemed ready to end the war as soon as spring returned.[13]

★ Three armed men of Major Robert Rogers's (1732–1795) Rangers came to the house of Adolph de Grove, Jr. (1750–55 to post-1800) near Fort Constitution between 11 and 12 on Saturday morning, February 22, 1777. After knocking, they asked the way to the fort and asked to come in and warm themselves. Mr. de Grove invited them in and they asked for something to eat. He told them he would order them some food. When they saw his musket, they seized it and took him prisoner. They demanded his cash and he gave them what he had in his desk which was only a small sum. They put a pair of pistols to his head, threatened his life, and demanded more, telling him they knew he had more money. Mr. de Grove told them he had no more in the house and they left him. Mr. de Grove immediately went to the fort and got a guard to pursue the Rangers. The following morning, the guard surprised one of the Rangers at the house of Thomas Searle about 27 miles from de Grove's. The man ran off and might have escaped had his tracks in the snow not encouraged the guard to continue the pursuit. The man threw

Photo NJ-7. Re-enactors portraying Hessian grenadiers

Photo NJ-8. Re-enactor portraying a Hessian jaeger

Photo NJ-9. Mortar, used for firing shells or bombs. Mortars are designed to fire the shells or bombs in an arc to get behind walls and other high obstacles that cannons cannot reach.

away de Grove's musket and his own great coat to facilitate his escape. His pursuers ran and tracked him for about a dozen miles before they caught up to him and captured him. They seized him and brought him back in irons.[14]

★ A party of about 70 Loyalists under the command of Captain Thomas Ward had evacuated the post at Bergen Point. They were joined by an equal number from New York, under the command of Captain George Harden on Monday morning, May 14, 1781. They landed at Bull's Ferry on the Jersey shore and proceeded to the English Neighborhood by way of Fort Lee and returned to Fort Lee that evening. A party of about 100 Whigs appeared a short while later and took possession of a stone house about 100 yards from Fort Lee. They maintained a constant fire from this location for almost an hour before the house was stormed and the occupants routed, leaving one man killed. The Loyalists captured two more prisoners.

★ About 100 Loyalists from New York seized a blockhouse at Fort Lee on Tuesday, May 15, 1781 and held off two companies of New Jersey militia under Colonel Richard Dey (1752–1811).[15]

★ The Whigs received a reinforcement of 300 militiamen and planned an attack in three divisions for the next morning. The Loyalists learned of the plan and took the offensive immediately, causing the Congressional troops to flee in great confusion. Many threw away their arms, leaving Colonel Cooper (who was also a Judge and Commissioner for selling the estates of the Loyalists) wounded on the field, along with two men killed.

On May 16th and 17th, the Loyalists erected works for a post on the site of Fort Lee. On the morning of May 18th, just after sunrise, an advance party of about 10 men prepared to resume their work and had nearly arrived at the works when they found them occupied by about 400 Congressional militiamen commanded by Colonel Richard Dey, who captured two of the party prisoners. The rest fired their muskets and ran down the hill with the militiamen in pursuit.

The combined fire from a Loyalist gunboat, the muskets, and Captain Harden's field piece forced the Whigs to return up the hill. Captain Harden advanced through a valley that led up the hill and charged the enemy's right flank, forcing them to evacuate the defenses in great confusion. They left one man killed and one wounded and brought several who were badly wounded with them. Captain Harden pursued the Whigs to the English Neighborhood but could not overtake them. The Loyalists only had one man slightly wounded and two captured.[16]

Leonia
Englewood
English Neighborhood (Oct. 19, 1776; Nov. 9, 1776; Dec. 20, 1776; Mar. 20, 1777; June 20, 1777; July 17, 1777; Oct. 13, 1777; Oct. 31, 1777; Mar. 27, 1778; Apr. 22, 1779; June 4, 1779; Apr. 15, 1780; July 21, 1780; Aug. 5[?], 1780; Apr., 1781; Mar., 1783)

Near Liberty Pole (Nov. 1, 1776; June 15, 1777; Sept. 22, 1778; Aug. 19, 1779; July 29, 1781)

Three Pigeons (Oct. 31, 1777; Jan. 29, 1778)

Prior's Mill (Jan. 29, 1778; Mar. 22, 1778; May 10, 1778; May 16, 1778; Oct. 6, 1778; June 17, 1779; Aug. 19, 1779; Aug. 25, 1780)

> English Neighborhood was near Fort Lee in what is now Leonia. The Sign of the Three Pigeons Tavern was in English Neighborhood, near Little Ferry, less than 5 miles from Bergen. Prior's Mill was near Bergen and Paulus Hook (Jersey City).
>
> Liberty Pole was at the head of English Neighborhood Creek and is now part of Englewood. A liberty pole was erected in 1766 near what is now the intersection of Lafayette and Palisade Avenues in Englewood to celebrate the repeal of the Stamp Act. The Liberty Pole Tavern also was in the area.

Colonel John Glover (1732–1797) in command of three Massachusetts regiments [his own 14th Continental infantry, Colonel Joseph Reed's (1741–1785) 14th Massachusetts and Colonel William Shepard's (1737–1817) 4th Massachusetts] advanced under cover to meet the Crown forces marching toward the country in an attempt to take Fort Lee on Saturday, October 19, 1776. Colonel Shepherd's men took position behind a wall in the English Neighborhood. They gave the grenadiers (see Photo NJ-10) and infantrymen an unexpected heavy fire from a distance of 30 or 40 yards. They followed with a second and third volley which broke the enemy line and sent them running away in confusion. They returned with field pieces and flanked the Massachusetts regiments, obliging them to retreat a short distance. They rallied and held their ground against the cannonade and troop advance. The militia lost 30 or 40 killed and wounded. Two Crown deserters reported they lost 1,000 men, but they probably lost about 150.[17]

★ About 11 AM on Friday, November 1, 1776, an advance party of Crown forces arrived with a number of field pieces at a hill about 2 miles north of Liberty Pole and about 1.5 miles above Major General Nathanael Greene's (1742–1786) headquarters.

Photo NJ-10. Re-enactors portraying Scottish Highlander grenadiers

They found the road from Fort Lee to New Bridge was still in enemy hands and began a furious cannonade which Colonel Henry Knox's (1750–1806) artillery promptly returned.[18]

Colonel William Malcom or Malcolm (1745–1791) and his artillery took a position at the head of a hollow on the Crown forces' left. Major Israel Keith galloped to advise him to quit the hill for fear that the Crown forces would move up the hollow and cut him off from the rest of his division.

Upon closer examination, however, there was a stone wall at the head of the hollow which could cover a body of troops. It would allow the Continentals to throw a heavy fire directly down the hollow while troops on both sides could fire obliquely. The initial order was countermanded and the colonel ordered to defend his post until reinforcements arrived. A strong regiment was sent to the head of the hollow to occupy the wall. Both sides kept up a brisk cannonade.

The Crown forces, realizing they could not make any impression, withdrew their pieces and circled around to the right of the Continentals where they were surprised to find some 12-pounders. After cannons discharged, the Crown forces retreated as fast as they could with their field pieces, leaving an artillery horse dead on the field. One cannon shot took off the head of a Hessian artilleryman. Their other losses are unknown. General Greene's division lost only one man killed from Lieutenant Colonel Levi Pawling's (1721–1782) regiment of New York troops.[19]

★ Colonel Robert Magaw's (1738–1790) men killed 13 Hessians and an officer in a skirmish near Fort Lee on Saturday, November 9, 1776.[20]

★ The British relied on Loyalist forces to forage in New Jersey. Lieutenant Colonel Abraham van Buskirk's (1750–1783) battalion of New Jersey Volunteers, mostly recruited from the Hackensack area, often foraged in small bands, burning buildings and arresting suspected Whigs. General Samuel Holden Parsons (1737–1789) and General George Clinton (1739–1812) set out about dusk on Tuesday, December 19, 1776 with 500 troops and Mr. Zabriskie as a guide. They headed to the English Neighborhood where they were informed Lieutenant Colonel Abraham Van Buskirk's (1750–1783) Regiment of New Levies and some companies of light infantry were quartered while they cut wood.

When they came to the first house in the English Neighborhood, they detached Colonel Jesse Woodhull (1735–1795) with 200 men with orders to march east of the settlement, through the fields to the edge of Bergen Woods, to place guards on the roads leading to Burdett's and Bull's ferries behind the enemy at the foot of the Palisades, below the site of Fort Lee.

Colonel Woodhull and the remainder of his force were to come in on the back of the enemy to prevent their escape while General Parsons and General Clinton would march through the Neighborhood from the north. They surprised and captured the advance guard about dawn about 1 mile from Bergen Woods. Immediately afterward, they began to advance to attack their main body. One of the Loyalist dragoons rode up and one of the soldiers challenged him and fired on him, alarming the rest of the Crown troops. They turned out and fired on the attackers who returned fire and drove them back. They fled before Colonel Woodhull and his party could reach the main road after a rough march. The attackers took 23 prisoners, 18 excellent new muskets, a wagon and eight horses and killed four or five. Had it not been so cold and had the men not been worn out from the long 28-mile march, they might have captured more and may have killed or captured the entire party.[21]

★ Colonel Joseph Barton led some of his Loyalist troops into the English Neighborhood on a very rainy Thursday, March 20, 1777. He attacked a post held by Lieutenant Colonel Levi Pawling (1721–1782) and captured four prisoners without firing a shot. They were probably asleep in a house some distance from the guard.[22]

★ Loyalists surprised party of 30 men at Liberty Pole on Sunday, June 15, 1777 and forced them to retreat.[23]

★ A scouting party of 30 New Jersey militiamen skirmished with a strong party of Loyalists at the English Neighborhood on Friday, June 20, 1777.[24]

★ A party of Whigs passed through the English Neighborhood on Thursday, July 17, 1777 and carried away about four people they suspected of being Loyalists.[25]

★ The Crown troops left Hackensack for New York on Tuesday, October 13, 1777. They went by way of the English Neighborhood. The light horsemen followed and captured some prisoners.[26]

★ A party of Whig militiamen appeared in the English Neighborhood on Friday, October 31, 1777. They took a number of cattle from the inhabitants and went as far as the Sign of the Three Pigeons.[27]

★ Major John Goetschius (1745–1826), commander of a party of rangers in Bergen county, ordered Abraham Brouwer (1763–1806) and John Lozier (1745–1784) to intercept Loyalist commerce between New Jersey and New York and to reconnoiter the picket at Paulus Hook on Wednesday, January 29, 1778. They lay in ambush at Prior's mill, near the enemy sentry, about 6 miles below the Three Pigeons (Pidgeons) Tavern. John Richards (d. 1778), a New York Loyalist who was returning from a visit to New Barbados Neck (Bergen) where his family was sick with smallpox passed them in a wagon along with one of his and one of Cornelius Van Vorst's (1728–1818) slaves. Even though John Richards had a pass from Colonel George Turnbull (1752–1807) to go to Bergen, Brouwer and Lozier took him and the two slaves to Major Goetschius for examination.

About 6 miles down the road from their place of capture, Mr. Richards and his slave grabbed Lozier's musket. Lozier, in the wagon with the prisoners, called to Brouwer, on horseback, for help. As Brouwer arrived, the slave grabbed Lozier; and Richards turned to seize Brouwer. Brouwer shot him dead on the spot and brought the slaves to Major Goetschius.[28]

Judge Thomas Jones's (1731–1792) version of the story says that Richards stopped at a tavern where a Whig recognized him, insulted him and demanded his watch. Richards refused to surrender it, whereupon the man drew a pistol and shot Richards through the head. The man then took the watch, money, and any other valuables. Richards's death infuriated New York City and Bergen County Loyalists in New York.[29]

★ A foraging party of six New Jersey militiamen under Captain William Johnston came down near Paulus Hook, as far as Prior's Mills on Sunday March 22, 1778. A party of Colonel George Turnbull's (1752–1807) New York Volunteers (Loyalists) pursued them as they tried to remove some cattle, forcing them to leave their plunder behind to avoid capture.[30]

★ On Friday, March 27, 1778, a party of Lieutenant Colonel George Turnbull's (1752–1807) New York Volunteers (Loyalists), under the command of Lieutenant Haines, were sent toward the English Neighborhood to search for some Whigs believed to be hiding there. They entered the house of one Degroote and seized four armed men, including a man called John Lozier (1745–1784) who was involved in the murder of Captain John Richards (d. 1778) and a sergeant in Captain Boorbaek's company of Brigadier General Oliver de Lancey's (1718–1785) first battalion. Richards's watch was found in Lozier's pocket.[31]

★ A party of Whigs seized two African American men who were taking a few eggs and a small quantity of butter to market at Prior's Mills on Sunday, May 10, 1778. Another party carried off some more African Americans on Friday and Saturday, May 15 and 16, 1778. A party from Paulus Hook pursued them and they fled.[32]

★ On the afternoon of Tuesday, September 22, 1778, 5,000 Crown forces [General Charles Cornwallis (1738–1805) and Major Generals Charles Grey (1729–1807) and Edward Mathew (1729–1805) with two British brigades, the grenadiers (see Photo NJ-10), the light infantry, the Guards, 200 dragoons, Lord Francis Rawdon's (1754–1826) Irish battalion, and 200 provincials] began disembarking from transports and flat-boats at Paulus Hook. [Major Carl Leopold Baurmeister (1734–1803) says they landed at Fort Lee.] A regiment of dragoons immediately overran the outpost at Liberty Pole which was defended by Captain Elias Romeyn's company of Bergen County militia and a detachment of southern troops under the command of a Lieutenant Hayes. The dragoons captured 29 prisoners and killed about 14 men while the Crown forces lost one dragoon and two horses killed. As they had received advance warning of the attack on their picket, the main body of Congressional forces at New Bridge withdrew to Paramus.[33]

That night, the Crown forces camped along New Bridge Road, between Liberty Pole and the bridge. Lord Cornwallis made his headquarters on Schraalenburgh Road at the junction of New Bridge Road. Lord Rawdon and his Volunteers of Ireland camped on the lower ground to the west between the light infantry and the Long Swamp Brook. Other regiments were stationed to the east from Schraalenburgh Road to a point almost at the edge of the Palisades.[34]

★ Young Mr. Bogaert, son of Nicholas Bogaert (1735–1793), a New York merchant was killed by some Crown forces in New Jersey a few days before October 6, 1778.[35]

★ Captain Joshua Bowman (1757–1827) of the North Carolina brigade with a party of Continental troops and a few New Jersey militiamen clashed with some British or Loyalist troops at De Groot's, in the English Neighborhood, about 7 miles from Hoebuck, on Thursday, April 22, 1779. He drove them but had three men wounded, two Continental soldiers and one militiaman. The losses of the Crown forces are not known; but one of them was taken prisoner and two or three were carried off dead or wounded.[36]

★ Lieutenant Colonel Abraham Van Buskirk (1750–1783), suspecting there were some spies and robbers near his post at Hoebuck, ordered out a small number of men on Friday night June 4, 1779. They discovered a party of Whigs in a rye field in the English Neighborhood about 3 AM. They took two prisoners, William Wirts and Henry Bastion.[37]

★ A party of Whigs came to Prior's Mill, within 1 mile of Paulus Hook, on Thursday, June 17, 1779. They fired some shots at some troops there. A few men were ordered out after them, and they fled into the bush.[38]

★ On the night of Tuesday, August 17, 1779, Captain Allen McLane (1746–1829) posted troops in the Bergen Woods to cut off communication between the Crown forces and upper Bergen County. About 10:30 in the morning of the 18th, Captain Levin Handy (1754–1799) and two companies of Continentals moved down from Paramus to New Bridge to join Major Henry "Light-Horse Harry" Lee (1756–1818) and his 300 Virginians. Together, they marched toward Paulus Hook, about 20 miles away, about 5 PM. They passed Liberty Pole and English Neighborhood and reached the Bergen Woods late that night, where they were joined by McLane's dismounted dragoons.

The Congressional forces were delayed for several hours because incompetent guides caused confusion. They arrived at the edge of the marsh which separated Paulus Hook from the mainland at 4 AM. They crossed the long causeway over the marsh without opposition because the picket of one noncommissioned officer and 10 men of the Erb Prinz Regiment thought they were Lieutenant Colonel Abraham Van Buskirk's (1750–1783) men returning from a raid.

Lee's Virginians rushed forward in deep silence at dawn on Thursday, August 19th with fixed bayonets. They surprised the sleeping invalids quartered in a blockhouse and attacked the Hessian noncommissioned officer in the rear and took him prisoner. They also captured almost the whole garrison in a short but desperate fight.[39]

Lee expected to take his prisoners across the Hackensack River, due west of present-day Jersey City, and go to New Bridge over the Polifly Road. This would put the river between him and his pursuers. However, the boats did not arrive on the Hackensack; so the troops had to go back over the English Neighborhood Road which followed the Hudson a mile or two inland. They were in danger of being attacked the entire time.

Meanwhile, the Congressional forces learned that Lieutenant Colonel Abraham Van Buskirk was on his way to attack them; so a party of 500 men from Brigadier General William Alexander's (Earl of Stirling, 1726–1783) brigade set an ambuscade near Paulus Hook and put a picket near this post. The picket was ordered to withdraw to the opposite side of the ambuscade as soon as it was attacked. Van Buskirk's detachment ran out and drove back the picket around midnight. The picket moved toward New Bridge with the Crown forces in pursuit.[40]

See also **Paulus Hook.**

★ Some of Van Buskirk's troops were returning from a raiding expedition at Paulus Hook and camped in a concealed location during the night, planning to attack the Congressional forces near Liberty Pole at sunrise on Thursday, August 19, 1779. When they saw Lee's troops returning to New Bridge, Van Buskirk's men thought that their plan had been discovered. They moved into the main road and attacked the Virginians. Lee had the planks removed from the bridge over the English Neighborhood Creek and then ordered a captain and a few men into the stone house which covered the bridge, thus blocking Van Buskirk's troops until Lee could withdraw his main force.[41]

★ April 15, 1780 see **Hopperstown.**

★ A small party of Loyalists skirmished with Congressional troops near Fort Lee on Friday, July 21, 1780. They repulsed the attackers but had four killed and six wounded. Captain Thomas Ward pursued the rear of the retreating army for more than 4 miles and retook 20 head of stolen cattle, killed one soldier, and captured two, including Brigadier General "Mad Anthony" Wayne's (1745–1796) servant. The Congressional troops were believed to have incurred higher casualties than the Loyalists.[42]

★ A party of militiamen engaged some British cavalry at the English Neighborhood in early August 1780 and killed one rider and captured four. The exact date is unknown but the skirmish occurred the week before August 9, probably on the 5th.[43]

★ General George Washington (1732–1799), Major General Marie Jean Paul Joseph du Motier Marquis de Lafayette (1757–1834), Major General Nathanael Greene (1742–1786), Brigadier General "Mad Anthony" Wayne (1745–1796), along with many other officers, and a large body of troops were in the vicinity of Bergen at the end of August 1780. They took all the forage from the inhabitants and left them destitute of almost everything for their winter subsistence. The officers were down as far as Prior's Mills on Friday, August 25, but did not seem inclined to make any attack. Most of their artillery, except for some field pieces, was with the baggage, about 20 miles in the country.

On Saturday, the Congressional forces burned Colonel William Bayard's (d. 1801) new house and barn at Castile on the north end of Hoebuck. They also destroyed all the forage and timber before leaving on Saturday night or Sunday morning.[44]

★ Captain John Outwater (1746–1823) led some militiamen against a British landing party at the salt marshes south of Hackensack near the English Neighborhood in April 1781. They killed seven and took one prisoner while losing only one man wounded.[45]

★ Major Thomas Ward and a party of Refugees went from Bergen Neck to Liberty Pole on Sunday morning, July 29, 1781. He detached Captain John Miller and a party of 20 horsemen toward New Bridge, near Hackensack, where they captured three "notorious rebels" by the name of Demareas, drove off their stock, and returned to the party without firing a shot.[46]

★ Captain John M. Hogenkamp (1742–1813) and 30 to 40 militiamen of different companies marched into the English Neighborhood in March 1783. They did not expect to meet with any enemy, as they thought that hostilities had ceased and peace was expected. They came under fire by a party of British and Loyalists who lay in ambush. Everyone escaped unhurt except for one man who was wounded in the knee and taken prisoner.[47]

Northern New Jersey (Mar. 24, 1777; Apr. 22, 1777)

A party of about 60 men from Sampton under Major Ritney skirmished with a larger party of British near one of their outposts on Monday, March 24, 1777. Faced with enemy reinforcements, Major Ritney, outnumbered three to one, retreated in good order without losing a man.

Lieutenant Colonel Henry Hollingsworth (1737–1803) brought a detachment of Maryland militiamen and some Virginia volunteers from Colonel Benjamin Rumsey's (1734–1808) battalion as reinforcements. His party of less than 130 men, entirely exposed in an open field, engaged more than 300 Regulars posted behind trees. Colonel Hollingsworth forced the enemy to retreat from the woods into their breastworks about half a mile away, leaving behind several hats, knapsacks, blankets, and one bloody handkerchief. The British were seen carrying some men off the field but the number of casualties is not known. Colonel Hollingsworth had nobody hurt and two rifles broken.[48]

★ On Tuesday night, April 22, 1777, Captain Thomas Combs or Coombs (d. 1785) led a force behind enemy lines and captured two British sentinels from whom he extorted the countersign. He then returned to attack the picket guard. One of his men deserted and informed the enemy of his intentions. They prepared themselves and gave Captain Combs a very warm reception. Captain Combs drove the pickets into the guard house where they fired through the door and windows. Combs ordered his men to charge the door with bayonets fixed. The enemy received them in the same manner but soon called for quarter. Combs took the entire picket guard of two subalterns and 30 men prisoners. Both of the officers and 14 men were killed and 16 men were brought in as prisoners. Combs was wounded in the foot and both his subalterns were wounded in the body. Nobody was killed and only three wounded, none mortally.[49]

Hackensack (Dec. 14, 1776; Dec. 25, 1776; Feb. 10, 1777; Mar. 22–24, 1777; June 10, 1777; Sept. 11, 1777; Sept. 14, 1777; Sept. 30, 1777; Oct. 5, 1777; Sept. 28, 30, 1778; Oct. 1, 1778; Feb. 7, 1780; Dec. 8, 1780; Apr. 1781; Aug. 29, 1781)

Hackensack Valley (Apr. 20, 1777; Apr. 21, 1779)

Manhattan Dutchmen crossed the Hudson River to establish a trading post on a lesser river about 4 miles west. They called the site New Barbados. The name was changed to Hackensack in 1921, a Native American term meaning "place of sharp ground." The village was a strategic point during the American War for Independence because of its location on the road that linked Manhattan and its bastion (see Photo NJ-11, NJ-12) at Fort Lee.

The Green at the south end of Main Street was the core of New Barbados. It contained the courthouse, the pillories, and the church. The church on the northeast corner of the Green was built in 1696 and is one of the oldest in the state. Reconstructed several times since, its Dutch Colonial architecture served as a prototype for several churches in the area.

Photo NJ-11. Earth bastion, Fort George, Castine, Maine

Photo NJ-12. Stone bastion, the northeast bastion of Fort Ticonderoga. Mount Independence is in the background.

After the fall of Fort Lee (November 18, 1776), General George Washington (1732–1799) began his retreat across New Jersey. He made his headquarters at Hackensack from November 19 to 21.

Major General William Heath (1737–1814), in charge of a small detachment, led a raid on the town of Hackensack on Saturday, December 14, 1776. They captured the eight-man British garrison and a large quantity of military supplies the Loyalist militia were storing there. Heath abandoned the post two days later when he learned of the approach of two British columns.

★ December 25, 1776 see **Paramus.**

★ The British returned to Hackensack on February 10, 1777 and again on March 22–24 when they burned Whig houses and the courthouse. Local militiamen and a regiment of Pennsylvania Continentals put up some resistance but were no match for the raiders. The Redcoats then went on to raid Paramus (today's Ridgewood).[50]

★ Small Loyalist raiding parties led by Claudius Smith (1736–1779) operated in the county murdering and plundering, mostly at night. At one time, 35 of these men were confined in the Morris jail. Two of them were hanged and the remainder branded in the hand and released. On Sunday, April 20, 1777, Captain Samuel Ryerson and 44 New Jersey Loyalists skirmished with a guard of Continentals in the Hackensack Valley and had two men wounded.

★ A party of light horsemen skirmished with over 200 Loyalists at Hackensack on Tuesday, June 10, 1777.[51]

★ In September 1777, while General George Washington (1732–1799) was maneuvering along the Brandywine, Lieutenant-Colonel Aaron Burr (1756–1836) was at Suffern, in temporary command of Colonel William Malcom's or Malcolm (1745–1791) regiment. Three British detachments from around Manhattan marched on Hackensack on Wednesday, the 10th and Lieutenant Colonel Burr went south to meet them. He found some badly disorganized local militiamen at Paramus and rallied them to help defend the area in case the British came north. Burr surprised and defeated the Crown troops at Hackensack in a night attack on Thursday, September 11, 1777. He then sent an express to reassure the militia commander.[52]

★ About 10 PM on Sunday, September 14, 1777, Lieutenant Colonel Aaron Burr (1756–1836) led a detachment of 24 men in a night attack against a British picket guard less than 3 miles from Hackensack. Colonel Burr went forward alone to reconnoiter and found the pickets lying on the ground guarded by two sentinels. He was near enough to hear their watchword and determined that this picket was so far in advance of the main body as to be out of hearing. He returned to his regiment less than an hour before daybreak. He woke his men and informed them of his intentions to attack the picket.

He ordered his men to follow at a distance and forbade them to speak. When they arrived, he led his men between the two guards at the moment when they were farthest apart. A sentinel challenged Burr when he got within 10 yards. Burr immediately shot him dead and then gave the signal to attack. They captured one officer, a sergeant, a corporal, and 27 privates. Only one of the pickets besides the sentinel made any resistance. He received two bayonet wounds and was overpowered. He attempted to march away with his comrades but was compelled to lie down exhausted and fainting from loss of blood after going a short distance.

Colonel Burr sent an express to Paramus to order all the troops to move and to rally the inhabitants. The people were so encouraged by his exploit that they turned out quickly and put themselves under his command. The enemy retreated the next day, leaving behind most of their plunder.[53]

★ Brigadier General William Maxwell (1733–1796) received intelligence on Saturday morning, September 27, 1777 that General Henry Clinton (1730–1795) had come from New York to Staten Island the evening before and that a large body of troops were lying on their arms on the island.

About 3,000 Crown troops from New York were seen at 10:30 PM headed for Crane's Ferry with 11 or 12 brigs, sloops, and galleys, followed by their flat boats. As the weather was hazy, General Maxwell could not see their rear and supposed they were coming in force. He ordered the alarm guns and signals to be fired. The militia mustered and the general marched with his brigade to meet them. But the Crown forces turned about and went up to Newark Bay and then up the Hackensack River to plunder Bergen County and to construct some earthworks on the other side of the New Bridge beyond Hackensack.

They began a smart firing with small cannon or large swivels (see Photo NJ-1) from their vessels at the sentries at Dehart's Point, near Elizabethtown on Sunday night but did not injure anybody. The Congressional troops returned a brisk fire and assumed they wounded several Crown troops.

★ On Tuesday September 30, 1777, some 3,000 Crown troops under General Henry Clinton (1730–1795) landed near Hackensack to plunder and forage. They sent about 100 vessels, such as sloops, shallops, row-galleys, and flat-bottomed boats, up the Hackensack and Passaic Rivers to carry off the plunder.

★ A band of men armed with guns and bayonets entered the store of John Varick (1723–1809) at Hackensack on Sunday, October 5, 1777. Mary Thomas was alone at the store and was unable to prevent the raiders from stealing everything. They even took the owners' bed and bedding. It took almost seven years before the case came to trial.[54]

★ Major General Charles "No Flint" Grey (1729–1807) was headed to Old Tappan to attack Colonel George Baylor (1752–1784) and the 3rd Continental Dragoons ("Mrs.

Washington's Guards") which had been annoying the Crown forces' foraging parties. As they approached Baylor's position near the Overkill Road (River Vale Road today) about 2 AM on Monday, September 28, 1778, a party of regulars surprised a guard of about a dozen of Baylor's dragoons at the Hackensack Bridge. They slaughtered the guards and continued toward Baylor's camp which they struck at 3 AM.[55]

See **River Vale/Westwood (Old Tappan)** (September 27–28, 1778).

A great body of militia mustered to reinforce Brigadier General William Maxwell (1733–1796) to drive the "freebooters" back to the place from whence they came. Several boats returned and four, "loaded with forage and the petticoats of old women," were captured and burned.[56]

★ Captain von Donop led a patrol of about 80 Hessians and chasseurs about daybreak on Wednesday, September 30, 1778. They had gone less than 2 miles when they were surrounded by a party of 100 light horsemen and infantrymen. A party of 12 to 16 mounted jaegers had advanced too quickly and became separated from the rest of the patrol. Their lieutenant was severely wounded and captured. Captain von Donop retreated, leaving two dead and 17 wounded to be taken prisoners.

The following day, the chasseurs marched at 9:30 PM, taking only their blankets and a light field piece with about 30 rounds but without a powder wagon. They marched through the woods and over stony roads in silence in the darkness. A party of the advance guard was suddenly challenged about 3 AM. When they did not respond quickly enough, a party of light horsemen fired and galloped away. The chasseurs, eager for spoils, set out in pursuit, nearly shooting each other in the dark. One of the men shot an old woman through the leg as she came out of her house. Some of the men took some blankets and woolen coats left behind by the light horsemen.

The chasseurs regrouped and took possession of a hill behind the house where they stayed until daybreak. They then proceeded across a valley along a high hill. They came under fire of more than 40 musket shots and could hear the bullets whiz over their heads. The advance guard ran at full speed to attack their flank but were ordered back.[57]

★ General Charles Scott (c. 1739–1813) was stationed at North Castle, New York at the end of September 1778. He sent a detachment of light infantrymen to New Jersey to check British foraging along the east bank of the Hudson. On Thursday October 1, 1778, two days after Baylor's massacre (Colonel George Baylor (1752–1784) on September 30, 1778), Colonel Richard Butler (1743–1791) with 300 men and Captain Henry "Light-Horse Harry" Lee (1756–1818) with some of his dragoons surprised a party of 150 Hessians at Hackensack. They killed 10 of them and captured 19, without any losses of their own. General Scott commented that "this in Some Measure Compliments For poor Baylor."[58]

★ Lieutenant Colonel Abraham Van Buskirk (1750–1783) sent off Captain Joseph Ryerson (1760–1854), Lieutenant Jacob Van Buskirk (1760–1834), and Ensign Earle with a detachment of 42 Loyalists of the 4th Battalion of New Jersey Volunteers on Wednesday, April 21, 1779. They fell in with an advance guard of Continentals about daybreak. They immediately charged the Continentals and routed them. They killed and wounded a considerable number whom they passed on the field begging for mercy. They pursued the rest until the Continentals were reinforced by their main body, consisting of about 100 Carolina troops and 60 militiamen. As his men were very tired, Captain Ryerson withdrew to a nearby hill. Instead of attacking Ryerson's party, the Continentals withdrew. Ryerson lost only one man missing and two wounded.[59]

★ On Monday morning, February 7, 1780, Mr. Justice Ogden drew a sketch of the roads from Newark and Elizabethtown to General George Washington's (1732–1799) headquarters at Morristown, several miles northeast of his camp near Hackensack. The following morning, William Smith (1728–1793) got Mr. Milledge, Deputy Surveyor of Morris County to sketch the roads from Paulus Hook to Morristown. He sent the sketch to General William Tryon (1729–1788) with a letter suggesting a plan to capture General Washington during the night and perhaps to attack the Continental camp.

Snow fell on February 7 and 8 which still lay heavy on the camp and headquarters about two weeks later. A rider brought General Washington a dispatch on the night of February 11 in which Major General Arthur St. Clair (1737–1818) reported four hostile parties had made an incursion into Continental positions—three from Staten Island and one from Paulus Hook. The largest force from the island headed to Elizabethtown, but withdrew rapidly after they found the small Continental guard on the alert. The detachments that went to Woodbridge and Rahway did little more than steal some cattle and plunder a few houses. About 300 dragoons set out from the British outpost on Paulus Hook on Saturday, February 12, 1780 and headed to Hackensack. Using maps supplied by William Smith, they intended to kidnap General Washington from his headquarters in Morristown. However, they encountered unexpectedly deep snow that forced them to abandon their plan.[60]

★ Militiamen captured five horse thieves of Captain Thomas Ward's party at Dow's Ferry near Hackensack on Friday night, December 8, 1780 as they were headed to New York. There were eight in the party and each had stolen a horse but three of them had already crossed the river before the militiamen caught up with them.[61]

★ April 1781 Salt Marshes south of Hackensack, NJ see **Bergen County, Little Ferry, Moonachie** (April 10, 1781).

★ A party of Captain Thomas Ward's plunderers from Bergen Neck came to the Hackensack area on Wednesday night, August 29, 1781. They collected a number of cattle which the inhabitants retook. They also killed and wounded several of the raiders.[62]

Closter (Apr. 21, 1777; Mar. 28, 1779; May 9, 1779; May 10, 1779; May 17, 1779; May 18, 1779; July 10, 1779; Mar. 23, 1780; May 25, 1780; June 8, 1780; June 10, 1780; Mar. 12, 13, 1781; Sept. 12, 1781)

Closter is on the Hudson River about 25 miles from Bergen and 5 miles north of Fort Lee. Isaac Naugle's House (80 Hickory Lane, Block 2103, Lot 7) was sacked three times by the British during the American War for Independence.

Captain William Van Allen raided Closter with about 50 Royal Bergen Volunteers on Monday, April 21, 1777. They were searching for a party of Whigs who learned of their approach and left. Captain Van Allen pursued them for several miles when they overtook three Whig sutlers and took seven wagon loads of rum, sugar, coffee, chocolate, and other supplies without losing a man.[63]

★ Captain David Peek and Lieutenant Wiert Banta (1753–1834), led a party of about 30 of Lieutenant Colonel Abraham Van Buskirk's (1750–1783) Loyalists stationed at Hoebuck to Closter to steal horses and rob the inhabitants on Sunday night, March 28, 1779. Lieutenant John Huyler and nine militiamen routed them. They left their plunder behind, along with one of their officers, dead on the field. Another officer was wounded in the arm, and Lieutenant Wiert Banta was shot through the knee. Lieutenant John Huyler's mother and Wiert Banta's father were sister and brother.[64]

This may have been the same engagement that began when Sergeant John Huyler (Captain Huyler's nephew) and three men fell in with a party of Loyalists, "drew up near them . . ., fired, fell on the ground till their shot passed over us, then rose and retreated till we met a party of our company and a part of Captain Thomas Blanch's (1740–1823) company, had a fight, killed two [and] took two prisoners." James I. Blauvelt's arm was shattered by a musket ball in that engagement.[65]

★ In another engagement, at about the same time, "Henry Cooper got wounded, taken prisoner and taken to New York, where his leg was taken off by a surgeon. He recovered and returned home."[66]

★ A large party of Loyalists came up the Hudson by boat to the Closter Dock (about 8 miles above Fort Lee) on Sunday morning, May 9, 1779. They moved down the heavily wooded Closter Dock Road unobserved until they were almost upon the little settlement that, according to James Rivington (ca. 1724–1802), abounded "with many violent rebels, and persecutors of loyal subjects, and who are almost daily affording some fresh instance of barbarity." Consequently, Loyalists were always ready to attack the settlement.

Captain John Huyler's militia company was stationed a few miles to the west in Schraalenburgh that morning. When they received the alarm, they hurried to Closter to engage the raiders, retook about 90 head of stolen cattle but were too late to do much more. The Loyalists burned several dwelling houses and barns, killed two, wounded about five and captured four.[67]

★ Lieutenant Colonel Abraham Van Buskirk led 100 Loyalists on a raid a few miles north of Hackensack on Monday, May 10, 1779. They entered by way of Closter and carried off a number of inhabitants, burned buildings, abused many women, and destroyed life. Another detachment brought desolation on the 17th, destroying all the Whig houses and killing Abraham Allen (d. 1779) and George Campbell (d. 1779). Jacob C. Zabriskie (1724–1804) was stabbed in 15 places and two African American women were shot. The militia and a few Continental troops pursued the Loyalists so closely that they took no cattle.[68]

★ General Henry Clinton (1730–1795) mounted a full-scale military expedition through Closter against the Congressional troops at Paramus Church. Captain Patrick Ferguson (1744–1780) and three detachments headed to the northern end of Manhattan on Monday evening, May 18, 1779. They crossed the river at night to attack the outpost quickly. The 63rd Regiment crossed the river farther south, at Fort Lee, earlier in the evening, to cover Ferguson's flank. Lieutenant Colonel Abraham Van Buskirk's corps came up from Paulus Hook to support the 63rd.[69]

Captain Ferguson was delayed in the embarkation and landed about 1 mile below the Closter landing place at daylight. He had only seven boats with him instead of 12. He waited a considerable time for the other five boats which went down the river; but the men never joined him. With his force so much reduced, Captain Ferguson marched two or three miles above Closter and seized some cattle.[70]

The regiment which had landed at Fort Lee moved toward Hackensack and New Bridge where a party of about 40 Whigs tried unsuccessfully to take up the planks of the bridge. Both sides exchanged several shots without doing any damage. Two companies of Regulars and 50 of Van Buskirk's corps held New Bridge while two other companies were posted at Liberty Pole. Guards were placed at the Little Ferry and on the road to the Three Pigeons Tavern. The 64th Regiment arrived from New York the next day to guard the lower ferries over the Hackensack. Ferguson's detachment and the 63rd joined at New Bridge and held the heights a quarter mile to the west.[71]

The whole force marched to Hoboken the following morning and recrossed the Hudson to New York.[72]

★ On Sunday afternoon, July 10, 1779, a party of about 20 Loyalists under Lieutenant Waller landed at Closter Dock. They collected and drove off a considerable number of cattle and horses to bring them back to their sloop. Captain David Harring and Captain Thomas Blanch (1740–1823) led a few of their neighbors to recover all the cattle except two and a calf. They also retrieved all the horses except one and an old mare which the raiders got on board before Captain Harring's arrival. They killed two of the plunderers and wounded two others. Captain Harring took two prisoners, seven stand of arms, and three suits of clothes and forced Lieutenant Waller to cut his cable, conceal his men below deck, and let their vessel drift with the tide. There were more than 20 vessels in the river which tried to protect the Loyalists by cannonading Captain Harring.[73]

★ Toward the end of March 1780, a party of about 400 British, Hessians, and Loyalists passed through Hackensack on their way to attack some Pennsylvania troops at Paramus. They entered the lower part of the town about 3 AM on Thursday, March 23 and found everything quiet. A small company of 20 or 30 militiamen under Captain John Outwater (1746–1823) had retired for the night. Half of the Crown forces marched quietly through town; but when the rear units, consisting mostly of Hessians, arrived, they broke open the doors and windows, robbed and plundered, and took a few inhabitants prisoners, including Mr. Archibald Campbell (d. 1798). Mr. Campbell had been confined to bed with rheumatism for several weeks. The soldiers forced him into the street and ordered him to follow them, often threatening to shoot him if he did not quicken his pace. Mr. Campbell later escaped in the confusion and hid in the cellar of a house opposite the New Bridge. He lived until 1798, and never again experienced any rheumatism.

The Hessians burned two dwellings and the courthouse on the west side of the green, eight or ten rods from Campbell's tavern. The family threw water on the roof of the tavern and the west wind blew the sparks over the green, saving the house. The commotion aroused the militiamen who hastened across the fields, mounted horses, and alarmed the troops at Paramus.

By the time the Crown forces arrived at the Red Mills, 4 miles from Hackensack in Arcola, they realized that Captain John Outwater and the militia were on their way to meet them. They met at the Red Mills where a withering fire from behind the mills and every available tree routed the advancing columns. The Crown forces returned toward Hackensack and headed north toward New Bridge. Their large flanking parties kept the militia at a distance. When they arrived at the Hackensack River, they found the planks of the bridge had been torn up. During the two-hour delay to replace the planks, the flanking parties skirmished with the people.

After they crossed the river, the Crown forces marched down the east side of the Hackensack through the English Neighborhood while the militiamen pursued them down to Bergen Woods—12 miles to a considerable distance within their lines. They lost many killed and wounded while none of the militiamen were killed. The wounded included a young man wounded by a spent ball which cut his upper lip, knocked out four front teeth, and was caught in his mouth. Captain Outwater received a ball below the knee which was never extracted. He carried it for many years to his grave.[74]

★ Another party of about 30 Loyalists landed at Closter to plunder cattle on Thursday, May 25, 1780. Captain Thomas Blanch (1740–1823) attacked them while they were collecting the cattle. He recaptured the cattle, killed one and wounded two of the plunderers and drove them to their boats without any loss.[75]

★ Local militiamen attacked a party of 30 to 50 Loyalists on a foraging raid collecting horses, cows, and sheep at Closter about 4:30 AM on Thursday, June 8, 1780. They targeted the area around Isaac Naugle's house, about 2 miles south of the New York–New Jersey line, on the road to Sneden's Landing at Closter. Captain Thomas Blanch (1740–1823) and Lieutenant John Huyler gathered the local militia and attacked the raiders, killing one, wounding several, and driving the others off "in such confusion that they dropped several of their greatcoats and many other articles."[76]

★ Two days later, on Saturday, June 10, Captain Thomas Blanch (1740–1823) reported the capture of the foraging sailors. He wrote to Governor William Livingston (1723–1790), "With pleasure I can acquaint you, that . . . the *Vulture* of sixteen guns came up [the Hudson] as high as Closter where it landed [thirty] men." Captain Blanch had taken command of a number of new Bergen County militiamen that very morning and captured "a mate shipman" and 11 sailors prisoners. They were taken to Morristown and imprisoned in the provost.

Captain Blanch made it clear that he did not have the men or the resources to continue fighting off the raiders. He wrote: "The *Vulture*, commanded by Captain Sutherland [remains] opposite the dock. The miserable situation we are in I cannot express. We have no assistance in this quarter, only . . . our too small company." He said that all the other militiamen, except Captain Logan of the Somerset militia posted near Hackensack, had been ordered out of the county. Captain Blanch was wounded shortly after this incident.[77]

★ A soldier of the Jersey brigade was executed for desertion on Saturday, June 17; and three spies shared the same fate on Monday the 19th.[78]

★ A large plundering party of 200 British and Loyalists under Captain Thomas Ward, of the Associated Loyalists, was on a two-day expedition to Closter on Monday and Tuesday, March 12 and 13, 1781. They brought two field pieces with them and stripped the town of everything movable. Major General William Heath (1737–1814) sent some Continental troops to drive them off, but Captain John Outwater (1746–1823) and his militia drove the Loyalists away before the Continental soldiers arrived. They also recaptured the cattle.[79]

★ Loyalist Captain William Harding and a party of 11 men went from Fort DeLancey on Bergen Neck to Closter on Wednesday evening, September 12, 1781. They captured a Whig guard of six men and 15 cattle and brought them to the fort.[80]

Paramus (Dec. 16, 1776; May 12, 1777; June 11, 1777)

Ridgewood

Hopperstown (Dec. 25, 1776; Dec. 27, 1776; Apr. 26, 1777; Apr. 21, 1779; Mar. 23, 1780; Apr. 16, 1780)

Garret Hopper's (1735–1814) neighborhood, or Hopperstown, was in what is now Paramus. It was about 8 miles north of New Bridge. Paramus is about 6.5 miles northeast of Paterson.

Major General William Heath (1737–1814) and General George Clinton (1739–1812), who had followed General Heath down Schraalenburgh Road with some of his officers and a small detachment of Continental light horse, retired to Paramus on Monday morning, December 16, 1776. They brought their prisoners and captured stores in the face of a strong British troop movement toward Hackensack. They assumed that the troops were heading toward them but they were only going into their long-delayed winter quarters.[81]

★ About 500 (some say 800) Crown troops, consisting of Highlanders and Lieutenant Colonel Abraham Van Buskirk's (1750–1783) Regiment, entered Hackensack Wednesday evening, December 25, 1776. They abused and imprisoned the few inhabitants they found there. General George Clinton (1739–1812) sent out scouting parties to protect the inhabitants in and around Paramus and to discover the enemy movements.[82]

★ During the night of Friday, December 27, 1776, a British and Loyalist force stationed at Hackensack raided Hopperstown and Paramus. They took Garret Hopper (1735–1814) and six or seven other Whig farmers prisoners and confined them in the Hackensack jail.[83]

★ Colonel Joseph Barton, Lieutenant Colonel William Drummond (d. 1814) and Major Robert Timpany (1742–1844), and about 200 new Loyalist recruits surprised Captain Wynant Van Zandt and three others at Garret Hopper's neighborhood, a little after sunrise on Saturday, April 26, 1777. They captured 12 muskets, five or six horses, one wagon, a chest and cask of goods. The neighbors either hid themselves or ran away and escaped.[84]

★ Colonel Joseph Barton's force of more than 300 Loyalist levies decided to take the road to Paramus to destroy some stores there, guarded by 80 to 100 men. They drove the Whigs from their strongholds, and forced them to retreat to the woods. They also intended to attack General Nathaniel Heard (1730–1792) and a small party of militiamen at Pompton on a foggy Monday morning, May 12, 1777. General Heard learned of the plan and changed his camp. Because they were delayed, the Loyalists attacked Captain Peter Fell's command of about 30 militiamen quartered at Garret Hopper's (1735–1814) house at Paramus Church instead. They marched that night to Benjamin Oldis's (1710–1791) house, about a quarter of a mile farther on the Pompton road, and surrounded Garret Hopper's house at daybreak. The Loyalists entered General Heard's former camp by different routes and mistook each other for the enemy. The confused levies fired smartly at each other and killed five of their own men before they realized it. As they retreated, General Heard's men killed two more and wounded several others who were carried off. General Heard lost one man killed and another taken prisoner.[85]

The Norwich Packet states that Lieutenant John Zabriskie led a small reconnoitering party that fought with the raiders for some time and then retreated. Captain Fell ordered his men to fire a volley which threw the Crown forces into disorder and they ran back. Captain Fell, afraid of having his avenue of retreat cut off, left a few of his men to secure the retreat while he sallied out with about 18 men and drove the Crown forces back in confusion. They followed the Regulars for 6 miles, killed five and wounded 17. More likely, it was the British who drove the militiamen, outnumbered 10 to 1, from their position.[86]

★ Colonel Joseph Barton and a party of 200 Crown troops went from Bergen to Paramus without any opposition on Wednesday, June 11, 1777. They were pursuing a party under Frederick Frelinghuysen (1753–1804) but ran away when they found him.[87]

★ On Wednesday, April 21, 1779, Captain Jonathan Hopper (1752–1779) of the Bergen County militia was killed by Loyalist raiders at Hopperstown. He found "a party of ruffians from New York . . . breaking open his stable door and hailed them, upon which they fired and wounded him; he returned to the house, they followed, burst open the door and bayoneted him in upwards of twenty places." One of the raiders, Stephen Ryder (or Rider), had been one of Hopper's neighbors before the war and was convinced that it was more profitable to steal horses from Whigs than to buy them and run them through the Continental lines.

Rivington's Gazette saw Hopper's death not as a warning against horse thieves but as a lesson to purchasers of confiscated Loyalist property, as Captain Hopper had purchased the house of Major Robert Drummond, a Loyalist, at public auction. Captain Hopper might have survived had he not tried to defend his property.[88]

★ During the night of Wednesday, March 22, 1780, two detachments of Crown forces crossed the Hudson River into New Jersey. Lieutenant Colonel John Howard, of the British Guards, led one detachment of 300 men of the Brigade of Guards from Kingsbridge. They landed at Closter several miles above Fort Lee. The other detachment, of equal force, comprised British and German troops from New York under the command of Lieutenant Colonel Duncan Macpherson of the 42nd Regiment (Black Watch). They embarked at the Hay Wharf on Manhattan Island with 600 men at 7 PM. They landed at Weehawken a little before 10 PM and marched to the Little Ferry on the Hackensack River where they were transported across in a small whaleboat (see Photo NJ-1) and a canoe between midnight and 3 AM.

Lieutenant Colonel Howard had orders to penetrate into the country to the north of Hopperstown and to attack the rear of the Continental camp. He was to have moved from Kingsbridge at the same time that MacPherson left the Hay Wharf; but he was delayed for several hours. The boats did not arrive at Spuyten Duyvil until 10:30 and didn't reach Closter Landing until midnight. They then had to march at least 17 miles to Paramus Church to come in the rear of the enemy pickets. He arrived near Hopperstown two hours after daybreak on the 23rd.

Colonel Howard ordered Lieutenant Colonel Stuart to take 50 men to march on the east side of Saddle River while Lieutenant Colonel Francis Hall and 60 light infantrymen proceeded to Hopper's house. Colonel Howard took 190 men along the west side of Saddle River toward Paramus. He surprised two pickets, and attacked one of the camps, forcing the officer and his men to leave their arms behind. He captured and destroyed more than 30 stand of arms. The main body of 200 to 300 men put up a show of resistance at the church but retired quickly when they saw an attack imminent. Howard's Guards pursued them for more than a mile and captured several prisoners.

Meanwhile, Colonel Macpherson's force crossed the Hackensack to surprise that town where a company of militia was quartered. Colonel Macpherson sent a subaltern and 25 men of the 43rd Regiment to the end of the town, next to New Bridge, to prevent anybody from escaping. The remaining part of the detachment of the 43rd Regiment and 50 Anspachs were ordered to follow Loyalist guides and to attack every house they pointed out and to seize every man they found. They then attacked the front of the camp at Paramus but found it abandoned; so they went to join Colonel Howard at the church, having taken a few prisoners who were then brought to Zabriskie's Mill.

As it was futile to pursue the enemy, both detachments returned to Zabriskie's Mills where they were joined by the party left at Hackensack which had taken several prisoners. The troops returned by way of New Bridge and the English Neighborhood. Lieutenant

Colonel Howard's detachment embarked near Fort Lee, while Lieutenant Colonel Macpherson's force continued marching, with the prisoners, toward Weehawken where boats were waiting to transport them.

One man of the Guards was killed and a few men were wounded on the march toward the English Neighborhood. Congressional forces, in loose parties, kept up an irregular fire upon their rear and some men dropped behind from fatigue. A clergyman [Warmoldus Kuypers (1732–1797)] and another resident (probably Mr. Periam, the Paramus schoolmaster) were taken prisoners by mistake during the march. They were dismissed and accidentally shot by the militia. Mr. Periam was badly wounded in the shoulder.

The Crown forces burned the courthouse in Hackensack and one or two dwelling-houses. They plundered Mr. Campbell, a tavern-keeper, of a large sum of Continental hard money and captured 64 prisoners—24 Continental troops, a captain, 26 militia-men, and 13 deserters from Paramus. The number of Congressional killed and wounded is unknown. The Crown forces reportedly had three or four wagons full of killed and wounded. Their retreat was so hurried that they did not stop to pick up any of their dead and wounded who fell off the wagons.[89]

The Crown forces marched out of Hackensack at daybreak on Thursday, March 23, 1780. They proceeded 2 miles to Pollingtown where they hoped to capture a Congressional command of about 250 to 300 of the 5th Pennsylvania Regiment. However, the Congressional troops learned of their movements from spies and took positions behind a stone wall in front of the church. When the Crown forces formed to attack, the militia fled. The Crown forces pursued them for 1.5 miles before being ordered back to Paramus Bridge to join Lieutenant Colonels Stuart and Hall. Lieutenant Colonel Stuart surprised a corporal and six men. Another picket of an officer and 20 men in an adjoining house ran off, leaving 30 stand of arms. Lieutenant Colonel Hall surprised a picket of nine men, one of whom escaped. The main body at Hopper's house escaped half an hour earlier.

Meanwhile, MacPherson's party marched to Zabriskie's Mills where they arrived at 6:30 AM and continued marching toward Paramus without any opposition. They arrived about 7:30 to find Colonel Howard and his Guards pursuing the enemy. The two forces rejoined here.

Meanwhile, the Hessians found themselves attacked from all sides, forcing them to return to Hackensack or be taken prisoners. Lieutenant Colonel Andreas Emmerich (1737–1809), who crossed the North River beyond Kingsbridge the day before, came with reinforcements of 400 light infantrymen and jaegers to cover their flank, as they withdrew slowly under steady fire which lasted more than six hours.

The Hessians discarded most of the furniture they had taken and arrived at New York about 8 PM, having been pursued to the shore of the North River. The Crown forces lost three Scots, 11 English and Hessians killed and one private captured. The Congressional troops lost two wounded and 65 captured.[90]

★ A cavalry detachment of about 120 men, composed of the 17th dragoons, Queen's Ranger hussars, Diemar's hussars, and Lieutenant Stuart's volunteers from Staten Island together with a body of 312 foot soldiers, composed of 12 jaegers, 150 men of the regiment von Bose, 100 men of the regiment Mirbach [Major General Werner von Mirbach Regiment von Mirbach (later Jung von Lossburg) (1780)], and 50 men of the Loyal American Regiment, from York Island, landed in New Jersey on Saturday, April 15, 1780. Major Johann Christian DuPuy of the regiment von Bose commanded the detachment. The cavalry went near the end of Bergen Neck, while the infantry went near Fort Lee. They joined forces in the English Neighborhood and marched north to New Bridge on the Hackensack. They arrived there between 2 and 3 AM on the 16th after encountering a Whig patrol there. They took the commanding officer and three of his men prisoners. The others escaped.

The Crown forces continued marching to Paramus. Major DuPuy saw the church a little after daybreak. He attacked a detachment of 200 Continental troops, under the command of Major Thomas Langhorne Boyles (d. 1780) or Biles or Byles, of the Pennsylvania line, stationed at Paramus. Major Boyles, had sent out two parties, each with a commissioned officer, that morning in addition to his usual patrols. The Crown troops fell in with one of the patrols, surprised a picket guard posted at the bridge upon Saddle Creek near where Maple Avenue crosses the Ho-Ho-Kus Brook. The picket fired. The advance guard of cavalry immediately charged and captured an officer and three men.

The cavalry pushed forward to Hopperstown. When they arrived a short while later, they attacked a larger body of Continentals who had just finished parading and were dismissed when the alarm was sounded. The horsemen advanced so rapidly that the Continentals had no time to reassemble. The major tried to defend his quarters with only a small guard. Both sides kept up a brisk fire. The stone house, with three windows below and two above, was soon completely surrounded. Nine men, mostly servants of the officers, fired from another house about 20 yards away. Corporal Bart and six or eight men were ordered to dismount and fire in the windows of the first house at random. Corporal Bart placed two men at the door and took the rest and broke the second house open. The people in it then surrendered.

Some of the men from the first house began to cry for quarter; others continued to fire from the windows. The Regulars chided them for asking quarter and continuing to resist. They demanded that the Continentals come out to receive quarter. Major Boyles surrendered and received a mortal shot in the left breast when he did not present the hilt of his sword in front. He died three days later.

The Regulars plundered and burned the house and mill of Mr. John Hopper and that of his brothers. Mrs. Abraham Brasher, who lived in one of the houses with her family, begged the commanding officer on her knees to spare the house. He damned her and bid her to be gone, declaring they all deserved to be bayoneted. As the Regulars withdrew, some Continentals and a few militiamen harassed them with a continual fire from different directions. Their constant scattered fire from different quarters annoyed the marchers but had little effect. The harassment continued all the way to Fort Lee, their place of embarkation. The infantry arrived between 3 and 4 PM while the dragoons returned by the same route by which they advanced.

The Continentals re-took four wagons with plunder and 19 horses. They lost one major, two captains, four lieutenants, and about 40 to 70 privates killed, about 10 wounded left behind, and 51 prisoners, many of them wounded. One of the officers was killed on the spot. The major in command and another officer were left badly wounded while two captains, two lieutenants and two ensigns were taken prisoners.

The Regulars acknowledged comparable losses: three dragoons killed and eight wounded, four infantrymen killed and 23 wounded, four wagons, and a number of horses. The 17th light-dragoons lost one horse killed and three privates and one horse wounded. The Queen's Ranger hussars lost three soldiers and three horses killed, one soldier and two horses wounded. Diemar's hussars lost two men and one horse wounded. The Staten Island Volunteers had two privates wounded and the jaegers, one wounded.

Major General Werner von Mirbach lost one killed and 11 men wounded while Lieutenant Colonel Carl Ernst Johann von Bose (d. 1778) lost two killed, one sergeant and five privates wounded. The Loyal Americans lost one killed and five wounded, giving a total of 25 men and 6 horses killed, two sergeants, 63 men and 5 horses wounded.[91]

Polifly (Sept. 22, 1778)

Polifly is about 3 miles north of Passaic.

Brigadier General William Winds (1727–1789) captured the Crown fort at Polifly on Tuesday, September 22, 1778.[91a]

River Vale/Westwood (Old Tappan)

Herringtown (Apr. 17, 1777; Sept. 28, 1778)

Baylor's Massacre (Sept. 27–28, 1778)

The site of Baylor's Massacre is at the intersection of Old Tappan Road and Rivervale Road in Westwood (see Photo NJ-13). The entrance to the site is on Rectenwald Court, a short distance from the intersection. Some sources refer to the engagement as the Old Tappan Massacre.

Major Blauvelt [probably Johannes Joseph Blauvelt (1714–1789)], of Tappan, was seized at his home on Thursday, April 17, 1777, by a dozen Loyalists, led by Captain David Peek of Schraalenburgh. The band of Loyalists included several of Blauvelt's relatives, Cornelius Johannes Blauvelt, Jacob Johannes Blauvelt and Garret Smith, his neighbors John Straat and Jacob Straat, and Abraham Parcels and Parcels' brother, all of

Photo NJ-13. Site of Baylor's Massacre

Schraalenburgh. John Straat, when arrested for the affair, testified that "he understood that . . . Peter T. Herring, as he was going down to the English Neighborhood with but-ter in order to procure some salt, was taken by a party of American troops near the Tiene Fly [Tenafly], and carried prisoner somewhere to the westward. . . . Some time last spring . . . David Peek, who lives at Schraalenburgh, sent word to him . . . to come to the house of . . . [Herring] to assist to take Major Blauvelt in order to have him exchanged for Herring and by that means to effect Herring's releasement." Straat told the messenger, Isaac DePew (1758–1825), that "he would not come and assist, for that Major Blauvelt was a very clever man," but DePew threatened that Peek would come and take him and carry him off to provost jail in New York. This statement intimidated Major Blauvelt who went to Herring's house unarmed but "kept at a distance without giving the party any assistance and as soon as he conveniently could went off privately to his own house." Curiously enough, Captain Johannes Jacobus Blauvelt and others testified that they be-lieved that Straat and some of the others were telling the truth when they said they had acted solely from fear of Peek, and they were released.[92]

★ General Henry Clinton (1730–1795) needed food for the troops he planned to send from New York to the West Indies. He sent Lieutenant General Wilhelm von Knyphausen (1716–1800) and his troops up the eastern bank of the Hudson on a for-aging expedition while General Charles Cornwallis (1738–1805) and approximately 5,000 men proceeded toward the Paulus Hook peninsula on the western bank of the Hudson on Tuesday, September 22, 1778.

General Cornwallis's force consisted of the 3rd and 4th British brigades, the grena-diers (see Photo NJ-10), the light infantry, the guards, and the Volunteers of Ireland. They captured the posts at Liberty Pole (Englewood) and New Bridge, forcing the main body of the Congressional forces to retreat. General Clinton and his staff joined General Cornwallis on September 25th as they headed north through New Jersey.

General George Washington (1732–1799) had sent Colonel George Baylor (1752–1784) and the 3rd Regiment Light Dragoons ("Mrs. Washington's Guards") to annoy the Crown forces in their foraging mission, capture enemy scouts, and intercept messen-gers. Baylor's dragoons had received 200 new uniforms on September 27 and made an excellent military appearance when they set out in pursuit of Cornwallis. They occupied the house and barns of a Loyalist farmer named Cornelius Haring that night in Old Tappan, New Jersey, near the Overkill Road (Rivervale Road today).

Baylor and his officers bedded down for the night in Haring's house, while the sol-diers slept in the three barns on Haring's property. A sergeant and 12 men guarded a bridge over the Hackensack River. Despite occupying the property of a Loyalist, Baylor was confident his men were safe because his intelligence reports indicated the near-est Crown troops were at least 10 miles away and Brigadier General William Winds (1727–1789) and a force of 400 New Jersey militiamen were stationed only 2.5 miles away in New Tappan, New York.

General Cornwallis saw an opportunity to strike at Baylor's outpost. He selected four regiments—the 2nd Light Infantry, the 2nd Grenadiers, the 33rd Regiment, and the 64th Regiment—to attack Baylor and Winds. Local Loyalists provided Cornwallis with accurate intelligence. They and 50 dragoons also accompanied Cornwallis's main col-umn under Major General Charles "No Flint" Grey (1729–1807). General Knyphausen was supposed to send a detachment across the Hudson to attack Winds's New Jersey militia at the same time as Cornwallis struck Baylor; but a lack of boats canceled this attempt.

As he did in the attack at Paoli the year before, General Grey had his men remove the flints from their muskets so no weapon would fire and warn the enemy. Guided by Loyalists, Grey marched toward Old Tappan at 10 PM on Sunday, September 27, 1778. They headed north on Kinderkamack Road. They then took Piermont Road to reach Overkill Road (today's Rivervale Road). Cornwallis left two hours later with a supporting column. They took a different road and arrived too late to help.

General Grey struck at 3 AM on Monday, September 28. He sent six companies of the light infantry with orders to take no prisoners. The light infantrymen eliminated the guard at the bridge and surrounded the barns where Baylor's dragoons were sleeping. The rest of the troops attacked the Haring buildings.

Baylor's dragoons, caught without warning, could not put up an effective defense. In one of the barns, 16 of them resisted for a short time. Grey's men soon overpowered them and bayoneted and killed nine. Lieutenant William Barren was the only dragoon to escape on horseback. Captain Robert Smith (1752–1838) and 10 of his men managed to escape into the swamps.

The attackers trapped Baylor and his officers in the Haring house. They tried to escape up the chimney of a Dutch oven but Grey's men caught them and bayoneted Major Alexander Clough (d. 1778), Baylor's second in command. He died of his wounds. Baylor was severely wounded in the lungs. Six years later, in 1784, complications from his wounds proved fatal. Many of the Continental dragoons who did surrender were bayoneted, many with multiple stab wounds. Seventeen men were left for dead. Local residents came to collect the bodies the next day and cared for them. Somehow, 13 of the 17 wounded recovered. Some of them were taken to the church in New Tappan, New York, a short distance away. The church would later serve as the site of the trial of Major John André (1751–1780).

Captain Smith, the ranking surviving officer in command of the 3rd Dragoons returned to the Haring farm the next day. He was accompanied by the 37 remaining dragoons, including some who were wounded. He found one dead dragoon with 16 bayonet wounds. Three others had 12 wounds each. Some of the dead were buried on the field. Others were placed in a mass grave in the tanning vats of Blauvelt's tannery along today's Rivervale Road in Old Tappan. The archaeologists excavating the site found some of the skulls crushed by the butt plates of muskets. The massacre left 67 dead and wounded while the attackers had no significant casualties.

Captain John Swan (1731–1790) and his 4th troop were captured and taken back to New York with a total of 39 prisoners. They also took Baylor and regimental surgeon George Evans (1756–1832).

General William Winds had learned of General Cornwallis's advance but neglected to inform Baylor. He marched his men in a safe direction and was not attacked that night, but Cornwallis pursued him the following morning.

General Washington appointed Major William Washington (1752–1810) of the 4th Dragoons to command Baylor's dragoons. William Washington was promoted to lieutenant colonel on Friday, November 20, 1778. He then took his regiment to winter quarters at Fredericktown, Maryland.

General Clinton gathered the necessary grain, cattle, and forage for his West Indies expedition, but very few Loyalists joined his ranks. Many Loyalist families used the opportunity to join their husbands or fathers then serving in the army, while some of the country people made a profit by their produce. Those not inclined toward the British lost much of what they had.[93]

Bergen County
Little Ferry (Apr. 12, 1779; May 1779)
Moonachie (Apr. 10, 1781)

> The road to Hackensack turned due west toward the Little Ferry over the Hacken-
> sack River. The north and south road continued on to Liberty Pole, Tenafly, Closter
> and Tappan.
> Moonachie is about 1 mile south of Little Ferry.

A detachment of about 60 Loyalists under Captain William Van Allen seized an outpost at Little Ferry near New Barbados in Bergen County on Monday, April 12, 1779. A party of about 20 men crossed the river by lashing two canoes together. They marched about 3 miles through the swamps and woods during a violent storm to get in the rear of the guard which consisted of two noncommissioned officers and 12 privates of the Carolina Brigade and one militiaman [Lucas Brinkerhoff (1754–) of Major Richard Dey's (1752–1811) troops]. They came to the sentry at the door undiscovered. The sentry challenged them and they rushed in, killed two, wounded two who tried to escape and took the rest prisoners with all their arms and accoutrements. They returned to New York after sunrise on Wednesday morning with their prisoners and their pockets full of paper dollars.[94]

See **Closter.**

★ Several hundred foragers stripped the neutral ground from Little Ferry to the New York line in May 1779.[95]

★ A British gunboat brought a party of foragers up the Hackensack River to Moonachie Point on Tuesday, April 10, 1781. The foragers took about 20 head of cattle. Local militiamen routed the foragers and recaptured the cattle. The British lost seven men killed and one prisoner. Militiaman John Lozier (1745–1784) was shot through the thigh with a musket ball. Corporal Abraham Vreeland (1759–1826) tore up his shirt to stop the blood and to dress the wound. He carried Lozier out of the salt marshes, where the action occurred, to the home of George Doremus, about 11 miles from Pompton. It took Lozier almost a year to recover from his wound.[96]

Paterson
Wagaraw (Apr. 21, 1779)

> Wagaraw is on the Passaic River opposite present day Paterson

A Loyalist raiding party murdered Captain Jonathan Hopper (1752–1779) of the Bergen County militia, on Wednesday, April 21, 1779. Hopper was born at Hopperstown but lived on a farm in Wagaraw which he bought from the commissioners for seized Loyalist estates.

See **Hopperstown.**

Newfoundland
Charlotteburg (Apr. 27, 1779)

> Charlotteburg is off the Paterson–Hamburg Turnpike (NJ 23) in Newfoundland on
> the eastern shore of the Charlotteburg Reservoir.

A "party of robbers and well-armed Villains" surrounded a house at Hibernia Furnace on Tuesday April 27, 1779. Three of the robbers entered about 9 PM while the family was at supper and stayed nearly two hours. They pointed a pistol at each family member, ordered them to give up their arms and surrender themselves prisoners in the King's name or they would be killed. The three workmen around the house were in bed and could not come to the family's assistance. The robbers posted a sentry at each door and then proceeded to plunder the house, loading five horses with their spoils.

They went to Doctor Jonathan Chuver's house, near Charlotteburg iron-works, intending to murder him. While they were surrounding his house, he escaped out a window. They fired at him but missed. He ran six or seven miles, wearing only his shirt, to alarm the townspeople. The robbers plundered his house, threatened to murder his wife, and made her go down on her knees twice to beg for her life. They left before the militia arrived.[97]

Weehawken (Nov. 21, 1777; Apr. 17, 1779; Aug. 19, 1779)

> Weehawken is on the western shore of the Hudson River between 45th and 48th Streets in West New York.

A detachment of Orange County militiamen under Captain William Johnston skirmished with the British or Loyalists near Weehawken in November or December 1777, probably around November 21, 1777. Garrett C. Oblenis (1760–1839) was wounded by a shot that went through his left arm and broke two of his ribs.[98]

★ On Saturday, April 17, 1779, two Bergen County militiamen and several others had been out as a reconnoitering party. They saw a boy running toward a house on the bank of the Hudson River, about 1 mile above Weehawken, and suspected that some members of a gang of robbers were hiding there. One of the party advanced as fast as possible to the house and discovered five or six in the house, several of them armed. He pretended he had a large party accompanying him and called out to them, fired his musket and killed the leader of the gang on the spot. When he retired to reload, the rest of the gang ran away but were fired upon by the rest of the reconnoitering party. One of the gang was believed to be wounded.[99]

★ After the capture of Paulus Hook on Thursday, August 19, 1779, Major General Charles Lee (1731–1782) and his men marched toward Dow's Ferry where they expected to join with Brigadier General William Alexander's (Earl of Stirling, 1726–1783) covering party of 300 men and board boats to return to New Bridge. Lee's troops were tired from marching 30 miles "through mountains, swamps and deep morasses, without the least refreshment" and fighting a battle. They were 14 miles from New Bridge and had no dry cartridges. They feared that Lieutenant Colonel Abraham Van Buskirk's (1750–1783) foraging party might return to the Hook soon and attack them.

When they arrived at the rendezvous point, they found the boats were not there. Captain Henry Peyton (d. 1781) was in command of that operation with the first company of Captain Henry "Light-Horse Harry" Lee's (1756–1818) Legion. Expecting the rendezvous to occur several hours earlier, he assumed that the plan had been abandoned when the troops did not arrive at the appointed time. So he took the boats back to Newark.

Lee realized his situation was desperate. He ordered his troops "to regain the Bergen road and shove on to the New Bridge." He also sent an express to Stirling to come meet him. He divided his force in three near Weehawken and divided the prisoners among the three detachments. Captain Levin Handy (1754–1799) led one part on the road over the hills. Major Jonathan Clark (1750–1811) took the second part along the Bergen road and Lee took the center route with the rest. Captain Thomas Catlett (1741–1780) and 50 Virginians arrived at this time with dry ammunition. Lee assigned some of the Virginians to each column to act as rear guards.

Colonel Ball arrived a short while later with a detachment from Stirling. Van Buskirk and his raiders arrived almost at the same time and attacked the column's right flank as it reached the Liberty Pole (Englewood). Lee's rear guard faced about and Lieutenant Rudulph placed a party of the Legion in a stone house and Van Buskirk retired. The entire command assembled with all their prisoners at the New Bridge at 1 o'clock in the afternoon of the 19th. The expedition had no military value, but it captured some prisoners and improved the morale of the army. Lee received much praise for his exploits and Congress voted to thank him by awarding him a gold medal. It also appropriated $15,000 in Continental paper to be divided among the troops. Rudulph was brevetted captain.[100]

See **Leonia, Liberty Pole.**

New Bridge (Jan. 28, 1776; Dec. 9, 1776; Dec. 25, 1776; Sept. 11, 1777; Sept. 12, 1777; Sept. 14, 1777; Sept. 16, 1777; Nov. 17, 1777; Feb. 5, 1778; Apr. 16, 1780; July 29, 1781)

Zabriskie Mills–New Bridge (May 30, 1780)

New Bridge is about 2 miles north of Hackensack. Zabriskie's Mills was about 4 miles from Hackensack. Paramus Church was about 5 miles beyond Zabriskie's Mills. Easton Tower Historic Site occupies the location of Zabriskie Mills, which was the location where the Crown forces jailed nearly all the men they captured in their attack on Hackensack on March 23, 1780.

Colonel William Malcom or Malcolm (1745–1791) led a party to New Bridge on Sunday, January 28, 1776 and raised a "terrible uproar among the Tories as well as in the enemy's little camp." They also captured a Loyalist named Pierson.[101]

★ Colonel William Malcom's or Malcolm (1745–1791) militia at Tappan raided Loyalist troops near New Bridge on Monday December 9, 1776, and captured two.

See also **Bridgewater, Two Bridges.**

★ A Whig scouting party took Peter Quackenboss and Benjamin Babcock prisoners near New Bridge on Wednesday night, December 25, 1776. They had just come from the British lines and had assisted them in moving their baggage to Hackensack. Benjamin Babcock had an original letter from Governor William Tryon (1729–1788) and a receipt signed by Babcock to a Mr. Grant, for eight pounds for assisting to bring in recruits to the British Army.[102]

★ Brigadier General Alexander McDougall (1732–1786) and his brigade marched to Tappan on Thursday, September 11, 1777. Colonel William Malcom or Malcolm (1745–1791) and his regiment and a few Orange County militiamen went to Paramus while Brigadier General "Mad Anthony" Wayne (1745–1796) proceeded to the Acquackanonk River with the Jersey militia. The Crown forces received notice of their approach and retreated.

★ That same day, while they were encamped at New Bridge, Lieutenant Colonel Aaron Burr (1756–1836) and a party of 24, including officers of Colonel William Malcom's or

Malcolm (1745–1791) regiment rushed, with fixed bayonets, on an enemy picket guard of 23. They killed 13, wounded and captured five with two other prisoners. The other three escaped to their camp.[103]

★ On Friday, September 12, 1777, the day after General William Howe's (1732–1786) crushing defeat of General George Washington (1732–1799) at Brandywine, General Henry Clinton (1730–1795) invaded New Jersey with 2,000 troops as a diversion for General Howe's Philadelphia campaign. He divided his force into four columns which were to rendezvous at New Bridge. Brigadier General John Campbell (d. 1806) led one column, including 200 of Lieutenant Colonel Abraham Van Buskirk's (1750–1783) 4th New Jersey Volunteers and 40 marines. They landed at Elizabethtown Point and headed toward Newark, driving cattle, disarming the inhabitants and preventing any enemy forces from proceeding to Acquackanonk.

A small corps landed at Schuyler's Ferry with cannon. Captain Drummond took another corps with two field pieces, 250 recruits of the 71st Regiment and some convalescents by way of Schuyler's Ferry to occupy the high ground around Newark. General Clinton went up Newark Bay to Dow's Ferry at Schuyler's Landing on the Hackensack River. The cannon were landed and ordered to proceed, over the Belleville Turnpike and through the cedar swamp, to the high ground near Schuyler's house where Captain Drummond had been for some time with his 250 men. Meanwhile, General Campbell landed at Tappan without opposition about 4 AM, with orders to remain there and to fall back on New Bridge if pressed. During the night, General Campbell arrived with his detachment and the cattle he had collected en route. They occupied Schuyler Heights, commanding the environs of Newark, to secure the retreat route over the Passaic River to Acquackanonk.

Major General John Vaughan (1738?–1795) landed at Fort Lee with a company of Captain Andreas Emmerich's (1737–1809) chasseurs, five companies of grenadiers (see Photo NJ-7) and light infantry, the 54th and 63rd and Prince Charles's Regiments, with five pieces of very light artillery. He met some resistance along the Passaic River. After a long day exchanging fire with Congressional troops, he withdrew to New Bridge and sent outposts up the Schraalenburgh Road toward Tappan to prevent any attack from the north. He moved rapidly by way of New Bridge and Hackensack toward the heights over the Passaic at Slotterdam to the southwest. He left some troops at Hackensack and secured the very important pass at New Bridge with one battalion and two artillery pieces.

★ While the Crown forces were encamped at New Bridge, Lieutenant Colonel Aaron Burr (1756–1836) and 24 officers from Colonel William Malcom's or Malcolm (1745–1791) regiment, with fixed bayonets, rushed on an enemy picket guard of 23 on September 14. They killed 13, wounded and took seven others prisoners, but three escaped.

The militiamen, informed of the landing at Elizabethtown Point, were removing their cattle when the troops arrived about noon. The number of militiamen increased and they brought one artillery piece. They also gathered all the boats on their side of the river. Both sides fired muskets and cannon the whole day with little or no loss on either side. Sporadic firing was heard beyond Newark and General Henry Clinton (1730–1795) received a private report that night that Brigadier General John Campbell (d. 1806) had taken possession of that town and was on his way to Acquackanonk. General Clinton ordered him to halt until morning.

By daybreak the next day, the militia, reinforced by Continental troops, had gathered in some force and had three cannon in a battery on their side of the ravine about noon. General Clinton ordered Lieutenant Colonel Abraham Van Buskirk's (1750–1783) 4th New Jersey Volunteers (mostly Dutch Loyalists) to march through a cornfield to flank the militia posted behind a stone wall which would have been difficult to remove by a frontal attack. The militia left the place without firing a shot and retired to the neighboring woods in the evening. The New Jersey Volunteers won a citation for their action.

The Congressional troops retired to the nearby woods in the evening. General Clinton waited for a squadron of dragoons to arrive from Paulus Hook and ordered them to assist General Campbell in surrounding the enemy and to capture the cannon if possible. Meanwhile, Major General John Vaughan (1738?–1795) sent a letter to General Clinton to inform him that the Congressional troops were assembling in great force at the Clove (Ramapo Valley). General Clinton assembled his troops as soon as possible and occupied New Bridge in some force.

They were to cross the river when the captured cattle were on the other side and remain there with their cannon.

The various columns assembled at New Bridge on the 15th. General Clinton ordered the small corps on the Heights of Schuyler, reinforced with two companies of grenadiers, to fall back and cover the entry of the defile while the army withdrew with the cattle because of threatening weather and the soldiers had no tents or blankets. General Campbell continued his march to English Neighborhood at dawn. He marched his force from the English Neighborhood to raid Bergen Point on the 16th. He captured 400 cattle, including 20 milk cows, 400 sheep, and a few horses taken from the people of Essex and Bergen before crossing over to Staten Island. General Vaughan went to Fort Lee and crossed the North River. The entire expedition had returned to their former stations by 2 PM. The Crown forces lost eight privates killed, one lieutenant and 17 privates wounded, one drummer and nine privates missing, and five privates taken prisoners.[104]

See also **Newark, Elizabethtown,** and **Slotterdam.**

★ A party of Loyalists overran a Congressional post near New Bridge on Monday, November 17, 1777.[105]

★ A party of four Loyalists captured a man called Brower, of New Barbados Neck (Bergen Neck), one of the slayers of Loyalist John Richards (d. 1778). He was secured under a provost guard at New York on Thursday afternoon, February 5, 1778.[106]

★ Colonel Johann Christian DuPuy and a force of 300 Hessian infantrymen and more than 100 dragoons struck an outpost at New Bridge at 1 AM on Sunday, April 16, 1780. The post was garrisoned by a captain and 30 men. The attack, about 2 AM, killed five defenders and captured 20. Lieutenant Bryson received several wounds as he defended himself with his spontoon (see Photo NJ-14) against four horsemen. Outnumbered and overpowered, he surrendered to an officer. The Crown forces then marched to Hopperstown (Paramus), where they attacked Major Langhorne Boyles (d. 1780) and 270 men of the 5th Pennsylvania Regiment. DuPuy's forces killed four, wounded six, and captured 40 of them.[107]

See **Paramus.**

★ On Tuesday night, May 30, 1780, two detachments of 300 Loyalists under Colonel Abraham Van Buskirk raided New Bridge to murder and carry off the militia. They

Photo NJ-14. Members of the Brigade of the American Revolution marching in a column of four. The sergeant leading the column is carrying a spontoon.

arrived at the house of Joost Zabriskie about 1 AM and mistook each other for the Whig guard. They engaged in a furious exchange of gunfire and "made a dreadful slaughter, the ground round the house being in a measure covered with blood." Realizing their mistake, they retreated over the bridge and took up the planks to prevent the enemy from pursuing them.[108]

★ Major Thomas Ward and a party of Refugees went from Bergen Neck to Liberty Pole on Sunday morning, July 29, 1781. He detached Captain John Miller and a party of 20 horsemen toward New Bridge, near Hackensack, where they captured three "notorious rebels by the names of Demareas, drove off their stock, and returned to the party without firing a shot.[109]

Hoboken
Bull's Ferry (May 28, 1780; July 21, 1780)
Block House (July 21, 1780)

Bull's Ferry is almost 4 miles above Hoboken on the New Jersey shore, approximately opposite 80th Street in New York City. The Bull's Ferry blockhouse site is at John F. Kennedy Boulevard and 74th Street, North Bergen. The blockhouse had three sides built against sheer rock. The open side had three lines of defense: an abatis, a log wall with portholes for cannons and muskets, and a deep ditch that attackers would have to cross if they got past the other two defenses. The only entrance to the fort was a tunnel wide enough for only one man.

A number of New York Loyalists had "taken post and erected some works of defense" in the upper part of Bergen township, near Bull's Ferry. Captain John Huyler and Captain Thomas Blanch (1740–1823) reported to Governor William Livingston (1723–1790) on Saturday, May 27, 1780 that they could not determine their number or strength with any certainty. They decided to take about 50 militiamen to test their strength.

Huyler, Blanch and Ensign Banta set out from Closter with 30 militiamen that night. They joined forces with Ensign John Terhune's (1759–1839) 19 militiamen from Hackensack at the Liberty Pole about 2 AM and marched to within half a mile of the blockhouse (see Photo NJ-15) erected in the highest part of the mountain about half a mile below Bull's Ferry Road. It was above a ravine running back from the Hudson at Bull's Ferry, protected on two sides by the perpendicular cliffs of the Palisades and in the front by abatis and stockades, a ditch and parapet. However, there was no possibility of retreat for the occupants. When the Congressional troops reached the heights overlooking Bull's Ferry, they abandoned any thoughts of trying to attack the blockhouse and returned by the main road. Along the way, a party of six Loyalists attacked their left flank. The militiamen killed one of the Loyalists on the spot, the noted murderer and thief John Berry (d. 1780) who went by the alias John the Regular. The militiamen mortally wounded another who died a little while later. They also captured two prisoners, a lieutenant and a private of the New York Militia taken near Bergen Woods. They had only one man wounded.

The prisoners informed their captors that the blockhouse, commanded by Lieutenant Colonel Abraham C. Cuyler (1742–1810), had two 6-pounders and about 100 to 200 men. They also employed 12 or 14 horsemen every night as a patrol to scout the English

Photo NJ-15. Blockhouse at Fort Halifax in Winslow, Maine, the oldest blockhouse in the United States. Notice the loophole and the dovetail construction on the corners.

Neighborhood. The State Treasurer paid Captain Blanch $1,000 to distribute among the noncommissioned officers and privates of the militia who had assisted in Berry's demise "as a Reward for their bravery, Zeal, and Activity."[110]

★ Although the war was in a stalemate in the north after 1779, occasional skirmishes and conflicts continued. One of these skirmishes occurred at Bull's Ferry on July 21, 1780. General George Washington (1732–1799) ordered Brigadier General "Mad Anthony" Wayne (1745–1796) to eliminate the blockhouse on July 19. Captain Thomas Ward's unit of 70 Regulars and Loyalists used it as a base for wood-cutting and foraging raids and other attacks.

General Wayne arranged his troops to guard the different landing places on the Bergen shore where the Crown forces from Staten Island might be expected to land to intercept his retreat. He sent the cavalry to drive off the stock while he proceeded to the blockhouse with 2,000 Pennsylvanians from the 1st, 2nd, and 10th Regiments and four 6-pounders on Saturday morning July 21, 1780. General Wayne intended to destroy the blockhouse which was protected on two sides by a ravine and by huge rocks, to seize cattle and horses, and to lure the Crown forces into an ambush near Fort Lee. They arrived at New Bridge about 9 PM where the local militia, which had recently been reinforced by four officers and 90 militiamen from Morris, Essex and Sussex Counties, joined them. They rested for four or five hours before continuing the march to Bull's Ferry where they arrived about daybreak.

Brigadier General William Irvine's (1741–1804) brigade moved along the top of the ridge while the 1st Brigade, the dragoons and the artillery took the direct road. The dragoons and a detachment of infantrymen guarded the fork of the road leading to Paulus Hook and Bergen to prevent any surprise. General Irvine took a position north of the blockhouse where he could intercept any attempt to land near Fort Lee. Two regiments of infantry occupied the ravine to hold the pass until General Irvine supported them in the event of a landing.

General Wayne's remaining force surrounded the blockhouse about 10 AM, seized the landings on the Hudson below the Palisades and the wooden boats and sloops tied up there, and began the attack. His infantry surrounded the blockhouse on three sides and began a heavy musket fire, while the field pieces were brought up within 60 yards of the entrance. Wayne began firing his field pieces at it about 11 AM and continued for an hour; but they were too light to penetrate the log walls.

The Continental troops were under constant fire from the loopholes (see Photo NJ-15) of the blockhouse and had no chance of breaching the walls with cannon. Despite the officers' efforts to restrain them, the 1st and 2nd Regiments rushed through the abatis to the foot of the stockade to try to force an entrance. They found it impracticable and suffered heavy casualties from the musket fire at close range from a secure location. Fifteen men were killed at the entrance and 46 were wounded. The Crown forces suffered about 21 total casualties. Wayne lost a total of three officers wounded (one of whom died), 15 noncommissioned officers and privates killed, and 46 noncommissioned officers and privates wounded.[111]

When he received news that 3,000 troops were on their way, General Wayne ceased the attack. Some reports said that the Loyalists had only one round of ammunition left when the ceasefire was called. The Continentals destroyed some boats and seized some cattle before hurrying over the Hackensack River to their camp at Totowa to avoid entrapment. The Loyalists pursued them for a good distance back toward New Bridge. Major John André (1751–1780) parodied the incident in his poem "Cow Chase." The

Crown forces abandoned and burned the fort two months later when they moved their woodcutting operation to Fort Delancey.

Staten Island (before Nov. 20, 1775; Feb. 12, 1776; Apr. 7, 1776; Apr. 14, 1776; July 2, 3, 4, 1776; July 23, 24, 1776; Oct. 13, 1776; Oct. 16, 1776; Jan. & Feb., 1777; Mar. 14, 1777; Aug. 19, 1777; Aug. 22, 1777; Aug. 23, 1777; Aug. 27, 1777; Nov. 18–21, 1777; Nov. 27, 1777; Dec. 26, 1777; June 10, 1778; June 24, 1778; Nov. 3, 1778; Nov. 28, 1778; Feb. 8, 1779; Mar. 18, 1779; June 29, 1779; June 30, 1779; Aug. 6, 1779; Jan. 14, 1780; Jan. 18, 1780; Feb. 12, 1780; Aug. 25, 1780; Sept. 3, 1780; Sept. 19, 1780; Nov. 8, 1780; Mar. 26, 1781; Apr. 9, 16, 1781; May 8, 1781; Aug. 23, 1781; Nov. 8, 1781; Mar. 15, 1782; May 22, 1782; June 21, 1782)

After the siege of Boston, the British moved to New York in April 1776. General William Howe (1732–1786) occupied Staten Island with his army of 31,600 men in June and early July 1776. The island became a haven for Loyalists. The island's proximity to New Jersey made it a very good starting point for many of the raids into that colony. Even though most of the engagements at Staten Island involved New Jersey, the island is part of New York and is treated in that volume.

See *The Guide to the American Revolution in New York.*

Hibernia (Apr. 27, 1779)

Hibernia is about 9 miles north of Morristown.

See **Charlotteburg.**

Montague (July 1779)

Montague is near the Pennsylvania border, about 8 miles southwest of Minisink.

A band of Native Americans raided the fort at Montague in July 1779, at the time of the Battle of Minisink.[112]

Morris County
Parsippany (June 22, 1779)

Parsippany is north of Morristown.

A party of Loyalists had been conspiring to capture or assassinate Governor William Livingston (1723–1790) when he returned from the General Assembly. One of the governor's sons led one of them to believe that the governor would arrive on Tuesday, June 22, 1779. Toward the evening of that day, a report circulated that the governor had returned. Expecting that the conspirators would attack the house that night, the governor's son prepared to receive them.

The Loyalists were discovered within 50 yards of the governor's house about 2 AM the next morning. They fled into the woods when a patrol fired on them. The suspected leader disappeared, was pursued, captured and imprisoned in the Morristown jail.[113]

Pompton (Apr. 17, 1777; Sept. 1, 1781)

Pompton is on Hamburg Turnpike (US 202) just south of Pompton Lake.

Apr. 17, 1777 see **Hoboken.**

★ Constant Cooper, an express rider, was captured by the British at Pompton on Saturday, September 1, 1781 and taken to New York.[114]

★ Pompton was also the site of a mutiny on Saturday, January 27, 1781 when 200 to 300 soldiers mutinied. Three of the ringleaders were taken, tried by court-martial on the spot, and sentenced to be shot immediately by twelve of their comrades. Two were executed and buried where they fell, in a secluded spot, a mile or two northeast of Pompton. The third man was pardoned.[115]

Saddle River (May 12, 1777; Apr. 16, 1780)

> Saddle River contained what is now Manchester prior to the formation of Passaic County. It was then shaped like a saddle, hence its name.

A detachment of about 300 Loyalists, under the command of Lieutenant Colonels Joseph Barton and Edward Vaughan Dongan (1748–1777), marched from Bergen Town on Monday afternoon, May 12, 1777 to attack General Nathaniel Heard (1730–1792), who lay at Pompton with 350 New Jersey militiamen. The Loyalists were unable to reach their destination by the intended time due to the morasses and other impediments.

After consulting his fellow officers, Colonel Barton decided to take the road to Paramus, and destroy some stores there, guarded by 80 to 100 men. Colonel Dongan was previously detached to Saddle River and Slotterdam with a small party to surprise a party of Whigs, under the command of Captain David Marinus (1751–1778) and two others. Colonel Dongan arrived at Saddle River at daybreak, made the attack, captured the Point, and took the captain, his lieutenant, and three others prisoners. He also took a small cask of powder, some cannon and musket balls, eight or nine stand of arms, a drum, and some other articles. Captain Hardnut was wounded in the groin by a bayonet in this skirmish but the wound was not mortal.

Colonel Barton then marched to Paramus, drove the Whigs from their strongholds, and forced them to retreat to the woods.[116]

See also **Hopperstown.**

★ April 16, 1780 see **Hopperstown.**

Sussex County (Mar. 11, 1779; Mar. 31, 1779; Sept. 3, 1779; Apr. 16, 1781)

Ogdens, Sussex County

Sussex Courthouse (Mar. 11, 1779; Aug. 24, 1779; June 4, 1780; June 21, 1780)

Four armed men were seen passing through the mountains in the eastern part of Sussex County on Thursday, March 11, 1779. The inhabitants, on receiving intelligence of it, set out in pursuit of them with several excellent dogs for tracking. They pursued them along different routes for more than 30 miles before the dogs found them. Two of them escaped, and the other two were captured and taken to the Continental troops stationed at Minisink. They proved to be spies sent by the British commander in New York with dispatches to Walter Butler (ca.1752–1781) and Joseph Brant (1742–1807), Mohawk Chief Thayendanagea.[117]

★ A number of armed Loyalists broke into the house of the Honorable Robert Ogden, Esquire (1714–1787) in Sussex County, on Wednesday night, March 31, 1779 and robbed him of a considerable amount of money. A party of militiamen pursued the Loyalists who fled to the mountains.[118]

★ A band of Native Americans appeared within 12 miles of Sussex Courthouse on Tuesday, August 24, 1779. This caused 70 militiamen to march out in pursuit until they were surrounded and cut off. Fifteen officers of this detachment were lost and one had his arm broken.[119]

★ Mr. Maxwell's Elizabethtown brigade was cut to pieces and "terribly maull'd" by Joseph and his Brethren (Native Americans) in Sussex County on Friday, September 3, 1779.[120]

★ About 1 AM on Sunday morning, June 4, 1780, Major Robert Hoops discovered a man and a woman near his house and began to question them. The woman lied; and the man stumbled for answers, making Major Hoops suspicious. He asked them to walk into the house to verify what they had told him. On his way to the house Major Hoops turned around to see the man running away. He pursued the man and captured him after wounding him in the arm with a small sword. When he saw a cocked pistol in the man's hand, he found him to be a levy soldier in the corps of Jersey Volunteers dressed in his regimentals. When they came into the light, the major took one of the pistols he had taken from the man and pointed it to his head, declaring he would shoot him if he did not disclose his plans.

The man said that he came out with Lieutenant James Moody (1744–1809) and another man from New York about three weeks earlier. He had received instructions from Lieutenant General Wilhelm von Knyphausen (1716–1800) but kept them secret. He only revealed that he was to capture some person within 2 miles of Morristown. Finding that the man was not at home and would not return before June 15th, they came to Sussex Courthouse to pass their time until the person returned. He said that he had left Lieutenant Moody in the road near the Moravian mills and that he had permission to go visit his uncle, Matthew Lowry. He was on his way there when Major Hoops apprehended him. He was expected to meet Lieutenant Moody and his companion on the top of Jenny Jump Mountain on Thursday night, when they were to proceed on their intended expedition.

Major Hoops left the man under guard and gathered some friends and neighbors to pursue Lieutenant Moody, but they could not find him.[121]

★ Loyalist Lieutenant James Moody and a party of new levies from Staten Island took the Sussex County jail during the night of Wednesday, June 21, 1780 and released all eight prisoners there. A few hours later, four of them returned on their own. The militia tried unsuccessfully to recapture the others.[122]

★ Some Native Americans killed private Joseph Jobs (d. 1781) during a skirmish in Sussex County on Monday, April 16, 1781.[123]

Wantage
Decker's Fort (1779)

Decker's or Gardner's Fort was in northwestern New Jersey in what is now Wantage.

Native Americans raided Decker's or Gardner's Fort in 1779.[124]

Dumont
Bergenfield
Near Schraalenburgh (Apr. 17, 1777; week of Mar. 16 to 22, 1779; June 2, 3, 1780; June 14, 1780; Oct. 1781; late June 1782)

> Northern Schraalenburgh is now the town of Dumont and Southern Schraalenburgh is the town of Bergenfield.

April 17, 1777 see **River Vale/Westwood.**

★ About 1,500 men, mostly Associated Loyalists, made an excursion to Schraalenburgh, a small village in the neighborhood of Hackensack during the week of March 16 to 22, 1779. They burned some houses, abused the inhabitants, and plundered their effects. The militia mustered in a hurry and forced the raiders to retreat quickly, taking little plunder and only a few cattle. They stabbed an old man, about 90 years old, named Talman (ca. 1689–1779) in an attempt to make him reveal where his money was. He died from his wounds a short time later. They also killed Mr. Zabriskie (d. 1779), by frequently stabbing him with their bayonets, and an African American girl as she was driving off some cattle.[125]

★ New York Loyalists encamped in the upper part of Bergen Township in late May and conducted a series of raids in the area. Major John Goetschius (1745–1826) and his men had to guard three different places: Barbados, New Bridge and Closter and had to change quarters every night after 9 PM. Two of his men were badly wounded in an engagement at the blockhouse on Friday, June 2, 1780. The following night, Ensign Huyler and 4 men met the horse thieves at Schraalenburgh and killed two of them on the spot, Mr. Miller (d. 1780) and Mr. Kille (d. 1780) who took five of the best horses from near Wallkill in New York. The Loyalists pillaged Major Goetschius's farm on Wednesday, June 14, 1780.[126]

★ Lieutenant Robert Campbell (1735–1777) and his party of 30 men failed to attack a party of Loyalists near Schraalenburgh on a very dark night in October 1781. Lieutenant John Van Orden and a soldier attacked the party and re-captured one lieutenant and a private, one wounded, and seven horses and took them to Captain James Christie's (1744–1817) headquarters.[127]

★ Three militiamen on patrol encountered some Loyalists near Schraalenburgh in late June 1782. The Loyalists killed one militiaman.[128]

2
CENTRAL NEW JERSEY

See the map of Central New Jersey.

Jersey City
Paulus Hook (Apr. 8, 1776; July 12, 1776; July 21, 1776; July 22, 1776; Sept. 7, 1776; Sept. 13–18, 20–23, 1776; Feb. 22, 1777; Aug. 19, 1779; Dec. 21, 1779)

> Paulus (Powle's, Poole's) Hook (Hoeck) is now Jersey City. The site of the main British fortification is presumed to be around the intersection of Washington and Grand Streets where Paulus Hook Park is located. Commercial development has long since obliterated the site of "Light-Horse Harry" Lee's victory.
> In the 18th century, Paulus Hook was a small island separated on the west from Harsimus Island by a marsh with a stream. It was several feet above water level and was separated from the land at its west by a creek that was navigable at high tide. It was later connected with the mainland by a causeway, an earthen embankment (now lower Newark Avenue), over the marsh to Harsimus Island, then a road (now Railroad Avenue) westward over Harsimus to Prior's Mill bridge and the mainland. This quickly became a busy part of the main post road from New York to Philadelphia.

General George Washington (1732–1799) ordered two forts built at Paulus Hook (also spelled Powles, Powle's, Poole's Hook and pronounced Poole's Hook) early in the war. The hook was a large spit of land jutting out into the Hudson River. Washington saw this site as a crucial location for defending the Hudson or launching an attack into New York, as it was the closest point in New Jersey to New York City. However, the Continental Army abandoned the fort in September 1776 when it retreated through New Jersey. The Crown forces took it over and occupied it for the rest of the war.

Joshua Barns, from Phillipsburgh in Westchester County, was enlisting men to serve as Governor William Tryon's (1729–1788) Life Guards. Six of his new recruits landed on the Jersey shore near Paulus Hook on Monday evening, April 8, 1776 and were captured and imprisoned.[129]

★ The British entered the lower bay on Saturday, June 29, 1776 and soon took possession of Staten Island. Brigadier General Hugh Mercer (1725–1777), who was in command in New Jersey, had his flying-camp at Bergen. He placed a guard of 500 men on Bergen Neck to prevent the enemy's approach by that pass. He also made arrangements for the proper disposition of the Pennsylvania militia as they arrived at Paulus Hook.

The British remained on the island awaiting reinforcements. By Friday, July 12th, their forces amounted to 30,000 men and the harbor was filled with ships. That afternoon, Captain Hyde Parker, Jr.'s (1739–1807) 40-gun frigate *HMS Phoenix* and Captain James Wallace's (1731–1803) 20-gun frigate *Rose,* their decks protected by sand bags and accompanied by three tenders, headed up the Hudson River toward New York. As they passed Paulus Hook, the shore battery opened a lively fire upon the ships, which returned several broadsides. Neither side suffered much damage.

★ Shore batteries fired on the HMS *Phoenix* and *Rose* again as they moved up the river on Friday, July 21, 1776. The ships returned fire.[130]

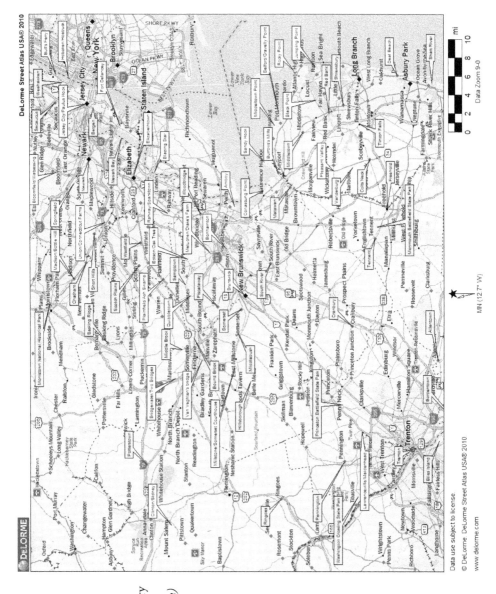

Central New Jersey: Map for The Guide to the American Revolutionary War in New Jersey
© 2011 DeLorme (www.delorme.com)
Street Atlas USA®

★ Lieutenant William Quarme of HM Brig *Halifax* saw some people on the shore at Paulus Hook at 7 AM on Saturday, July 22, 1776. Mistaking them for Loyalists, he sent a yawl and a whaleboat (see Photo NJ-1) to them. As the boats approached the shore, the Whigs began a heavy firing of small arms about 9 AM which the sailors returned. At noon, the *Halifax* fired several 4-pound shots at the Whigs and got all the boats safely on board.[131]

★ Batteries at Paulus Hook bombarded (see Photo NJ-4, NJ-5) British ships heading up the North River on Saturday, September 7, 1776.[132]

★ At 3 PM on Friday, September 13, 1776, Admiral Richard Howe's (1726–1799) ship fired a signal gun for the HMS *Phoenix* and *Roebuck,* each with 44 guns, and the 30-gun frigate *Orpheus* to weigh anchor and head up the East River. As they proceeded, they came under a very hot fire from all the shore batteries.

★ During the evening of Saturday September 14, 1776, four other frigates and two transports went up the East River to join those that went the day before. That same evening, the *Roebuck* came down river. As she passed Paulus Hook, she was fired upon and received three shots which did no material damage.[133]

★ On Sunday, September 15, 1776, the British ships-of-war *Roebuck*, *Phoenix*, and *Factor* made another attack upon Paulus Hook. They raked the Hook with grape shot and killed one horse. The garrison under the command of Colonel John Durkee (Durkie) (1728–1782) did not surrender. That same day, the *Asia*, and two other ships-of-war proceeded up the North River and came under heavy fire from a battery at Paulus Hook. The following morning, around daylight, the *Asia* came down river faster than she went up. Three British warships were nearly all destroyed by four fire ships that sailed in among them. A sudden gale of wind that sprung up at that moment prevented their total destruction.[134]

★ The following day, Captain Francis Banks's HMS *Renown* passed Paulus Hook about 5 AM on her way to New York when she came under fire from New Jersey regiments under Colonels John Durkee (Durkie) (1728–1782) and Duyckinck. The Whigs kept a constant fire on the *Renown*, inflicting minor damage to her sails and rigging. When the *Renown* came abreast of the Whigs, she fired several broadsides at them.[135]

★ On Wednesday morning, September 18, 1776, Captain Francis Banks took the *Renown* up the North River again. Whigs on shore at Paulus Hook fired at her five or six times but without effect.[136]

★ Colonel John Durkee's (Durkie) (1728–1782) regiment exchanged fire with the HMS *Renown* again on September 20, 1776. The Regulars made an unsuccessful attempt to invade Paulus Hook on the 21st but successfully occupied it on Monday night, the 23rd. The militia had previously taken off all the cannon and stores. This was the first territory in New Jersey to be occupied by the Crown forces, marking the beginning of the New Jersey Campaign.[137]

★ A large field of ice forced Lieutenant James Clark to bring HMS *Dependence* to shore at Paulus Hook about 4 PM on Saturday February 22, 1777. The crew tied her to a tree. A party of Whigs tried to cut the lines around 9 PM. The *Dependence* fired four 4-pound round shots at them. When the ice floes had passed, the *Dependence* cast off from shore at 10 PM and returned to her anchorage.[138]

★ Major Henry "Light-Horse Harry" Lee (1756–1818) had discovered that the strong Crown fort at Paulus Hook was negligently guarded. He proposed to make a surprise attack on the fort during a night march. While it was impractical to hold such a position with the Crown forces in New York, the exploit would "give éclat to the Continental arms." General George Washington (1732–1799) did not favor the project at first but eventually yielded.

Lee left his camp at New Bridge around 4 PM Wednesday afternoon, August 18, 1779 with about 300 Congressional troops. They took the lower road which intersected the Hackensack road near the English Neighborhood church. He took the precaution to send Captain Henry Peyton (d. 1781) ahead with instructions to have boats ready at Dow's Ferry at a certain hour of the night to take his troops over the Hackensack River. Lee also detached patrols of horsemen to watch the communications along the North River and posted Major General William Alexander (Earl of Stirling, 1726–1783) at New Bridge to cover his retreat, if necessary.

Major Lee reached Prior's Mill at 3 AM on Thursday morning. Daybreak was approaching along with the rising tide that would fill the ditch and overflow the road between Warren and Grove Streets. Lee ordered his troops to advance in the order which they then held. Lieutenant John Rudulph (1744–1836), who had been sent forward to reconnoiter the passage of the ditch, reported that all was silent within the works and that the canal was passable.

The operation was conducted with such secrecy that Lee's troops arrived at the fort undiscovered, despite having wandered three hours in the woods between Union Hill and the fort, due to their guide's ignorance or treachery. They were also in danger of encountering Lieutenant Colonel Abraham Van Buskirk (1750–1783) who had left the fort at Paulus Hook about the same time that Major Lee had set out to raid the English Neighborhood.

Lieutenants McCallister and Rudulph led the forlorn hope, marching in silence with trailed arms. They reached the ditch at the intersection of Newark Avenue and Warren Street at 3:30. They encountered no opposition, except for a shot or two fired from the sentries on the left. The 200 soldiers garrisoning the fort were either asleep or took the approaching force to be Colonel Van Buskirk's men returning from their raid.

The Continentals entered between the post of the gate and the abatis. They surprised the guard in the blockhouse (see Photo NJ-15) and captured them before proceeding to the main redoubt where the cannon was. They entered the blockhouse and redoubt easily and took possession of them, as the guards in the other blockhouses had deserted their posts.

The main body came pouring through the abatis and took the fort in a few minutes before a piece of artillery could be fired. Unfortunately, in crossing the ditch their ammunition was destroyed, rendering their firearms useless.

Major William Sutherland, the Commandant, along with a captain, subaltern and about 30 Hessians took refuge in the Round Redoubt on the left. As daylight arrived, Major Lee was anxious about the boats at Dow's Ferry. Moreover, the firing had aroused the British in New York, and Major Lee feared reinforcements from New York City would trap him, as a large body of troops could be ferried across the river in a few minutes. He therefore made no attempt to take the Round Redoubt and ordered an immediate retreat without burning the barracks, spiking the cannon, destroying the powder magazine or doing any material damage. Moreover, the soldiers in the redoubt would be able to fire grapeshot at his troops. They left about an hour after taking the fort, killing three men and taking 159 prisoners.

Major Lee sent Captain Forsyth to Prior's Mill to muster able-bodied men to take a position on Bergen Heights to cover the retreat. Lee rode forward to look after the boats at the ferry and was dismayed to find there was not a single boat there. Captain Peyton had removed them to Newark because he thought Major Lee had changed his plans. Lee immediately countermarched his troops to the Bergen road en route to New Bridge. He communicated with Lord Stirling at New Bridge and returned to the rear guard at Prior's Mill.

His prospects were now discouraging. His troops were tired and their ammunition destroyed. The 14-mile retreat route left him vulnerable to be intercepted by troops from New York, with no way of escape. Moreover, he was encumbered with prisoners.

Along the way, the Continentals met some 50 soldiers who may have been stragglers from Lee's command who had become lost during the earlier night march to Paulus Hook. The retreating troops received some dry ammunition from these stragglers. Major Lee sent one party to the rear, on the Bergen road, and one to move along the bank of the river to prevent a sudden attack.

Major Sutherland had followed Lee and was about to overtake his column at the Fort Lee Road when 200 Virginia Continentals arrived to reinforce Lee. A body of Crown troops appeared on the right shortly afterward and opened fire. Lee quickly dispatched two groups of soldiers who caused the Crown forces to withdraw. This gave Lee's force time to cross the English Neighborhood creek at the Liberty Pole, now Englewood. They arrived safely at New Bridge about 1 PM.

Lieutenant Colonel Abraham Van Buskirk and 120 men left the garrison in New York that evening to surprise the Continental pickets near New Bridge. A captain and 50 Hessians were sent to Paulus Hook to strengthen the post in Van Buskirk's absence.

See also **New Bridge.**

The Continentals lost two dead and three wounded. Although there are no reports of Crown casualties, we know they lost 159 prisoners, including officers. The raid suffered many setbacks, but it disrupted the British fortification at Paulus Hook and helped raise Continental morale. The Second Continental Congress awarded Lee a gold medal for his exploits. Major William Sutherland, the British commander, was court-martialed.[139]

★ In December 1779, Brigadier General "Mad Anthony" Wayne (1745–1796) marched down from Tappan to Bergen to observe enemy operations at Paulus Hook for a while before going into winter quarters at Westfield, Union County. The raids on both sides caused the inhabitants of Bergen great suffering. Some buried their money and their valuables; but often renegade Loyalists revealed the hiding places to the enemy.

On Tuesday night, December 21, 1779, a detachment from General Anthony Wayne's brigade exchanged shots with the picket of the garrison at Paulus Hook. Finding the garrison prepared to receive them, General Wayne's brigade retreated.[139a]

Irvington
Camptown (June 4, 5, 1776)

> Camptown, now Irvington, is equidistant between Newark and Connecticut Farms (Union).

In early June 1777, General George Clinton (1739–1812) gave permission to three young men to go to Shawangunk where they claimed to have acquaintances. They said they lived below Paramus and pretended to be fleeing from the British. They proved, rather, to be impostors who really intended to purchase horses for the British Army. They had already purchased 13 horses and were returning when Major Albert Pawling (1750–1837) learned of them. He detached a party of the Orange light horse at 9 PM on Wednesday, June 4 and sent them to Camptown to intercept the impostors. The light horsemen captured the impostors and took them prisoners.

★ The following night, June 5, General Clinton learned of another party on a similar mission. They were returning through Easttown with a larger drove. General Clinton sent a party after them.[140]

New Brunswick

Brunswick (Dec. 1, 1776; Dec. 3, 1776; Dec. 17, 1776; Jan. 16, 17, 1777; Feb. 4, 1777; Feb. 26, 1777; Mar. 3, 4, 5, 1777; Mar. 8, 1777; Mar. 9, 1777; Mar. 14, 1777; Mar. 18, 1777; Mar. 21, 1777; Apr. 13, 1777; June 13, 1777; June 14, 1777; June 19, 1777; June 21, 1777; June 22, 1777; Oct. 21, 1779; Oct. 26, 1779; Aug. 5, 1781; Jan. 2, 1782; Jan. 7 or 9, 1782; before June 19, 1782)

Near Brunswick (Jan. 1777; Feb. 15, 1777; Oct. 24 or 26, 1779)

Bennett's Island or Lawrence Island (Feb. 18, 1777; Apr. 1777)

Highways and corporate complexes have obliterated almost all of colonial Brunswick. The town was strategically important for its access to the Raritan Bay.
  The Buccleuch Mansion (see Photo NJ-16) (800 George Street), built in 1739 and one of the finest houses in town, was seized by the British when they occupied New Brunswick from December 2, 1776 to June 22, 1777. A legend says that two officers of the Enniskillen Guards fought a duel in the house and one of them was killed. The interior of the house supposedly bears the scars of the duel. General George Washington (1732–1799) also stayed here later in the war. General William Howe's (1732–1786) headquarters was at the Neilson house. Built before 1733, the house stood at 265 Burnet Street near Route 18. It was torn down in the 1870s. The site was where Route 18 northbound runs today.

Photo NJ-16. Buccleuch Mansion, New Brunswick. According to legend, two officers of the Enniskillen Guards fought a duel in the house and one of them was killed.

The Hessian commander, General Leopold Philip von Heister (1707–1777), had his headquarters in the Van Nuis house which was built by John Van Nuis, in 1727.

When General Washington made a brief stop in the city, he made his headquarters on the southwest corner of Albany and Nielson Streets.

Bennett's Island (also known as Lawrence Island) was 2 or 3 miles south of New Brunswick.

When the Crown forces entered New Brunswick, they built fortifications on the hill beyond the Theological Seminary and erected two important outposts: one at Raritan Landing on an eminence overlooking the river, the other on Bennett's Island, 2 miles below the city. Many of the officers were quartered in the houses of the inhabitants and on the property of William Van Deursen (1736–1816), below New Street. A redoubt was constructed for their protection and that of the encampment there.

Brigadier General William Alexander (Earl of Stirling), (1726–1783) and his brigade were cannonaded at Brunswick by the Crown forces on Sunday, December 1, 1776. Thomas Contee (1729–1811), of Prince Georges County, Maryland, recorded in his diary for December 1, 1776:

> We rode out to the bridge to see Smallwood's (General William Smallwood (1732–1792), of Maryland) battalion. Met General Washington and some other generals, and were informed the enemy were advancing. We rode to Brunswick to see the officers of Smallwood's battalion. They were ordered to their post on an alarm. General Chamberlain (James Chamberlain (1745–1819)) and myself rode up the hills above the town. We saw the enemy's light horse approach towards the ferry at Brunswick. In a short time the field pieces appeared, and they fixed upon a hill and began to cannonade the town. We saw the first fire and remained until several shots were exchanged from our side. The enemy fired six to our one.

Major Mordecai Gist's (1743–1792) Maryland Continentals, now reduced to 190 effective men, together with Brigadier General Lord Stirling's and General Adam Stephens's (ca. 1730–1791) brigades were ordered to cover the retreat. Lord Sterling lost two men killed and two wounded.

The following day, the Crown forces took control of the whole town, appropriating all the public buildings for their own use. They compelled many of the citizens to abandon their residences, suspended all business, and interrupted public worship. They removed the furniture from the Dutch Reformed Church on Neilson Street and converted it first into a hospital and later into a stable. They also burned the Presbyterian Church on Burnet Street. General George Washington (1732–1799) retreated to Trenton where he arrived on December 4th and transported his baggage and supplies across the Delaware River.[141]

★ On Sunday, December 3, 1776, a Whig concealed on a pier under the bridge shot and killed Captain Weiterhausen (d. 1776) of the grenadiers (see Photo NJ-10) as he crossed the bridge over the Raritan.[142]

★ On Friday, December 17, 1776, some Congressional forces attacked the picket guards in an attempt to destroy the enemy's magazine and supplies. They were repulsed and lost about 30 men in killed, wounded, and captured.[143]

★ A party of Congressional forces attacked a "large body of the enemy" about 3 miles up the Raritan River from Brunswick in January 1777. They captured almost 600 head of cattle, more than 50 wagons, and a number of horses that were so emaciated they could hardly walk.[144]

★ Major General John Vaughan (1738?–1795) narrowly escaped being killed on the road near Brunswick on Thursday, January 16, 1777. A Whig had concealed himself behind a fence to ambush the general; but one of the light horsemen leaped the fence after him and immediately cut him down. A detachment of 200 Congressional troops attacked a picket guard at Brunswick the following night. They were repulsed, losing about three men killed, and about 30 captured.[145]

★ On Tuesday, February 4, 1777, between 20 and 30 prisoners, including two commissioned officers, were brought to New Brunswick.[146]

★ A scouting party of Congressional forces captured 15 British soldiers near Brunswick on Saturday, February 15, 1777 and took them to Trenton. A battery of six 32-pounders at Brunswick fired on some British boats coming up the Raritan River to deliver supplies on Tuesday, February 26, 1777.[147]

★ Colonel John Neilson (1745–1833) organized a secret expedition against the British outpost on Bennett's Island, also known as Lawrence's Neck and Island Farm, near Weston's Mills about 3 miles south of New Brunswick. He picked 200 New Jersey militiamen and secretly approached the defenses some time before daybreak on Tuesday morning, February 18, 1777. The clear, cold night and fresh snowfall made the undertaking very hazardous. They managed to reach their objective without being discovered.

Colonel Neilson was the first man to leap the stockade. The sentinel was ready to discharge his musket into Neilson's breast when Captain Lodowick Farmer, Jr. (1757–1816) fired his weapon and killed the sentry. The engagement lasted only a few minutes when Major Richard V. Stockton, who was the Acting Commander of the post in the absence of Colonel John Skinner (ca. 1750–1827), surrendered. Neilson captured one captain, several subordinate officers and 51 privates of the 6th Battalion, New Jersey Loyalists and a quantity of munitions of war. Colonel Neilson had only two men wounded. He sent Major Stockton to Philadelphia in irons. When General George Washington (1732–1799) heard of it, he directed that he should be treated as a prisoner of war.

As only a few guns were fired, the British knew nothing of this occurrence until later that morning. But Neilson and his men were well on their way toward Princeton to deliver their spoils and prisoners to General Rufus Putnam (1738–1824). General Washington paid Colonel Neilson and his men a very high compliment for the wisdom with which they had planned and the secrecy with which they had executed this successful expedition. Colonel Neilson was appointed brigadier general of militia on Friday, February 21, 1777 in recognition for his services. General Sir William Howe (1732–1786) made his headquarters in Colonel Neilson's house in New Brunswick during the winter of 1777.[148]

★ A party of Congressional troops from Brunswick executed a bayonet charge and captured a picket of 100 men of the Free Corps (a band of about 1,000 men under Brigadier General Montfort Brown) on Monday, March 3, 1777, without firing a shot. The following night they intended to undertake a similar attack on a picket of 60 Hessian jaegers and 40 Hessian grenadiers. The Hessians fired one round and retreated hastily, as they were outnumbered. They lost two jaegers who were captured.[149]

★ March 5, 1777 see **Quibbletown.**

★ The Crown forces sent two battalions of the 71st Regiment and a battalion of Hessians at 5 AM on Saturday, March 8, 1777, to cover the boats that were taking in salt hay about 3 miles up the Raritan. The flank corps and the 3rd brigade went ashore to the foraging place at 10 AM with two field pieces and some wagons. The grenadiers and part of the light infantry were posted on the Woodbridge Road when 300 or 400 Congressional troops passed their front to the left and soon after fell in with part of the 52nd Regiment and Major Normand Lamont's battalion of the 71st Regiment from Bonhamtown. They skirmished for more than two hours before the Congressional forces were driven back. The 52nd had three wounded and three missing. The 71st, five or six killed and wounded.[150]

★ Some Congressional forces attacked General William Howe's (1732–1786) troops at Brunswick on Sunday afternoon, March 9, 1777, as he headed to Amboy on the way to New York. A party of troops routed them.

★ On Friday, the 14th, a party of Whigs from the Jersey shore fired on some boats that were captured while foraging at New Blazing Star on Staten Island. Major Robert Timpany (1742–1844), Major of the Fourth Battalion of the Bergen Volunteers (New Jersey Loyalists), crossed the river with about 40 men and drove the Whigs 3 miles inland and captured 10 head of cattle and about 30 sheep without losing a man.[151]

★ On Tuesday March 18, 1777, Congressional forces captured several wagons and eight prisoners. They killed four or five in a skirmish while losing four killed and eight captured. Another skirmish occurred on Friday, three days later, when the Crown foraging party returned to Brunswick and was driven off.[152]

★ The Crown forces came out from Brunswick early Sunday morning, April 13, 1777. They intended to surprise Major General Benjamin Lincoln (1733–1810) at Bound Brook. They might have accomplished their plan due to the carelessness of a militia guard at one of the fords on the Raritan River. However, the general got notice of their approach in time to withdraw himself and most of his men to the mountain behind the town. His main loss was two artillery pieces and Lieutenant Charles Turnbull (d. 1795) and Lieutenant William Ferguson and about 20 men from Colonel Thomas Proctor's (1739–1806) regiment. They could not possibly escape due to a party of horsemen who rushed them. The Regulars stayed about an hour and a half before returning to Brunswick.[153]

★ The British killed Private William Sodin (d. 1777) during a raid at Bennett's Island in April 1777.[154]

★ The British Army assembled at Brunswick on Friday, June 13, 1777 while the main body of the Continental Army was encamped on the mountain above Quibbletown and a corps of 2,000 men were at Princeton. General William Howe (1732–1786) decided to move from Brunswick in two columns in the morning of the 14th. He left Brigadier General Edward Mathew (often misspelled Matthews) (1729–1805) to guard that post with 2,000 men. General Charles Cornwallis (1738–1805) and the 1st division advanced to Hillsborough while General Leopold von Heister (1707–1777) took the 2nd division to Middle Bush to draw the Continentals down from the mountain into a general action. The Continentals maintained their strong position that would have been imprudent to attack.[155]

★ General Howe returned to his camp at Brunswick on Thursday, June 19, 1777 and prepared to march to Amboy on the 22nd, where he intended to embark his troops to cross to Staten Island. The force evacuating Brunswick between June 19 and 22 was so large that parties of Continental troops hovered nearby to see what mischief they could do. Had it not been for the rainy weather, the British would have met with rougher treatment than they actually received. Brigadier General "Mad Anthony" Wayne (1745–1796), Colonel Daniel Morgan (1736–1802) and their officers and men constantly advanced upon them. The British were far superior to them in numbers and well secured behind strong redoubts.

Major General John Sullivan (1740–1795) advanced from Rocky Hill to Brunswick with his division, but he did not receive his marching orders until very late at night, so he did not arrive until some time after the British had departed. Brigadier General William Maxwell (1733–1796) never got his orders; so Major General Nathanael Greene's (1742–1786) force had to give up the chase. General Wayne then withdrew. This conflict was intended not to engage the Crown forces into a battle but to harass them. It suffered from lack of coordination which prevented more Congressional units from joining the fight.[156]

★ As the preparations were complete to cross to Staten Island, General Howe received intelligence that the Continentals had moved down from the mountain and taken post at Quibbletown, intending to attack the British rear as it left Amboy. Brigadier General William Alexander (Earl of Stirling, 1726–1783), Brigadier General William Maxwell (1733–1796) and General Thomas Conway (1733–1800) and 3,000 men and 8 field pieces and another corps of about 700 men and one cannon advanced to the left. The Continentals fired at long range but did little damage. Some battalions in the woods harassed General Charles Cornwallis's rear guard. He dispersed the Continentals, killing nine and wounding about 30, with the loss of only two men killed and 13 wounded.

★ Colonel George Taylor lost four of his New Jersey Loyalists in a skirmish with some Whigs in Northern New Jersey on Saturday, June 21, 1777.[157]

★ Congressional troops took possession of Brunswick on Sunday, June 22, 1777, when the British left to go to Amboy. Brigadier General William Maxwell (1733–1796), General Samuel Holden Parsons (1737–1789) and his brigade and Major General William Alexander (Earl of Stirling, 1726–1783) with his division pursued the British for some distance while the main body of the Continental Army—about 6,000 men—camped in the city.

Advised that Lord Stirling with Generals Maxwell and Thomas Conway (1733–1800) were advancing on his left with 3,000 men and eight field pieces and a smaller corps of 700 men and one cannon, Howe tried to provoke a general engagement.

★ General George Washington (1732–1799) intended to move his whole army closer to the British the day after the evacuation of Brunswick but was prevented from doing so by the rain. He sent an express to Brigadier General Maxwell to inform him of Major General Greene's movement toward Brunswick. The messenger never arrived and was probably captured. Had Maxwell received his orders, the whole rear guard would have been cut off from the main army and eventually captured.

One of General Howe's adjutants later expressed the opinion that if General Washington had attacked the retreating column in force at several points simultaneously, they would have inflicted severe damage, as the column was too unwieldy and too cramped for space in the narrow road. The main body of the Crown forces proceeded toward Amboy, burning houses and barns along the road. Nicholas Cresswell (1750–1804), an English civilian who accompanied the army, recorded: "All the Country houses were in flames as far as we could see. The Soldiers are so much enraged" at being called upon to retreat "that they will set them on fire in spite of all the Officers can do to prevent it."[158]

When the rain stopped on June 24, General Washington moved down from the hills to the vicinity of Quibbletown. He sent Lord Stirling to the Short Hills with a strong detachment and stationed light parties close to the British lines.[159]

★ On June 26th, General William Howe (1732–1786) sent out two columns. The right, under the command of General Charles Cornwallis (1738–1805) with Major-General James Grant (1720–1806), Brigadier Generals Edward Mathew (1729–1805) and Alexander Leslie (1740–1794), and Colonel Donop, took the route by Woodbridge toward Scotch Plains. The left column under Lord Howe with Major Generals Sterne, John Vaughan (1738?–1795), and Charles Grey (1729–1807), and Brigadier-Generals Samuel Cleveland and James Agnew (d. 1777), marched by way of Metuchen where a junction was to be made by the two columns. Four battalions were detached with six pieces of cannon to take up a post at Bonhamtown. General Cornwallis and his men fell in with the small Continental wing soon after passing Woodbridge. The firing that ensued gave the alarm to the main army at Quibbletown which retreated to the mountains. Lord Cornwallis shortly after came up with the division commanded by Lord Stirling who made an heroic struggle to maintain his position but was forced to retreat with a loss of three brass cannons, three captains, and 60 men killed, and over 200 officers and men wounded and taken prisoners. The British loss was reported at five men killed and 30 wounded, among the latter being Captain John Finch (d. 1777) of the Light (Coldstream) Guards who died in Amboy on June 29th.

The Crown forces pursued the Continentals as far as Westfield but the day was so hot that the soldiers marched with great difficulty. The Continentals took the opportunity to escape in the thick woods until night allowed them to join the main army in the mountains. The British lay at Westfield that night, returned next day to Rahway and the day following to Amboy.

See also **Short Hills.**

★ After the Crown forces left New Jersey on June 30, 1777, they continued to make frequent predatory excursions to Woodbridge, Rahway, Elizabethtown, and up the Raritan. As the Queen's Rangers approached Brunswick on their return from a raid at Bound Brook on Thursday, October 21, 1779, they found 170 Congressional troops on the hill near the barracks, ready to receive them. The Rangers charged immediately and dispersed the Congressional troops with great slaughter, killing Major Edgar (d. 1779), Captain Peter Voorhees (d. 1779) and another captain and many other officers.

The Queen's Rangers then proceeded along the road toward South Amboy where they joined forces with the infantry. They took 27 prisoners, including John Hampton, during the expedition. They lost only one man killed and four taken prisoners in addition to Colonel John Graves Simcoe (1752–1806) who was taken to Brunswick. The 27 prisoners captured by the Queen's Rangers were taken to New York Friday night, October 29.[160]

See **Bonhamtown, Brunswick, Bound Brook, Elizabeth,** and **Somerset Courthouse.**

★ October 24 or 26, 1779 see **Van Veghten's Bridge.**

★ A party of about 100 of Lieutenant Colonel John Graves Simcoe's (1752–1806) light dragoons went up the Newark River and landed at Sandy Point above Amboy on Tuesday night October 26, 1779. They set fire to Continental guard houses on Wednesday morning. They proceeded to Bound Brook where they burned some stores before heading to Van Veghten's bridge where they burned 18 boats and then to Somerset Courthouse which they also burned. The militia turned out to annoy them. They killed the horse of the commanding officer, a colonel, and made him a prisoner, along with a private and two or three horses. The dragoons lost three killed, six prisoners and a considerable number of wounded. The militiamen pursued the dragoons so closely on their return that they dropped a great number of their caps, coats and other articles. They returned to South Amboy by way of Brunswick.[161]

★ Captain Adam Hyler (1735–1782) or Huyler went from New Brunswick to Long Island in an armed boat on Sunday, August 5, 1781. He marched 3 miles into the country and halted. He captured Captain Jeromus Lott, a lieutenant colonel of militia, and John Hankins, a captain of a vessel. He then brought his prisoners safely back to New Brunswick.[162]

★ About 300 British and Loyalist troops from New York landed at the lower end of Brunswick about 4 AM on Wednesday, January 2, 1782. The guards discovered their approaches on the river and alarmed the people about 15 minutes before they landed. A small party attacked the troops while they landed and killed 2 men. Lieutenant Colonel John Taylor's (1751–1801) Middlesex militia went to support the guards but the troops had already landed and gained the heights by the time they arrived. Outnumbered, they were forced to retire.

The Crown troops then took possession of the town with very little difficulty, as the darkness of the morning and the troops landing in different places, prevented the inhabitants from assembling in force. The troops maintained possession of the town more than an hour and received little opposition.

When the light of the morning began to appear, they retired to their boats and a smart skirmishing commenced which would have been much more severe had not many of the Continental muskets been rendered useless by the falling snow and rain. The militia had only five wounded and six inhabitants taken prisoners. Losses of the Crown forces could not be determined; but they lost two men killed at their first landing and left two dead in the town and carried several others with them when they withdrew. The well-directed fire of several parties assembled on the shores from Piscataway and South River probably inflicted more casualties on their return. The troops accomplished their objective of taking three whaleboats (see Photo NJ-1). The Crown troops executed "a well concerted plan" and generally did not mistreat the inhabitants. They did not insult the people or burn property and only plundered two houses.[163]

★ Captain George Beckwith (1753–1823) and a party of light infantrymen, the 40th and the 42nd Regiments from Staten Island boarded six boats at New York and went up the Raritan River to New Brunswick either on Monday, January 7, 1782 or on Wednesday, January 9. They set out in pursuit of Captain Adam Hyler (1735–1782) or Huyler whom the British were determined to capture. They landed at the lower end of New Brunswick at 5 AM the following morning and captured all of Hyler's whaleboats. This was a hard blow to the venturesome captain. New Yorkers quipped that Captain Hyler wouldn't be able to fit out as many whaleboats for several years due to the scarcity of wood and iron. However, Captain Adam Hyler immediately rebuilt his little navy and resumed his harassment of the Crown troops early in June.

Colonel George Taylor (1734–1799) commanded a detachment of New Jersey militiamen at Brunswick but ran off when he received information about the approach of the troops. The mission was accomplished in 24 hours with very little loss. The Crown troops covered a distance of almost 100 miles and the boats met with three cross tides.[164]

Brunswick: account under **Scotch Plains.**

★ Captain Adam Hyler (1735–1782) or Huyler of Brunswick captured an 18-gun cutter and blew her up after securing his prisoners and a few articles on board before June 19, 1782.[165]

Basking Ridge (Dec. 13, 1776)

The Widow White's Tavern was located at the southwest corner of South Finley Avenue and Colonial Drive in Basking Ridge. The tavern was razed about 1950 and there is no marker to identify the site. There is a blue marker on Lord Stirling Road to mark the site of Brigadier General William Alexander's (Earl of Stirling, 1726–1783) estate.

Lieutenant Colonel William Harcourt of Major General John Burgoyne's (1732–1792) light horse and 30 dragoons surrounded the headquarters of Major General Charles Lee (1731–1782) at the Widow White's Tavern at Basking Ridge on Friday, December 13, 1776. They killed two men, wounded two others and captured General Lee and four others without losing a single man. The prisoner was supposedly taken and confined under a strong guard first to Amboy, then to New Brunswick, and finally to New York where he arrived on January 22, 1777.[166]

Bonhamtown (Jan. 6, 1777; Jan. 16, 1777; Jan. 23, 1777; Feb. 23, 1777; Mar. 8, 1777; Apr. 14, 1777; Apr. 15, 1777; Apr. 20, 1777; Apr. 21, 1777; May 10, 1777; June 23, 1778; June 25, 1777; Oct. 21, 1779)

Bonhamtown is about 2 miles south of Metuchen and 4.5 miles west of Perth Amboy.

The Crown forces had placed three field pieces on a hill, about 50 yards from the bridge at Bonhamtown to prevent the Congressional forces from crossing. When the Continentals found it impossible to cross there on Monday, January 6, 1777, they went down the river, broke through the ice, waded across the river up to their middles, flanked the enemy, routed them, and took 43 baggage wagons, 104 horses, 115 head of cattle, and about 60 or 70 sheep. They lost four or five men, killed or wounded about 24 or 25, and took 12 prisoners. British reports claimed they were attacked by 3,000 of General George Washington's (1732–1799) troops and lost 35 or 36 men, but the Continentals lost 300.[167]

★ About 350 Congressional troops attacked a party of about 700 Crown troops near Bonhamtown, between Brunswick and Amboy, on Thursday, January 16, 1777. They had retreated to a small brush due to a lack of artillery after supposedly killing a colonel and 20 men and mortally wounding a lieutenant colonel and 30 or 40 privates.[168]

★ A force of 350 Congressional troops attacked 700 Crown troops at Bonhamtown on Thursday, January 23, 1777. They killed 21, wounded 30 to 40 others, and claimed the victory.

★ About 2,500 Crown troops attacked the Continental advance guard near Bonhamtown on Sunday, February 23, 1777. They drove in the guard but Brigadier General William Maxwell (1733–1796) assembled his troops as quickly as possible, formed ranks and attacked, forcing the Crown forces to retire. The militiamen pursued the Crown troops to Amboy. They captured seven prisoners and found two dead. The farmers whose wagons were impressed to carry the dead and wounded reported that a great many fell. General Maxwell had only five killed and wounded.[169]

★ General William Howe (1732–1786) was at Bonhamtown on Saturday, March 8, 1777, attempting to open communication with New Brunswick, which had been cut off by the Whigs. He failed. Intending to return to Amboy, he sent out a guard of 3,000 troops who posted themselves, their artillery and wagons in battle array on "Punk Hill" or "Spunk Hill." The wagons were to disguise their intentions and to make it look as if they were foraging, but there was no forage in that area.

Brigadier General William Maxwell (1733–1796) and his troops were a good distance away on rising ground to the northward, in plain view but too weak to attack General Howe's forces. He sent out advance parties under Colonels Samuel Potter, Sr. (1727–1802) and Edward Cook (1738–1808) of Pennsylvania and Colonel Nathaniel Thatcher of Massachusetts when a skirmish ensued. General Maxwell sent a party to the left and a strong party to the right on the heights toward Bonhamtown, his real objective. He wanted to attack their flank.

The two parties joined about half a mile lower down between Carman's Hill and Woodbridge and met a strong enemy advance party. Both sides received reinforcements which led to a more general engagement which extended from Punk Hill at Amboy to Bonhamtown and Metuchen.

The Crown forces lost an estimated 20 killed and 40 wounded, four prisoners, three field pieces and a baggage wagon.[170]

See also **Woodbridge.**

★ General Adam Stephen (ca. 1730–1791) attacked Crown forces pickets near Bonhamtown on April 14th, 15th, 20th, and 21st. On Monday April 14, 1777, he killed a captain and seven privates, and captured 16 prisoners.

★ A detachment of Captain Alexander Patterson's (1743–1822) 12th Pennsylvania Regiment commanded by Colonel Edward Cook (1738–1808) attacked a British picket guard of 25 men at 2 AM on Tuesday, April 15, 1777, about 400 yards from Bonhamtown. Lieutenant Frazier, of the 75th Regiment (d. 1777), was killed on the spot in the brief but obstinate engagement which killed nine of the guard and made the remaining 16 prisoners. Colonel Cook lost Lieutenants William McElhatton (McAlhatton) and John Reily wounded but not mortally. The Crown forces held a favorable position but did not attempt to support their guard. They hastily retired to their earthworks.[171]

★ A party of 16 men of Colonel William Cooke's (1732–1804) regiment, under the command of Lieutenant James McCabe (1735–1795) attacked a Crown forces picket guard at Bonhamtown Sunday night, April 20, 1777. They drove the guard in, killed one man, and wounded two who were left on the field. Lieutenant McCabe's men kept up their fire and maintained their ground until daybreak, despite enemy reinforcements. They then retreated in the morning. In another attack on the 20th, the Regulars killed or captured the entire raiding party of 25.[172]

★ Some Pennsylvania troops under Lieutenant Benjamin Lodge (1749–1801) attacked the same British picket guard at Bonhamtown on Monday, April 21, 1777. The guard had been doubled and Lieutenant James McCabe reinforced Lieutenant Lodge. Together, they drove the guard, killing one and wounding two. With only 32 men, they kept the Crown troops in Bonhamtown under arms all night.[173]

★ General Adam Stephen's (ca. 1730–1791) division was being hastily assembled from different posts in early May 1777. On Saturday afternoon, May 10, he attacked the 42nd or Royal Highlanders' Foot Regiment; the 2nd Battalion of the 71st or Highland Foot, commanded by Major Simon Foster, and the 33rd Regiment and six companies of light infantry posted within 2 miles of Bonhamtown and about the same distance from Brunswick. The British had large camps at Brunswick, the Landing, and Amboy which could have easily reinforced these troops.

The action continued for about an hour and a half. The Continental troops drove in the picket at Bonhamtown, attacked and drove the Highlanders out of a wood they had taken possession of near Piscataway. The Highlanders were too proud to surrender and lost two officers and 26 men killed and wounded. The British were reinforced but again forced to retreat. They were reinforced a second time. This time the Continentals retired with minor losses.[174]

★ The Crown forces set out toward Amboy at daybreak on Tuesday, June 23, 1778. The Congressional forces had alarmed all their outposts throughout the night and a great number of riflemen, supported by light cavalry and guns, followed them so closely that they withdrew to the vicinity of Bonhamtown under constant skirmishing. The Queen's Rangers, assigned to cover the right flank, strayed too far from the army, and were attacked so severely by a superior force that half of the corps was killed or wounded. Captain Carl August von Wreden's detachment also suffered very much.

The army deployed near Bonhamtown to support the rear, as they expected the entire Continental army to make vigorous attacks. General Alexander Leslie (1740–1794), the 71st Highland Regiment and Captain Johann von Ewald's (1744–1813) jaegers (see Photo NJ-8) were sent to secure a pass which the army had to march through. They discovered that it was held by 600 men and several light guns.

General Leslie immediately ordered the jaegers and the Highlanders to attack. After a hard fight under heavy enemy fire, they took the pass. They captured several officers and about 30 privates.

General Leslie's corps erected some earthworks on Bordentown Creek and fired some cannon at the Congressional forces during the evening. They crossed Bordentown Creek the next morning and marched through Bordentown. They exchanged a few cannon shots at troops who tried to molest them as they pulled down a drawbridge to join General Henry Clinton (1730–1795) at Crosswicks.[175]

General Stephen attacked while they were at dinner, catching them totally by surprise. Major McPherson (d. 1777), three subalterns, three sergeants, and about 60 privates were killed and Captain Stewart of the light infantry and 120 privates were wounded, 40 of them so critically that they were brought to New York. Stephen lost two men killed and a captain, three subalterns, and 11 privates wounded. One subaltern was seriously wounded and taken prisoner with 12 of his men. The Crown forces then reinforced these posts with one battalion of Hessians and the 10th and 55th British regiments.[176]

★ General William Howe (1732–1786) marched out of Amboy with part of the army under his command about 1 AM on Wednesday, June 25, 1777. The division under General Charles Cornwallis (1738–1805) fell in with a body of about 3,000 Continentals near Bonhamtown. The British soon put the Continentals to flight, killing about 100 and taking 70 prisoners along with three pieces of artillery.[177]

★ Lieutenant Colonel John Graves Simcoe (1752–1806) led a raid on Bonhamtown, Elizabethtown, Bound Brook, and Somerset Courthouse on Thursday, October 21, 1779. The Queen's Rangers, along with their dragoons and 10 light horsemen under the command of Captain John Stewart landed at Amboy about 2 AM. They proceeded as far as Bonhamtown where the infantry returned to Amboy and Colonel Simcoe's 70 dragoons advanced to Bound Brook where they destroyed 18 large flat-bottomed boats and some supplies. They then proceeded to Somerset Courthouse, 28 miles from Amboy, released the Loyalists confined there, set fire to the courthouse, and destroyed a large quantity of forage and supplies destined for the Continental army.

As they returned on the south side of the Raritan, a large body of Whigs, who lay in ambush in woods within 2 miles of Brunswick, fired on them. The dragoons immediately charged and dispersed the Whigs; but Colonel Simcoe's horse was shot from under him. He received a bruise in the fall which stunned him. His dragoons, thinking him killed, left him on the field and proceeded to Brunswick.[178]

See **Brunswick, Bound Brook, Elizabeth,** and **Somerset Courthouse.**

Metuchen
Drake's Farm (Feb. 1, 1777)

> Drake's Farm was in what is now Metuchen.

The British Army had more than 10,000 troops at New Brunswick and Amboy at the end of January 1777. General George Washington (1732–1799) had his small force spread out to the north and west with its center at Morristown. He also had a detachment of about 600 men camped at Quibbletown (New Market) in Middlesex County to the south.

Brigadier General William Erskine (1728–1795) left Brunswick early on Saturday morning, February 1, 1777 with a foraging party of 180 men from the 42nd (Black Watch) Regiment and eight artillery pieces. They marched northeast toward Metuchen which is equidistant—about 6 miles—from Brunswick and Quibbletown. They joined forces with Lieutenant Colonel William Harcourt and about 850 men, also from Brunswick. The heavy snow that fell during the night of January 29th was beginning to melt as the troops headed to Drake's farm in Metuchen. The Black Watch stood guard over the fields where haystacks were still standing as Harcourt's men gathered the hay and loaded it into wagons.

Colonel Charles Scott (ca. 1739–1813), of the 5th Virginia Regiment, left Quibbletown about 10 AM that same morning with 600–700 Virginia and Connecticut troops. They marched about a quarter of a mile southeast along the Quibbletown–Metuchen road. Colonel Scott led an advance scouting party of 90 men early in the afternoon to reconnoiter the area when he encountered a picket of five of Erskine's light horsemen guarding the foraging party. Scott ordered his men to attack the guard. They fired and pursued the dragoons, all of whom escaped except for the commanding officer whom they captured.

The Crown forces finished gathering the hay about 2 PM when Colonel Scott's advance column came over the hill to their left (north) and attacked the Black Watch, partly in front, partly in flank. Harcourt ordered the Hessian grenadiers (see Photo NJ-7), who had been gathering hay in the fields south of the road, to take up a position to the right of the Black Watch. This increased the force opposing Scott to 230. It took them about 10 minutes to get in position with the 1st battalion of grenadiers on the right of the Hessians and on Scott's flank. A heated skirmish ensued for 15 minutes before Scott's men drove the grenadiers back. They soon returned with 300 fresh men and a field piece, forcing Scott to retreat about 300 yards up the hill toward a small wood to reform.

Colonel Andrew Ward (1727–1799) of Connecticut and the remaining Congressional troops, who had not yet been involved in the engagement, now advanced over the hill in three columns. One of Ward's men remembered Colonel Scott's advice. Fearing that the men would fire too high, which is likely to happen at the beginning of an action, Scott told them:

Take care now and fire low bring down your pieces fire at their legs, one man
Wounded in the leg is better [than] a dead one for it takes two more to carry him off
and there is three gone leg them dam 'em I say leg them.

The first of Ward's three columns, on the right, faced the grenadiers. The second and
third columns had trouble covering the ground and failed to take the flank of the Crown
forces. Erskine ordered his light infantry alongside the grenadiers to outflank both ends
of Scott's line, forcing them to take shelter at the edge of the wood while Ward's men hid
behind fences and walls at the northern edge of the hayfield about a quarter of a mile
from the foraging party. Erskine also brought up a field piece which not only hastened
the retreat of the Congressional troops but also kept them out of effective musket range
by dominating the open field in front of the Crown forces' position. Some accounts say
the Continentals formed again; others say they soon dispersed with sporadic shots fired
from behind rail fences.

There were five men lying on the field wounded during the retreat, plus Lieutenant
William Kelly (1750–1790), adjutant to Scott's 5th Regiment, and Lieutenant John
Gregory, Jr. (1747–1777), both Virginians. Some of the men tried to help Kelly off
the field. As he was wounded in the thigh and could walk only with great difficulty, he
ordered the men to retreat and surrendered. His captors clubbed him to death with his
own musket and bayoneted Lieutenant Gregory and the other wounded. One account
says that several British soldiers "dashed out their brains with their muskets and ran
them through with their bayonets, made them like sieves." The dead privates were buried on the field, but the officers' bodies were brought back to Quibbletown for burial.
The Congressional forces lost one officer and seven men killed and 22 wounded and
two more officers and five men killed after the retreat. The Crown forces lost one officer
(Lieutenant G. A. Cunninghame of the 22nd Regiment Light Company) and six men
killed, and 23 wounded.[179]

Metuchen and New Brunswick (Mar. 8, 1777)
See **Bonhamtown.**

Dismal Swamp (May 17, 1777)

Dismal Swamp was between Metuchen and New Brunswick.

General Adam Stephen (ca. 1730–1791) ordered 800 Jersey, Pennsylvania, and Virginia troops to muster at Colonel Edward Cook's (1738–1808) quarters, about 9 miles
from the Metuchen meetinghouse under Brigadier General William Maxwell (1733–
1796), on Saturday, May 17, 1777.

They marched over Dismal Swamp in the afternoon and advanced to the Crown
forces' picket. The Crown forces observed their movements and assembled 300 troops
who engaged the advance guard for some time. The guard feigned a retreat over a narrow
causeway, turned suddenly upon the Crown troops, and repulsed them.

Reinforced with six companies of light infantry and other troops, the skirmish became general and lasted for some time before the Crown troops gave way. They received
a large body of reinforcements and artillery from Brunswick and forced the Congressional troops to retreat to a hill but did not pursue them.

The next morning, General Maxwell sent a flag of truce to Bonhamtown to request
a list of his men captured. That afternoon, he learned that they had one subaltern,
whose leg had been amputated, and 23 privates prisoners, most of whom were wounded.

They also reported two men killed. The Crown forces lost about 100 killed and many wounded, victims of the many riflemen and excellent marksmen posted in the woods and other suitable places firing at them in the open field, and frequently in confusion.[180]

Piscataway
Quibbletown (New Market, Piscataway, or Squabbletown)
(Jan. 16, 1777; Jan. 24, 1777; Jan. 30, 1777; Feb. 1, 1777; Feb. 8, 1777; Feb. 20, 1777; Feb. 21, 1777; Mar. 5, 1777; Mar. 8, 1777; Mar. 10, 1777; May 10, 1777; May 11, 1777; June 22, 1777; June 25, 1777; June 26, 1777; July 6, 1777; Sept. 13, 1777)

Near Bonhamtown (Jan. 16, 1777)
Near Quibbletown (Mar. 24, 1777)
Near Piscataway (ca. Apr. 20, 1777)

> Quibbletown was also known as Squabbletown and New Market. It is now called Piscataway.

General Philemon Dickinson (1739–1809) and about 400 militiamen engaged a Crown forces foraging party at **Quibbletown** on Thursday, January 16, 1777. They took nine prisoners but did not count the enemy dead and wounded.[181]

★ Colonel Mordecai Buckner (1721–1800) and 300 to 400 Virginia troops attacked about 600 Crown troops conveying a number of wagons from Brunswick to Amboy. Colonel Richard Parker's advance party engaged them at Quibbletown on Friday, January 24, 1777. In a little more than 20 minutes, they inflicted heavy casualties, killing the commander and mortally wounding the second in command while suffering only four wounded and two prisoners. Colonel Buckner was placed under arrest and tried for dereliction of duty for not coming to Colonel Parker's assistance and possibly routing the enemy.[182]

★ Lieutenant Colonel Josiah Parker (1751–1810) and 300 Virginia troops engaged a large British foraging party with six cannons near Quibbletown on Monday, January 30, 1777. The foragers lost 25 killed and several wounded; Parker had seven dead.

A letter, dated January 22, 1777, reported that a large number of British light-horsemen came to a farmer's house one afternoon. A colonel and about a dozen other officers took possession of the parlor and bedrooms, except the one where the farmer's aged mother lay very sick with a fever. They fed their horses with the farmer's hay and grain then plundered the cellar of about 50 pounds of sugar, 60 pounds of butter, a quantity of cheese, hogs' fat, candles, and meat. They then killed all the poultry, except three chickens, leaving the family with nothing to eat, despite the pleas of the sick woman's daughter.

The colonel and his officers spent the evening feasting and drinking. When the farmer came home the next morning, he found the soldiers had drawn off two hogsheads of his cider, eaten and destroyed all his winter apples, stolen several coats, his boots, a table cloth, pillow-cases, towels, silver stock buckle, and several other things. He was obliged to beg food from one of his neighbors. The letter's author noted that the light-horsemen were noted to be the best bred part of the army.[183]

★ A force of 700 Congressional troops and about 1,000 Crown troops skirmished at Piscataway around Saturday, February 1, 1777. The Crown forces lost 36 men dead and three field pieces and were forced to retreat. Reinforced with new troops and 3 additional guns, they renewed the attack. The Congressional troops withdrew with a loss of nine killed and 14 wounded in both affairs.[184]

★ February 1, 1777 see **Metuchen, Drake's Farm.**

★ At daybreak on Saturday, February 8, 1777, General Charles Cornwallis (1738–1805) set out with an advance guard of 50 jaegers supported by 400 light infantrymen, 400 Scots, 100 dragoons, several 6-pounders, 400 English grenadiers (see Photo NJ-10), two Hessian grenadier (see Photo NJ-7) battalions, and 400 British troops drawn from several regiments. They headed to Quibbletown to forage. At the first plantation, the jaegers (see Photo NJ-8) ran into a post of riflemen who withdrew after stubborn resistance. Several of them were killed or captured as they retreated.

The jaegers pursued the riflemen so swiftly that both parties arrived in Quibbletown at the same time. Riflemen were positioned behind the stone walls around the gardens and at the houses on both sides of the ravine running through the town. They put up strong resistance; but, when artillery was brought up, they withdrew into the nearest wood on the other side of the village. The light infantrymen and the Scots pursued them, and a battery was erected on the hill on this side.

The jaegers skirmished steadily with the riflemen as the foraging continued. Although they were outflanked on both sides, they did not worry about being cut off because the Crown troops occupied Quibbletown. The foragers completed their work about 3 PM and the Crown forces headed back to camp. No sooner had they begun their march than "a vast swarm of riflemen" attacked them from all sides.

They reached the village where the battery covered the crossings over the bridges. The militia occupied the houses on the other side and set up cannon behind stone walls and a stubborn fight ensued. The jaegers were ordered here to form the rear guard with two companies of light infantry. Several cannon were placed along the road to cover the retreat. The road ran 500 to 600 paces from the village to the wood where the foragers were unprotected. The riflemen and militiamen kept on their rear until they reached the camp.

From that time on, the Crown forces procured their forage from New York to prevent the gradual destruction of the army. Crown forces' casualties are not known but they killed 12 and captured a captain and five privates prisoners who were brought back to New Brunswick with the forage.[185]

★ On Thursday, February 20, 1777, a party took 20 wagons loaded with forage from Crown troops near Quibbletown. They drove in their picket guard, killed two light-horsemen, and narrowly escaped being taken, but sustained no losses. They brought in the horses and accoutrements. The same day, an artillery lieutenant was captured and taken to Major General John Sullivan's (1740–1795) quarters, with seven other prisoners, most of them Highlanders.[186]

The following day, the troops set out from Quibbletown to forage at Drake's farm in Metuchen. The dead officers from that skirmish were brought back to Quibbletown for burial.

See **Metuchen.**

★ A couple of foraging parties had a small skirmish at Quibbletown on Friday, February 21, 1777. The New Jersey militiamen beat back the Crown picket guard, killed eight men and brought off 15 loads of hay without losing a man.[187]

★ On Wednesday, March 5, 1777, 500 Continental troops attacked the Hessian picket guard near Brunswick. They drove the pickets into the town, took 11 milk cows, two horses, and 15 to 20 loads of hay which the Crown forces had stacked up within their lines. After the Hessians escaped, a number of light horsemen came out and drew their sabers but did not attack the troops removing the hay.[188]

★ Brigadier General William Maxwell (1733–1796) attacked a foraging party of the 42nd (Highland Watch) Regiment near Quibbletown on Saturday March 8, 1777. He had three men slightly wounded, none killed or taken. The foragers left four dead on the field and carried off about 20 wounded. General Maxwell pursued their rear so closely that they left one wagon behind.[189]

★ Another foraging party of Crown forces ran into local militiamen at Quibbletown on Monday, March 10, 1777. The Crown forces left four dead and carried off about 20 dead and several wounded. The militiamen had three wounded but none killed. The militiamen pursued their rear so closely that they left a wagon behind and three prisoners were taken.[190]

★ A party of 60 men from Samptown, under Major Ritney, fell in with a party of British troops near one of their outposts near Quibbletown, within half a mile of the British breastworks, on Monday, March 24, 1777. A skirmish ensued; but Major Ritney's party was outnumbered three to one by the British who were continually reinforced. Major Ritney was compelled to retreat but was soon reinforced by Lieutenant Colonel Henry Hollingsworth (1737–1803) with a detachment of Colonel Benjamin Rumsey's (1734–1808) battalion of Maryland militia and Virginia volunteers. About 130 Congressional troops, in an open field, now forced about 300 British from an advantageous position in a wood where they were posted behind trees. They drove the Crown troops into their breastworks, leaving behind them several hats, knapsacks, blankets and one bloody handkerchief. Several Regulars were seen carrying some of their comrades off the field. Major Ritney had two rifles broken but nobody injured.[191]

★ A party of 200 Congressional troops skirmished with Crown troops near Piscataway around Sunday, April 20, 1777. They lost six killed and 16 wounded.

See also **Closter.**

★ Brigadier General Adam Stevens (1718–1791) and Brigadier General William Maxwell (1733–1796) commanded a body of 2,000 New Jersey troops at Quibbletown, Samptown, Westfield, and Chatham. They attacked the picket guard of Lieutenant Colonel Thomas Stirling's (d. 1808) 42d (Royal Highland) Regiment; the 2nd Battalion of the 71st or Highland Foot, commanded by Major Simon Foster; and the 33rd Regiment and six companies of light infantrymen posted at Bonhamtown and around Piscataway about 4 PM on Saturday May 10, 1777. General Stephen attacked while they were at dinner, catching them totally by surprise.

The British had large camps at New Brunswick, the Landing, and Amboy which could have easily reinforced these troops. Two companies soon came to support the Highlanders who were on picket duty at Piscataway. They advanced into the woods where they held their ground despite being greatly outnumbered. When they were joined by the rest of the regiment, the Highlanders began a heavy fire that caused the Congressional troops to retreat toward their left in great confusion.

As they withdrew, the Highlanders encountered the light infantry, quartered between Piscataway and Bonhamtown, who were going to support them. The entire Congressional force now gave way and fled in a hurry with the British troops in hot pursuit. The British pursued them close to their encampment on the heights near Metuchen Meetinghouse. The Congressional troops began to strike their camp in great terror. The British officers had great difficulty in restraining their men from storming the encampment.

As night approached, the British were ordered to return to their cantonments. The Highlanders lost Major McPherson (d. 1777), three subalterns, three sergeants, and about 60 privates killed. Captain Stewart of the light infantry and 120 privates were wounded, 40 of them so critically that they were brought to New York. One of the British wounded was Lieutenant Stewart who been attacked three times when commanding the picket at the same post.

General Stephen lost two men killed and a captain, three subalterns, and 11 privates wounded. One subaltern was seriously wounded and taken prisoner with 12 of his men. The Crown forces found 40 Congressional dead in the woods the next day and took 36 prisoners. They then reinforced these posts with one battalion of Hessians and the 10th and 55th British Regiments.[192]

See also **Bonhamtown.**

★ There was a skirmish at Piscataway between portions of the regiments of Colonels Edward Cook (1738–1808) and Hendrick, and the 71st Regiment of Scots on Saturday, May 10, 1777. The Regulars were forced to withdraw and the Continentals took possession of their quarters. When reinforcements arrived from Bonhamtown, the Highlanders regained their quarters with considerable losses. The provincials lost 26 or 27 men killed, wounded and captured. The skirmish drew out a number of Regulars from Amboy, but they returned soon afterward.[193]

★ Early Sunday morning, Brigadier General William Maxwell (1733–1796) and about 500 men attacked and drove out the guards near Piscataway. When the guards were reinforced and formed ranks, a hot engagement began and lasted about half an hour before the British gave way and the militiamen pursued. The British received a second reinforcement very quickly and the militiamen were obliged to give up the pursuit and retreated because they were nearly surrounded. A flag of truce reported that the British held one major mortally wounded, one captain, two lieutenants, and 65 privates.[194]

See also **Bonhamtown.**

★ A large part of the Continental army pursued General William Howe (1732–1786) from Brunswick toward Amboy as they evacuated Brunswick June 19–22, 1777. They took a post at Quibbletown, while General George Washington (1732–1799) and the rest of the army remained at Middle Brook. Colonel Daniel Morgan (1736–1802) led the advance along the right bank of the Raritan where his riflemen encountered a Hessian picket guard at the New Brunswick bridge about dawn on Sunday, June 22, 1777. They forced the Hessian pickets to retreat with Morgan in hot pursuit until they came to the British rear guard at Brunswick.

Major General Nathanael Greene (1742–1786) and Brigadier General "Mad Anthony" Wayne (1745–1796) charged and drove the enemy through the town and across the bridge to their redoubts on the east side of the river. They forced them out of the redoubts and pushed them as far as Piscataway.

★ Early Monday morning, June 25, General William Howe (1732–1786) marched his whole army very rapidly toward the passes in the mountains behind Quibbletown, on the left of the Continental Army. He intercepted Brigadier General William Alexander's (Earl of Stirling, 1726–1783) party and had a smart skirmish. General Alexander made a safe retreat to Westfield and took a position in the mountains behind Scotch Plains intending to attack the rear of the army leaving Amboy to cross to Staten Island.

Meanwhile other parties engaged the British flanks in light skirmishes until they joined the main body which also continued marching to Westfield. They halted there until the next day when they retired to Amboy, plundering and burning houses along their march. Several small parties of Continentals harassed the British as they retreated. The British captured three cannon at Quibbletown.[195]

See **Scotch Plains.**

★ General George Washington encamped at Quibbletown to be "nearer the enemy" and "act according to circumstances." Major General William Alexander (Earl of Stirling, 1726–1783) took a strong detachment to the Short Hills near Metuchen where the Crown forces would attack him on Thursday, June 26, 1777. Meanwhile, Washington's troops were pursuing the Crown forces, in the summer of 1777, as they withdrew to Staten Island where they would get transportation to Philadelphia.

See **Short Hills.**

★ Brigadier General William Maxwell's (1733–1796) brigade attacked the rear of the Crown forces' army at Quibbletown on Sunday, July 6, 1777 and took several prisoners.

★ A party of Whigs captured two Loyalists, James Illif and John Moor, during a raid at Piscataway on Saturday, September 13, 1777.[196]

Woodbridge (Feb. 11, 1776; Dec. 11, 1776; Dec. 22, 1776; Dec. 1776; Jan. 23, 1777; Feb. 12, 1777; Feb. 23, 1777; Mar. 8 or 28, 1777; Mar. 20, 1777; Mar. 22, 1777; Apr. 19, 1777; June 22, 1777; June 26, 27, 1777; July, 1778; Aug., 1778; Feb. 2, 1779; Feb. 16, 1779; June 22, 1779; June 28, 1779; June 29, 1779; Aug. 16, 1779; Feb. 1, 1780; May 10, 1780; June 1, 1780; July 30, 1780; Sept. 17, 1780; Mar. 21, 1781; before June 19, 1782)

Strawberry Hill (Mar. 8 or 28, 1777; July 1778)

> Trinity Episcopal Church (see Photo NJ-17) (Trinity Lane) remained Loyalist during the war but its cemetery contains the graves of many soldiers from both sides. The cemetery of the First Presbyterian Church of Woodbridge (next door, at 600 Rahway Avenue) contains about 75 more graves of soldiers, including that of Captain Nathaniel Fitz Randolph, a local legend, and that of Colonel Nathaniel Heard (see Photo NJ-18) who arrested royal governor William Franklin.

A foraging party of Congressional troops captured 400 cattle and 200 sheep behind enemy lines at Woodbridge on Sunday, February 11, 1776.[197]

★ The New Jersey militia units spent their time observing the activities of the Crown forces and attacking them at weak points after the fall of Fort Lee (November 18, 1776) and before the battles at Trenton and Princeton (December 26, 1776 and January 3, 1777). They usually executed swift raids to seize livestock the enemy commissaries collected. One of these raids occurred on Wednesday, December 11, 1776 at Woodbridge which was located deep within the British lines. The New Jersey militia drove off 400 cattle and 200 sheep the Redcoats had collected. British reports claim that they lost over 700 cattle and 1,000 sheep and hogs in militia raids during this brief period.

★ A party of Crown troops left Amboy on Sunday, December 22, 1776 to bring in the property of a Mr. Barns (Joshua Barns?). The militia stationed near Woodbridge attacked them and had a small shooting match while they were retiring with Mr. Barns's effects. About the same time, a party of Loyalists tried to land some boats on Woodbridge Neck and to take some cattle and hay from Smith's farm. However, the militia took the cattle and burned the hay.[198]

★ One of the most respectable gentlemen in Woodbridge was alarmed by the cries and shrieks of his daughter near Woodbridge one day in December 1776. When he rushed

Photo NJ-17. Trinity Episcopal Church, Woodbridge. Its cemetery contains the graves of many soldiers from both sides.

to her aid, he found a British officer in the act of raping her. The man immediately killed the officer. Whereupon, two other officers rushed in with fusils and fired two balls into the father.[199]

★ A detachment of 300 Congressional troops attacked two British regiments near Woodbridge, on Thursday, January 23, 1777. They killed between seven and 30 privates and several officers and wounded several others. They had no casualties but they had two men captured.[200]

★ On Wednesday, February 12, 1777, Loyalists set out from Staten Island on simultaneous raids in New Jersey. They struck at Woodbridge, Rahway, and Elizabethtown.[201]

★ Brigadier General William Maxwell (1733–1796) and about 700 Congressional troops were informed about 9:30 AM Sunday, February 23, 1777, that about 1,900

Photo NJ-18. Gravesite of Colonel Nathaniel Heard at First Presbyterian Church of Woodbridge. Colonel Heard arrested Royal Governor William Franklin, son of Benjamin Franklin.

Crown troops, mostly those who had left Rhode Island and were going to reinforce the army at Brunswick, were marching from Amboy to Ash Swamp by way of Rahway. Soon after receiving the news, the Congressional forces heard firing. The scattered troops assembled as quickly as possible but the Crown forces arrived before they could all muster together.

Firing began around 9:30 AM about 2 miles from Ash Swamp between two small parties. When the main body of Crown troops arrived with six field pieces, the Rhode Islanders retired into Ash Swamp where a heavy fire of field pieces and small arms continued for a considerable time. It ended about 10:15 when it seemed that all the trees in the swamp were on fire and the noise of the guns was like one continuous explosion. This continued with little interruption until sometime after noon. The Congressional troops then retired to the hills in back of the swamp and formed. The Crown troops did not pursue them but returned to a hill about 1.5 miles from the Congressional camp and appeared to be moving even farther away. General Maxwell then sent a party on the right and eventually met the enemy near Woodbridge.

Colonel Eleazer Lindsly (1737–1794) and Major Joseph Morris (1732–1778) pursued the enemy closely about 1 PM and kept a continual fire on their rear guard. The party on the right engaged the Crown forces a little further down for about 15 minutes or more and General Maxwell came up behind them. A very heavy discharge of small arms ensued which continued for a few minutes with great fury. The Crown troops then went off very briskly and were followed to a hollow where the pursuit ended about dusk when the Congressional forces could no longer see where the enemy were.

The Congressional troops lost two men killed and about 10 or 12 wounded, one of whom had his thigh amputated on Tuesday afternoon, the 25th.

Edward Kelly, a sailor at Amboy who was at Major General John Vaughn's (1738?–1795) quarters to get a pass to go to Brunswick when the officers came to his quarters the next morning to report on the previous day's affair, reported that when the British troops arrived there the evening after the battle, he heard them say that they must not think of going out with 1,900 men and six field pieces because the Congressional forces would attack them on all sides. The officers told the general that they had between 400 and 500 men killed and wounded and that they had left 14 officers killed. He saw five wagons loaded with the dead come in at once.[202]

See also **Ash Swamp.**

★ On Saturday, March 8 or Friday March 28, 1777, 2,000 Redcoats occupied Strawberry and Carman's hills between Bonhamtown and Woodbridge. They paraded and "made a grand rattling of Drums," making them a tempting target. They also "brought a number of Waggons on pretence of Forraging where there was nothing left worth notice." Brigadier General William Maxwell (1733–1796) soon realized that their real intent was to "make a shew of something out into the Country . . . to secure Genl. Howe a safe passage" from New Brunswick to Amboy.

General Maxwell decided to attack the troops on the two hills with whatever soldiers he could muster and hoped reinforcements would come soon. He placed his men "on a rising ground" north of the Crown forces "in plain sight" and "at a good distance" because the enemy was "too well situated to attack." He "sent a party to the left to a Muse them" and sent Colonel William Cooke (1732–1804) and his Pennsylvanians to the right along the ridge toward Bonhamtown. He also sent a "strong party to examine their lines . . . and to fall in near the End of them that I might get on their flank." This party consisted of Colonel James Potter's (1729–1789) Pennsylvania militia and Colonel Nathaniel Thatcher's Massachusetts militia.

As the first guns fired, General Maxwell sent Colonel Ephraim Martin's (1733–1806) and Lieutenant Colonel Eleazer Lindsley's (1737–1794) New Jersey troops as support. When he saw two groups of British soldiers separated, Maxwell sent other men to drive a wedge between them; and they "gave way in great confusion." Maxwell might have pursued the retreating troops to Amboy; but he feared the large number of British troops at Bonhamtown "near us on our right" might force him to do further battle on "a plain open ground."

The engagement on the hills between Bonhamtown and Woodbridge was hardly more than a skirmish. Casualty reports are unreliable. Maxwell reported 20 killed and 40 wounded, while the British claimed to have killed several Americans and taken 15 captive. The action did not accomplish much. A British officer reported afterward that the Redcoats had encountered a "nest of American hornets."[203]

See also **Bonhamtown.**

★ A young woman was passing an evacuated house in Woodbridge on Thursday morning, March 20, 1777, when she saw, through the window, a drunken Hessian soldier who had straggled from his company. As there were no men within a mile of the town, she went home, dressed herself as a man, and returned to the house armed with an old firelock. She entered the house and took the Hessian prisoner and disarmed him. As she was leading her prisoner away, she met the patrol guard of a New Jersey regiment, stationed near Woodbridge and delivered her prisoner to them.[204]

★ Joseph Bloomfield's (1753–1823) New Jersey regiment was involved in sharp action with a large British force attempting to plunder the property of the Barnes family near Woodbridge on Saturday, March 22, 1777. The militia drove them off, allegedly inflicting over 150 casualties and suffering "inconsiderable" losses of about five killed and about five more wounded.

★ British troops captured Isaac Cotheal (1743–1812), a private in Captain Christopher Marsh's (1743–1810) company of light horse at Woodbridge on Saturday, April 19, 1777.[205]

★ As the Crown forces advanced from Amboy to Westfield on Sunday June 22, 1777, General Charles Cornwallis's (1738–1805) division encountered Colonel Daniel Morgan's (1736–1802) rangers at Woodbridge. A hot contest ensued for half an hour, inflicting a considerable number of casualties.

★ As General William Howe's (1732–1786) troops moved in the Westfield and Scotch Plains area, a small skirmish occurred at Woodbridge on Thursday, June 26, 1777. The main action is the battle of Short Hills.

See **Short Hills.**

★ A party of Continental riflemen surprised the Crown Forces near Woodbridge on Friday, June 27, 1777, the day after the battle of Scotch Plains. When General George Washington (1732–1799) heard their fire, he immediately withdrew to the Middlebrook passes and regained the heights before the superior forces of the enemy cut him off. This left both armies in the same positions.

★ Captain Christopher Marsh's (1743–1810) militia company routed a Crown foraging party at Strawberry Hill in July 1778. They captured 42 Hessians.[206]

★ Colonel Samuel Potter, Sr. (1727–1802) and 300 New Jersey militiamen attacked an enemy force from Amboy near Woodbridge in August 1778.[207]

★ Captain Samuel Ryerson, of Lieutenant Colonel Abraham Van Buskirk's (1750–1783) regiment, and a party of new levies from Staten Island, came to Woodbridge about 3 AM on Tuesday, February 2, 1779. They marched into town undiscovered and went to the house of Charles Jackson where a scout of 12 Continental soldiers from Bonhamtown was spending the night. The sentinel did not discover them in the dark until they had almost surrounded the house. He fired and ran away. The others, being asleep, were taken by surprise without making any resistance.

Captain Ryerson's main objective was to capture Captain Nathaniel Fitz Randolph (1747–1780) who lived at this house. Captain Fitz Randolph had just returned from Staten Island, where he had spent most of the night with a small party. He had been in the house only a few minutes when the sentinel's shot alarmed him and the Loyalists rushed into the house and seized him and Mr. Jackson along with the rest of the scouting party. They left without doing any other damage before the neighbors could gather. They plundered the house of a few small articles, taking the shoe buckles out of the women's shoes but Captain Ryerson restrained his men from further plunder or damage. The prisoners were exchanged Sunday, February 14.[208]

★ February 8, 1779 see **Staten Island** in *The Guide to the American Revolution in New York.*

★ The militia in the vicinity of Woodbridge and Brunswick assembled on Tuesday, February 16, 1779 when they learned that the enemy were collecting a number of boats at Billop's Point on Staten Island.[209]

See also **Staten Island** in *The Guide to the American Revolution in New York.*

★ A detachment of about 50 Regulars from Colonel Joseph Barton's 37th Regiment and an equal number of Loyalists went from Staten Island to Woodbridge on Tuesday night, June 22, or Monday, June 28, 1779 to raid Woodbridge and Rahway. The following night, they surprised a party of militiamen at the Six Roads or Crossroads Tavern, killed their commanding officer, Captain Richard Skinner (1740–1779) of a troop of light horse, and another man. They also took Captain Samuel Meeker (1740–1804), Christopher Marsh (1743–1810), Joseph Stephens, Benjamin Willis (1735–1789), David Craig (1756–1841), Stephen Ball (1750–1781), Lewis March, Jotham Moore, Jesse Whitehead, John Tharm, Thomas Bloomfield, Jeremiah Corey (1740–1805) and David Hall (1759–1843) prisoners. A few militiamen gathered immediately and prevented them from committing any further mischief. Several Crown troops were wounded, including one who was captured and died later in the day.[210]

★ Unknown persons fired upon a party of two captains and Congressional militiamen going from Monmouth County to Elizabethtown as they marched near Woodbridge on Monday, August 16, 1779. The commanding officer was wounded in the thigh and the rest were routed and several of them wounded.[211]

★ Lieutenant Colonel John Graves Simcoe (1752–1806) received orders to send a party to surprise the Congressional posts at Woodbridge or Rahway around Tuesday, February 1, 1780. His party of 200 Queen's Rangers was to cross the ice at 1 AM and return about 9 or 10 o'clock. Major Armstrong would cover his return with some infantrymen, the cavalry, and cannon on the heights at the Old Blazing Star.

The snow made marching difficult and Colonel Simcoe found no posts in Woodbridge. He proceeded until he encountered a Congressional patrol at the cross roads from Amboy to Elizabethtown and halted his troops. Another patrol on horseback approached his flank and fired. The Queen's Rangers' bugle-horns, drums, and bagpipe sounded the alarm in succession and the party returned toward Woodbridge.

A chance shot from the sentinels killed one of the soldiers. The patrol assembled in Colonel Simcoe's rear. When the Rangers passed Woodbridge creek around 8 o'clock, the snow was so deep that they had difficulty leaving the road. They occupied orchards or trees a short distance from the road and checked the enemy who pressed upon their rear.

As he approached the Sound, Colonel Simcoe could hear the enemy planning to occupy the houses at the ferry and to fire on the Rangers as they passed by. He sent Sergeant Wright to gallop over the ice to Major Armstrong with a request to point his cannon at the ferry house. He then sent Captain David Shank's (d. 1831) detachment across the ice ahead of the troops to conceal themselves behind the ridges of the ice floes to cover the retreat of the party which would pass between their fire and that of Major Armstrong's cannon.

As the Congressional troops approached, the Rangers suddenly turned about and charged them, causing them to flee. The Rangers pursued until they passed over a small hill, when the Rangers returned to cross the ice. The Whigs returned when the Rangers were halfway across. Some of the militiamen occupied the houses while others followed on the ice. The fire from Captain Shank's ambuscade drove them back, while the cannons fired at the houses. Some of the Congressional troops were killed; but the Queen's Rangers returned unharmed, except for the man killed earlier and a few wounded. The militia had six wounded.[212]

★ Some 30 Loyalists from New York, landed at Stony Point on the Raritan River and proceeded to Woodbridge Thursday evening, May 10, 1780. They captured Justice Henry Freeman, Mr. Edgar, six other whites and two African Americans. The prisoners were brought to New York. Some accounts date this event as occurring on Thursday June 1, 1780.[213]

★ A party of Loyalists from Staten Island took Dr. Moses Bloomfield (1729–); Jonathan Bloomfield (1759–1828), a town collector; and Ensign Britton Moores, all of Woodbridge, prisoners on Sunday, July 30, 1780.[214]

★ Some Loyalists from Staten Island came to Woodbridge on Sunday night, September 17, 1780, and carried off Mr. Thomas Brown and two other inhabitants.[215]

★ During 1781 the "Cow Boys" made frequent forays along the Jersey border opposite Staten Island to plunder and imprison the inhabitants in unprotected localities with impunity. One Wednesday night in March, possibly the 21st, a party of them from the Island entered Woodbridge and kidnapped nearly a dozen of its residents and stole all the available property along the way.[216]

The noted horse thief William Clarke (d. 1782) was shot somewhere in the vicinity of Woodbridge while he was on one of his excursions before June 19, 1782. He had stolen more than 100 valuable horses from Monmouth and other counties and found ready buyers in New York and Long Island. He had eluded the vigilance of the Whig guards and scouts for more than five years. The stratagem that led to his demise was a letter sent to him as if from one of his accomplices in Sussex. The letter notified Clarke that if he came over at an appointed time, he would find two excellent horses tied in a certain field, ready to be conveyed to Staten Island with little trouble or risk. Clarke went to the appointed location and was immediately shot by the people who lay in wait for him.[217]

Trenton and vicinity (Dec. 8, 1776; Dec. 17, 1776; Dec. 18, 1776; Dec. 19, 1776; Dec. 21, 1776; Dec. 25, 1776; Dec. 25, 1776; Jan. 2, 1777; Mar. 23, 1780)

Titusville

Coryel's Ferry (Dec. 9, 1776; Feb. 28, 1778; Apr. 4, 1778)

Vessels (McKonkey's Ferry) (Dec. 17, 1776)

Howell's Ferry, Trenton (Dec. 20, 1776)

Pennington (Dec. 13, 1776; Dec. 16, 1776; Dec. 17, 1776; Dec. 18, 1776)

Washington Crossing (Dec. 25, 1776)

Trenton Ferry (Dec. 27, 1776)

Five Mile Run (above Trenton) (Jan. 2, 1777)

The Old Barracks Museum (see Photo NJ-19) (**www.barracks.org**) on Barrack Street in Trenton is the only surviving colonial barracks in the United States. Constructed in 1758, it was occupied at various times by British, Hessian, and Continental troops and by Loyalist refugees. Colonel Johann Gottleib Rall and 1,400

Photo NJ-19. Old Barracks, Trenton is the only surviving colonial barracks in the United States. It was occupied at various times by British, Hessian, and Continental troops and by Loyalist refugees.

Hessians, including elements of General Knyphausen's and von Lossberg's regiments, were quartered here. These barracks were General Washington's objective at the Battle of Trenton. A cultural history museum includes a restored officers' quarters with 18th-century furnishings and permanent and changing exhibits. The history laboratory provides interactive experiences.

The Sons of the American Revolution erected 12 stone obelisks, in 1914, to mark Washington's retreat route from Trenton to Princeton.

Number One is at the southwest corner of South Broad Street and Hamilton Avenue.

Number Two is 0.7 miles east of Number One on the left side of Hamilton Avenue.

Number Three is in Hamilton Township in the vicinity of the intersection of Greenwood and Ward Avenues near the northwest side of Greenwood Cemetery.

Number Four is near the Mercer County Geriatric Center at Jencohallo Avenue and Chewalla Boulevard (off Nottingham Way) in Hamilton Township.

Number Five is near the Veterans of Foreign Wars Post on Christine Avenue off Klockner Avenue.

Number Six is about 2 miles away from Number Five on the left side of Quaker Bridge Road.

Number Seven is 1 mile north of Number Six off Youngs Road east of Quaker Bridge Road.

Number Eight is 0.5 miles north on Hughes Drive in the Van Nest Refuge, just west of Quaker Bridge Road.

Number Nine is on Quaker Bridge Road in the Mercer Mall just north of the intersection with Route US 1.

Number Ten is almost 2 miles north of Number Nine on Quaker Bridge Road in a wooded area owned by the Institute for Advanced Study in Princeton Township.

Number Eleven is in a field on the right side of Quaker Bridge Road 1 mile north of Number Ten.

Number Twelve is in the woods behind the Clark House at Princeton Battlefield State Park.

Trenton Ferry operated below Trenton and a smaller one just above the town. There were two other ferries 4 miles north of Trenton: Howell's Ferry, near the foot of Upper Ferry Road, and Yardley's Ferry, now Yardley, Pennsylvania. Johnson's or John's Ferry operated 8 miles north of Trenton on the New Jersey side and McKonkey's Ferry on the Pennsylvania side at what is now Washington Crossing. Vessels's Ferry is what the British called McKonkey's Ferry.

A marker on US 206, about 1 mile south of its intersection with NJ 546 in Lawrenceville, marks the site of Shabakunk Creek.

Coryel's Ferry is now New Hope, Pennsylvania. The New Jersey end of this strategic crossing was in today's Lambertville.

Washington Crossing State Park (**www.state.nj.us/dep/parksandforests/parks/ washcros.html**) is in/near Titusville, New Jersey. From Trenton go 8 miles northwest on State Route NJ 29, then northeast on County Road 546 to the entrance (355 Washington Crossing–Pennington Road). Washington Crossing State Park is an 800-acre park which runs along the Delaware River. The visitor center/museum contains a large collection of Revolutionary War artifacts. An interpretive center contains exhibits. Continental Lane, over which the Continental troops marched on Christmas night in 1776, extends nearly the length of the park.

The Ferry House at the south end of Continental Lane (see Photo NJ-20) in Washington Crossing State Park is across the Delaware River from McConkey's Ferry, Pennsylvania. George Washington stayed here until all his men had crossed the Delaware on the night of December 25, 1776. It has been restored as a Dutch farmhouse. A taproom, a kitchen, and a bedroom contain period furniture which was probably not in the building in 1776.

Photo NJ-20. Ferry House, Washington Crossing State Park was General George Washington's headquarters during the famous crossing of the Delaware

> The Nelson House, across NJ 29 near the river bank, is a small museum that has historical exhibits. There is a separate Washington Crossing Park on the Pennsylvania side of the river.

The Continental Army marched in a single column to Trenton on Friday morning, December 8, 1776, arriving in the afternoon. General William Howe (1732–1786) and Brigadier General James Grant (1720–1806) occupied Trenton where there were two ferries: Trenton Ferry below the town and a smaller one just above the town. General Charles Cornwallis (1738–1805) was at Maidenhead (Lawrenceville), almost directly east of another principal ferry crossing, 8 miles north of Trenton. There were two ferries, possibly three here also: Johnson's or John's Ferry on the New Jersey side and McKonkey's Ferry on the Pennsylvania side at what is now Washington Crossing. If the Continental Army tried to cross the Delaware, it would probably do so at one or more of these places.[218]

Brigadier General William Alexander's (Earl of Stirling, 1726–1783) brigade skirmished with General Cornwallis's advance troops near Trenton on Sunday, December 8, 1776 and inflicted several casualties. The Hessian jaegers (see Photo NJ-8) were sent immediately to Falls Ferry to capture the rear guard of the Continental Army at the crossing; but they arrived too late. They were still about 300 yards away as the last boats left the shore. The Continentals, on the right bank of the Delaware River, fired 18 heavy guns at the Hessians until they were all dispersed. The artillery did little damage and only killed one jaeger.

The jaegers were then assigned posts in a small wood near Falls Ferry to protect the crossing over the Delaware, as the Hessian army was quartered in and around Pennington and Trenton. The troops were to rest in their positions until the Delaware froze and was covered with ice. The army would then cross the river and capture Philadelphia, expecting to end the war, as General George Washington (1732–1799) only had about 3,000 men, most of them dispirited.

In the event of a mild winter, a fleet would sail into the Delaware to destroy the Continental fleet lying off Philadelphia. The army would then cross the river on a pontoon bridge.[219]

★ Major General Karl Emil Kurt von Donop (1740–1777) received information during the night of Sunday, December 9, 1776, to be on his guard. A corps of Continentals had passed the defile at Crosswicks, behind the left flank of the army, in order to attack and cut off the light infantry at Trent Ferry and the jaegers at Falls Ferry. Captain Johann von Ewald (1744–1813) took a Hessian patrol along the Delaware and Captain Lorey patrolled beyond Crosswicks with 12 mounted jaegers and an officer with 30 dragoons. However, all this was a false alarm, but scouting parties exchanged fire 2 miles south of Coryel's Ferry that day.[220]

★ Sixteen young women fled to the woods to avoid the brutality of part of the British Army under the command of General Charles Cornwallis (1738–1805) which was stationed at and near Pennytown (Pennington) on Friday, December 13, 1776. However, they were captured and carried off. The wife and only daughter (a child of 10 years of age) of one man were ravished. Another girl of thirteen years of age was taken from her father's house, brought to a barn about a mile away and raped repeatedly by six soldiers.[221]

★ The British and Hessian troops went to winter quarters on December 14, 1776. Major General Count Karl Emil Kurt von Donop (1740–1777) based half of his 3,000 men in Trenton (a small town of about 100 houses) and the other half at Bordentown and Burlington, respectively 7 and 17 miles downstream to the southeast. Headquarters was located at New Brunswick, 27 miles north. General William Howe (1732–1786) settled in New York and General Charles Cornwallis (1738–1805) prepared to return to England.

While General William Howe (1732–1786) rested comfortably in New York, General George Washington (1732–1799) desperately sought to reconcentrate his forces and redeem the defeat in New York. Major General Charles Lee (1731–1782) had the misfortune of getting captured by the British on December 12, 1776 and his 2,000 remaining men then made haste to join General Washington. Eight decimated regiments were also pulled from the Northern Army and, with some Pennsylvania militiamen, Washington was able to assemble a force totaling about 7,000 by the last week of December 1776. If he was to use this force, he would have to do so before the enlistments expired on December 31.

★ December 14, 15 and 16 were quiet in Trenton. Some Whigs came over the river in boats on Saturday the 16th, but accomplished nothing. The 20th Light Dragoons arrived from Princeton for duty on the 16th and six of them were sent on patrol to Pennington and McConkey's Ferry the following day. One of General Philemon Dickinson's (1739–1809) scouting parties crossed in three boats during a cannonade of 18-pounders. They attacked the six chasseurs who were recently driven from the house near the river at Trenton and "deadly wounded" a jaeger at Pennington on the road to Maidenhead about 10 miles from Trenton. The Hessians could not impede the landing and were forced to retire to await reinforcements. The militia withdrew, taking a pig which the chasseurs had just killed.[222]

★ General George Washington (1732–1799) crossed the Delaware River at Vessels's Ferry (McConkey's) with a large force of Brigadier General William Alexander's (Earl of Stirling, 1726–1783) corps late Sunday afternoon, December 17, 1776. Lord Stirling's troops were quartered about 2 miles north of the ferry. They landed on Colonel Johann Gottlieb Rall's (1720–1776) right flank to join with Major General Charles Lee's (1731–1782) troops. They engaged the Hessian dragoons in a skirmish.[223]

★ Brigadier General James Ewing's (1736–1805) Pennsylvania militia attacked the jaeger picket post at the ferry south of Trenton on Sunday, December 17. He began a "strong cannonade and under the cover of the fire, some 30 or more men were landed." The artillery barrage continued for two consecutive days. The jaegers withdrew across the river before Colonel Johann Gottlieb Rall (1720–1776) could send reinforcements. Prior to the attack, the picket consisted of one officer and six jaegers. After this attack, Colonel Rall reinforced the post with six more jaegers and stationed an officer and 30 infantrymen at Dr. William Bryant's house nearby [15 Market St., Trenton, NJ 08611 phone: 609-989-3027, formerly the home of William Trent (1653–1724)].[224]

★ The Continentals attacked the jaeger detachment at the ferry again at dawn the following day. They began with a barrage of "18 cannon shot" which forced the jaegers to withdraw out of range. Colonel Rall received an urgent message notifying him that a landing party of about 50 to 100 men from Dickinson's New Jersey militia had landed "four miles above Trenton at Howel's Ferry." He sent 12 jaegers on foot and two dragoons to investigate. The militia killed one dragoon in the skirmish and quickly returned to the other side of the river.[225]

Rall immediately sent out a large force of 220 men to destroy the scouting party, but they had already disappeared. After this second attack at the ferry, Colonel Rall ordered the staff officer of the day to take about 70 men and two cannon down to the lower ferry every morning before daybreak. They would remain there behind the hill until 10 AM to await another attack.[226]

★ Militia under Colonel David Chambers (1748–1842) of Hunterdon County, one of General Philemon Dickinson's (1739–1809) scouting parties, captured three grenadiers (see Photo NJ-7) of the Lossberg regiment on Tuesday, December 19th. They were on a foraging expedition 2 miles from Trenton not far from the road to Maidenhead.[227]

★ Colonel Johann Gottlieb Rall (1720–1776) sent Lieutenant Friedrich von Grothausen and a party of 20 jaegers and four dragoons from The Hermitage on patrol to Howell's Ferry 4 miles upriver from Trenton on Friday, December 20, 1776. There, they "met a rebel detachment of 150 men" of the Hunterdon militia commanded by Captain John Anderson (1731–1797). The jaegers killed one man and captured two or three others in the skirmish. One dragoon had his horse killed.[228]

★ Lieutenant Abraham Kirkpatrick's (1749–1817) Virginia militia fought with a band of Hessians near Trenton on Thursday, December 21, 1776. They killed one Hessian and captured another.[229]

★ As the men of Colonel Johann Gottlieb Rall's (1720–1776) regiment were settling down to rest about 8 PM on Wednesday, December 25, 1776, they heard shots north of the town. The last picket post on Pennington Road was under attack. The soldiers formed ranks and Lieutenant Colonel Brethauer and Colonel Rall led them up High Street on the double. Lieutenant Colonel Brethauer halted his regiment on "the rising ground where the Maidenhead and Pennington roads come together." Colonel Rall sent part of his regiment and 20 dragoons to reconnoiter the area near where the attack occurred. They found no sign of the enemy on Pennington Road or on the road to Johnson's and McKonkey's ferries.

When the reconnoitering party returned, Rall reinforced the picket "with nine men and a noncommissioned officer." This increased the guard to 20 men under Lieutenant Wiederholt, minus the four wounded. The troops then marched back to Trenton. The pickets sent out several patrols to guard against another surprise attack, but the night passed quietly. The identity of the attacking party of about 30 men has never been established satisfactorily. Despite General George Washington's (1732–1799) order that he "would not have any troops harassed," hit-and-run attacks became an almost daily occurrence around Trenton prior to the assault on the town, either to harass the enemy or to cover spy activities.[230]

First Battle

★ General Washington formulated a plan for a surprise dawn strike on the Hessian garrisons at Trenton and Bordentown on Thursday, December 26, 1776, when the troops might be expected to relax their guard for holiday revelry. Washington had all the boats on the river removed in order to escape into Pennsylvania and to prevent General William Howe's (1732–1786) further advance. This was the only time in the war that Washington commanded naval superiority over the British.

General George Washington personally commanded his force of 2,400 men across the Delaware River during the night of Wednesday, December 25, 1776. They crossed from Pennsylvania to New Jersey at McKonkey's Ferry, Pennsylvania, 9 miles upstream from Trenton. Washington stayed at the Ferry House (see Photo NJ-20) on the New Jersey side until all his men had crossed.

The troops would then proceed in two columns by different routes, converging on the opposite ends of the main street of Trenton in the early morning of December 26, 1776. A second force of about 1,900 men, mainly militiamen, under Colonel John Cadwalader (1742–1786) was to cross south of Trenton near Bordentown to attack the Hessian garrison there. A third force of 700 men, also militiamen, under Brigadier General James Ewing (1736–1805), was to cross directly opposite Trenton to block the Hessian route of escape across Assunpink Creek. Christmas night was cold, windy, and snowy and the Delaware River was filled with blocks of ice. It took nine hours for the 2,400 men to make the crossing from Pennsylvania to New Jersey.

Elisha Bostwick recalled the difficulties of crossing and re-crossing the Delaware:

> When crossing the Delaware with the prisoners in flat bottom boats the ice con-
> tinually stuck to the boats, driving them down stream; the boatmen endevering to
> clear off the ice pounded the boat, and stamping with their feet, beconed to the
> prisoners to do the same, and they all set to jumping at once with their cues flying
> up and down, soon shook off the ice from the boats, and the next day re-crossed
> the Delaware again and returned back to Trenton, and there on the first of January
> 1777 our yeers service expired, and then by the pressing solicitations of his Excel-
> lency a part of those whose time was out consented on a ten dollar bounty to stay
> six weeks longer, and altho desirous as others to return home, I engaged to stay that
> time and made every exertion in my power to make as many of the soldiers stay
> with me as I could, and quite a number did engage with me who otherwise would
> have went home.[231]

Colonel Cadwalader got some of his men across but not his artillery, so the attack on Bordentown never occurred. General Ewing could not get his men across, leaving the Hessians with an escape route to the south. Driven on by Washington's indomitable will, the main force did cross as planned and the two columns, commanded respectively by Major General Nathanael Greene (1742–1786) and Major General John Sullivan (1740–1795), converged on Trenton at eight o'clock Thursday morning, December 26, taking the 1,400 Hessians, commanded by Colonel Johann Gottlieb Rall (1720–1776), largely by surprise, even though Loyalist sympathizers had warned Colonel Rall that the Continentals were planning an attack and even gave him the day and time. Rall ignored them because the patrol activities of the Continentals on December 25 convinced him that he need not fear a general attack but only a patrol.

The Hessians celebrated all Christmas day and into the night. Rall did not get to bed until about 6 AM, drinking and playing cards at the home of a Loyalist townsman. A farmer named Wall delivered a message concerning the movements of the enemy troops, but Rall put the note in his pocket and forgot about it.

The guard on duty the following morning consisted of hung-over pickets and their officers who did not expect anything out of the ordinary. When Washington attacked, the Hessians tried to form for battle, but they faced artillery batteries commanded by Captain Thomas Forrest (d. 1825) and Captain Alexander Hamilton (1755–1804), fir-ing down the streets. The Hessians withdrew in disorder as Brigadier General William Alexander's (Lord Stirling, 1726–1783), men charged down the streets to capture two guns that had been hastily emplaced.

The Continentals had superior numbers and the advantage of surprise. The artillery under Colonel Henry Knox (1750–1806) was placed at the end of King and Queen Streets, dominating the town. Firing as rapidly as possible, they kept the Hessians from forming to defend themselves.

Colonel Rall rallied his troops for a charge, but the Continental infantry now occupied houses along both sides of the street, firing on the Hessians. Colonel Rall ordered a retreat and was mortally wounded. The Hessians surrendered about 9:30 after a fight that lasted either 35 minutes or an hour and three quarters, depending on which account of the battle you read. Continental casualties totaled four killed, three of whom supposedly froze to death during the withdrawal, and three wounded. General Howe reported Hessian casualties as 40 men killed and wounded, besides officers, and 918 prisoners, including 30 officers. About 500 escaped over the Assunpink to Bordentown because Ewing was not in place to block their escape. Washington reported, on December 28, the total number of prisoners numbered about 1,000.

Part of the British Army under the command of General Charles Cornwallis (1738–1805) burned the elegant house of Daniel Coxe, Esq.; at Trenton Ferry on Wednesday, December 27, 1776. Mr. Coxe supported the Loyalists in that region.[232]

General Washington met with his senior officers and decided not to defend Assunpink Creek and risk losing most of his army. General Cornwallis ceased attacking when it became too dark to see, deciding to wait until the following day to capture Washington who was cornered with the river behind him.

Since there were not enough boats around Trenton to cross into Pennsylvania, trying to retreat across the Delaware would risk losing most of the army. Instead, Washington slipped away during the night, moving in the opposite direction. He left a group of some 400 men to keep the campfires burning brightly, guard the creek, work noisily at digging entrenchments, then slip away at daybreak.

The Continentals muffled the gun wheels with old rags and marched quietly across Cornwallis's front. A cold northwest wind froze the roads, so the army did not encounter the mud which slowed the Crown forces during the day. They followed deserted and little known back roads toward Princeton. At daybreak, Brigadier General Hugh Mercer (1725–1777) and a brigade of 350 men seized the Stony Brook Bridge 2 miles from Princeton to delay Cornwallis's pursuit while the main body under Washington and Sullivan continued the retreat from Trenton to Princeton.[233]

See also **Princeton.**

Second Battle

★ The Crown forces began to advance on the Congressional forces at Trenton on Thursday, January 2, 1777 and engaged in the second Battle of Trenton which comprised three separate skirmishes at Shabakunk Creek, Stockton Hollow and Assunpink Creek.[233a]

Five Mile Creek or Run is the name frequently given to the main battle of Colonel Edward Hand's (1744–1802) delaying action on the eve of the Battle of Princeton. Colonel Hand's 1,400 Continental troops and 3,500 militia engaged General Charles Cornwallis's (1738–1805) 6,000 advance troops as they headed toward Trenton on Thursday, January 2, 1777. Hand's men occupied advance posts and defended key artillery positions. Colonel Edward Hand deployed the riflemen, artillery personnel, and regular infantrymen with muskets to oppose the jaegers and light infantry who led the advance of the Crown forces. Despite being outnumbered, Hand's men killed one Hessian. The decisive skirmish occurred about a mile farther south at Shabakunk Creek.[233b]

Colonel Hand's troops delayed the march of the Crown forces for two hours, causing them to bring up artillery. This gave General George Washington (1732–1799) time to prepare his defenses at Assunpink Creek.[233c]

★ Colonel von Donop and his troops were returning to Trenton from near Princeton about 8 AM on Thursday, January 2, 1777. The order of march was as follows: two jaeger companies, 100 Hessian grenadiers (see Photo NJ-8), and two troops of light dragoons from the 16th Regiment in front and on the flanks. Then came the light infantry and several 6-pounders followed by the Hessian and British grenadiers, the remnants of the Hessian Brigade, two British brigades and the rest of the 16th Dragoons. The troops lost considerable time getting on the road and there were large gaps between units. They were delayed further by the rain and thaw during the previous night which made the roads and fields very muddy.

Brigadier General Alexander Leslie's (1740–1794) 2nd brigade was late in starting, leaving a large gap between him and the main force. Leslie's brigade consisted of about 1,500 men from the 5th, 28th, 35th, and 49th Regiments of Foot, plus two troops of the 16th Regiment of dragoons. Because of the tardiness of General Leslie's departure from Princeton, Lieutenant Colonel Charles Mawhood (d. 1780) only learned about noon that his 4th brigade could take over the garrison. They did not arrive in town until evening.

The main British army passed through Maidenhead about noon and encountered a Congressional picket which shot a mounted jaeger from his horse. A small party of Congressional pickets still at Five Mile Run, Little Shabakunk, heard the shot and waited for the picket to arrive. They then retired to the main advance position at Shabakunk Creek where they moved after the skirmish at Five Mile Run the day before.

Colonel Edward Hand of the Pennsylvania Rifle Regiment, commanded a very advantageous position at the Shabakunk. The south side of the creek was "covered with close wood a mile in depth [while the north side] presented open fields." His men pulled down the wooden bridge after the Five Mile Run detail crossed the Shabakunk. Colonel Hand placed his men on both sides of the road, slightly back from the creek's edge and concealed by the trees. Major Miller commanded the force on the left facing the enemy and Colonel Hand, the force on the right. They waited for the jaegers to come "within point blank shot" before firing. The ambush forced them back to the main body in great confusion with the riflemen in pursuit.

The Crown forces prepared for battle and brought up the artillery which "scoured the woods for half an hour." During this time, General Washington, accompanied by Major General Nathanael Greene (1742–1786) and Brigadier General Henry Knox (1750–1806), rode out to the Shabakunk to encourage the men. Before departing, Washington told Hand that "it was important to retard the march of the enemy until nightfall."

After the cannonade, the Crown forces began to push across the creek in force. The skirmish lasted two hours before Colonel Hand could no longer hold his position and was forced to abandon his position between 3:30 and 4 PM. His men retreated slowly, loading and firing, retreating while reloading, then firing again.

★ In a second skirmish at Stockton Hollow later that same day, Colonel Hand's troops killed at least 10 of General Cornwallis's advance guard, wounded 20, and captured 25. Hand lost about six killed, about 10 wounded, and one deserter.

★ Before going out to Shabakunk, General Washington had posted his troops at Assunpink Creek with Brigadier General John Cadwalader's (1742–1786) troops "stationed in a field on the right about a mile from town, on the main road to prevent the enemy from flanking." This was near the present intersection of Hudson Street and Hamilton Avenue. Cadwalader had five pieces of artillery.

Colonel Daniel Hitchcock's (1740–1777) brigade guarded the Assunpink bridge and Brigadier General Thomas Mifflin's (1744–1800) brigade was held in reserve. Brigadier

General James Ewing's (1736–1805) Pennsylvania militia and Colonel Silas Newcomb's (1723–1779) New Jersey militia flanked Hitchcock on each side of the bridge. These forces had about 20 cannons and howitzers distributed among them, most of them placed on the high ground to the east of Assunpink Bridge.

Brigadier General Hugh Mercer's (1725–1777) brigade was stationed with two cannons about 2 miles up the creek, on high ground south of Pond Run, just east of current Olden Avenue. Brigadier General Arthur St. Clair's (1737–1818) New England troops with two pieces of artillery defended the fords of the Assunpink at Henry's Mill (near the Clinton Avenue crossing of the Assunpink) and Philips's Mill (near Whitehead Drive). The water at Henry's Mill was rapid and high, making it scarcely passable for horses. Philips's Mill, about 1 mile higher, was a better ford; so St. Clair placed most of his 1,400 men there. If they could hold the ford, they could prevent a flanking movement as the swamps, deep water, marshy land or other obstacles such as high banks along the Assunpink in 1777 made the crossing by large bodies of troops and artillery extremely difficult and hazardous except for Philips's Mill and the Assunpink Bridge in Trenton.

Major General Count Karl Emil Kurt von Donop (1740–1777) and the Hessians crossed the Shabakunk under cannon fire from General St. Clair's brigade and returned fire. He took part of the force and marched toward Trenton while the remaining Hessians faced Colonel Hand's second holding position at Stockton Hollow, "a ravine, which crosses the road at right angles, and descends to the plain of the Assanpink." A battery of two field pieces dominated a strategic position overlooking the hollow (about one third of a mile from the present battle monument, now approximately Bond Street, Trenton). The guns dominated the road to Trenton and fired at the enemy "for about twenty or twenty-five minutes" before they brought up their own artillery and answered with a counter-barrage. The head of the column reached Trenton about 4 o'clock, while their rear was as far back as Maidenhead (Lawrenceville).

The gunfire was so effective that the Crown forces directed their main effort near Assunpink Creek about sundown. They pressed on with such force that they compelled the Virginians to withdraw which, in turn, forced Colonel Hand to give up his position to avoid being outflanked. General Washington ordered Colonel Hitchcock's brigade "back across the Assanpink . . . to cover the retreat" of Colonel Hand and his men. They marched through the main street of town and proceeded a short distance up Bridge Street (now North Broad) when they saw Colonel Hand's troops coming toward them.

Hitchcock's men opened ranks to let them pass. The artillery passed with great difficulty as the street leading to the bridge was narrow. Hitchcock's brigade then closed ranks and marched up the street to meet the von Linsing and Block grenadier battalions and jaeger corps which were the first ones to enter the town. Hitchcock's men engaged the Hessians in Bridge Street, while the British light infantry passed Bridge Street (near the present battle monument) and advanced "between the main street [now North Warren Street] and the Delaware."

The British light infantry came down toward the Assunpink and moved in obliquely on Hitchcock's brigade, firing into their "flank at every space between the houses." Hitchcock's brigade, under fire from the front and flank, turned and ran in confusion as the enemy unsuccessfully tried to cut off their retreat from the bridge. Part of the American-German battalion was ordered to remain on the north side of the bridge to cover Hitchcock's retreat; but they were forced to retreat also.

As the British light infantry approached the ford below the bridge to pursue the American-German battalion, General Washington shouted an order for the Hitchcock brigade to re-form to block them. The men did not hear the order until Washington pointed to "a little meadow at a short distance, on the south side of the creek or river and between the road and the Delaware." The troops then started to move in that direction, re-formed and advanced to the edge of the stream. They soon withdrew a short distance under the cover of the houses which allowed their cannon to fire on the fording place and prevented the enemy from trying to cross.

The British light infantry repulsed, the Hessian grenadiers tried to force the bridge. Washington ordered Lieutenant Colonel Lambert Cadwalader's (1743–1823) light infantry to hurry there from their position about 1 mile away. The Hessians had placed "2 field ps in the Main Street and 2 field ps secreted behind Mr. Waln's house opposite the Mill and some Riflemen in the Mill, and artillery all along the creek." They then advanced toward the bridge, keeping up a heavy fire with the artillery and muskets in front and flank for about 12 minutes. They advanced about halfway over the bridge before being repulsed by the cannonade at the bridge which ended about 7 PM, about an hour after dark.

The British light infantry losses were considerable but unknown. The Hessians had "8 killed, 24 wounded and 29 taken prisoner." The Congressional forces had about 20 wounded but did not give a figure for their dead. The Crown forces halted and built their fires on the north side of Assunpink Creek with the Congressional forces on the south side. Both sides cannonaded each other until dark but did little damage.

The Congressional forces stoked their fires about midnight and left guards at the bridge in Trenton and other passes on Assunpink Creek. They then marched to Princeton by a round-about road, arriving about sunrise. They found only three regiments and three troops of light horse there, two of which were on their march to Trenton.[234]

★ A party of light horsemen from the British Army at Philadelphia captured Captain Samuel Dunham (1723–1789) and his two sons along with 127 bullocks at Coryel's Ferry on Saturday, February 28, 1778. The cattle were destined for the Continental Army.[235]

★ A party of the King's troops skirmished with some Whigs at or near Coryell's Ferry on Saturday, April 4, 1778. The Whigs were "very severely handled."[236]

★ A detachment of about 200 Crown troops under the command of Lieutenant Colonel McPherson, of the 42nd Regiment descended upon Trenton by way of Little Ferry at 4 AM on Thursday, March 23, 1780. Shortly after they entered the town, they burned the courthouse and the homes of misters Boyd and Chapple and then proceeded to Paramus, intending to surprise the detachment of Continental troops under the command of Major Christopher Stuart.

The British troops were joined at Paramus by another force of equal size which landed at Closter and marched by Wearimus. They probably would have succeeded in their purpose had not Major Stuart received information of their approach. Along the way, they plundered and abused the inhabitants indiscriminately and took about 20 or 30 of them prisoners. Captain John Outwater (1746–1823) of the New Jersey militia and Henry van Geison (1745–1805) were slightly wounded but not captured. The British had a number of killed and wounded in this excursion and had about 20 men taken prisoners. The militia pursued their rear closely as the British retreated from Paramus to Fort Lee where they embarked.[237]

See also **Paramus.**

Princeton (Dec. 20, 1776; Dec. 30, 1776; Jan. 3, 1777)
Rocky Hill (Jan. 2, 1777)

Princeton Battlefield State Park (**www.state.nj.us/dep/parksandforests/parks/ princeton.html**) is at 500 Mercer Road, south of town. A monument at Mercer, Nassau, and Stockton streets commemorates the battle. A tile map on the battle-field interprets the action.

The Thomas Clark House still stands on the crest of the battlefield and British and Continental graves lie in the distance marked by the Ionic columns from the portico of an 1836 Philadelphia mansion.

Princeton University's Nassau Hall, completed in 1756, was the university's only building in 1776. It housed classrooms, dormitories, teachers' quarters, and dining rooms. Both sides used it as barracks and as a military hospital during the American War for Independence. The Continental Congress met in Nassau Hall in 1783 when mutinous Continental soldiers drove its members from Philadelphia. The Congress also received the news of the treaty of peace with Great Britain here.

Rocky Hill is about 4 miles north of Princeton.

Colonel Johann Gottlieb Rall (1720–1776) sent two dragoons to Princeton with letters on Wednesday, December 20, 1776. About an hour after leaving, one dragoon returned to report that his companion had been killed from ambush northeast of Trenton, New Jersey. Rall then sent a captain and 100 men with one field piece to deliver the letters. One of the letters requested General Alexander Leslie (1740–1794) to station 200 men at Maidenhead (Lawrenceville) to keep the lines of communication open and to patrol Howell's and Johnson's ferries. General Leslie denied the request and criticized Colonel Rall for his extravagant use of manpower. The Hessians never held Howell's or Johnson's Ferry during their entire stay at Trenton, presenting a constant threat to the troops there.[238]

After several attacks by General Philemon Dickinson's (1739–1809) militia, Major Justus Matthaeus of the Rall regiment appealed to Colonel Rall, suggesting that it was "necessary for Pennington to be held by a detachment from which there could be detailed scouts to John's [Johnson's] ferry and in this manner they could watch the movements of the enemy." Rall replied, "What if the detachment should be lost and would the major like to be sent there?" The major answered that he would go if ordered, but Rall thought it too dangerous, unless it was a force of at least 200 men, which he could not afford.

Apparently, General Dickinson's and Brigadier General James Ewing's (1736–1805) militia attacks from the north and south were not planned and scheduled. Each commander seems to have acted independently in selecting the appropriate time to harass the enemy movements or to cover a spy crossing. Since most of Dickinson's and some of Ewing's force lived in the area, they knew every hiding place and could stay on the New Jersey side and return when they deemed it safe.[239]

★ A party of British dragoons accompanying a forage party near Princeton on Monday, December 30, 1776 left their weapons to go "attacking and Conquering a Parcel of Mince Pyes." A Congressional light horse unit under Colonel Joseph Reed (1741–1785) surrounded them and captured 10 or 12 of them.[240]

★ Encouraged by his success at the Battle of Trenton on Thursday, December 26, 1776, General George Washington (1732–1799) determined to make another foray. By an impassioned appeal to the patriotism of the men, supplemented by an offer of a $10 bounty in hard money, he was able to persuade at least part of his old army to remain for six more weeks. With a force of around 5,000, Washington crossed the Delaware River again on the night of December 30, 1776.

When General William Howe (1732–1786) heard the news of the Battle of Trenton, he canceled General Charles Cornwallis's (1738–1805) leave and ordered him to take command in New Jersey. He hurried south from New York City, reaching Princeton Wednesday evening, January 1, 1777. The next morning, he marched toward Trenton with 5,500 men to confront Washington.

Heavy rain during the night filled the roads with mud, slowing Cornwallis's travel. Large bands of Continental troops commanded by Colonel Edward Hand (1744–1802) and Major General Nathanael Greene (1742–1786) delayed him further. The British had reached Washington's main line of defense south of Assunpink Creek late in the afternoon of January 1. Cornwallis decided to wait until daylight the next morning to cross the creek, believing that he had the Continentals in an inescapable trap: Washington had his back to the river and no apparent line of retreat.

That night, Washington met with his senior officers and decided not to defend Assunpink Creek and risk losing most of his army. As there were not enough boats around Trenton to cross into Pennsylvania, trying to retreat across the Delaware River was also deemed to be risky. Instead, Washington devised a plan to slip away during the night, moving toward New York, the opposite direction from that which the British expected. At daybreak, Brigadier General Hugh Mercer (1725–1777) and a brigade of 350 men seized the Stony Brook Bridge, 2 miles outside Princeton, to delay Cornwallis's pursuit, while the main body under Washington and Major General John Sullivan (1740–1795) continued toward Princeton itself, planning to outflank the Crown forces, destroy a rear guard, and capture a vital supply depot in Brunswick, even though his troops had little food and some lacked shoes.

While Washington closed on Princeton, a regiment of British infantry reinforced by some dragoons and a part of another regiment (800 men in all) commanded by Lieutenant Colonel Charles Mawhood (d. 1780) was marching toward Trenton to join Cornwallis. Mawhood had just crossed the Stony Brook Bridge when he discovered Mercer's force behind him. He turned his men around and crossed back over the bridge in double-time. Both Mercer and Mawhood recognized the tactical value of a hill on the east side of the brook and raced toward it.

Mercer, realizing he could not reach the heights first, turned to join Sullivan's men who were coming down a road (no longer in existence) that cut across the battlefield at a diagonal toward Nassau Hall in town. A small detachment of Redcoats fired on Mercer's men from behind a fence, so Mercer led a charge that drove them back up the slope. Mawhood now realized how small a force Mercer had. He turned and charged across the field from the other side of present Mercer Road. The Continentals could not reload fast enough to fire another volley before they received Mawhood's bayonet charge that drove them back in confusion. General Mercer tried to rally his men but was bayoneted seven times and left for dead near the Thomas Clark house. According to legend, Mercer refused to be removed from the field and was placed under a white oak tree. He died of his wounds in the Clark house nine days later.

As Mercer's and Colonel John Cadwalader's (1742–1786) troops were retreating under Colonel Mawhood's advance, General Washington galloped onto the field. Disregarding his personal safety, he rode within 30 yards of the British line, calling the retreating men to return to the fight. A volley rang out filling the air with smoke and hiding Washington from view. When it cleared, the men saw him on his white horse, encouraging them to go forward.

Continental troops from Sullivan's column arrived, formed a line, and advanced. With the reinforcements, the Continental troops outnumbered the British and drove them into Princeton where some took refuge in Nassau Hall of the College of New Jersey (the original name of Princeton University). Captain Alexander Hamilton (1755–1804) brought an artillery piece and fired two shots into the building. The first glanced off. The second went through the main room on the ground floor. He then ordered a charge, and about 200 Redcoats promptly surrendered. Colonel Mawhood abandoned his guns, ordered a charge, and personally led it straight through the Continental ranks. He then turned about and gained the road to Trenton. Washington pursued Mawhood for several miles and captured about 50 prisoners.

The battle lasted less than half an hour. The Continentals lost 23 killed, including General Mercer, and 20 wounded. The Crown forces lost 28 killed, 58 wounded, 187 missing, and 323 captured. Washington wanted to continue on to the main British supply base at New Brunswick, but his troops were exhausted. They had been under arms for 40 hours in bitterly cold weather with practically no food. He did not want to risk a pitched battle with Cornwallis's fresh troops marching back from Trenton.

Cornwallis's soldiers marched into Princeton at the same time that the Continental rear guard marched out, ending Howe's campaign to destroy the Continental Army, capture Washington, and take Philadelphia. Washington proceeded toward Morristown where his army went into winter quarters on Howe's flank, threatening any move the British might make through New Jersey or up the Hudson.

The British had had enough of winter warfare. General William Howe (1732–1786) drew in his outposts in New Jersey to New Brunswick and Perth Amboy and settled in for the winter. He found that, despite his smashing rout of the Continentals in New York, he was left with little more than that city, a hold in New Jersey, and the port of Newport, Rhode Island.

The battles of Trenton and Princeton saved the Continental Army and temporarily saved Philadelphia, the capital of the colonies. They also cleared most of the enemy out of New Jersey, except for New Brunswick and Amboy (now Perth Amboy) where they posed no threat. These battles against an army of professional, trained, and battle-tested soldiers offset the worst effects of the disastrous defeats in New York and restored Washington's prestige as a commander with both friend and foe alike. In the execution of the two strokes east of the Delaware, Washington had applied the principles of offense, surprise, and maneuver with great success and finally achieved stature as a military commander. If these victories did not assure him that he could recruit such an army as Congress had voted, they did at least guarantee that he would be able to field a force the following year.[241]

See also **Trenton.**

★ After the battle at Trenton on Thursday, January 2, 1777, and the battle of Princeton, General George Washington (1732–1799) remained at Princeton a short while. He then retreated by way of King's Town, destroying the bridge behind him. He marched his army across the Millstone River at a bridge under Rocky Hill to occupy a strong position, staying several hours march in front of General Charles Cornwallis's (1738–1805) troops. He expected to join the rest of his troops and prepare for a general attack on the Crown forces to prevent them from reaching New York. Lord Cornwallis, seeing it was futile to continue his pursuit, returned to Brunswick with his whole force. Washington then went to Morristown.[242]

★ After the battle at Princeton on Friday, January 3, 1777, General George Washington (1732–1799) noticed a wounded British soldier lying on the field. He went up to him, inquired into the nature of his wound, commended him for his gallant behavior, and assured him that he would do what he could for him. After the general left, a soldier, thinking he was dead, came up to strip him. General Washington returned to tell the soldier to leave and ordered a sentry to guard the wounded prisoner until he could be brought to a house and cared for.[243]

Lawrenceville

Maidenhead (Dec. 19, 1776; Jan. 2, 1777; Jan. 4, 1777; Oct. 14, 1779)

Maidenhead, now Lawrenceville, is about 4 miles southwest of Princeton.

One of General Philemon Dickinson's (1739–1809) scouting parties captured three men of General Friedrich Wilhelm von Lossburg's (b. ca. 1720) regiment on Friday December 19, 1776. They were foraging 2 miles from Trenton not far from the road to Maidenhead.[244]

★ When the Continental Army received intelligence that the British Army was advancing from Princeton to Trenton on Thursday, January 2, 1777, two brigades, under brigadier generals Adam Stephen (c. 1730–1791) and Matthias Alexis Roche de Fermoy (ca. 1737–after 1778), which had been detached to Maidenhead several days before, were ordered to skirmish with the enemy during their march and to retreat to Trenton if necessary. Colonel Edward Hand (1744–1802) and a body of men were also ordered to impede the enemy's march to give the Continental forces sufficient time to form and prepare for the British Army's arrival. They placed two field pieces on a hill a small distance above the town. They fired on the enemy for some time before being ordered to join the main force at the south part of the bridge over the little river which divides the town in two and opens into the Delaware at a right angle.

Lieutenant Colonel Charles Mawhood (d. 1780) and the 17th and 55th Regiments were marching to join Brigadier General Alexander Leslie (1740–1794) at Maidenhead on Friday morning, January 3, 1777. His forces suffered much from incessant musket fire from behind houses and barns as they passed through the town.

The Continental Army was drawn up in order of battle on the south side of the bridge. The artillery fired briskly from the hill, followed by a heavy discharge of musket fire which continued for 10 to 15 minutes. A party of men were detached from the Continental right to secure part of the river where they expected the Crown forces to ford. Finding the ford blocked, the Crown forces made a feeble attempt to cross the bridge which was also aborted. The engagement ended about 6 PM as darkness approached.[245]

★ General George Washington (1732–1799) occupied part of Trenton and General William Howe (1732–1786) the other part with the main body of the British Army. Informed that General Howe was advancing with 4,000 men on Friday, January 3, 1777, General Washington went to intercept him at midnight. The two armies met at Maidenhead and an engagement ensued early in the morning. After half an hour of smart fire, General Howe withdrew. General Washington pursued him to Princeton. The 40th Regiment took refuge in Nassau Hall. General Washington summoned them to surrender or else he would burn the building and them in it. They all surrendered. The Continentals also captured 300 prisoners on the road with eight field pieces. Captain

John Stryker (1740–1786) and 20 dragoons also captured three British soldiers and numerous wagons. General Washington then sent two brigades to help the part of his army he left behind in Trenton. When they learned of General Washington's victory, the Crown forces in Trenton left toward Pennytown.[246]

★ Major Joseph Brearley (1742–1805) of Maidenhead, aware of a band of robbers in the neighborhood, gathered a small party of men on Thursday, October 14, 1779 and waited to ambush them on a lane he expected them to pass. The robbers came along about midnight when the major and his men seized them all and brought them to the jail. They included Dr. John Hunt, whose real name was Abraham Whitmoro; John Carr, a notorious horse thief; and Samuel Slack who escaped from the Philadelphia jail. They were all well-armed and had stolen two horses that night. They were on their way to rob another house when they were captured. One of them confessed and revealed a number of accomplices, several of whom were later captured with a considerable quantity of stolen goods.[247]

Cranbury (Mar. 12, 1777)

Cranbury is about 9 miles east of Princeton Battlefield State Park.

A party of Middlesex militia drove off an enemy plundering party at Cranbury on Wednesday, March 12, 1777.

Springfield/Union

Springfield (before Dec. 18, 1776; Aug. 10, 1780)

Connecticut Farms (Jan. 5, 1777; ca. Jan. 15, 1777; Jan. 19, 1777; Feb. 1, 1777; Nov. 4, 1780)

Battle of Connecticut Farms (June 7, 1780; June 23, 1780)

The Battle of Springfield is also known as the Battle of Connecticut Farms. (Connecticut Farms is now called Union.) A curbside marker reads: "Connecticut Farms—Settled by Yankees 1667—Scene of Hardest Fighting Against Invading British and Hessians June 6, 1780. Became Union in 1880."

Another plaque on the front of the Connecticut Farms Presbyterian Church, built in 1791, identifies it as standing on the site of a former church "where was fought a battle on June 7, 1780, between American forces under General Maxwell and Colonel Dayton and the British army in its advance to Springfield. The church and the village were burned by the British during their retreat on June 23, 1780. The British second advance here formed into two columns and advanced to Springfield where they were repulsed." The plaque also lists the names of 72 men who served in the militia and the army during the American War for Independence and are buried at Connecticut Farms.

Reverend James Caldwell lived in the Hutching House [126 Morris Avenue (NJ 82), Union, New Jersey], built about 1750 and better known as the Cannonball House because it was struck in the side by a cannonball. It is one of the four surviving buildings in Union and headquarters of the Springfield Historical Society. Visitors can see the cannonball among the exhibits. Despite the devastation of this portion of New Jersey in 1780, several important structures of the Revolutionary and earlier period remain, particularly in Elizabeth.

Some New Jersey militiamen skirmished with a body of British troops under General Alexander Leslie (1740–1794) near Springfield before Wednesday, December 18, 1776. Both parties retired. The militia had several killed and wounded.[248]

★ Major Crewe tried to cut off a detachment of New Jersey militiamen on a foraging party near Springfield on Sunday, January 5, 1777. They had a brief exchange and the Crown forces took four or five prisoners before heading to Newark to avoid being cut off. They arrived on Monday when Lieutenant Mesnard, of the 17th Regiment, marched out with about 12 light horsemen and 50 Waldeckers to search for the enemy. They marched about 4 miles and halted when they came to a hollow. They spotted some militiamen and proposed to return. They advanced a little and came under fire. The Waldeckers tried to retreat up the hill but found their route impeded. They retreated to a house, where they sustained some fire but were all taken prisoners. His escape route cut off, Lieutenant Mesnard and about 10 light dragoons marched toward Springfield. As he marched through the town, he came under a smart fire and had several of his men and horses wounded. He managed to escape with all his men except for a servant.[249]

★ Colonel Oliver Spencer (1736–1811) and 300 New Jersey militiamen skirmished with less than 100 Germans at Connecticut Farms around January 15, 1777. They killed one and captured about 70.

★ The militia killed and wounded eight or 10 Waldeckers near Springfield on Sunday morning, January 19, 1777. They captured the rest of the party, 39 or 40, including two officers, without suffering any casualties.[250]

★ A party of about 4,000 Continental troops under Major General John Sullivan (1740–1795) tried to take a hill from Brigadier General William Erskine's (1728–1795) 42nd Regiment (Highlanders) on Saturday, February 1, 1777. Both sides fought hard in hand-to-hand combat; but the Highlanders prevailed. They reported 18 killed and wounded while claiming 250 Continentals "killed on the spot."[251]

★ Lieutenant General Wilhelm von Knyphausen (1716–1800) was in temporary command in New York City while General Henry Clinton (1730–1795) was in Charleston, South Carolina. He ordered 5,000 men from British, Hessian, and New Jersey Loyalist units to march toward the Continental Army encamped at Morristown on Wednesday, June 7, 1780. Some historians do not know why he launched this large raid, but some think that Knyphausen planned to exploit the news of mutinies among the Continentals. Others think he believed Loyalist sympathies were increasing and that the local populace would greet his men with open arms. Others think it was to draw General George Washington (1732–1799) and his army out of Morristown.

General Knyphausen realized his error when he got to Elizabethtown (now Elizabeth) where local militiamen and farmers rushed to block his advance. Colonel Elias Dayton (1737–1807), in command of a regiment of 2,500 men including local militia, prevented Knyphausen from crossing the bridge over the Rahway River at Springfield. The strong Continental resistance surprised the Crown forces who retreated to the high ground just to the northwest of Connecticut Farms, now Union, in a heavy thunderstorm during the night of June 7 and entrenched. The Continentals received reinforcements and pursued the Crown forces who burned most of the homes at Connecticut Farms as they continued retreating to De Hart's Point near Elizabethtown on June 9. His operation a failure, Knyphausen evacuated part of his force to Staten Island and then lay on his arms waiting for Sir Henry Clinton to return to New York from Charleston, where he had beaten the Continentals under Major General Benjamin Lincoln (1733–1810).

Meanwhile, Washington moved the main body of his army from Morristown to Short Hills, just to the northwest of Springfield. Delighted with the performance of Dayton and the New Jersey militia, he was unsure of Knyphausen's intent. He thought the Crown forces might be planning a major march up the Hudson River Valley, so he scattered his troops throughout the area to prepare for any eventual attack.

★ General Henry Clinton (1730–1795) returned to New York City on Saturday, June 17, 1780. He examined the situation and feared that General George Washington (1732–1799) might head north to join a French force on its way across the Atlantic headed for Newport, Rhode Island. Clinton planned a second strike toward Springfield with another column marching on the main objective: Morristown. Both sides were considerably reinforced as the Crown forces approached Springfield on Friday, June 23, 1780 but this time they met a well-organized opponent.

The Crown forces now numbered about 6,000 men while the Continentals had about half that number. Major General Nathanael Greene (1742–1786) commanded about 1,000 Continental regulars and militia at Springfield while Washington moved his main force to Pompton because British ships moving up the Hudson on June 20 threatened West Point. Mounted troops, including Captain Henry "Light-Horse Harry" Lee's (1756–1818) Legion screened the country between Springfield and Elizabethtown while Brigadier General Edward Hand (1744–1802) commanded a task force of 500 men to harass the beachhead at De Hart's Point.

Knyphausen approached the Raritan River just east of Springfield with half his army while the other half proceeded (along what is now Vauxhall Road) to envelop the Continentals. Here, they encountered Lee's dragoons, reinforced with two regiments of New England regulars and militiamen who prevented them from attaining their objective.

Colonel Israel Angell's (1740–1832) Rhode Island Continentals defended the Springfield Bridge preventing Knyphausen's troops from crossing for 40 minutes. Angell and the Rhode Islanders then withdrew through the village to join Colonel William Shreve's (1737–1812) New Jersey militia around the "Second Bridge," just west of the village while Greene concentrated the rest of his force on the high ground around the Connecticut Farms Presbyterian Church.

The formidable Continental force caused General Knyphausen to discontinue the action. His troops burned all but four of the buildings in Springfield before withdrawing to Staten Island, leaving only their dead, wounded, some stragglers, and some prisoners of war. General Washington had already ordered the evacuation of supplies from Morristown and proceeded to support Greene when he received news that no help was needed at Springfield. The Continentals lost 13 killed, 61 wounded, and 9 missing. Crown losses are not reported but contemporary journalists estimated them at about 150.[252]

The "Fighting Parson"

Reverend James Caldwell, pastor of the First Presbyterian Church in Elizabeth, had delivered a memorable series of sermons at Connecticut Farms in 1774 and became known as the "high priest of the Revolution" by the Loyalists and as the "fighting parson" by the Whigs. Caldwell's wife Hannah (d. 1780) and their children took refuge in the parsonage at Connecticut Farms as the Crown forces advanced on June 7. She was killed on that day and became a martyr. The inscription on the monument in Elizabeth to Reverend Caldwell and his wife reads: "killed . . . by a shot from a British soldier, June 25th, 1780, cruelly sacrificed by the enemies of her husband and of her country."

Not only is the date wrong, but some of the other details may be questioned. While we can never know for certain what really happened, there is evidence that she may have been murdered by a former servant for revenge.[252a]

After the first skirmish in Springfield, Reverend Caldwell went to Connecticut Farms to serve Colonel Dayton's regiment as chaplain when he learned of his wife's death. During the battle of June 23, Continental soldiers reportedly had run out of wadding for their muskets and Caldwell is said to have gone into the church to get an armful of Watts' hymnals (see Photo NJ-21) to give to the men. He reportedly encouraged them by yelling "Give 'em Watts, boys—give 'em Watts!" as they tore pages out, but primary sources make no mention of this.

Photo NJ-21. Watts hymnal and key to the Connecticut Farms Presbyterian Church. Pages of similar hymnals were used as wadding for the cannons during the Battle of Connecticut Farms.

Reverend Caldwell was shot dead by James Morgan, a Continental sentry, in Elizabethtown on Saturday, November 24, 1781 (see Photo NJ-22). The apparent cause was an argument over the soldier's strict interpretation of the special orders prescribed for his guard post. There was evidence, however, that Morgan had been bribed to kill Caldwell whenever he found an opportunity. Morgan was tried in a building where the Presbyterian Church now stands at Broad Street and Mountain Avenue in Westfield, New Jersey. He was found guilty of murder and hanged at Morgan's or Gallows Hill on Broad Street at the northeast side of town.

Photo NJ-22. Grave of Rev. James Caldwell, the "fighting parson," and his wife Hannah in the cemetery of the First Presbyterian Church (Broad Street and Caldwell Place), Elizabeth

★ Four armed men looted the house of John Black, Jr. in Springfield Thursday evening, August 10, 1780. They took a large sum of hard currency and continental money and clothing. They then proceeded to the house of Caleb Shreve, Esq. (1721–1786), taking a certain Mr. Lloyd with them as their guide or to prevent him from alerting the neighborhood. They robbed Mr. Shreve of a small sum of hard and continental currency and then went to the house of Mr. Cleayton (Clayton) Newbold (1737–1812). They robbed Mr. Newbold of a quantity of plate, a gold watch, and money. They then went to the house of Mr. William Newbold (1770–1841) where they observed several people about the house. They pretended to be Whigs in pursuit of horse thieves and made no attempt to rob.

Mr. Lloyd managed to escape, or was released, and immediately went to alarm the neighborhood. Colonel William Shreve (1737–1812) and a number of inhabitants immediately set off in pursuit of the villains and caught up with them at Borden's Run on the edge of a pine grove in a thick swamp. Mr. John De Cow (1745–1813) or De Cou hailed their sentinel who answered by firing his musket and running into the swamp. Mr. De Cow returned fire and pursued the sentinel so closely that he threw away his musket and plunder, which included all Mr. Newbold's plate and Mr. Black's continental money and clothing.[253]

★ Loyalists John Smith Hatfield or Hetfield, Cornelius Hatfield, Cornelius Blanchard and others came over from Staten Island to Elizabethtown, on Saturday night November 4, 1780. Informed that Colonel Matthias Ogden (1754–1791), of the 1st Jersey Regiment, and Captain Jonathan Dayton (1760–1824), of the 3rd, were lodging that night at William Herd's, at Connecticut Farms, they hurried there, captured the two men in bed and brought their prisoners to Staten Island unmolested. The prisoners were jailed for a short time and released. Dayton got his revenge the following year when he led ambushes against bands of Loyalists from Staten Island who were raiding northern New Jersey.[254]

Bergen and vicinity (July 12, 1776; July 18, 1776; July 21, 1776; Aug. 26, 1776; Oct. 5, 1776; Dec. 20, 1776; Mar. 21, 1777; Apr. 17, 1777; Apr. 22, 1777; May 12, 1777; July 6 to 12, 1777; July 28, 1777; Sept. 10, 1777; Nov. 19, 1777; Dec. 5, 1777; Mar. 21, 1778; Sept. 28,1778; Sept. 30, 1778; Nov. 1, 1778; Nov. 28, 1778; Jan. 13, 1779; Mar. 14, 1779; Apr. 2, 1779; Apr. 22, 1779; May 17, 1779; July 23, 1779; Aug. 17, 1779; Nov. 2, 1779; Aug. 21, 1780; Oct. 7, 1780; Mar. 30, 1781; May 4, 1781; Nov. 29, 1781; Dec. 6, 1781; Dec. 23, 1781; Feb. 7, 1782; Mar. 29, 1782; June 7, 1782; Sept. 1, 1782)

Bergen Neck (Aug. 12, 1779)

Bergen is a narrow neck of land west of Paulus Hook accessible on three sides by water and exposed to a variety of attacks in different places at the same time. A large body of troops could capture it whenever they pleased.

Bergen Woods is now North Hudson.

Bergen Point Fort Site is at the southernmost tip of Bayonne in Hudson County under the Bayonne Bridge where the Kill Van Kull meets the Newark Bay. The property is now occupied by oil refineries.

A historical marker on Avenue B in Bayonne tells the story of Fort Delancey (West 52nd Street between Avenue B and Avenue C). Built by the Continental army in 1776 in what was then called Bergen Neck, it passed to the Loyalists after October

5, 1776 when the Continentals evacuated the area. They held it from the fall of 1776 until 1782. The Loyalists abandoned Bergen Point in 1780 and built a more substantial fort with a log fence. The new fort was called Fort Delancey in honor of Brigadier General Oliver de Lancey (1718–1785), a prominent Loyalist in New York. It became the main center for woodcutting operations when the Crown forces abandoned the blockhouse at Bull's Ferry.

See **Bull's Ferry.**

Admiral Richard Howe's (1726–1799) fleet began arriving off the coast of New Jersey on June 29, 1776 and within two days, the fleet swelled to 130 men-of-war and transports. The troops landed on Staten Island and the fleet anchored at the mouth of Kill von Kull. The Rebels feared the Regulars would occupy Bergen Point and surround New York.

On Thursday, July 4, 1776, General George Washington (1732–1799), fearing an attack from Staten Island, ordered Brigadier General Hugh Mercer (1725–1777) to station a guard of 500 men at Bergen Neck and to guard the ferries over the Hackensack and Passaic rivers. The next day, he sent an engineer from New York to supervise the construction of a fort, later renamed Fort DeLancey by the Loyalists, a short distance below the canal at Bayonne.

The British attack did not materialize, so General Mercer prepared to attack them. However, the plan was aborted because of bad weather which prevented his forces from crossing the Kill von Kull. The British troops soon grew to 30,000.

As the 40-gun frigate HMS *Phoenix* and the 20-gun *Rose* patrolled the harbor on Friday afternoon, July 12, 1776. Continental guns opened fire on them from the sandhills of Paulus Hook. The vessels responded with a broadside as they glided by the fort comparatively unharmed.

★ A large barge carrying troops landed at Bergen Point on Friday, July 18, 1776 only to be driven back. Congressional troops fired a great many shots at a British barge full of men as they tried to land at Bergen Point on Sunday, July 21, 1776. A tender continued a smart fire for a considerable time without doing any damage. Two deserters reported that the cannon and musket fire killed a captain and two privates on board the barge.[255]

★ The two sides traded shots between Bergen Point and a battery on Staten Island again on Monday, August 26, 1776. General Washington asked the militia to fortify the spot on August 30 as part of the "flying camps" he was setting up to place soldiers around the New York City area and at locations from which they could be moved quickly to wherever fighting occurred.

★ When New York fell in the autumn of 1776, the flying camps disintegrated and the men joined Washington in the retreat through New Jersey. Bergen remained Washington's headquarters until October 5, 1776 when he found it necessary to collect his forces in preparation for his retreat to the Delaware. He detailed the reasons in a letter written on October 4:

> Bergen is a narrow neck of land accessible on three sides by water, and exposed to a variety of attacks in different places at one and the same time. A large body of the enemy might infallibly take possession of the place whenever they pleased, unless we kept a stronger force than our numbers will allow. The spot itself is not an object of our arms: if they attack it would but cut off those who defended it and secure the grain and military stores. These have been removed, and when we are gone a naked spot is all they will find… We go to Fort Constitution [later renamed Fort Lee] as

soon as we have seen the troops marched off. We shall leave a guard of observation
behind us: this may prevent the enemy's discovering our removal for a day or two.

The Loyalists then occupied the area. The fort became the site of small skirmishes throughout the war as Whigs rowed over from Elizabethtown to harass or to try to capture Loyalists.

★ With information that Lieutenant Colonel Abraham Van Buskirk's (1750–1783) regiment was at or near Bergen Woods, the Continentals decided to attack them. General Samuel Holden Parsons (1737–1789) and 250 Continental troops and General George Clinton (1739–1812) with 250 New York militiamen marched from Paramus Church at 8 PM on Thursday, December 19, 1776. Meanwhile, a covering party of 300 men went to Tappan.

The detachment reached Bergen about 1 AM, completely surprised the guard, and captured 22 prisoners, 16 new muskets, six horses, and one wagon. As the Loyalists were gathering, the detachment withdrew, content with their victory. They returned to Paramus about 1 PM after marching more than 40 miles. They lost one man and reported several enemy killed.[256]

★ March 21, 1777 see **Weehawken.**

★ When the British occupied New Jersey, they imprisoned many Congressional troops. Within six months, both sides began to capture and imprison civilians in the neutral area. Samuel Beal (1714–1778) reported to General Adam Stephen (ca. 1730–1791) one such British seizure on the night of Thursday, April 17, 1777. A few days later, on the 22nd, a Loyalist raiding party of 25 captured John Fell at Paramus, not far from the New York State line, and took him to Lieutenant Colonel Abraham Van Buskirk (1750–1783) at Bergen Point and later to General Sir Robert Pigot (1720–1796) at New York. Fell was then sent to the Provost Jail with Captain William Van Allen. He was paroled in January 1778, exchanged for Governor Philip Skene (1725–1780) in May, and allowed to go home.[257]

See also **Paramus** and **Slotterdam.**

★ A detachment of 300 Provincial troops under the command of Lieutenant Colonels Joseph Barton and Edward Vaughan Dongan (1748–1777) marched from Bergen on Monday afternoon, May 12, 1777, to attack Nathaniel Heard (1730–1792) who was at Pompton with 350 men. Morasses and other impediments prevented the troops from reaching the place at the intended time; so Colonel Barton held a consultation and decided to take the road to Paramus, and destroy some stores there guarded by 80 or 100 men.[258]

See also **Ridgewood, Paramus** and **Passaic, Slotterdam.**

★ Colonel Philip Van Cortlandt (1749–1831) and his regiment came as far as Bergen during the week of July 6 to 12, 1777. They took 250 sheep, 150 fat oxen, and 90 wagons and horses from the town and the adjacent neighborhood. Several of the wagons were loaded with poultry, mutton and veal destined for the Loyalists of New York.[259]

★ A party of Whig light-horsemen came down as far as Bergen Point on Tuesday night, July 28, 1777, and returned toward Hackensack the next morning. They visited Hoebuck on their way and carried off a great number of cattle from the inhabitants.[260]

★ Three detachments of British, one from New York, another from Kingsbridge, and another from Staten Island conducted a successful foraging raid into "the Jersies" in the Bergen area on Wednesday, September 10, 1777. They took a number of prisoners and a very large drove of oxen, sheep, and other cattle before returning the following Tuesday.[261]

★ A party of Congressional troops went to Bergen on Friday night, November 19, 1777. They took some horses and other property from Mr. Cornelius Aeltse Van Riper, the blacksmith.[262]

★ A party of 12 Congressional troops and some officers went to Bergen Point on Friday night, December 5, 1777, to seize Mr. Van Buskirk. As they returned, Colonel George Turnbull (1752–1807), commander at Paulus Hook, fired on them, and killed one officer and captured another.[263]

★ A party of Colonel George Turnbull's (1752–1807) New York Volunteers captured four Congressional troops near Bergen on Saturday, March 21, 1778.[264]

★ September 28, 1778 see **River Vale, Baylor's Massacre.**

★ Lieutenant General Wilhelm von Knyphausen (1716–1800) sent patrols from both wings of his camp to the front on Wednesday, September 30, 1778. Captain von Donop and 50 dismounted jaegers occupied the road to Dobbs Ferry while Lieutenant Mertz rode ahead with 15 mounted jaegers. The mounted jaegers encountered some Congressional troops on the Jersey side of Dobbs Ferry and saw many more [Colonel Richard Butler (1743–1791) and 250 men and Major Henry "Light-Horse Harry" Lee (1756–1818) with 200 dragoons] in ambush on their right. When Lieutenant Mertz tried to go for reinforcements, the Congressional troops cut in on the road behind him. He attacked the superior troop of dragoons and beat his way through.

Lieutenant Mertz halted briefly and was attacked again. He received several cuts in the face in a heated skirmish and was forced to surrender. He lost two jaegers killed, one was left severely wounded, and one escaped. Lieutenant Bickell's men proceeded on foot along the North River and lost only one noncommissioned officer and one jaeger wounded. The New Jersey militia had only one man killed.[265]

★ Lieutenant Colonel Eleazer Lindsley (1737–1794) led a party of men as far south as Bergen Point on Sunday, November 1, 1778. They killed a British guard and took 2 prisoners and 20 horses. Colonel Christian Febiger (1746–1796) reported from Hackensack on Saturday, November 29, that he had sent a captain and a force of 36 men down to Hoboken, Weehawken, and Bergen the day before to intercept traffic to the ferries.[266]

★ A detachment from the British 26th Regiment captured Ensign Allen and three Jersey militiamen at Bergen Point on Wednesday, January 13, 1779.[267]

★ Lieutenant Colonel Abraham Van Buskirk (1750–1783) received intelligence that a captain and lieutenant were at the Three Pigeons tavern in Bergen Woods with a party of Carolina troops on Sunday morning, March 14, 1779. He sent a lieutenant and a band of Loyalists to search for them. The Carolinians learned of their approach and escaped. The Loyalists pursued them 12 miles into the country before overtaking them. They fired a few shots and captured two prisoners, one of whom was wounded. The rest escaped in sleighs.[268]

★ A detachment of the British 64th Regiment from Paulus Hook captured 12 privates and Lieutenant James Paul from Colonel Israel Shreve's (1739–1799) 2nd New Jersey Regiment on Bergen Neck on Friday night, April 2, 1779.[269]

★ Captain Joshua Bowman (1757–1827), of the 1st North Carolina brigade, with a party of Continental troops and a few militiamen had a smart skirmish with the enemy near De Groot's [English Neighborhood], about 7 miles from Hoebuck, early in the morning of Thursday, April 22, 1779. The Congressional troops drove them off, suffering two Continentals and one militiaman wounded. Crown losses are not known for certain, but one of them was taken prisoner and two or three were carried off dead or wounded.[270]

★ Lieutenant Colonel Abraham Van Buskirk (1750–1783) and a detachment of 1,000 Loyalists from several different corps landed in Bergen County on Monday, May 17, 1779. They destroyed all the Whig houses along their route and killed several occupants. They also killed two African American women who were driving off some cattle belonging to their masters and stabbed Mr. Joost Zabriskie in 13 different places. They hurriedly withdrew to their boats and returned to New York when a considerable number of militiamen began to gather.[271]

★ Captain William Van Allen and a company of New Jersey Volunteers (Loyalists) chased three Whigs a short distance from Bergen on Friday, July 23, 1779. They captured two of them, David Ritzema Bogert and John Lozier (1745–1784) who was involved in the murder of Captain John Richards (d. 1778).[272]

★ Bergen Neck Aug. 12, 1779 see **Little Ferry** April 12, 1779.

★ Aug. 17, 1779 see **Englewood, Liberty Pole.**

★ Brigadier General "Mad Anthony" Wayne (1745–1796) moved his troops on a huge forage expedition on the morning of Tuesday, November 2, 1779. They went as far south as the "Overpeck Creek between Fort Lee and Paulus Hook," where they collected "upward of one hundred head of fat cattle and a considerable quantity of grain." The conduct of the troops had not been very good before the forage and got even worse on the forage. One of Wayne's staff wrote, "They have indiscriminately stripped the neighbors of their corn, milk, ducks, fowls, &c, &c, and that too even in the sight and under the very noses of the owners." [273]

★ Captain William Harding and about 40 Loyalists from the Refugee Post on Bergen Neck went to Newark on Monday, August 21, 1780. They took four prisoners and about 30 cattle which were brought to Fort De Lancey.[274]

★ General George Washington (1732–1799) ordered a captain's command to remain at Sneden's Landing to guard the blockhouse, to patrol and guard the landing places and avenues leading to the post, and to observe enemy movements to avert a surprise attack. The forage around Tappan, Harrington, and Schraalenburgh was exhausted. Major Henry "Light-Horse Harry" Lee's (1756–1818) light horsemen had been harassing the woodcutters in the upper Bergen Township and some Pennsylvania light infantrymen had been posted in and around Liberty Pole.

The main body of the Continental Army left camp at 3 PM on Saturday, October 7, 1780, a cold, wet day. They moved westward through Paramus toward Preakness. After crossing the New Bridge in the rain, a party of about 200 light infantrymen and horsemen attacked the Refugee post at Bergen Point, under the command of Captain Thomas Ward. The garrison gave them a smart fire of artillery and musketry, assisted by a cannonade from the galleys, forcing them to retreat. The Continentals captured about 30 Refugees and took quarters in the barns between Hackensack and New Bridge that night before proceeding toward Preakness in the morning.[275]

★ A party of Whigs went from Newark to raid and plunder Bergen on Friday night, March 30, 1781. They captured two sloops lying near the Refugee Post on the Bergen shore. They also took eight prisoners from the sloops and sent them to Morristown.[276]

★ Captain John Ward (1753–1846) and a party of about 50 men, consisting of the Loyal Refugees and a number of Morrisania Loyalists, embarked at Bergen Point at 1 PM on Friday, May 4, 1781 and landed on the Jersey shore. The Whigs fled in a hurry as the Loyalists approached. When they were reinforced a short while later, the Whigs tried to prevent the Loyalists from executing their plans. They received such a warm reception that they fled to the dense woods where a heated engagement continued for about two hours. The Whigs lost three killed and several wounded. The Loyalists had no casualties and returned about 6 PM with a considerable quantity of goods.[277]

★ November 29, 1781 see **Newark Bay.**

★ Captain Baker Hendricks (1756–1789) and a small party of men in whaleboats (see Photo NJ-1), went down Newark Bay, near the Kills, on Thursday night, December 6, 1781. They landed on Bergen Neck, near the Refugee Post, where they boarded and stripped two boats and took one prisoner. They landed a small party of men near the Loyalist post (Fort Delancy) on Bergen Neck and took two prisoners. On their return, they captured three more "noted villains" with all kinds of provisions.[278]

★ They captured eight more at Bergen on Sunday, December 23, 1781.[279]

★ Captain Bowmay and a detachment of about 200 men of the Jersey Brigade were joined by a party of militiamen on Thursday morning, February 7, 1782. They crossed the sound on the ice to the Refugee Post, Fort Delancy, on Bergen Neck. They attacked the fort before sunrise, captured three Loyalists and bayoneted the advance sentinel, an African American who refused to surrender.[280]

★ A party of Whigs from Newark landed at Bergen Neck on Friday night, March 29, 1782. They captured seven prisoners lodging in houses along the shore. The commanding officer sent a party to intercept the raiders. Both parties arrived at the whaleboat almost simultaneously. The Loyalists hailed the Whigs who fired on them. The Loyalists returned fire, not knowing that the Whigs had some of their oar men along with them. They killed two of their own men who were held prisoners and wounded two others. They also killed one Whig [John Yates (d. 1782) or Yeaters] and mortally wounded two others.[281]

★ Captain Baker Hendricks (1756–1789) captured seven Loyalists at Bergen on Thursday, June 7, 1782.[282]

★ Around September 1, 1782, Fort Delancy was evacuated and burned. On Saturday, October 5th, Major Ward and his band of Loyalists embarked for Nova Scotia, bringing with them farm implements and one year's provisions.[283]

Rahway

Spanktown (ca. Sept. 5, 1776; Jan. 5, 1777; Jan. 6, 1777; Jan. 8, 1777; Feb. 23, 1777; Mar. 8, 1777; Mar. 14, 1777; Mar. 16, 1777; Apr. 4, 1777; May 17, 1777; June 27, 1777; July 6, 1777; June 29, 1779; Jan. 30, 1780; Feb. 11, 1780; Mar. 1, 1781; Mar. 21, 1781; Sept. 25, 1781; Mar. 14, 1782)

Samptown (Mar. 9, 1777; June 26, 1777)

Rahway was called Spanktown in the 18th century. Samptown is now Rahway, located north of New Brunswick.

Captain Benjamin Cory's (1740–1821) company skirmished with Crown forces at Spanktown about September 5, 1776. They took one prisoner but lost two men killed.[284]

★ A party of about 90 New Jersey militiamen attacked Lieutenant Cameron, of the 46th Regiment, and about 20 of his men near Spanktown about half an hour before sunrise on Sunday, January 5, 1777. Though outnumbered, the Loyalists continued skirmishing for two hours and lost one dead and three slightly wounded. They sent dispatches to Woodbridge and Amboy for reinforcements. Two regiments hastened to their relief; but the Hessians encamped at Woodbridge refused to go, thinking that the

New Jersey militiamen were at Spanktown in large numbers. The two regiments arrived just in time to save their comrades from total disaster. The militiamen took about 1,000 bushels of salt and fled, leaving nine dead behind, when Lieutenant Colonel Edward Vaughan Dongan (1748–1777) and about 20 Jersey Volunteers from Colonel William Luce's Battalion came to Lieutenant Cameron's assistance.[285]

★ The Continental Army marched from Pluckemin to Morristown on Monday, January 6, 1777. Brigadier General William Maxwell (1733–1796), who had marched toward Elizabethtown with a considerable body of Continental troops and militiamen, sent for reinforcements. When he received them, he advanced and took possession of the town, captured 50 Waldeckers and 40 Highlanders stationed there. He also captured a schooner with baggage and blankets on board. About the same time, Continental troops secured 1,000 bushels of salt at Spanktown, about 5 miles from Woodbridge.[286]

See also **Woodbridge.**

★ A party of Jersey militiamen attacked a regiment of British troops at Spanktown on Wednesday, January 8, 1777. The British received support which saved them.[287]

As the forage wars continued, General Henry Clinton (1730–1795) had to increase the size of the guards for those soldiers assigned to gather forage. This required the Continental commanders to also deploy a greater number of troops to offer effective resistance.

★ Lieutenant Colonel Charles Mawhood (d. 1780) left Amboy with 1,500 troops at 8:30 AM Sunday morning, February 23, 1777. His force consisted of the 3rd British brigade, the 3rd battalion of grenadiers (see Photo NJ-10), and a regiment of light infantry. One British officer noted that, in addition to foraging, Mawhood expected to "surprize, surround and extirpate the Rebel Army." This Rebel Army was Brigadier General William Maxwell's New Jersey militia at Spanktown. In addition to Maxwell's brigade, they consisted of Lieutenant Colonel George Stricker's (1732–1810) Maryland regiment, Colonel Edward Hand's (1744–1802) 1st Pennsylvania Regiment and part of Colonel Daniel Brodhead's (1736–1809) 8th Pennsylvania Regiment.

This mixed force of Continentals and militia was posted near Rahway Meetinghouse, 5 miles north of Woodbridge. As the British force marched, Maxwell's scouts withdrew before it. British light infantrymen and grenadiers marched as flankers through the snow as the wagon train creaked along the frozen road.

The Crown forces split into two columns 7 miles out of Amboy. Lieutenant Colonel John Campbell (d. 1806) took the left fork of the road with 500 troops to serve as a decoy while Mawhood marched to the right with the remaining men to forage. This maneuver also put Maxwell's troops in the middle of the two prongs. One of Mawhood's parties could come to the aid of the other or it could seal off the Whigs.

Colonel Campbell encountered "a pretty large body" (about 600) of Maxwell's troops in a wood and behind a rail fence. An attempt to flank them failed, and an unsuccessful frontal attack cost them dearly. He started to fall back after exchanging a few volleys. One of his officers recorded: "in a few minutes our attention was awakened with a rattling of small arms upon our right, which we soon discovered to be our other Division driving the enemy before them. This was the signal for us to advance, which we did with all expedition inclining to the left in order to cut off their retreat."

Maxwell's troops evaded pursuit by heading into the woods. Confusion in the British ranks prevented them from following. As it was late afternoon, Mawhood ordered the return to Amboy. Maxwell's troops now numbered more than 1,000. They followed Mawhood's force "in small parties keeping up a constant fire from all quarters." They also prepared an ambush further down the road, near Baker's Farm, at the junction of the Woodbridge-Rahway road with the road to Short Hills. Forewarned, Mawhood had his men ready to do battle again. A British officer commented, "the rascals gave way almost instantaneously, we followed them as far as was necessary, returned and continued our march homewards. Tho' I enjoyed this affair upon the whole, at least equal to a fox chase, I was a good deal vexed at one time when we might have made it I think a good deal more compleat."

Maxwell's troops fired on the British from all sides as they retreated back to Amboy. The foraging party had not eaten the whole day and had "marched at least 28 or 30 miles over fences woods and ditches every step up to the ankles in mud or snow, and some part of it at run." They were very tired by the time they reached Amboy at 8 PM. Captain William Cornwallis Hall said of the expedition:

> As the body proceeded, the enemy, discovering its force, withdrew their advanced parties, but when we had completed our forage and were returning, having collected, they attacked us in our retreat, and behaving much better upon this occasion than they had been accustomed to do, they pressed hard upon the rear of the detachment, notwithstanding the fire of our field-pieces, which occasionally played upon them whenever they showed themselves in numbers. It was dark before the detachment reached the garrison, having been marching through deep snows for ten hours, losing in the action four officers and near one hundred killed and wounded.
>
> Lieutenant Peebles, out of twenty grenadiers that flanked with him that day, alone escaped, keeping his ground in the action till the whole of his party was either killed or wounded, and then joining the grenadiers unhurt.[288]

A Whig account made the British force 2,000 strong, with six field pieces. It stated that the action began at 9:30 AM and lasted all day. The Continentals retreated five or six miles; but, reinforced by 1,400 men of General Maxwell's brigade, they eventually claimed a victory with only five men killed and 12 wounded. The British loss was estimated at 500 but was probably closer to 100 as Captain Hall noted.

A contemporary letter states that the officer in command was placed under arrest for not having proceeded immediately toward New Brunswick instead of marching out of his way, hoping to capture General Maxwell and his troops at Rahway.[289]

★ On Saturday, March 8, 1777 or Friday, March 14, 1777, a British relief expedition of 2,000 men went out from Amboy in a second attempt to reinforce their brethren cooped up in Brunswick. The party failed to reach its destination because the officer in command made a detour of about 14 miles to capture Brigadier General William Maxwell and his party at Spanktown instead of marching directly to Brunswick. He realized his mistake too late when he discovered that he had surrounded Colonel Patten's battalion of Pennsylvania militia; a part of Colonel Nathaniel Thatcher's New England troops; Colonel Edward Cook's (1738–1808) Pennsylvanians, together with Colonel Ephraim Martin (1733–1806) and Lieutenant Colonel Eleazer Lindsley (1737–1794), of the Eastern Battalion of Morris County, Jersey Militia. They soon put the Crown forces to flight and pursued them to Amboy where they boarded their ships. The troops never ventured to reinforce their cooped up brethren in Brunswick again.[290]

See also **Amboy.**

Major William Butler (1759–1820) stationed near Samptown, skirmished with some Crown troops on Sunday, March 9, 1777. He drove in their picket guard, killed four men and captured seven horses.[291]

★ A party of the King's troops under Major General John Vaughan (1738?–1795) was escorting General William Howe (1732–1786) on Sunday morning, March 16, 1777, as they marched from Amboy to Spanktown to surprise a party of Congressional troops who had been plundering in that neighborhood for several days. They came under fire from the Congressional troops at Spanktown. Lieutenant Colonel Charles Mawhood (d. 1780) was ordered to cut off their retreat, while the main force attacked the front. However, the roads were so bad that the plan could not be executed. General Vaughan's main body engaged a detachment of the Congressional troops, killed some, and took 15 prisoners who were brought to town that day.[292]

★ A skirmish on Friday, April 4, 1777, resulted in five Crown troops killed and one Continental rifleman wounded.[293]

★ May 17, 1777 see **Dismal Swamp**.

★ A force under the command of General Sir William Howe (1732–1786) and General Lord Charles Cornwallis (1738–1805) fell in with Colonel Daniel Morgan's (1736–1802) corps of rangers at Samptown on Thursday, June 26, 1777 and took heavy casualties.[294]

★ General Charles Scott's (ca. 1739–1813) light horsemen and Colonel Daniel Morgan's (1736–1802) Rangers harassed the British on Friday, June 27, 1777, after their evacuation of New Brunswick.[295]

★ A party of Crown forces captured "near a dozen" residents of Spanktown during a raid on Sunday, January 30, 1780.[296]

★ About 600 of General Cortlandt Skinner's (1728–1799) Loyalists made an excursion from Staten Island to plunder Elizabethtown and Rahway on Friday morning, February 11, 1780. Although the guards in town were vigilant enough not to be surprised, they were too few to make any effective resistance as they were only a captain's guard.

The Loyalists threatened and beat women and children. An aged widow who was blind was stripped and plundered with insults and threats. In some houses, they destroyed elegant looking glasses (mirrors) and other furniture which they could not carry off. After a short stay, they retired, taking seven inhabitants with them. They were later returned on their parole.[297]

★ Loyalist Captain Cornelius Hatfield or Hetfield, Jr. found his way to Spanktown by night on Thursday, March 1, 1781. He carried off John Clawson, Esq., one of the commissioners for selling the confiscated estates, against whom he had a peculiar grudge.[298]

★ On the night of Wednesday, March 21, 1781, a band of Loyalists from Staten Island crossed over to Spanktown to plunder and kidnap everyone they encountered. They captured about a dozen inhabitants as prisoners.[299]

★ A party of Loyalists, hidden behind a fence, fired upon Captain John Pain's (d. 1781) company as they reconnoitered near Spanktown on Monday, September 25, 1781. Sergeant Joshua Marsh (d. 1781) was killed.[300]

★ Loyalist Lewis Robbins led a raid on Spanktown on Thursday, March 14, 1782. He captured 7 prisoners.[301]

Bound Brook (Jan. 6, 1777; Apr. 13, 1777; May 26, 1777; June 14, 1777; June 17, 1777; June 18, 1777; Oct. 21, 1779; Oct. 23, 1779; June 12, 1780; Mar. 12, 1781)

Middletown (Feb. 13, 1777; May 26, 1777; May 27, 1778; Apr. 26, 1779; May 15, 1779; May 16, 1779; May 18, 1779; June 1, 1779; Mar. 30, 1780)

Near Middlebrook (June 1, 1777)

Bound Brook is about 8 miles northwest of New Brunswick. The Battle of Bound Brook Monument (in the cemetery at Hamilton and High Streets) is about 2 blocks from the site of the battle which occurred at the intersection of the road through the railroad underpass and East Main Street near the conflux of Green Brook and the Raritan River.

Landing Bridge is 6 miles east and the Van Veghten Bridge 4 miles to the west. A granite monument commemorates the site of the April 13, 1777 skirmish. Originally placed in an intersection just north of the bridge, it was moved to the side yard of the Pillar of Fire Temple at 519 Main Street. There are historical markers east of the road leading to the bridge from Main Street; but traffic conditions make sightseeing by car dangerous. General Washington's Middlebrook encampment was a short distance north of Bound Brook about 1 mile north of exit 14B off I-287 (see Photo NJ-23).

After the battles of Trenton and Princeton in early January 1777, the Continental Army camped at Morristown, while the British camped at New York City and the Hessians at Brunswick, during the winter and early spring of 1777. Both armies had detached outlying units which were vulnerable to quick attack. Major General Benjamin Lincoln (1733–1810) commanded one of these units, a force of 500 Continentals, at Bound Brook, on the Raritan River, a river which could be forded at numerous places. His men took up a position near the northern approach to the Queen's Bridge and constructed a blockhouse nearby to guard the bridge and the roads leading to it. His patrols covered the three river crossings from the Landing Bridge, 6 miles east, to the Van Veghten Bridge, 4 miles to the west, to protect as many of the inhabitants as possible. His men were also to harass the Crown forces and to guard the mountain pass that covered the route to Morristown. They were observing the Hessians but paid little attention to other enemy forces.

A party of British light horsemen raided Bound Brook on Monday, January 6, 1777. A Loyalist named Stewart shot Benjamin Booney hiding in his cellar.[302]

★ Crown forces killed Lieutenant John Whitlack (d. 1777) in a skirmish at Middletown on Thursday, February 13, 1777.[303]

★ General Charles Cornwallis (1738–1805), annoyed by constant raids on his pickets and aware of Major General Benjamin Lincoln's (1733–1810) overextended force, decided to attack it. He marched from New Brunswick between 8 and 9 PM on Saturday, April 12, 1777 with

Photo NJ-23. Site of the Middlebrook encampment, a short distance north of Bound Brook

Brigadier General James Grant (1720–1806) and Brigadier General Edward Mathew (often misspelled Matthews) (1729–1805) with the 1st battalion of grenadiers, one battalion of light infantry, a detachment of the guards, the light horse, two battalions of Hessians and the jaegers, commanded by Major General Count Karl Emil Kurt von Donop (1740–1777). He left 2,000 troops in Brunswick on Palm Sunday, April 13, 1777, and caught Lincoln in a surprise attack.

Between 4,000 and 5,000 Crown troops, who may have received intelligence from a local farmer, crossed the Raritan River in 3 columns led by General Cornwallis and Brigadier General Grant with a detachment of Hessians. Brigadier General Mathew commanded the reserve corps. The expedition was conducted with so much secrecy that the inhabitants did not learn of their departure until the following morning. One column crossed the Raritan about 1 mile above Major General Nathanael Greene's (1742–1786) headquarters, the second division came up in front of the town, the third to the left of the town and crossed the river. They avoided the roads and got close to the Continental entrenchments before daybreak.

The militia should have detected General Cornwallis's movements, but General Lincoln received no warning of the attack which converged on the blockhouse from three directions about 5 AM. Colonel Richard Butler's (1745–1781) 300 excellent marksmen had a good fire upon the heads of one of their columns for a considerable time. The Crown forces waited until the Continentals fired their morning gun to begin the attack. With little or no time to put up any organized resistance, the Continentals fled to the wooded hills behind the blockhouse. General Lincoln barely had time to draw off the troops from between the heads of their two flank columns which kept up a warm fire as the Continentals passed between them. He managed to withdraw himself and most of his men to the mountains behind the town but lost his artillery detachment consisting of three 3-pounders and the ammunition belonging to them. Most of the men belonging to the artillery and two of the officers were made prisoners (about 20 artillerymen).

Accounts of casualties range from two to 30 Continentals killed or wounded and 20 to 80 captured, including Lieutenants Trumbull and William Ferguson, with a small party of Colonel Thomas Proctor's (1739–1806) Pennsylvania regiment along with two brass field pieces. General Greene noted that the Continentals lost "about 40 battalion men kild, wounded and missing. General Lincoln had one aid de camp made Prisoner and lost almost all his papers." A British account lists the losses as:

> Casualties - upward of 100; prisoners taken - 73, among them one aide-de-camp, one captain, one lieutenant, 70 men, and one man in irons who had been sentenced by the rebels to be shot on Sunday; three brass cannon, a quantity of arms, two wagons loaded with ammunition, a number of horses, 120 heads of cattle, sheep and hogs, 300 barrels of flour, several hogsheads of whiskey and New England rum, and several other articles that the rebels cannot very well spare.

The Crown forces had one man killed and two jaegers wounded.

General Cornwallis was driven back and counter-attacked by the militia the same night at Raritan Landing. He withdrew before Major General Nathanael Greene (1742–1786) arrived from Middlebrook with a greater number of reinforcements. The event persuaded General George Washington (1732–1799) to evacuate some of his more vulnerable detachments before the beginning of the spring and summer campaign.[304]

See also **Brunswick**.

★ Major General Benjamin Lincoln received intelligence that the Regulars were marching toward Bound Brook with about 700 troops. He met them about 100 yards from the bridge on Monday morning, May 26, 1777, with a force of similar size and reported a "brush with the Philistines." The Continentals gave the Regulars "pretty little threshing" and drove them almost 3 miles back to their lines. They killed eight Regulars: three light horsemen, four Highlanders, and a lieutenant colonel while only having three wounded, one mortally. The officer was killed by a 6-pound shot.[305]

★ Lieutenant William Martin (d. 1777) led 10 men from Captain David Lyons's (1745–1802) company in a skirmish with a party of 15 Hessians and British light horsemen near Middlebrook on Sunday, June 1, 1777. The first volley killed the commander. His troops rallied and routed Lieutenant Martin's men. Martin himself was left on the field and soon surrounded. He called out for quarters but was bayoneted 17 times.[306]

★ The disposition of General Washington's troops in June 1777 prevented General William Howe (1732–1786) and the Northern Army from getting any communication or intelligence by land. His position on the rugged heights above Bound Brook made him formidable to the Jersey army. General Howe could make no advances toward the North or the Delaware and he couldn't leave so large an army in his rear. He tried a feint to the Delaware, hoping to draw General Washington into a general engagement. He marched his army of about 14,000 British and Hessian troops in two divisions early Saturday morning, June 14, 1777. The first division under General Charles Cornwallis went to the right while the second under General Leopold Philip von Heister (1707–1777) went left. The 1st division took its post on the heights of Millstone the same day. They skirmished and retired with the light infantry suffering some losses.

The 2nd division halted at Middle Bush, where General Howe made his headquarters with the line of his 1st and 2nd columns extending 5 miles. When a deserter brought information that General Washington intended to attack the part of the army lying over the Millstone River, General Howe sent a patrol of the Queen's Light Dragoons, supported by five companies of light infantry toward Van Veghten's Bridge to discover whether General Washington had made any preparations for crossing a large body of troops. The patrol advanced within 400 yards of the bridge and found the Continental troops in an advantageous position. Both sides exchanged a few shots and the patrol withdrew.

When the patrol returned to camp, General Howe ordered another on the road to Flemington, located about 18 miles southwest of Millstone. The dragoons seized a resident within 6 miles of Flemington, extorted information about the disposition of the Continental troops, and returned to camp with their prisoner. The army maintained its position the next day and built redoubts to strengthen the posts and to preserve communication. The prisoner taken the previous day was released and laid an ambuscade that killed one sergeant and one private.

★ The Continentals tempted a Hessian picket guard with a few sheep on the 17th. When they took the bait, seven grenadiers (see Photo NJ-7) and jaegers (see Photo NJ-8) were killed and wounded. The following day, two grenadier officers were surprised and captured when they tried to prevent some soldiers from marauding. The army was ordered to march to the left at 3 AM and arrived in Brunswick without any opposition. The troops remained there for a few days before going to Amboy.[307]

★ May 27, 1778 see **Sandy Hook, Burrows's Mills.**

★ April 26, 1779 see **Shrewsbury.**

★ A party of almost 200 Loyalists landed at Middletown about 2 AM on Saturday, May 15, 1779 to plunder. The militia gathered quickly and skirmished before the raiders returned to their boats. They plundered only two or three families.[308]

★ A party of Loyalists from Staten Island landed at Middletown on Tuesday, May 18, 1779. They plundered several houses and took four or five inhabitants prisoners.[310]

★ The Queen's Rangers, their cavalry, and 10 light horsemen, under the command of Captain John Stewart, left Staten Island and landed at Amboy about 2 AM Thursday morning, October 21, 1779. They proceeded as far as Bonhamtown, when Lieutenant Colonel John Graves Simcoe (1752–1806) and 70 foot and the cavalry returned to Amboy.[312]

★ A party of about 100 of Colonel John Graves Simcoe's (1752–1806) Queen's Rangers landed at Sandy Point, north of Amboy on Tuesday night, October 23, 1779. They started out by seizing all the good horses they could find. They said they were a detachment from General George Washington's army to prevent any alarm from spreading. It was only after they left Quibbletown that a man who recognized Colonel Simcoe sent an express to Colonel John Neilson (1745–1833) at New Brunswick. Neilson immediately ordered out his regiment and marched them to the bridge at the Raritan Landing.

Colonel Simcoe went to Bound Brook where he set fire to some forage and burned 18 large flat-bottomed boats and some stores. He then proceeded rapidly to Colonel Gabriel Peterson Van Horn's (d. 1815) house, at Middlebrook, where he was disappointed not to find the governor there. (Governor William Livingston (1723–1790) was in New Brunswick.)

The Queen's Rangers then went to Millstone (Somerset), 28 miles from Amboy, where they released the Loyalists confined there and set fire to the courthouse and jail and destroyed a large quantity of forage and supplies collected for the Continental Army. Colonel Neilson noticed the smoke of the buildings and thought Colonel Simcoe and his rangers would try to pass Van Veghten's bridge on the Raritan River in their retreat; so he remained there, expecting to engage them on their retreat. He sent Captain Moses Guest (1750–1837) and 35 men with orders to "endeavor to fall in with them and annoy them as much as possible."

Soon after getting on the road leading from Millstone village to the bridge, an express informed Captain Guest that the enemy was only a few hundred yards away. He barely had time to find a clearing in the woods before they arrived and Guest and his men attacked. Captain William Marriner arrived with a few more men and joined the fray.

On the south side of the Raritan, less than 2 miles from Brunswick, the New Jersey militia lay in ambush in the woods and fired on the Rangers. Colonel Simcoe's horse received five musket balls, fell on him and bruised him badly. One man was killed and several wounded. The militia left a physician with Simcoe and proceeded on. Simcoe's party halted on the west of Brunswick and sent Dr. John Ryker and Mr. John Polhemus, his servant, with a flag to request permission to tend to Colonel Simcoe. The permission was granted but the doctor and his servant were considered as prisoners because the rangers continued to retreat during the parley which is contrary to the rules of war.[313]

See also **Staten Island** in *The Guide to the American Revolution in New York*.

Captain Peter Sanford (ca. 1755–1812) took over command of the Queen's Rangers and continued on to South Amboy around what is now the corner of Throop Avenue and Sanford Street. As they approached Brunswick, they discovered 170 militiamen on the hill near the barracks waiting for them. The rangers charged and defeated the militiamen, inflicting many casualties. They took nearly 30 prisoners and lost one man killed and four taken prisoner in addition to Colonel Simcoe. Colonel Simcoe was captured near where DeRusey's Lane meets the old Amwell Road.[314]

Captain Peter Voorhees (d. 1779) of the 1st New Jersey Regiment, had just returned from Major General John Sullivan's (1740–1795) army and, with a few militia horsemen, pursued the rangers so closely that the rangers dropped a great number of their caps, coats and other articles. A detachment sallied out. Captain Voorhees tried to leap over a fence but his horse missed and fell on the rails. The rangers caught up with him and hacked him with their sabers, leaving him for dead, captured three of his men, and proceeded to South Amboy. Voorhees was later found lying in the road mortally wounded. He was brought to Brunswick where he died a few hours later. He was to have been married the next day.

The death of Captain Voorhees angered the people to seek vengeance, but Governor William Livingston (1723–1790) issued an order to prevent them from harming Colonel Simcoe. It read:

> The Governor being informed that some people have a desire to abuse and insult Lieut.-Col. Simcoe, a British captive, and wounded in a skirmish that happened this day between our militia and the British horse; though the Governor is not inclined to believe a report so great a disgrace upon the people of this State as that of the least inclination of revenge against a wounded enemy in our power; yet, to prevent the execution of any such attempt, it is his express order to treat the said officer according to the rules of war known and practiced among all civilized nations; and as it is his desire to be carried to Brunswick, it is his further order that no molestation be given to him in his being carried hither, and that while there he be treated with that humanity which the United States of America always observed towards their prisoners.
>
> Brunswick Landing,
William Livingston,
2nd October, 1779

Colonel Simcoe was transferred from Brunswick to Bordentown on Thursday, October 28, 1779, where he was kept in a tavern owned by Colonel Hoagland of the New Jersey Militia. He was brought to the Burlington jail on November 7 and was exchanged for other prisoners on December 31st. The militia killed three rangers, made six prisoners, and wounded a considerable number in the affair.[315]

★ March 30, 1780 see **Tinton Falls.**

★ A band of Loyalists killed Private Joseph Murray (1720–1780) as he was working in his cornfield behind the barn in Middletown (at today's Poricy Park) during a raid on Monday, June 12, 1780 (Some sources say it was June 8).[316]

★ About 50 Crown troops appeared at Bound Brook on Monday March 12, 1781. The local militia assembled and forced them to retire. A man by the name of Olisby, of Lyon's Farms, later discharged his musket, killing Mr. John Calhoun (d. 1781) of the same place.[317]

Monmouth County

Freehold <small>(Jan. 2, 1777; June 21, 1778; June 28, 1778; Jan. 26, 1779)</small>

Monmouth County <small>(Jan. 17, 1777; Jan. 21, 1777; week of Apr. 6 to 12, 1777; Feb., 1779; Feb. 13–19, 1780; June 9, 1780; Aug. 21, 1780; June 21, 1781)</small>

Monmouth Battlefield State Park (see Photo NJ-24) (**www.state.nj.us/dep/seeds/ monbat.htm**) is in/near Freehold, New Jersey, 3 miles west on Business Route NJ 33 (1.5 miles west of the Freehold Circle). The visitor center features displays that trace the troops' movements during the battle. On the grounds is the Craig House, built in 1710 and restored to its 18th-century appearance.

Photo NJ-24. Re-enactors parading on Comb's Hill, Monmouth Battlefield State Park. The cornfield is in the middle ground and the cherry orchard in the background.

Major John Mifflin and his 120 Pennsylvania troops arrived at Monmouth Courthouse Thursday evening, January 2, 1777. Informed that 200 Loyalists under Lieutenant Colonel John Morris, Second Battalion, New Jersey Volunteers, were in the town, Major Mifflin planned to attack them about half an hour before nightfall.

However, Colonel Morris learned of Major Mifflin's arrival and had his baggage loaded and his men ready to go to Middletown, about 18 miles away. They had proceeded about half a mile when Major Mifflin caught up to them about a quarter of an hour before nightfall and engaged them.

Both sides kept up a very heavy fire. After about eight minutes, the Pennsylvanians retreated quickly in the dark. They killed four men and captured 23 as well as seven wagon loads of stores and 12 horses.[318]

★ A large scouting party took 90 wagons loaded with stores in Monmouth County on Friday, January 17, 1777.[319]

★ An inferior number of Congressional troops attacked a large foraging party of Crown troops in Monmouth County on Tuesday, January 21, 1777. They drove off the foragers and captured four soldiers of the 71st Regiment, two of the 40th, three of the 28th, one of the 55th and two marines and most of the wagons. Some accounts state that there were 96 wagons loaded with baggage belonging to the Loyalists which they were transporting to a place of greater safety. The next day, four of the 3rd Regiment of Guards were captured.[320]

★ A party of Loyalists escaped from Monmouth County during the week of April 6 to 12, 1777. They encountered a party of Whigs at Freehold and attacked them, killing one and taking two prisoners with them to Staten Island.[321]

★ Loyalist Colonel George Taylor (1734–1799), on a plundering raid in Freehold on Saturday, June 21, 1778, lost two men killed and two taken prisoners, one white and the other African American. The rest of his party were swimming toward a boat that was coming to get them when the militia fired at them and killed one and wounded another. They were both hauled into the boat. The Crown forces looted the town three days later, on the day before the battle of Monmouth.[322]

★ As General Henry Clinton (1730–1795) prepared to depart Philadelphia in 1778, General George Washington (1732–1799) had high hopes of winning the war by a cooperative effort between his army and the French fleet. Admiral Comte Jean-Baptiste-Charles-Henri-Hector d'Estaing (1729–1794), with a French naval squadron of 11 ships of the line and transports carrying 4,000 troops, left France in May to sail for the American coast. D'Estaing's fleet was considerably more powerful than any Admiral

Richard Howe (1726–1799) could immediately concentrate in American waters. The strategic initiative passed from British hands for a brief period in 1778 and General Washington hoped to make full use of it.

Sir Henry Clinton had already decided, before he learned of the threat from d'Estaing, to move his army overland to New York, largely because he could find no place for 3,000 horses on the transports along with his men and stores and the hundreds of Loyalists who claimed British protection. He began evacuating Philadelphia on Thursday, June 18, 1778. At the same time, he sent 5,000 men to attack St. Lucia, an important French harbor in the West Indies. He also sent 3,000 men to Florida and smaller detachments to Bermuda and the Bahamas.

Clinton headed toward New York with 10,000 to 17,000 men in very hot and humid weather with frequent downpours. His men carried 80-pound packs, and their heavy woolen uniforms were soggy and painful to wear. He also had an immense baggage train of 1,500 wagons and 5,000 horses. The wagon train stretched 12 miles along the road. Lieutenant General Wilhelm von Knyphausen (1716–1800) commanded the guard which required almost half the army.

General Washington had gathered about 12,000 men by the time Clinton left Philadelphia. He immediately occupied the city and began to pursue Clinton, undecided as to whether he should risk an attack on the British column while it was on the march. His Council of War was divided, though none of his generals advised a "general action." The boldest, Brigadier General "Mad Anthony" Wayne (1745–1796), and the young Major General Marie Joseph de Motier Marquis de Lafayette (1757–1834), urged a "partial attack" to strike at a portion of the Crown forces while they were strung out on the road. The most cautious, Major General Charles Lee (1731–1782), who had been exchanged and had rejoined the army at Valley Forge, advised only guerilla action to harass the enemy columns.

At the same time, Major General Horatio Gates (1728–1806) advanced from the north to prevent Clinton from crossing the Raritan River to Amboy. Clinton, taking personal command of the rearguard, turned right and headed toward Sandy Hook at the mouth of the Hudson River where ships were waiting to carry them to New York.

On June 23, Washington sent an additional 1,500 men to help the New Jersey Militia harass the Crown troops. Later in the day, he sent another 1,400 men and Colonel Daniel Morgan's (1736–1802) 600 riflemen, bringing the number of men pursuing Clinton to over 5,000.

Washington's much less heavily encumbered army moved faster, closing in on Clinton's left flank and harassing him, threatening to overtake him. Patrols demolished bridges ahead of him. The Continentals were close to trapping Clinton, who covered less than 30 miles in five days, when he turned northeast toward Monmouth Courthouse on Thursday, June 25, 1778. The mid-day heat grew more intense. The soldiers, in their thick woolen uniforms and weighed down by their heavy packs, became more exhausted and ill-tempered.

On June 26, Washington decided to take a bold approach, though he issued no orders indicating an intention to bring on a "general action." He sent forward an advance guard, composed of almost half his army, to strike at the rear of the Crown forces when Clinton moved out of Monmouth Courthouse on Saturday morning, June 27. Washington met with Lee, Lafayette, Wayne, and others that afternoon. They decided to move against the enemy. Lee claimed the command from Lafayette when he learned the detachment would be so large. He was to attack east of the town while Washington supported him with the main body of the army.

At 4 AM on June 28, Clinton sent Von Knyphausen's division ahead with the baggage train. Cornwallis would follow with a larger force of three brigades: the guards, two battalions of British grenadiers (see Photo NJ-10) and the Hessian grenadiers (see Photo NJ-7), two battalions of British light infantry, the 16th dragoons, and Colonel John Graves Simcoe's (1752–1806) Queen's Rangers, a Loyalist unit.

Washington received a report of enemy movements by 5 AM, but Lee wasn't ready to move until 7 AM. As the Crown forces passed Monmouth County Courthouse on that hot Sunday, General Charles Lee's 5,000 men advanced over rough ground that had not been reconnoitered and made contact with Clinton's rearguard. Clinton outnumbered Lee by about three to two. He sent an urgent message to Knyphausen for reinforcements and ordered an attack, hoping to gain the advantage before Washington arrived. Lee's 12 guns opened artillery fire. Clinton reacted quickly and maneuvered to envelop the Continental right flank. Lee, feeling that his force was in an untenable position, began a retreat that became quite confused in the appalling heat. The British grenadiers pressed hard against the Continental front, while the light infantry and 16th light dragoons raced round their left flank.

There was much confusion among Lee's commanders and aides. Lafayette withdrew from one position to take another. The other commanders, uninformed of the order, interpreted this action as a retreat and ordered their units back as well. This caused a general withdrawal which Lee could not stop. Washington rode up amidst the confusion and, exceedingly irate to find the advance guard in retreat, exchanged harsh words with Lee. Washington then assumed direction of what had to be a defense against a counterattack. He rallied the disorganized troops and formed a new line along the road that now borders the cemetery (just past the intersection of County Road 522 and U.S. 9). He held his position until the main body arrived to take up positions 0.5 miles to the west. The Continentals met the attacking Crown forces with volleys of musketry and artillery. The battle that followed in the afternoon heat involved the bulk of both armies and lasted until nightfall with both sides holding their own in one of the longest battles of the American War for Independence.

When Lee ordered a retreat, Mary Ludwig Hays's (1754–1832) husband John served on the gun crew. The temperature was around 100 degrees. Molly brought pitcher after pitcher of cool water from a spring to the troops, earning her the nickname of Molly Pitcher. She also tended the wounded and once hoisted a disabled soldier on her shoulders and carried him to safety. On one of her water trips, Molly found her husband with the artillery, replacing a casualty. John fell wounded, leaving the gun crew with too few men to serve it. They were about to drag it to the rear when Molly took the rammer staff from her husband's hands and joined the crew, swabbing the barrel under heavy fire. Joseph Plumb Martin (1760–1850) recorded the event:

> [W]hile in the act of reaching for a cartridge and having [one foot] as far from the other as she could step, a cannon shot from the enemy passed directly between her legs without doing any damage than carrying away all the lower part of her petti-coat. Looking at it with apparent unconcern, she observed that it was lucky that it did not pass higher, for in that case it might have carried away something else, and then she continued upon her occupation.[323]

Clinton sent strong forces to attack both of Washington's flanks. One column marched up Wemrock Road to attack Greene who turned his artillery on Comb's Hill against them. The troops that attacked the left flank were beaten back by a wild bayonet charge that some historians believe was the turning point of the battle.

Meanwhile, the British grenadiers tried to break the center of the line with repeated assaults. Eyewitnesses reported an entire line of grenadiers collapsed from exhaustion in the intense heat as they charged up the slope. The Continentals pushed the Crown forces back and pursued them. Washington urged them on, riding up and down encouraging his men, seemingly unconcerned for his safety. He was only 30 or 40 feet from the enemy at times.

For the first time, the Continental troops, trained by Major General Friedrich Wilhelm von Steuben (1730–1794), fought well with the bayonet as well as with the musket and rifle. Their battlefield behavior generally reflected their Valley Forge training. Nevertheless, Washington failed to strike a telling blow at the Crown forces for Clinton slipped away in the night and, in a few days, completed the retreat to New York. General Charles Lee demanded and got a court-martial at which he was judged guilty of disobedience of orders, poor conduct of the retreat, and disrespect for the Commander in Chief. He was suspended from command for 12 months. Congress later approved the sentence which prompted Lee to write an insulting letter to the Congress, which expelled him from the army and ended his career.

The Continentals lost about 369 men (76 killed, 161 wounded, and 132 missing). The Crown forces lost about 358 killed and wounded. Many of the missing dropped because of heat exhaustion and later rejoined their units. About 37 Continentals and 60 Crown troops died of sunstroke (or heat exhaustion). Washington recorded that his men buried more than 249 enemy dead. Some historians believe the Crown forces lost more than 1,200 men in this one battle—about one-quarter of the troops involved in the battle if half of Clinton's army of 10,000 was occupied protecting the wagon train. The Continentals almost lost some people who would become notable. Alexander Hamilton almost got killed when his horse got shot out from under him. Lieutenant Colonel Aaron Burr (1756–1836) recklessly pursued the enemy until their guns began killing the men around him.[324]

★ Captain Benjamin Dennis (1740–1799) and his New Jersey Militia pursued three of the most noted Pine-Banditti (Stephen Bourke, alias Emmaus; Stephen West and Ezekiel Williams) on Tuesday, January 26, 1779. They were preparing to go to New York to sell their plunder when Captain Dennis was informed of the time of their intended departure and of the course they would take to their boat. The captain and a small group of militiamen positioned themselves at Rock Pond, near the seashore, and shot Bourke, West and Williams on the spot.

★ The Crown forces landed on the Jersey shore in Monmouth County in February 1779 and bayoneted some of Brigadier General William Maxwell's (1733–1796) men.[324a]

★ During the week of February 13–19, 1780, the New Jersey Militia captured a force of 22 "convention troops" and two African Americans along with Joseph Hayes, their guide, as they passed through Monmouth County on their way to New York. They were all imprisoned in the county jail.[325]

★ Colonel Tye (ca. 1753–1780), an African-American slave named Titus who lived in Monmouth County, escaped from his master and fled to Virginia early in the war. He joined the British Army in 1778 and led a band of about 20 African Americans and whites on a raid of Captain Barnes Smock's (1739–1829) house in Monmouth County on Friday afternoon, June 9, 1780. They took Captain Barnes Smock and Gilbert Vanmater (1762–1782) prisoners and spiked the iron 4-pounder at Captain Smock's house but took no ammunition. They also took two of the artillery horses and two of Captain Smock's horses.[326]

★ A colonel and Major John Smock (1727–1808), of the Monmouth County militia, were captured on Tuesday, August 21, 1780 and taken to New York the following day. One of the prisoners belonged to the Retaliators upon the Tories.[327]

★ A large body of about 1,000 new recruits, British and German troops under General Cortlandt Skinner (1728–1799), marched into Monmouth County on Thursday, June 21, 1781 to plunder a place called Pleasant Valley. They arrived there about 11 AM with little or no opposition. The inhabitants had already driven off their stock; so the raiders found very little booty.

The local militiamen were beginning to gather by this time and they kept up a pretty smart skirmish through the remainder of the day. The raiders began their retreat about sundown and did not stop until they got to Garret's Hill where they stopped for the night. A militia officer descended upon them during the night and rescued several stolen sheep. The raiders embarked the next day, taking with them about 40 cattle and 60 sheep. They burned two houses but did not harm the inhabitants. They lost one man killed, a number deserted and an unknown number of wounded. The militia lost one man killed and three or four wounded. As the Crown troops came out in such force, the militiamen expected they planned to go further into the country. The militias of the neighboring counties were called upon to prevent them from doing so.[328]

Morristown (Apr. 22, 1777)

Near Morristown (Jan. 23, 1777; Feb. 23, 1777; Apr. 23, 1777)

A large number of wagons under an escort of 600 men of the 28th and 37th Regiments and two cannons were proceeding from Brunswick to Amboy on Thursday, January 23, 1777 when they were spotted by the 6th Virginia Regiment near Morristown. The Virginians were an advance party of 400 men commanded by Colonel Mordecai Buckner (1721–1800). Lieutenant Colonel Josiah Parker (1751–1810) posted his advance party of 600 men in an advantageous position.

The Crown forces advanced in a column 10 abreast. When they got within 100 yards, Lieutenant Colonel Parker ordered his men to fire a volley. Colonel Preston (d. 1777), the commander of the Crown forces, was killed. The Congressional troops maintained an incessant fire for 20 minutes. Lieutenant Colonel Parker, realizing he was unsupported, retreated. The Crown troops had 25 killed on the spot and 40 wounded. They carried off their dead and wounded, except for 13 who were later cared for by a Whig surgeon. In addition to the colonel killed, the second in command was shot through the body and carried off speechless. In addition, one captain was killed and another wounded.

Colonel Buckner, who got panic struck and left Lieutenant Colonel Parker unsupported, was arrested and court-martialed. The Congressional forces had not a single man either killed or wounded. Later, Colonel Charles Scott (ca. 1739–1813) led 200 Virginians to the same area, engaged the British and Germans, and lost eight men killed.[329]

★ Colonel Charles Mawhood (d. 1780), commander of the 17th Regiment, led a foraging party near Morristown on Sunday, February 23, 1777. They encountered a body of Continentals and began a running engagement which drove the Continentals for several miles at the point of the bayonet. Colonel Mawhood ordered his men to return and the Continentals tried to form an ambuscade along the way. The Highlanders discovered the ploy, fired a volley, and then immediately charged with the bayonet. The Continentals fled with considerable losses. The King's troops lost Captain John Hall (d. 1777) of the 46th Regiment and three or four privates killed and about 40 wounded. Instead of flanking a fence, the troops marched up to the front of it and received enemy fire. The brigade returned to foraging and loaded the wagons with a large quantity of livestock and forage.[330]

★ Captain Thomas Combs or Coombs (d. 1785) and a party of men crossed enemy lines near the Continental camp at Morristown during the night of Tuesday, April 22, 1777. They captured two sentinels from whom they extorted the countersign. They then attacked the picket guard; but one of Combs's men deserted and alerted the Crown troops of his intentions; so the Crown forces were prepared to give Combs a very warm reception. Combs drove them into the guard house where the guards fired through the door and windows. Combs ordered his men to charge the door with bayonets. The guards received them with drawn bayonets but were soon obliged to call for quarter and were all taken prisoners. Combs captured the picket guard of two subalterns and 30 men. Both of the officers and 14 men were killed and 16 were brought in prisoners. Combs was wounded in the foot and both his subalterns in the body, none seriously.[331]

★ Lieutenant Colonel Charles Mawhood's (d. 1780) British brigade skirmished with some Congressional troops near Morristown on Wednesday, April 23, 1777. He lost five killed and perhaps 40 wounded.

See also **Amboy.**

Millstone (Somerset Courthouse) (Jan. 20, 1777; Jan. 23, 1777; June 17, 1777; June 19, 1777; Oct. 28, 1779; Jan. 2, 1782)

Middlebush (June 18, 1777)

Millstone is about 8 miles west of New Brunswick and 5.5 miles south of Somerville. Middlebush is west of Somerset.

Somerville's occupation with commerce, county government and industry exemplifies its position in the transitional zone between city and county. The area was first settled by Native Americans who later negotiated with European settlers for a peaceful withdrawal. Later, soldiers of the Continental Army frequented the area, then called Raritan and stayed at the Middlebrook encampment. General George Washington made his headquarters at the Wallace House (Wallace House State Historic Site, 71 Somerset St., Somerville) during the winter of 1778–79.

Rockingham State Historic Site, 5 miles north on CR 518 east of Rocky Hill in Franklin Township, was Washington's headquarters from August to November 1783, while the Continental Congress was in session at Princeton. He wrote his "Farewell Orders to the Armies" at this site. The restored house contains period furnishings.

The site of the burned courthouse is now a private home at 13 South River Road in Millstone near the intersection of Main Street (Route 533) and Amwell Road (Route 514). South River Road intersects with Amwell Road about 100 yards east of Main Street. The site is marked by a large boulder with a bronze plaque mounted on it.

After the battles of Trenton and Princeton, the Crown forces concentrated 18,000 men in Brunswick and Amboy (now Perth Amboy). General George Washington's (1732–1799) strategy in early 1777 was to disperse the army to strategic positions around New Jersey. He kept one division at Morristown and placed the others around the colony but not so far away that they could not return quickly to Morristown. They were headquartered as follows:

Major General John Sullivan (1740–1795): Chatham and Scotch Plains

Major General Israel Putnam (1718–1790): Princeton

Major General Nathanael Greene (1742–1786): Basking Ridge

Major General Benjamin Lincoln (1733–1810): Bound Brook

Brigadier General William Alexander (Earl of Stirling, 1726–1783): Quibbletown (New Market)

Adam Stephen (ca. 1730–1791): near Metuchen with Brigadier General William Maxwell's (1733–1796) division nearby

General Philemon Dickinson (1739–1809) and the New Jersey Militia: Somerset Courthouse

Brigadier General Nathaniel Warner had other militiamen at Millstone, to the west of Bound Brook

These divisions guarded all the roads leading out of the Crown forces' camps. The generals had full freedom to make operational decisions in the field and were even encouraged to attack the enemy whenever possible. The many skirmishes and small battles that ensued in subsequent months improved the soldiers' skills and morale. General Adam Stephen commented:

> Fighting is now become so familiar that unless it is a very great affair we do not think it worth mentioning . . . my Division is an Excellent School for a young soldier— We only fight eight or ten times a Week—in short I have got my men in such Spirits that they only ask where the Enemy come out, & where they are, without enquiring into their Numbers, & so fall on.[332]

First battle

General Philemon Dickinson (1739–1809) led a force of 400 New Jersey militiamen, two companies of Continentals and 50 Pennsylvania riflemen against a foraging party of approximately 600 men about 2 miles from Somerset Courthouse on the Millstone River on Monday, January 20, 1777. The militiamen had one field piece against three British guns. Unable to cross the bridge because the British defended it with their three guns, the militiamen sought a ford below. They broke the ice, waded through the river, flanked the enemy, and routed them. They captured 43 baggage wagons, 104 horses, 118 cattle, 60 or 70 sheep, and 12 prisoners. They lost only four or five men while the Crown forces' killed amounted to five or six times that number.[333]

★ Three days later, Colonel Preston (d. 1777) led a similar British detachment with two pieces of cannon. The detachment was attacked by an advance party from the 6th Virginia Regiment commanded by Lieutenant Colonel Josiah Parker (1751–1810) as they marched to Amboy from Brunswick. Colonel Parker, not having support from his superior, Colonel Mordecai Buckner (1721–1800), was forced to retreat after a brief but sharp engagement of 20 minutes. He did not have any losses; but the British had 65 killed and wounded, including Colonel Preston killed and his second in command seriously wounded. They also lost several wagons of supplies. The skirmish boosted the morale of the New Jersey Militia who defeated a force of Regulars of equal size.[334]

See also **Morristown.**

Second Battle

★ By June 1777, General Sir William Howe (1732–1786) was complaining about the New Jersey militiamen who shot at any man who strayed outside the camp. His troops found themselves in a fight every time they went out in force.

General Howe left Amboy on Friday, June 13 with 18,000 troops; and General Charles Cornwallis (1738–1805) left Brunswick on the same day with most of his force. General Cornwallis led the first column to Somerset; General Leopold von Heister (1707–1777) led the other to Middlebush near Somerset. Howe was traveling light and hoped for a quick victory. His troops, a much superior force to General George Washington's (1732–1799), began building earthworks along the spread-out line, hoping to lure Washington down from Middlebrook and to cut Major General John Sullivan (1740–1795) off from the main Continental Army. Washington remained cautious and pulled his troops back from Princeton in time. He also ordered Sullivan to retire to Rocky Hill to get him out of danger. There, he could cover the retreat route for the main army and "harrass the Enemy by incessant parties when they attempt to march thro the country."

As the Regulars attempted to cross the Millstone River at Somerset Courthouse on Saturday, June 14, a force of 200 of Colonel Daniel Morgan's (1736–1802) riflemen engaged them, killing 18 Hessians and taking several prisoners. Morgan and his 500 Virginia riflemen harassed the Crown soldiers constructing redoubts near Somerset Courthouse on Tuesday, June 17, 1777. Lieutenant Jacob Ten Eyck (d. 1777) was killed in the skirmish. The riflemen continued to harass the Regulars for the few days that they camped there.[335]

The Redcoats had left all their heavy baggage at Brunswick, including the bateaux and the portable bridge for crossing the Delaware. General Washington strengthened his right flank, his most vulnerable point, with 1,000 militiamen and 1,000 Continentals from Major General John Sullivan's (1740–1795) troops. He posted them at Steel's Gap in the Sourland Mountain, about 2 miles from Middlebrook and about 7.5 miles southwest of Somerset Courthouse. The Redcoats could cross the Raritan without baggage, boats, and bridge. Even if they brought them up, the Continentals still threatened their flank. A considerable force of Continentals and militiamen were posted on the opposite side of the Raritan and Washington was in their rear.

★ Congressional and Hessian patrols skirmished briefly at Middlebush on Wednesday, June 18, 1777.[336]

★ In another skirmish on Thursday, June 19, 1777, the British lost two officers and 14 men. They retreated from Middlebush and Somerset that night, returning toward their original positions in Brunswick "with marks of seeming precipitation." They began marching toward the port of Amboy on June 22, 1777. His troops burned Somerset Courthouse, meetinghouse, and many other houses and wheat before leaving. Along the way, they stole everything worth carrying off. They hung up three women who were presumed spies, two of them by the feet at the head of the army.

A few of the troops and the heavy baggage went to Staten Island to deceive General George Washington (1732–1799) into thinking they intended to evacuate the state. General William Howe's (1732–1786) real intention was to draw the Continentals out of their strong position.[337]

General Washington thought the movement was a final retreat and sent Major General Nathanael Greene (1742–1786) with his division of three brigades, reinforced by Brigadier General "Mad Anthony" Wayne's (1745–1796) brigade and Colonel Daniel Morgan's riflemen, to attack Howe's rear. He also sent orders to Major General John Sullivan (1740–1795) and Brigadier General William Maxwell to cooperate with Greene. Sullivan received his orders too late. The courier with General Maxwell's orders to close in on the enemy's left flank with his 1,500 troops either deserted or was captured and

Maxwell never received the orders. The rainy weather also hampered Washington's efforts to engage the retreating Redcoats. The Continentals did have several small skirmishes and inflicted a few casualties.

General Wayne's brigade encountered General Howe less than a mile from the bridge at Brunswick and pushed him from redoubt to redoubt, preventing him from forming his men. Had the troops on the west of the Raritan managed to arrive at that time, they might have annihilated the Crown forces.

Colonel Morgan's riflemen and General Greene's troops pushed General Howe to Piscataway and probably inflicted several casualties. General Howe was so greatly harassed along his return route that he could not cross over from Amboy to Staten Island until July 1. The Continentals lost three or four killed and about as many wounded.[338]

★ June 30, 1777 see **New Brunswick.**

★ Major John Graves Simcoe (1752–1806) raided Somerset, Bonhamtown, Bound Brook, and Elizabethtown on October 28, 1779 and was captured on his return.

See **Bound Brook.**

★ A force of 300 British Regulars and Loyalists landed at the lower end of Brunswick about 4 AM on Wednesday, January 2, 1782 to seize the whaleboats (see Photo NJ-1). Militia guards discovered them approaching on the river and alerted the town about 15 minutes before they landed. As they landed, a small party attacked them, killing two men. Reinforcements arrived to support the local residents; but the raiders outnumbered them and had already gained the heights, forcing the inhabitants to retire.

The Crown forces landed in different places, preventing the militia from assembling in force. They easily took possession of the town in the morning darkness and occupied it for more than an hour with very little opposition. When dawn broke, they retired to their boats.

Lieutenant Colonel John Taylor's (1751–1801) Middlesex militia began a smart skirmish which would have been much more severe had the falling snow and rain not rendered many muskets useless.

The Crown forces accomplished their objective, captured six inhabitants and only pillaged two families. They left two dead in the town, two more killed at the first landing, and were seen carrying off several others. They probably suffered more losses on their return from the well-directed fire of different parties assembled on the shores from Piscataway and South River. Colonel Taylor lost five men wounded.[339]

See **New Brunswick.**

Amboy (June 8, 1776; end of June 1776; July 5, 1776; July 25, 1776; Sept. 17, 1776; Sept. 27, 1776; Nov. 12, 1776; Jan. 1, 1777; Jan. 20, 1777; Feb. 1777; Feb. 12, 1777; Feb. 23, 1777; Feb. 28, 1777; Mar. 8, 1777; Apr. 19, 1777; Apr. 23, 1777; Apr. 24, 1777; Apr. 25, 1777; June 25, 1777; July 4, 1777; Aug. 19, 1777; June 12, 1778; Oct. 12, 1779; Oct. 21, 1779; Jan. 11, 1781; Jan. 16, 1781)

Spring Hill (Feb. 28, 1777)

East Jersey (early Mar. 1777)

Amboy was the seat of government for New Jersey and the residence of the principal royal officers during the American War for Independence. It had a commanding position and was a place of some interest to both parties. Highways and corporate complexes have obliterated almost all of colonial Amboy. The Proprietary House (see Photo NJ-25) (149 Kearny Avenue, Perth Amboy) was the home of William

Photo NJ-25. Proprietary House, the home of William Franklin (1731–1813), the last royal governor of New Jersey and Benjamin Franklin's son

Franklin (1731–1813), the last royal governor of New Jersey and Benjamin Franklin's (1706–1790) son. Colonel Hugh Mercer (1725–1777) used it as his headquarters before General William Howe (1732–1786) took control of the area and used it as his headquarters.

St. Peter's Episcopal Church (see Photo NJ-26) (183 Rector Street at the corner of Gordon Street), formed in 1685, is the oldest Anglican parish in New Jersey. It was friendly to the Whigs at a time when most Anglican churches favored England. The Whigs used the church's steeple as a watchtower to observe the activities of the Crown forces on Staten Island, less than a mile away, across the Arthur Kill. A small gun placed in the churchyard early in the war fired on ships of the Royal Navy on several occasions in June 1776.

Sandy Hook is a peninsula just southeast of Amboy that juts out into Sandy Hook Bay toward Staten Island.

Fort Hancock, off Rt. 36 at the Sandy Hook Unit of Gateway National Recreation Area is located near the tip of the Sandy Hook peninsula overlooking the entrance to New York Harbor. The fort played a key role in harbor defense and navigation since 1764 when the Sandy Hook Lighthouse was built on the grounds of the fort (**www.nps.gov/gate**). The lighthouse is the nation's oldest operating lighthouse.

The man-of-war HMS *Asia* (see Photo NJ-27) fired three times at two whaleboats full of men at noon on Saturday, June 8, 1776 as they passed over from Coney Island, New York to Amboy. The guns had little effect.[340]

★ When General William Howe (1732–1786) arrived at Staten Island with a large body of troops toward the end of June 1776, General George Washington (1732–1799)

Photo NJ-26. St. Peter's Episcopal Church, Amboy, is the oldest Anglican parish in New Jersey. It was friendly to the Whigs at a time when most Anglican churches favored England. The Whigs used the church's steeple as a watchtower to observe the activities of the Crown forces on Staten Island, less than a mile away, across the Arthur Kill. A small gun placed in the churchyard early in the war fired on ships of the Royal Navy on several occasions in June 1776.

formed a camp at Perth Amboy and placed Brigadier General Hugh Mercer (1725–1777) in command. Two armed British vessels and several armed whaleboats were stationed off Amboy in June 1776. One of these vessels was anchored in front of the

Photo NJ-27. HMS Victory, *a man-of-war or ship of the line*

town for some time. When a British tug-of-war entered the harbor and sailed into the Narrows, General Mercer's troops opened fire on it with an 18-pounder in St. Peter's churchyard. The British ship returned fire.[341]

★ Around Friday, July 5, 1776, a British brig-of-war, mounting 12 guns, entered the harbor and anchored off St. Peter's Church, about midway between Amboy and Staten Island. The Whigs procured an 18-pound gun from Woodbridge and placed it behind the breastwork by the church at night. When morning dawned, they opened fire on the vessel which returned fire. Because of her proximity to shore, she had to retire to avoid being sunk. Tradition says that one of the cannonballs broke the tombstone of Captain William Bryant in the rear of the church.[342]

★ On Thursday, July 25, 1776, the battery at Amboy fired several cannon at a number of boats from Staten Island bound to join the Royal Navy fleet at Sandy Hook. The encampment near Billop's Point (under some trees near Colonel Christopher Billopp's (ca. 1738–1827) house) on Staten Island began a cannonade which continued very hot on both sides for nearly an hour. "The boats got clear, but many of the Regulars were seen to fall, and several were carried off, supposed wounded." One soldier in the Philadelphia line was killed and one wounded. A horse in a carriage had his head shot off in High Street, a short distance south of the town well, and some houses were damaged.[343]

The two sloops leaving Staten Island at the Mill Creek, opposite Grass or Ploughshare Point, only had a hole torn in one of their mainsails by a passing ball. As they proceeded down the bay, guns were removed to another small battery near St. Peter's Church where firing resumed but with no effect.[344]

★ It seemed that the British were preparing to attack Amboy or attempting to cross the Sound in August 1776. As most of the troops had been sent to New York in early August when the British fleet menaced the city, the War Office ordered, on Friday, August 28,

1776, all the troops in Philadelphia or on their way to the camp to march to Amboy immediately. They planned to station 1,500 troops at Amboy, 400 at Woodbridge, and 500 at Elizabethtown.

Shortly after this order was issued, a fruitless peace conference was held in the Billopp house opposite Amboy on Wednesday morning, September 11th. A committee composed of Benjamin Franklin (1706–1790), John Adams (1735–1826), and John Rutledge (1730–1800) met with General William Howe (1732–1786) and his brother, Admiral Richard Howe (1726–1799). The Committee's report was entered into the *Journals of the Continental Congress* under the date of September 17, 1776.

★ On Tuesday afternoon, September 17, 1776, some Whigs at Amboy fired on HM Sloop *Tamar*'s boat which had taken a boat and four prisoners earlier that afternoon. They fired several shots at the boats from their batteries. The Hessians fired a number of shots at the Whigs.[345]

★ The HM Sloop *Senegal* was anchored in Amboy Channel on Friday, September 27, 1776 while a boat went to the Watering Place on Staten Island. Two of the men ran away with the longboat loaded with water about 3 PM. Captain Roger Curtis (1746–1816) sent his pinnace (see Photo NJ-28) after them. The pinnace's arrival on shore drew a party of militiamen who fired at the men aboard the pinnace, preventing them from taking the longboat.[346]

★ A party of 50 Congressional troops "went tory hunting" Tuesday night, November 12, 1776 but their prey had escaped before their arrival. The troops did observe that the Crown troops had "very numerous" fires in their camp. The guard left at the riverside opposite to the ships captured "a *red hot tory* coming from the enemy's vessels."

Photo NJ-28. HMS Victory's *pinnace (left). The pinnace was a 28-foot boat used to convey the captain or officers ashore or to other ships. It was generally rowed by eight oarsmen but could be rowed by four.*

Brigadier General William Alexander's (Earl of Stirling, 1726–1783) brigade and Colonel Edward Hand's (1744–1802) troops marched from Brunswick to be ready to prevent any attempts on the Amboy shore.[347]

★ Captain Stephen Mascoll (1744–1777), in the *General Putnam,* a privateer schooner from Salem, Massachusetts engaged the British ships *Nancy* and *Betsy* on Wednesday, January 1, 1777. Captain Mascoll was killed with one of his men as they tried to board a large ship off the western islands. After a struggle, the schooner sheered off.[348]

★ Jan. 20, 1777 see **Millstone (Somerset Courthouse).**

★ February 13, 1777 see **Amboy.**

★ About 2,000 Crown troops on a foraging party from Amboy, attacked some guards on Sunday, February 23, 1777 and drove them five or six miles. When Brigadier General William Maxwell (1733–1796) arrived with reinforcements of 1,400 troops, mostly militiamen, it was now the turn of the Crown forces to retreat in a hurry. They only had time to fire two volleys. General Maxwell took six prisoners and found two of British dead; but deserters who arrived later reported that they had about 500 killed and wounded. General Maxwell lost only three killed and 11 wounded.[349]

★ A large party of Whigs entered the house of Mr. Stephen Skinner at Spring Hill, near Perth Amboy, on Friday night, February 28, 1777. The raiders did much damage, plundered a large amount of his property, and threatened to set fire to the house. Mr. Skinner, Treasurer of East Jersey, had taken refuge with the King's troops almost two months earlier, but Mrs. Stephens and the family were home and were greatly terrified. When Major General John Vaughn (1738?–1795) was informed of their distress, he sent an escort to bring them and their remaining belongings to the British garrison at Amboy.[350]

★ The Congressional forces' foraging and scouting parties operating in the country between Amboy and New Brunswick, cut off all British communication with Brunswick during the month of February 1777, except by the Raritan River. A fleet of boats coming up the river from Amboy with supplies for General Charles Cornwallis's (1738–1805) headquarters at Brunswick and his detachment there were fired upon from a battery of six 32-pounders which the provincials had erected the night before on a high bluff below the town, overlooking the river. The cannonade devastated the boats, sinking four or five. The others returned to Amboy and then to New York. General William Howe (1732–1786) subsequently tried unsuccessfully to open the communication. He narrowly escaped capture, and Brunswick remained isolated until late March.[351]

★ A justice named Kemble (d. 1777) in East Jersey was murdered by a party of British troops in early March 1777 despite his protests that he was a Loyalist and had General William Howe's (1732–1786) protection. He was first shot through the body and then stabbed with a bayonet. He lived long enough to tell his story to a party of Continental soldiers who came to his house after the murderers had left.[352]

★ For the engagement on March 8, 1777 which spread from Punk Hill at Amboy to Bonhamtown and Metuchen, see **Bonhamtown** and **Spanktown.**

★ The British surprised Congressional forces in a raid near Amboy (probably Woodbridge) on Thursday, April 19, 1777. They captured 17 prisoners and killed two light horsemen without any loss.[353]

★ Captain Lacy marched from the neighborhood of Rahway with a detachment of 60 men and three subalterns to surprise the picket in the suburbs of Amboy on Wednesday night, April 23, 1777. They killed one sentinel and wounded another. Several Hessian soldiers ran into town from the barracks to sound the alarm. Expecting a general attack, all the troops were ordered out. They formed a semicircle extending from the water to the "parting roads."

★ The following night, a similar expedition of 20 or 30 men got lost in the dark and came within the lines and attempted to take a picket guard at Amboy on Thursday, April 24, 1777. Nobody escaped. A Whig attack on British guards at Amboy on Friday, April 25, 1777 resulted in a skirmish that left four of the attackers dead and the remaining 26 captured.[354]

After the evacuation of Brunswick, most of the Crown forces headed toward Amboy, burning houses and barns along the road on June 23, 1777.[355]

See **Woodbridge.**

★ Colonel Theodorick Bland's (1742–1790) Continental dragoons attacked the Crown forces near Amboy around 2 PM on Wednesday, June 25, 1777. A skirmish ensued. When the Continental infantry and artillery approached about 4 o'clock, the fighting became more intense, leaving four dead and three missing jaegers and about five dead and several wounded Continentals.[356]

★ Brigadier General "Mad Anthony" Wayne's (1745–1796) brigade marched down the east side of the Raritan River on Friday morning, July 4, 1777 while Brigadier General James Mitchell Varnum's (1748–1789) force proceeded down the west side. General De Boor's brigade followed General Wayne's as a support. As General Wayne approached at sunrise, the Crown forces abandoned their redoubts in a hurry. The redoubts were about 3 miles from Providence. General William Howe's (1732–1786) entire army of more than 7,000 immediately left Providence in the greatest haste and headed for Amboy. They encountered Colonel Daniel Morgan's (1736–1802) light troops about 9 AM. A smart skirmish ensued which left 300 Crown forces killed and wounded, while Morgan had only four or five wounded, none mortally. General Howe planned to burn the town before leaving it; but the quick advance of the Continental troops saved the place. The retreating troops did burn and destroy almost every house in their retreat, including 12 houses at Piscataqua.[357]

★ Aug. 19, 1777 see **Elizabeth.**

★ Brigadier General William Winds (1727–1789) and about 40 militiamen stationed at Elizabethtown went to Amboy where they fired on an armed brig on Friday morning, June 12, 1778. The brig had been terrorizing the people of Woodbridge and Amboy for three or four days and now lay between the church in Amboy and Colonel Christopher Billopp's (ca. 1738–1827) house on Staten Island. The gunfire did "great havoc among her rigging, and did considerable damage to her hull" and probably killed several sailors. The brig slipped her cables and departed with a fair breeze.[358]

★ A party of about 50 Loyalists came to Amboy from Staten Island early Tuesday morning, October 12, 1779. They collected more than 100 head of cattle and horses before any alarm was sounded. Captain William Davis, Sr. (1719–1791) and a small detachment of New Jersey militiamen marched from Elizabethtown and attacked them about 10 o'clock. The Loyalists fled, leaving most of their booty, taking only about 20 head of cattle. Captain Davis suspected that his men wounded several dragoons, but none of his were hurt.[359]

★ The Queen's Rangers proceeded along the road toward South Amboy after raiding Elizabeth, Bonhamtown, Bound Brook, Somerset Courthouse and Brunswick on Thursday, October 21, 1779. There they joined forces with the infantry. They took 27 prisoners, including John Hampton (1745–1843), during the expedition and lost only one man killed and four taken prisoners in addition to Colonel John Graves Simcoe

(1752–1806) who was taken to Brunswick. The 27 prisoners captured by the Queen's Rangers were taken to New York Friday night, October 29.[360]

See also **Bonhamtown, Brunswick, Bound Brook, Elizabeth,** and **Somerset Courthouse.**

★ A party of 10 or 12 New Jersey militia privates under Ensign Lewis Fitz Randolph (1756–1822) were surprised in Amboy by a British detachment around January 10 or 11, 1781. The entire party was captured and brought to Staten Island.[361]

★ About 4,000 or 5,000 Crown troops at Amboy embarked on several transports at Sandy Hook on Tuesday morning, January 16, 1781. They left under convoy of three men-of-war to give the impression of reinforcements from Europe. A party of Middlesex County militiamen skirmished with some British troops in South Amboy. The expedition returned to Staten Island and disembarked under the cover of night.[362]

Sandy Hook (Jan. 22, 1776; Mar. 10, 1776; Apr. 19, 1776; Apr. 23, 1776; Apr. 25, 1776; May 13, 1776; May 22, 1776; June 8, 1776; June 21, 1776; July 4, 1776; Nov. 12, 1776; Dec. 13, 1776; Feb. 10, 1777; Feb. 13, 1777; Mar. 1 or 8, 1777; Sept. 20, 1778; Jan. 7, 1779; Apr. 26, 1779; Jan. 12, 1780; Apr. 15, 1780; May 15, 1780; Oct. 5, 1781; between Apr. 17 and 24, 1782; June 12, 1782; before June 19, 1782)

Burrows's Mills (May 27, 1778)

> Sandy Hook is a peninsula just southeast of Amboy that juts out into Sandy Hook Bay toward Staten Island.
>
> Burrows's (Burrowes) Mills were near Keyport south of Sandy Hook.

Brigadier General William Alexander (Earl of Stirling, 1726–1783) and some people from the seaport towns captured the cargo ship *Blue Mountain Valley* at Sandy Hook, off Elizabethtown, on Monday, January 22, 1776. The ship's cargo consisted of "120 chaldron of coals, 100 barrels of porter, 300 sacks of potatoes, 10 pipes of sour crout, 4 four pounders, some powder and arms, and sundry other goods" for the ministerial army in Boston. Several men in a small vessel boarded her at night and brought her into port where they unloaded her. The vessel brought 80 hogs from London but many of them died on the voyage.[363]

★ The New York Provincial Congress resolved, on Tuesday, March 5, 1776, to dismantle the lighthouse at Sandy Hook and to make it useless. It appointed Major William Malcom or Malcolm (1745–1791) to execute their decision, instructing him to take the glass out of the lantern and to save it, if possible. Otherwise, he was to break all the glass. He was also instructed to pump all the oil out of the cisterns into casks and to bring it off. If he could not procure casks or was obstructed by the enemy, he was to pump it out on the ground.

Major Malcom, with the assistance of Colonel George Taylor (1734–1799) and some of his men, destroyed the glass on Sunday, March 10 because they did not have the necessary tools to remove it. They returned with eight copper lamps, two tackle falls and blocks and three casks and part of another cask of oil.[364]

★ Governor William Tryon (1729–1788) burned the pilot house at Sandy Hook on Friday, April 19, 1776. Mr. Adam Dobbs's property was confiscated and Mr. Dobbs and his servants were taken to New York.[365]

★ Congressional troops captured a watering party of 35 men from Captain George Vandeput's (d. 1800) HMS *Asia* at Sandy Hook on Tuesday, April 23, 1776. Another watering party fled into the lighthouse the next day and was captured. Sixteen men from one of the ships of war landed at Sandy Hook around Thursday, April 25, 1776 to get water. As they were all carousing in an upper room in the lighthouse, a party of the New Jersey Militia surprised them and took away the lower part of the stairs, making them all prisoners. The militiamen also burned their boat and filled up the well.[366]

★ Captain Hyde Parker, Jr.'s (1739–1807) HMS *Phoenix* fired several guns on Rebel troops who were attempting to seize a watering boat from the HMS *Asia* on Monday, May 13, 1776. He also sent armed boats to her assistance.[367]

★ Captain George Vandeput (d. 1800) heard the firing of guns at Sandy Hook on Wednesday morning, May 22, 1776. He sent the barge from the HMS *Asia,* manned and armed, as the Whigs were attacking his watering sloop. The barge returned that afternoon.[368]

★ Captain Charles Hudson's HMS *Orpheus* chased a sloop from the West Indies at 8 AM on Saturday, June 8, 1776. The *Orpheus* fired two 6-pounders and the sloop ran on shore. Captain Hudson sent out his boats after her but the surf prevented them from bringing the sloop back; so they destroyed her.[369]

★ About 300 militiamen, under the command of Colonel Benjamin Tupper (1738–1792) and Major Brooks attacked the lighthouse at Sandy Hook about 3 or 4 AM on Friday, June 21, 1776. The guard at the lighthouse, previously informed of the plan of attack, was strongly reinforced by a boat from Long Island. The Crown forces withdrew to the lighthouse which was so strongly fortified and cemented that the shot from Captain Drewry's two field pieces had little effect, even though they were not more than 150 yards away.

The HMS *Phoenix* and the *Liverpool* (some accounts say the *Lively*) with springs on their cables, poured a heavy fire in the militia's flank and rear while the troops at the lighthouse fired on their front. The skirmish continued for two hours with field pieces and small arms. Both sides kept up a smart fire the entire time. Seeing his men tired and exposed to the fire of the ships, Colonel Tupper withdrew his men about 2 miles to refresh them. Colonel Tupper sent out small parties to tempt the Crown forces to come on shore so he might attack them on a more equal footing; but they remained in the safety of the lighthouse. As evening approached and their provisions were nearly exhausted, the party returned to camp at the south end of the Cedar without the loss of a man and only two very slightly wounded.[370]

★ Some 500 Rebels with two brass pieces attacked the Sandy Hook lighthouse again on Wednesday, July 4, 1776.[370a]

★ Captain George Keith Elphinstone, Viscount Keith's (1746–1823) HMS *Perseus* exchanged fire with troops on shore at Sandy Hook on Tuesday, November 12, 1776. Foul weather drove one of their prizes, the brig *Roby,* on shore up the Amboy River. Captain Elphinstone manned and armed all his boats which he sent to retake the *Roby* from the Whigs. However, he had to detain the boats at noon because of the high winds.

The boats departed at 1 PM but found too many enemy on shore and returned to the *Perseus* at 3 o'clock. The *Perseus* came alongside the *Roby* and fired several shots at the Whigs. Captain Elphinstone then sent all his boats to destroy the *Roby* which they did at 6 PM while some guns and small arms fired several volleys from the shore.[371]

★ Marines from Captain Tobias Furneaux's (1735–1781) HMS *Syren* boarded a schooner that had run ashore at Sandy Hook on Friday morning, December 13, 1776. The marines took possession of the schooner at 5 PM and returned with 27 prisoners at 7 o'clock. The *Syren's* tender returned at 8 after firing several swivel guns (see Photo NJ-1) and small arms at the Whigs who were plundering the schooner. The tender returned to the schooner at 10 PM to burn it.[372]

★ February 13, 1777 see **Amboy.**

★ British troops under Major Andrew Gordon attacked Congressional forces at Sandy Hook on Wednesday, February 12, 1777. They killed 10 and captured about 70. The following day, Private John Bruce (d. 1777) was killed in a skirmish at the Loyalist camp at the Cedars near Sandy Hook.[373]

★ About 250 Congressional troops attacked the lighthouse at Sandy Hook on Saturday, March 1 or 8, 1777. The garrison and the guns of the warship *Syren*, at anchor nearby, beat them back with some loss. The Regulars had not a man either killed or wounded but two were reported missing.[374]

★ A party of about 70 Loyalists from Sandy Hook landed near Major Kearney's at Middletown Point on Wednesday morning, May 27, 1778. They marched to the house of Mr. John Burrows, the "Corn King," burned his mills, both his storehouses, all valuable buildings, and a great deal of his furniture and took him prisoner. They also took Lieutenant Colonel John Smock (1727–1808), Captain Christopher Little, Mr. Joseph Wall, Captain Jacob Covenhoven (1749–1812) (1746–1825), and several other persons. They killed two men and wounded another mortally before departing later that morning.[375]

★ Captain Priestman's 20-gun Letter of Marque ship *Brilliant* arrived at Sandy Hook from Liverpool on Sunday, September 20, 1778. During the passage, the *Brilliant* was attacked by a Whig frigate which she beat off.[376]

★ Some militiamen in row boats went from Jersey to Sandy Hook on Wednesday, January 7, 1779. They boarded four sloops, one of them armed, during the night and captured them. The unskilled pilots ran three of them ashore where they were burned. The other got safely to New Jersey with 19 prisoners. Each militiaman was awarded £400 for the exploit.[377]

★ Monmouth County militiamen, in response to British raids on Red Bank, Shrewsbury, Tinton Falls and Middletown, rallied and chased the Regulars to boats near the Loyalist camp at Sandy Hook on Monday, April 26, 1779. The British killed one and took several prisoners along with some cattle and horses.

See **Shrewsbury.**

★ Captain Michael Rudolph (ca. 1754–ca.1794) of Major Henry "Light-Horse Harry" Lee's (1756–1818) Rangers along with a sergeant, corporal and eight men, landed at Sandy Hook within half a mile of the lighthouse on Wednesday, January 12, 1780. They surrounded a house and captured seven Crown troops and confiscated 45,000 counterfeit Continental dollars, a quantity of hard money, and several parcels of dry goods without any loss.[378]

★ Captain John Patten (1746–1800) and 40 men surprised two British schooners and a sloop frozen in ice off Sandy Hook on Saturday, April 15, 1780. The men burned the vessels and took prisoners and plunder.[379]

★ When Captain Aplin learned, about 10 AM on Monday, May 15, 1780, that a party of Whigs had landed on Sandy Hook, he ordered the HMS *Swift* to fire a gun to signal all the boats to be manned and armed. He weighed anchor and set sail for Navesink and prepared the ship for action but later signaled the boats to return. The following afternoon, Captain Aplin ordered the *Swift*'s boats manned and armed to intercept the Whigs. As the boats approached the cove on the Jersey shore, they came under fire from several field pieces.[380]

★ Captain Adam Hyler (1735–1782) or Huyler, from New Brunswick, attacked five vessels with one gunboat and two whaleboats on Friday night, October 5, 1781. The vessels, two of which were armed—one with four 6-pounders and the other with six swivels (see Photo NJ-1) and one 3-pounder—were within a quarter of a mile of the guard ship at Sandy Hook. The engagement lasted only 15 minutes and all hands escaped safely to a small fort in longboats (see Photo NJ-29).

Despite constant fire from the fort's 12 swivel guns, Captain Hyler took the vessels without the loss of a man. One of the vessels, bound for New York, had aboard 250 bushels of wheat and a quantity of cheese belonging to Captain Richard Lippincott (1745–1826. Captain Hyler took 50 bushels of wheat, a quantity of cheese, several swivels, a number of fusils, one cask of powder and some dry goods. He then stripped the vessels of their sails and rigging as he could not bring the vessels into port due to a contrary wind and tide. He then set four of the vessels on fire. He spared the other vessel because it had a woman and four small children aboard.[381]

★ Captain Adam Hyler or Huyler (1735–1782), in an open boat, boarded and captured a 16-gun cutter manned with 46 men one calm and clear evening between April 17 and 24, 1782. She was anchored near Sandy Hook about a quarter of a mile away from the 64-gun man-of-war *Lion*. She was ready for sea, intending to cruise in Delaware Bay. The guard had been posted and Captain Robert White was on deck with three or four crewmen admiring the full moon when they heard several pistol shots fired into the cabins. When they turned around, a number of armed people at their elbows demanded their surrender. The captain and his crew were put in the hold and the hatches barred over them. The man-of-war, alarmed by the firing, wanted to know what was the matter. Captain Hyler told them, through the speaking trumpet, that all was well and

Photo NJ-29. Longboat of HMS Victory. *Longboats were used to ferry troops to and from shore.*

they made no further inquiry. As Captain Hyler was bringing the cutter away, she ran aground. He stripped her of her valuables and anything convenient to take away and then blew her up. He also took a sloop which he ransomed for $400.[382]

★ Captain Hyler destroyed several boats during another raid on Wednesday, June 12, 1782.[383]

★ Captain Adam Hyler (1735–1782) surprised a captain of the guard and half his men at the Sandy Hook lighthouse before June 19, 1782.[384]

At sea near Sandy Hook (June 1776; June 30, 1776; Aug. 9, 1777; Aug. 14, 1777; May 9, 1778; July 1778; July 18, 1778; June 11, 1779; June 13, 1779; June 15, 1779; Aug. 10, 1779; Sept. 11, 1779; Sept. 29, 1779; Nov. 1779; Nov. 27, 1779; Jan. 27, 1780; Feb. 1780; Apr. 15, 1780; Apr. 18, 1780; June 30, 1780; July 2, 1780; July 8, 1780; Sept. 9, 1780; Sept. 1780; Oct. 24, 1781; Dec. 12, 1781; Dec. 15, 1781; Dec. 28, 1781; May 25, 1782; June 1782; July 2, 1782)

One of the vessels in Commodore Ezek Hopkins's (1718–1802) fleet captured a transport ship from Greenock in June 1776. The transport had a company of the 42nd Regiment on board. After taking out the soldiers, except for the officers and their wives, the captors sent the transport to Newport, Rhode Island; but she was soon re-taken by the HMS *Cerberus* and was sent to Sandy Hook under the convoy of an armed sloop tender. The convoy met the Continental armed sloop *Schuyler* as they proceeded in back of Long Island. The *Schuyler* captured both the transport and the tender. The transport had on board five commissioned officers, two ladies and four privates as well as 80 butts of porter. The vessels and their cargo were brought safely to Philadelphia on Tuesday, June 18, 1776.[385]

★ Rebels captured a ship and 26 prisoners near Sandy Hook on Sunday, June 30, 1776.[386]

★ Captain Henry Johnson's 14-gun ship *Mary* sailed from Sandy Hook bound for Jamaica in company with Captain Mason's 10-gun sloop *Dolphin* on Saturday, August 9, 1777. That afternoon, they were attacked by the 18-gun Continental Navy sloop *Providence* full of men. A hot engagement continued for about three hours when the privateer withdrew with considerable losses. The other vessels returned to Sandy Hook for lack of ammunition. The *Mary* had only one man wounded.[387]

★ A Congressional privateer schooner appeared off Sandy Hook on Saturday, May 9, 1778. She had almost captured one of four pilot boats.[388]

★ The French fleet anchored 5 miles off Sandy Hook during the month of July 1778 and captured 14 to 17 prizes. On Saturday, July 18, the Allied forces exchanged cannonades with the British fleet off Sandy Hook.[389]

★ Captain William Havens's privateer *Beaver* forced a British sloop into port at Sandy Hook on Friday, June 11, 1779. The sloop had a cargo of about 60 hogsheads of rum and some sugar when she was captured.[390]

★ Two days later, on Sunday, June 13, 1779, Captain Peter Richards's (1754–) privateer *Hancock* engaged the 12-gun British schooner *Eagle* off Sandy Hook. The *Eagle* was returning from a cruise in which she had taken several prizes when she was captured by the *Hancock*. She was the ninth privateer from New York to be brought into the port of Sandy Hook since March 1, 1779.[391]

★ A British schooner laden with tobacco captured the privateer *Revenge* off Sandy Hook on Tuesday, June 15, 1779.[392]

★ Some Whig privateers captured the snow *Dashwood Pacquet* within sight of Sandy Hook as she was bound for that port on Monday, August 10, 1779. The following

Saturday, the 14th, some Jersey militiamen aboard a small 10-oar gunboat captured a fishing boat on the banks.[393]

★ The following month, on Saturday, September 11, 1779, three Congressional privateers, one of them an 18-gun brig full of men, chased Captain Buchannan's privateer brig *Dunmore* into Sandy Hook. The *Dunmore* was returning from a cruise in which she took three prizes which Captain Buchannan sent to Bermuda. One of them was a brig from St. Eustatia bound for Philadelphia.

★ An engagement the same day between the HMS *Active* and the brig *Mars* near Sandy Hook killed Elijah Matthews (1749–1779).[394]

★ On Wednesday, September 29, 1779, the sloop *Revenge* clashed with the HMS *Vengence* near Sandy Hook.[395]

★ Captain Jonathan Harridan's (Haradan or Harradan) (1744–1803) Congressional ship *Pickering* encountered a ship with 14 6-pounders, a brig with ten 4- and 3-pounders and a sloop with eight 4-pounders, all privateers bound from New York to Oporto in November 1779. The privateers fought well for three hours; but the *Pickering* captured all three vessels after killing and wounding a number of the crews. The *Pickering* had eight men wounded. Earlier, in the same cruise, the *Pickering* took the 12-gun *Pomona*, which got safely into Salem; the 14-gun brig *Hope*, and the 1-gun cutter *Royal George* which were sent to Boston.[396]

★ The Congressional privateer *Beaver* took the brig *L'Constance* a few leagues off Sandy Hook on Saturday, November 27, 1779.[397]

★ Captain George House, with 19 men in a small privateer schooner, captured a schooner from Madeira near Sandy Hook on Thursday, January 27, 1780. She was bound for New York with 108 pipes of wine. Captain House also took a pilot boat which came out from New York to pilot in the above schooner.[398]

★ In February 1780, three privateers (a 14-gun sloop of war, a 12-gun brig, and a 10-gun schooner) attacked the British packet ship *Grenville* (12 4-pounders and 45 men) two days after her departure. After a brisk action of about an hour, the *Grenville* sheered off and was engaged by the sloop which was the most powerful and nearest vessel. The sloop was obliged to break away and made signals of distress to her consorts which came to her assistance. The *Grenville* received no material damage, except two men wounded, one of them Mr. Steele, the first mate, "who lost his eye by a piece of an iron bolt weighing 13 ounces, which buried itself in the socket of his eye, and the upper part of his cheek bone turning his eye quite over his nose; the piece was extracted and the eye replaced by the surgeon Mr. Walpole." The bolt was supposedly sent to the British Museum; but it is no longer part of the museum's collection.[399]

★ The HMS *Galatea* drove the privateer brig *Rattle Snake,* of 8 guns and 52 men, ashore about half a mile from the lighthouse at Sandy Hook on Saturday, April 15, 1780. Captain Reed and his crew tried to escape into the country. The commanding officer at the lighthouse observed them and immediately sent a detachment to pursue them and they were taken prisoners.[400]

★ Captain Sutherland, of the HMS *Vulture,* drove another privateer brig, the *Black Snake,* on shore at Deal Beach, 12 miles off Sandy Hook the same day.[401]

★ Captain William Marriner left Amboy on Tuesday evening, April 18, 1780, with nine men in a whaleboat. About 4 AM on Thursday morning, he boarded the HM brig *Blacksnake* and captured her and her crew of 20 without opposition, even though he was near the HMS *Volcano*. The *Blacksnake* was a Rhode Island privateer taken by the HMS *Galatea*. Captain Marriner weighed anchor and headed out to sea where he fell in with the schooner *Morning Star* after 5 AM the same morning. Despite having the *Black-snake* in charge, Marriner engaged the *Morning Star* [four swivels (see Photo NJ-1), two cohorns, and 33 hands] in "an obstinate action" and boarded her. She lost three men killed, including her commander, Robert Campbell (d. 1780), and five wounded. Captain Marriner brought his prizes and 52 prisoners, mostly deserters from men-of-war, to Egg Harbor. One of the prizes had a large number of counterfeit Continental dollars on board.[402]

The British 8-gun sloop *Commerce* captured the schooner *Restoration,* mounting two 3-pounders, in a three-hour battle near Sandy Hook on Friday, June 30, 1780. Her prize was loaded with bar iron and cannon.[403]

★ A tender of the HMS *Raisonable* captured John Shaw's sloop *Hazard* on Sunday, July 2, 1780. The *Hazard* was loaded with lumber and bound from Egg Harbor to Rhode Island.[404]

★ Captain Daniel Moore's privateer brig HMS *Admiral Rodney (*16 carriage-guns and 83 men) had a severe engagement within pistol shot of a privateer brig of 16 6- and 9-pounders off Sandy Hook on Saturday, July 8, 1780. Captain Moore and several of his crew were dangerously wounded and six men killed in the three-hour engagement. The *Admiral Rodney* had her boom shot away and could not pursue the enemy.[405]

★ Two privateers attacked the HMS *Theresa* off Sandy Hook in September 1780 and some Congressional privateers attacked a British ship near Sandy Hook on Saturday, September 9, 1780.[406]

★ Captain Adam Hyler (1735–1782) or Huyler, of Brunswick, raided a Loyalist town near Sandy Hook on Wednesday, October 24, 1781. He went with one gunboat to surprise the town which harbored some horse thieves. He landed within three-quarters of a mile from the light horsemen but found that they were out in Monmouth County. He fell in with six other noted Loyalists whom he captured.[407]

★ Captain Hyler, commanding seven or eight stout whaleboats, manned with nearly 100 men, encountered two Loyalist sloops in the Narrows bound for Shrewsbury on Wednesday, December 12, 1781. One of the sloops, commanded by Shore Stephens, had on board £600 in specie and a large quantity of dry goods. The other had similar articles as well as sugar and rum. Both vessels were taken to Brunswick.[408]

★ Captain Adam Hyler and some militiamen in whaleboats captured two Loyalist mercantile ships off Sandy Hook on Saturday, December 15, 1781. They also captured five of the King's American Dragoons who were in sick quarters near Utrecht the previous night.[409]

★ Colonel Asher Holmes (1740–1808) and his men seized the privateer brig HMS *Britannia* at the mouth of Cheesequake Creek on Friday, December 28, 1781. She had dragged her anchors and run aground in a severe storm on Christmas day. The vessel did considerable damage to the wharves and some of the shipping. A large field of ice prevented any assistance getting to her. Colonel Holmes captured her crew who were exhausted from trying to save the vessel. The sails, rigging, hull, and cargo were sold at private auction.[410]

★ Captain Adam Hyler and some militiamen in armed boats attacked Captain John Schaak and 25 troops of the 57th British Regiment in the Shrewsbury River on Saturday, May 25, 1782. Captain Schaak and his men had been sent to intercept Hyler in passing through the Gut. As soon as Captain Hyler discovered them, he landed 13 of his men with orders to charge. They killed or wounded four and captured Captain Schaak and eight of his men. Several others may have been killed by fire from the gunboat.[411]

★ Captain Adam Hyler (1735–1782) destroyed several Loyalist boats during a raid on their camp at Sandy Hook in early June 1782. He captured one British captain and seven privates near the lighthouse at Sandy Hook and wounded some who were left behind. He captured four vessels near New York on Wednesday, June 5, 1782. One of the vessels was re-taken. The other three were run on shore and stripped.[412]

★ Captain Adam Hyler (1735–1782) or Huyler and Captain John Story, with a militia party in five boats, captured the schooner *Skip Jack*, a tender of eight guns (six carriage guns and two swivels), near Sandy Hook about noon on Tuesday, July 2, 1782. The *Skip Jack* was a tender to the admiral's ship. The guard ship got under way immediately but could not recover the prize because of little wind. The militiamen brought the *Skip Jack* to the Shrewsbury River where they burned her. They also captured the *Skip Jack*'s captain and nine or ten crewmen. The others escaped in their boats when they saw the whaleboats approaching. The *Skip Jack*'s sails, rigging, cabin furniture, two 3-pounders, and two African Americans named Thomas Prosper and Thomas Tucker and other effects were auctioned on Thursday, August 1.

At the same time, Captain Hyler took two fishermen (vessels), one of which he liberated, the other he carried off. Some boats from the guard ship re-took the vessel the next day.[413]

West Jersey (Apr. 11, 1777)
A force of 50 Crown troops lost five men killed in a skirmish with some Congressional troops in West Jersey on Friday, April 11, 1777.[414]

Plainfield
Ash Swamp
The Short Hills (Jan. 1777; Feb. 1777; Feb. 23, 1777; June 26, 1777)
Scotch Plains (June 16, 1777; June 23, 1777; June 26, 1777; June 16, 1780)

The Short Hills should not be confused with present-day Short Hills in Essex County. The site is the hilly region of the Hobart Gap, from Metuchen to Scotch Plains, ending in the first ridge of the Watchung Mountains.

Homestead Farm, the site of the battle of Ash Swamp is covered by the Ash Brook Golf Course. The entrance (Raritan Road, Scotch Plains) has a monument with an explanation of the battle. The Oak Ridge Golf Club, on Oak Ridge Road, occupies the site where the battle began.

General Charles Cornwallis (1738–1805) supposedly attracted by the odor of baking bread stopped at the Frazee Homestead (corner of Raritan and Terrill Roads, Scotch Plains) during the Battle of the Short Hills.

The Osborn Cannonball house (1840 Front Street) was struck by a cannonball fired by local militiamen during the skirmish. The Spence house (1461 Martine Avenue), less than a mile from the Battle of the Short Hills site is a Georgian mansion built in 1774. It was used by Congressional troops during the war. A strong room in the cellar is believed to have been used as a prison cell and supposedly has a beam with the name George Washington carved on it.

Militiamen under Captain McCoy skirmished with the Crown forces at Ash Swamp in January and February 1777. They had two killed and one wounded. A foraging raid at Ash Swamp ended in a skirmish on Sunday, February 23, 1777.[415]

★ During the inter-battle period between Connecticut Farms and Springfield, a "Party of Villains" came to Scotch Plains from Staten Island to steal horses before daybreak on Friday morning, June 16, 1780. Lieutenant Joseph Catterlin's (1750–1780) militiamen killed one of them and captured three with no losses. The three prisoners were court-martialed. The same morning, the militiamen captured a British lieutenant and six privates who came to steal poultry on the mountain near Scotch Plains.[416]

★ The British Army, under General William Howe (1732–1786), and the Continental Army had a series of skirmishes in the Woodbridge and Westfield area in late June 1777. The main action was the battle of Short Hills.

A large part of the Continental Army that pursued General Howe from Brunswick toward Amboy took post at Quibbletown, while the remainder went to Middle Brook. Howe came out of Amboy with his whole army early on Monday morning, June 23, 1777 and headed toward the passes in the mountains behind Quibbletown on the army's left. He intercepted a party under Brigadier General William Alexander (Earl of Stirling, 1726–1783) and "had a smart skirmish." General Stirling had fewer losses than the Crown forces and retreated safely to Westfield.

Other parties engaged in light skirmishes on the flanks of the Crown forces and joined the main body which also moved to the left to prevent General Howe from taking the passes. General Howe continued marching toward Westfield and halted until the next day, when he returned to Amboy, plundering and burning along the way. Several small parties harassed him during the march, but nothing of any consequence happened. The Continentals had few losses except for three pieces of cannon which were left at Quibbletown and taken by the enemy.[417]

The Crown forces assembled their army at Brunswick on Thursday, June 12, 1777 and marched in two columns on the morning of the 14th. Brigadier General Edward Mathew (often misspelled Matthews) (1729–1805) remained behind with 2,000 men to guard that post. General Charles Cornwallis (1738–1805) led the first division to Hillsborough. The second, under General Leopold von Heister (1707–1777), went to Middlebush, hoping unsuccessfully to draw the Continentals into a general action. They returned to the camp at Brunswick on the 19th and marched to Amboy on the 22nd, intending to cross to Staten Island.

General George Washington (1732–1799) sent Brigadier General William Alexander (Earl of Stirling, 1726–1783) with a strong detachment and two or three cannon to the Short Hills near Metuchen on Thursday, June 19, 1777. Some battalions went into the woods to harass the rear where Lord Cornwallis commanded. The Regulars soon dispersed the Continentals with the loss of two men killed and 13 wounded, while the Continentals had nine killed and about 30 wounded.

When the preparations for crossing the troops to Staten Island had been completed, General Howe received intelligence that the enemy had moved down from the mountain and taken post at Quibbletown, intending to attack his forces leaving Amboy. He also learned that two corps had also advanced to their left, one of 3,000 men and eight cannon under the command of Brigadier General William Alexander, Brigadier General William Maxwell (1733–1796) and General Thomas Conway (1733–1800). The other corps of about 700 men had only one cannon.

Howe wanted to draw Washington into a general engagement. He sent a diversionary force by sea as he marched his army out of Amboy in two columns at 1 AM on Thursday, June 26, 1777. The first column, under General Charles Cornwallis (1738–1805) headed to the right toward Scotch Plains by way of Woodbridge. The second under Major

General John Vaughan (1738?–1795), and accompanied by General Howe, marched toward Bonhamtown two hours later to join the rear of the right column in the road from Metuchen Meetinghouse to Scotch Plains. The two columns marched toward Scotch Plains and continued northward along parallel routes, intending to catch Stirling in a pincer movement and to gain control of the passes back to Middlebrook. This would force Washington to fight where he was by cutting off his retreat route to the heights. About 2 miles after joining forces, they intended to take separate routes to attack Washington's left flank at Quibbletown. The Crown forces detached four battalions with six cannon in the morning to take post at Bonhamtown.

Shortly after taking the road leading to Scotch Plains from Metuchen Meetinghouse, Lord Cornwallis met Lord Stirling's corps advantageously posted in a wood. Cornwallis's troops attacked Stirling's picket guard at 6 AM and pressed forward with such impetuosity that they dispersed the Continentals and drove them just beyond Woodbridge, leaving behind three brass field pieces, three captains and 60 men killed, and more than 200 officers and men wounded and taken. Cornwallis had five men killed and 30 wounded.

A messenger brought news of the advance to Washington at the Quibbletown camp and Washington hurriedly withdrew his troops back to Middlebrook. A force of 600 Continentals held the high ground at Short Hills until the Crown forces "approached them with some deployed battalions and cannon, whereupon they hurriedly withdrew into the woods behind them."

General Howe joined forces with General Cornwallis about 8:30 AM and a full-scale battle began to take shape. Stirling had 2,500 troops and six cannon. Brigadier General William Maxwell (1733–1796), who was familiar with the terrain, commanded Captain Robert Conway's brigade. The main body of Continentals under Maxwell and Stirling twice made a vigorous stand near Ash Swamp not far from Scotch Plains. They apparently were protecting some wagons which were being hastily removed to the hills. The Crown forces attacked furiously. William Gordon notes that "His lordship was in no hurry to retreat, but preferred engaging for a while, wherein he made a wrong choice, for he had been nearly cut off by the right column under Lord Cornwallis." [418]

The Crown forces greatly outnumbered the Continentals and overcame them, capturing three small French cannon and some 70–80 prisoners. The others fled to the mountain to avoid being surrounded. A Hessian officer noted that Stirling had his horse shot from under him and "General Maxwell was almost captured by the Hessian grenadiers, missing him only by a hair's breadth." Grapeshot from the Continental Army's cannons took its toll, but the Crown forces had overwhelming numbers and firepower, compelling Stirling to give orders "to Leave the Ground." Maxwell and his troops retreated to Westfield. The Crown forces headed in the same direction and were "continuously harassed by shots from single detachments, which were hidden in the bushes." The day was very hot and the soldiers found it difficult to continue their march. The intense heat and the long march claimed almost as many casualties from sunstroke as from the snipers, particularly among the more heavily clad and equipped Hessians.[419]

The Continentals retreated to the mountain at night. The Crown forces stayed at Westfield and plundered and burned the houses in the Westfield area before returning to Amboy unmolested. They began to cross over to Staten Island at 10 AM on Monday, June 30. Lord Cornwallis's rear guard crossed at 2 PM without any sign of the Continentals. By June 30, 1777, "the Province of New Jersey was entirely evacuated by the King's Troops."[420]

There are no accurate figures for the losses in this engagement which lasted an hour and a half. Both sides greatly exaggerated the casualties. Captain Karl Friedrich Hieronymus, Freiherr von Münchhausen (1720–1797) claimed a total of 400 Continental losses. The British claimed killing or wounding 100 Whigs and capturing 70 prisoners while suffering only 70 casualties on their side. Although we have no accurate records of casualties, we know that the Congressional troops lost three small but valuable French brass guns. Most conservative estimates are 20 killed, 40 wounded, and three field pieces lost for the Congressional forces and about 50 total casualties for the Crown forces.[421]

Hoboken

Bayard's Mill (June 27, 1777; Aug. 26, 1780)
Hoebuck (June 27, 1777, Mar. 28, 1778; July 8, 1778; Aug. 29, 1778; Sept. 5, 1778; Mar. 27, 1779; Apr. 17, 1779; Oct. 18, 1780)

Hoebuck is now Hoboken.

A party of about 40 Whigs raided Colonel William Bayard's (d. 1801) Mill near Hoebuck Ferry on Friday morning, June 27, 1777 and took some cattle. They were pursued by a detachment of the 57th Regiment stationed at Paulus Hook.[422]

★ A party of about 30 men from Lieutenant Colonel Abraham Van Buskirk's (1750–1783) corps of Loyalists stationed at Hoebuck went as far as Closter to steal horses and to rob the inhabitants on Saturday night, March 28, 1778. They were attacked and put to flight by Lieutenant John Huyler and 9 militiamen. They left their plunder behind them along with Ensign Peter Meyer dead on the field. Another officer was wounded in the arm. Lieutenant Wiert Banta (1753-1834) was shot through the knee.[423]

★ Colonel Stephen Moylan (1734–1811) and a party of his Continental light dragoons were foraging at Hoebuck on Wednesday, July 8, 1778. They captured a good amount of cattle and stores.[424]

★ A party of Whigs laying in ambush in the Meadows fired on a small boat from Kingsbridge as it passed close to the Jersey shore on Saturday, August 29 or September 5, 1778. They wounded some of the people in the boat which headed to shore. They captured the crew and burned the boat.[425]

★ A detachment of Lieutenant Colonel Abraham Van Buskirk's (1750–1783) regiment captured four privates: one of Colonel George Baylor's (1752–1784) light-horsemen, one Continental, and two militiamen in a raid. The prisoners were brought to Hoebuck on Saturday, March 27, 1779.[426]

★ A gang of Loyalist robbers stole 20 horses from the neighborhood of Pompton on Saturday, April 17, 1779. Some young men pursued them closely and recovered 11 of the horses. "The other 9 were carried off to the original den of thieves, at New-York." Four of the young men pursued the robbers as far as Hoebuck. Two of them went down a bank on the river side. One of them proceeded to examine a blockhouse in which he saw one of the robbers. He had a pistol in his hand and a carbine lying on each side of him. The young man rushed to the door, shot the robber dead, and took the carbines and pistol.

The discharge of the firelock brought the soldiers. The two young men loaded their weapons and the two carbines and prepared for a fight. They discharged their four pieces within about 60 yards of their attackers and put them to flight. The young men returned home safely.[427]

★ Another band came three years later on Saturday, August 26, 1780. They burned Bayard's new house and barn at Castle Point, on the north end of Hoebuck, and destroyed all the forage and timber. They then set fire to the grass, parched by the summer heat. The fire raged for two days and completely destroyed one of the most valuable orchards. Bayard's property was confiscated and sold to John Stevens (1749–1838) in March 1781.[428]

★ Lieutenant Seth Raymond of the New Jersey Militia went to Hoebuck with 20 men and captured six Loyalists and killed one around October 18, 1780.[429]

Shrewsbury (Oct. 18, 1776; Jan. 15, 1777; Feb. 12, 1777; Oct. 3, 1777; Jan. 26, 1779; Apr. 26, 1779; June 10, 1779; July 16, 1779; second week of Aug. 1779; Mar. 30, 1780; Apr. 24, 1780; Apr. 30, 1780; July 28, 1780; May 21 1781; July 26, 1781)

Red Bank (Apr. 26, 1779; June 9, 1780)

Tinton Falls (Apr. 26, 1779; June 9, 1779; last week in Mar. 1780)

Navesink (Feb. 13, 1777; June 9, 1779)

Shrewsbury Township (Mar. 30, 1782)

> Red Bank is in Eastern New Jersey about 1.5 miles north of Shrewsbury and about 14 miles northeast of the Monmouth battlefield. It should not be confused with the Red Bank which was the site of Fort Mercer, on the Jersey side of the Delaware River southeast of Philadelphia.
>
> Tinton Falls is 2.5 miles southwest of Shrewsbury. It contained about 25 dwellings, a furnace, a grist mill and a saw mill. The Grist Mill restaurant now occupies the site of the Tinton Falls mill which burned several times, so the foundation is possibly all that remains of the original structure. The building is located at the northeast corner of the intersection of Sycamore and Tinton Avenues. The Tinton Spring, a large natural spring which Native American people believed to be therapeutic, is a few hundred paces northwest from the Tinton Falls on a branch of the Navesink River.
>
> Shrewsbury Township is between Shrewsbury and Tinton Falls.

Colonel John Glover's (1732–1797), Colonel Joseph Reed's (1741–1785) and Colonel William Shepard's (1737–1817) Massachusetts regiments, under Colonel Glover, advanced under cover to meet the Crown forces at Shrewsbury on Friday, October 18, 1776. Colonel Shepard was well-covered under a wall. His regiment gave the British grenadiers (see Photo NJ-10) and infantry an unexpected heavy fire at 30 or 40 yards, followed by a second and a third volley which broke their ranks and sent them fleeing in confusion. They returned with field pieces and outflanked the Continentals, forcing them to retreat a short distance. The Continentals rallied and held their ground against the cannonade. They lost about 30 or 40 killed and wounded. Two deserters reported that the Crown forces lost between 700 and 1,000 and that General William Howe (1732–1786) had his leg shattered by a cannonball in the cannonade after the battle. The ball also killed a soldier standing near him.[430]

Monmouth County was bitterly divided over the American War for Independence. Many prominent Loyalists had their property confiscated during the war and afterwards. Roving bands scourged Monmouth County throughout the winter of 1778 and spring of 1779.

Loyalists from Sandy Hook destroyed the salt works at Shrewsbury on Wednesday, January 15, 1777. Private Amon Davis (d. 1777) of the Cumberland County Militia was killed.[431]

★ Colonel William Erskine (1728–1795) attacked Congressional troops in their quarters on Wednesday, February 12, 1777. He killed many of them and took 70 prisoners.[432]

★ Feb. 13, 1777 see **Amboy.**

★ Captain John Taylor, the Loyalist commander at the Sandy Hook lighthouse, went in search of some light horsemen that he heard were at Shrewsbury. He set out on Friday morning, October 3, 1777 and soon fell in with Captain John Dennis and his troop of light horsemen and a party of militiamen. A smart firing ensued and the light horsemen and militiamen were pushed back. Captain Taylor had one soldier wounded in the thigh after the ball went through the captain's coat. Captain Dennis was wounded and captured along with six of his men. They were sent to New York City the following day.[433]

★ A band of Loyalists called "Pine-Banditti" because they lived in caves in the pines, had been terrorizing the inhabitants of Monmouth County for some time. Captain Benjamin Dennis and a party of his militiamen went in pursuit of three of the most noted of them [Stephen Bourke (d. 1779), alias Emmans, Stephen West (d. 1779) and Ezekiel Williams (d. 1779)] on Tuesday evening, January 26, 1779. They caught up with them at Rock Pond in Shrewsbury on the eve of setting off for New York to sell their plunder. The militiamen killed the banditti on the spot.[434]

★ Captain Patrick Ferguson (1744–1780) and a force of 600 to 700 Regulars came up the Navesink River and landed about half a mile below Red Bank, in Monmouth County, about 1 mile from Shrewsbury, about 4:30 AM on Monday, April 26, 1779. The Regulars landed 400 men at Painter's Point at Shoal Harbor and about 40 of them marched to Shrewsbury and Tinton Falls while the rest went about half a mile to the west to cut off the retreat of nearly 300 Congressional troops posted there. The first division, which landed at Shoal Harbor, marched to Middletown where they arrived at daybreak. The other division went into the Shrewsbury River in flat-bottomed boats and landed at Red Bank, and then proceeded to Tinton Falls.

Lieutenant Colonel Benjamin Ford (d. 1781), when he learned of their landing, sent a detachment of 30 men under Captain Beall to observe their movements and to delay their march toward Tinton Falls which was assumed to be their primary target. The militia arrived at the bridge before the Regulars. Outnumbered about three to one, the militiamen retreated to Colts Neck to wait for reinforcements. The Regulars pursued Colonel Ford's troops, about 400 yards ahead of them, to the Falls, firing all the way, but could not overtake them. Unable to cut off the militia's retreat, they halted at Tinton Falls where they burned two houses belonging to militia officers and destroyed everything that they could in the other houses. They broke every pane of glass in all the windows. They then plundered and destroyed all the furniture they found and set fire to several houses. Some of the houses burned to the ground while others were extinguished by the inhabitants before they had suffered much damage.

The party which had landed at Shrewsbury crossed the river and went to Middletown where they arrived around midday and joined with the other division. They sent their boats around to the bay shore, near Harber's plantation. They had 13 sloops waiting there to take them off. Captain Hubbard Daniel Burrows (1739–1781), who had mustered 12 men, led the Crown troops to believe that they were surrounded by the militia at 8 PM. They remained in the village until 3 AM when they began to retreat. Captain Burrows and three other men kept a constant fire upon them for 2 miles when Colonel Asher Holmes (1740–1808) and 60 New Jersey militiamen came to reinforce him.

The raiders plundered the inhabitants and burned several houses and barns along their way. The militiamen pursued the enemy who boarded their boats at sunset and set sail immediately for New York. The militiamen had two men slightly wounded. The Crown troops left three dead behind and carried off their wounded, probably about 15.[435]

★ The Regulars returned to Shrewsbury, plundering all the way to Colonel Breeze's house. They robbed him of all his money and most of his plate. They plundered Justice Josiah Holmes's (d. 1790) house and destroyed everything they could lay their hands upon. They then withdrew to their boats at Red Bank with all the horses, sheep, and cattle they could find. Captain Beall's party harassed the raiders and re-took most of the stock.

Colonel Asher Holmes and his militiamen kept on the flanks of the Regulars who crossed over to Middleton where they stayed until evening. They joined a division of two Crown regiments, about 1,000 men, commanded by General Cortlandt Skinner (1728–1799). They burned a house and barn and plundered some of the inhabitants. Colonel Holmes had, by this time, assembled 140 militiamen who drove the raiders to their boats near the Gut dividing the Highlands from Sandy Hook. They boarded their boats at sunset and set sail immediately for New York. The militiamen had two men slightly wounded and killed one Regular, wounded about 15, and took another prisoner. The Regulars took several prisoners, some cattle and horses.[436]

See also **Middletown.**

★ A party of New Jersey Volunteers went down to Sandy Hook on Tuesday, June 9, 1779. A small detachment of Colonel Joseph Barton's regiment of Volunteers joined them there. The band of 56 Loyalists proceeded to the Gut, about 4 miles away. However, the boats failed to arrive due to the high winds; so the troops returned to the lighthouse. They set out again the following day and got as far as Tinton Falls, about 10 miles from the landing, where they halted about daybreak. They were near the militia headquarters at the back of the town but did not know which house the main guard occupied. So they surrounded three houses at the same time.

Captain Hayden, of General Cortlandt Skinner's regiment, proceeded to Captain Richard McKnight's house. Lieutenant James Moody (1744–1809), a member of the First Battalion of General Cortlandt Skinner's (1728–1799) Royal Greens went to Colonel Daniel Hendrickson's (1736–1797) house. Lieutenant Throgmorton went to Captain John Chadwick's (d. 1779).

Lieutenant Moody's party consisted of about 16 of his own men and six men and some guides under his friend, Mr. Hutchinson. They marched from Sandy Hook to Shrewsbury on Thursday, June 10, 1779. They eluded a Continental guard and arrived at a place called The Falls (Tinton Falls). All three parties arrived at the main guard's location about the same time but missed them because they were out scouting.

Lieutenant Moody's party captured Colonel Hendrickson, who secretly stored guns, gunpowder, flour and grains and other mill products for the Continental Army; Lieutenant Colonel Auke Wyckoff (1748–1820); Captains John Chadwick and Richard McKnight; and several privates. Going 1 mile farther, they took a Major Hendrick Vanbrunt.[437]

The raiding party collected about 30 horses, some sheep and horned cattle and destroyed a considerable magazine of powder and arms without damaging any private property. Mr. Hutchinson was charged with guarding the prisoners and whatever public stores they managed to plunder. Moody and his men covered the rear to defend them.

About 30 New Jersey militiamen quickly mustered and made some resistance but they were repulsed, losing two men killed (Captain Chadwick and Lieutenant Hendrickson) and 10 wounded. Lieutenant Moody placed his prisoners between his party and the militiamen to screen his men. Captain Chadwick and Lieutenant Hendrickson broke away and joined their friends and charged the Loyalists in another attack. Captain Chadwick had barely fired his first shot when a bullet struck him, killing him almost instantly.

As the Loyalists returned to their boats about 9 o'clock Friday morning, the militiamen harassed them as they retreated to the water side at Jumping-Point Inlet. Lieutenant Moody's Loyalists kept up a smart fire, checking and retarding the militia until Mr. Hutchinson's party got a considerable distance ahead with their booty. The party then advanced to the shore at Black Point (Sea Bright) where the militiamen could not flank them. The militia, now numbering 40 after the arrival of 10 reinforcements, entered into a warm engagement. Mr. Hutchinson and another man crossed the Inlet, behind which they had taken shelter, and came to Lieutenant Moody's assistance. The skirmish lasted for three quarters of an hour until the militia captain received two musket balls and fell. After expending all their ammunition—more than 80 rounds of cartridges—the Loyalists resorted to a bayonet charge. Only 10 men, three of whom were not wounded, could follow their leader in the charge. They pushed the militiamen back, killing three, wounding 14, and capturing seven.

Exhausted by a long harassed march in intensely hot weather, the Loyalists could not pursue. They managed to escape to New York with their plunder which sold for more than £500, which Moody gave to his men as a reward for meritorious service and good behavior.

The Loyalists then brought off their prisoners and a considerable number of cattle, sheep, and other stock.

After they had crossed the river, the Loyalists observed a man with a flag riding to ask permission to carry off the dead and wounded. Permission was granted and the man with the flag informed them that the entire party who were engaged were killed or wounded.[438]

★ About the same time, a northeast storm drove a British galley ashore near Shrewsbury. This leaky vessel had been ordered back to New York when she reached the eastern part of Long Island. Her crew of 30 men were made prisoners.[439]

★ A party of 50 African Americans and Loyalists plundered the inhabitants of nearly 80 head of cattle, 20 horses, clothing, and household furniture on Friday night, July 16, 1779. They also captured William Brindley and Elihu Cook.[440]

★ Two militia captains left Princeton to purchase some goods at Shrewsbury during the second week of August 1779. One of them was killed on the return trip.[441]

★ A party of Crown troops landed at Tinton Falls in Monmouth County the last week in March 1780. They took six or seven inhabitants prisoners. Another small party of Loyalists landed at Middletown and captured Mr. Browne who had been exchanged three days earlier and had just returned home.[443]

★ A party of African Americans and Loyalists from Sandy Hook landed at Shrewsbury to plunder on Thursday, March 30, 1780. Mr. John Russell (d. 1780) attempted to make some resistance, shot one of the ring-leaders, and was killed. His grandson had five musket balls shot through him and survived. The raiders captured Captain Warner, of the privateer brig *Elizabeth* and later released him. They also took nine militiamen prisoners, including Captain James Green (1728–1809 or 1738–1828) and Ensign John Morris (ca. 1740–1789).[444]

★ A party of New Jersey militiamen was patrolling the roads at Shrewsbury on Monday night, April 24, 1780 when they were attacked by several people believed to be from Sandy Hook. The Loyalists killed two of the militiamen and withdrew. A party of Loyalists and African Americans attacked both civilians and militiamen on Sunday, April 30, 1780 and captured two.[445]

★ June 9, 1780 see **Monmouth County.**

★ The militia captured several prisoners during a raid on Friday, July 28, 1780.

★ On Monday night, May 21, 1781, a party of New Jersey militia was patrolling the roads at Shrewsbury when they were attacked by several persons believed to be Loyalists from Sandy Hook. Two of the militiamen were killed.[446]

★ Captain Maffet, commander of a Philadelphia whaleboat (see Photo NJ-1), captured a sloop from New York off Long Beach on Thursday, July 26, 1781. The vessel was laden with fish. Captain Maffet also captured three Loyalist boats off Shrewsbury Point. These vessels had 30 plundered sheep and 23 sheep-stealers aboard.[447]

★ A party of militia light horsemen surprised Philip White (d. 1782), a Loyalist, at Shrewsbury on Saturday, March 30, 1782. White laid down his arms as a sign of surrender but took up his weapon again and killed a son of Colonel Daniel Hendrickson (1736–1797). The light horsemen captured him and brought him from Colts Neck to Freehold. Along the way, White tried to escape. The guard called on him several times to surrender but be continued running. White jumped into a bog that the horses could not cross and received a stroke in the head with a sword. He died instantly.[448]

Van Veghten's (Van Vechten) Bridge, raid (Oct. 26, 1779)
Hillsborough (Oct. 26, 1779)
South River Bridge (Oct. 26, 1779)

> Hillsborough and Van Veghten's (Van Vechten) Bridge are west of New Brunswick. The Van Veghten house (see Photo NJ-30), at the end of Van Veghten Road, off Finderne Avenue in Bridgewater, served as headquarters for Major General Nathanael Greene (1742–1786) and Brigadier General "Mad Anthony" Wayne (1745–1796) during the second encampment at Middlebrook. Wayne's regiment also camped on the house grounds. The current bridge over the Raritan River on Finderne Avenue (Route 533) is very near the site of Van Veghten's Bridge.

Lieutenant Colonel John Graves Simcoe (1752–1806) and 100 Queen's Rangers (Simcoe states that the command consisted of 22 of Buck's Dragoons, 46 of the Ranger hussars and a few others as guards) were on a raid from Perth Amboy through Woodbridge, Quibbletown, and Bound Brook on Sunday, October 24, 1779 (Simcoe's Journal gives the date as the 26th, probably the correct date) to destroy the boats collected at Van Veghten's Bridge and to take Governor William Livingston (1723–1790) prisoner.

Photo NJ-30. Van Veghten house in Bridgewater, served as headquarters for Major General Nathanael Greene and Brigadier General "Mad Anthony" Wayne during the second encampment at Middlebrook

The Rangers raided Van Veghten's Bridge on Tuesday, October 26, 1779. They burned boats being transported to General George Washington's (1732–1799) camp and a building containing army supplies. They also captured the personnel assigned to oversee the materiel. They then attacked the town of Hillsborough on their return, freed three Loyalist prisoners and burned the Somerset Courthouse. The raid drew out the militia who occasionally sniped at the raiders.

The raiders were later ambushed at the Battle of South River Bridge when Simcoe took a wrong turn in pursuit of the militia. He fell into an ambush where he and three of his men were captured. Only one militiaman was killed in the engagement.

See **Somerset.**

Newark (Nov. 28, 1776; Jan. 5, 1777; Apr. 16, 1777; Jan. 25, 1780; Feb. 19, 1780; May 16, 1780; May 26, 1780; July 17, 1780; Aug. 21, 1780; Nov. 21, 1780; Mar. 29, 1781; Aug. 15, 1781; Sept. 2, 1781)

> Military Park (Broad Street and Park Place) was a parade ground for the militia. General George Washington's (1732–1799) troops camped here on their retreat through New Jersey in 1776. Thomas Paine (1737–1809) supposedly began writing *The Crisis* here. *The Wars of America*, a giant sculpture by Gutzon Borglum (1867–1941), the designer of Mount Rushmore, is in the park.
>
>　Trinity Episcopal Church (now Trinity Cathedral), at the north end of Military Park, was a center for Loyalists. Both armies occupied it. Congressional troops damaged it so badly that the congregation petitioned Congress for war reparations and received them. The First Presbyterian Church (840 Broad Street), a center for Congressional forces, also suffered severe damage.

Washington Park, on Broad Street three blocks north of Military Park, was the site of the first Newark Academy which was the target of the Crown forces when they attacked on January 25, 1780. The academy supposedly stored arms and served as a barracks for Continental troops. The Crown forces burned the building in a surprise night raid. A plaque on a boulder in the park tells the story. The park also has a large bronze map of General Washington's retreat across New Jersey. Philips Park (Elmwood Avenue and Elwood Place) has a monument marking the site of his encampments.

Ann Van Wagenen, the mistress of Plume House (470 Broad Street at State Street), drove some Hessian pillagers from her property during one of their foraging parties. On another occasion, she locked a Hessian soldier in her ice house.

On Thursday morning, November 28, 1776, after the fall of forts Washington and Lee, the advance guard of General Charles Cornwallis's (1738–1805) army entered Newark as the rear of General George Washington's (1732–1799) army of less than 3,500 men left it.

★ On Sunday, January 5, 1777, Brigadier General William Maxwell (1733–1796) and his militia came down from the Short Hills and compelled the British to evacuate Newark. They skirmished at Springfield, drove them out of Elizabethtown and fought them for a few hours at Spanktown. The militiamen killed or wounded eight or ten Waldeckers and captured 39 or 40 prisoners at Springfield.[449]

See also **Springfield.**

★ A party of armed Loyalists arrived near Newark on Wednesday, April 16, 1777. The militia attacked them, killed a captain and two privates. The rest of the party fled.[450]

★ Judge Joseph Hedden, of Newark, issued a mandate in the summer of 1777 to banish a woman and her children because her husband was a Loyalist. When the guards he sent to execute his order arrived at the woman's house 6 miles from Newark, they found her very weak and unable to travel, as she had given birth to twins about fourteen days earlier. The guards, moved with compassion for her, did not execute their orders and returned without the woman.

Judge Hedden issued a new decree to have her brought to Newark regardless of her condition and then to be sent to Bergen. The captain of the guard protested that executing the order would result in the woman's death. Judge Hedden supposedly replied: "Let her die. There will be one damned Tory less."

The guard was sent a second time and brought the woman and her children to Newark in a wagon. She fainted, through weakness, on the wagon and was in such a deplorable condition when she arrived in Newark that she elicited the compassion of the residents. Some women enabled her to go through the last stage of her journey to Bergen the next day. The woman and her twins died there a short while later.[451]

★ January 25, 1780 see **Elizabethtown.**

★ A party of about 50 Crown troops invaded Newark about midnight on Saturday, February 19, 1780. They plundered several head of cattle and took two inhabitants prisoners. The alarm guns were fired to alert the militia who assembled so quickly that the raiders abandoned their cattle and retreated.[452]

★ A detachment of 150 men from the British 57th Regiment under Major Charles Brownlow landed at Newark Meadows at 2 AM on Saturday, May 16, 1780 to surprise, a small body of Congressional troops quartered in the town. They encountered a small patrol close to the town, one of whom ran off to give the alarm. This allowed most of them to escape, except for 33, four of whom were killed. The rest were taken prisoners. Major Brownlow only lost four men wounded.[453]

★ About 200 to 270 men of the 57th Regiment returned to Newark from Staten Island with one field piece about daybreak on Friday, May 26, 1780. They plundered some of the inhabitants and took about 20 of them prisoners. They tried to burn the jail, but some woman put it out. Captain Reading and a few militiamen fired on them from behind fences and buildings and pushed their rear and attacked their flanks very hard until they reached their boats and embarked. The militiamen wounded a few soldiers but lost a sergeant, a corporal and four men taken prisoners as well as two men of the Connecticut line. The sergeant was left behind to conduct some men returning from patrol to the main body, but he remained too long. Captain George Knox, who commanded the forlorn hope in the attack of Stony Point, was wounded in the face and had part of his tongue shot away and his jaw broken. He and another man were the only wounded.[454]

★ Lieutenant Ebenezer Ward and five Loyalists captured four prisoners at Newark on Monday evening, July 17, 1780. They were imprisoned in the Sugar House.[455]

★ Captain William Harding and about 40 Loyalists from the Refugee Post on Bergen Neck went to Newark on Monday, August 21, 1780. They took four prisoners and about 30 cattle which were brought to Fort DeLancey.[456]

★ About 100 New York Loyalists under Captain Thomas Ward embarked in two flat bottomed boats and one gunboat and proceeded to Roger's Ferry where they landed about 1 AM on Tuesday, November 21, 1780. They headed toward Newark with one 3-pounder which they posted on a hill halfway between the ferry and the town. They left "a number of musketeers to cover it and secure their return to their vessels, where they left one gun-boat to cover their passage over the marsh, should the enemy pursue them." Captain Ward then advanced at the head of 50 men. He got within 400 yards of the guard house undiscovered when Captain MacMichael and the advance party encountered a patrol which immediately fired on them. The Loyalists charged but found themselves flanked by men posted in different houses. They maintained their post in the center of town until their cannon was brought up.

The Loyalists obeyed strict orders against entering a house or plundering. When they first entered the town, some of Colonel Philip Van Cortlandt's (1749–1831) militiamen fired upon them from the upper windows of Mr. Robert Neil's house. A party of Loyalists set fire to the lower part of the house and the flames consumed the whole building but the occupants escaped.

Captain MacMichael brought up his 3-pounder and fired a few rounds of grapeshot which dispersed the Congressional troops for a little while. They took possession of the town for an hour and collected a number of hogs, cattle and sheep. Frustrated in their purpose, they retreated to their boats, as they expected the militiamen posted at Cranetown would march toward them.

Before they got out of town, they found a body of militiamen on their right flank trying to cut off their retreat. Meanwhile, others kept up a scattering fire at their rear. They retreated some distance when another party appeared on their left. These troops found it impossible to cut off their retreat, so they closed upon the flanks and the rear of the Loyalists who were forced to form a square to protect their field piece. They proceeded in this manner, keeping up a constant fire, until they got to their boats. They retook 89 head of cattle and most of the hogs and sheep along with two prisoners.

A little while later, the Congressional troops brought a 6-pounder to the edge of the marsh and kept up a constant fire upon them during their re-embarkation. Musketmen lined the banks of the river to harass the Loyalists but the troops in the gunboat kept them at such a distance that they did little damage. The Loyalists had six men wounded and two missing. They killed three and wounded seven, excluding those supposed to have been burned at Neil's house.[457]

★ A party of Crown troops from New York, dressed as peasants and impersonating New Jersey militiamen, came to the ferry nearly opposite Josiah Hornblower's (1729–1809) house in Essex county on Thursday, March 29, 1781. They called for the boat to carry them over. When the ferryman arrived, he observed G. R. (Georgius Rex or King George) on their cartridge boxes and let the boat flow downstream with the tide to give a hint to Mr. Hornblower's family that all was not right. Mr. Hornblower, Speaker of the Assembly, escaped out of the back door a few minutes before the kidnappers came in the front. Two of the raiders pursued Mr. Hornblower but were themselves captured. The others escaped after taking Mr. Hornblower's son-in-law, Mr. Cape, prisoner.[458]

★ A party of about 50 Loyalists from Bergen came to Newark before daybreak on Wednesday, August 15, 1781. They captured a sentinel but, as they approached a second sentinel, he fired on the Loyalists, killing one of them. The raiders took three inhabitants and about 30 head of cattle. The inhabitants returned home soon afterward.[459]

★ Captain Thomas Ward and "a party of black and white Negroes" came to Newark Neck on Sunday night, September 2, 1781. They concealed themselves until the following morning in order to kidnap people going into the meadows. They captured five or six prisoners and a number of cows before being discovered. The militiamen gathered and captured two of the raiders. The rest of the party embarked in a hurry under cover of their gunboats.[460]

Newark Bay (Nov. 29, 1781; May 29, 1782; June 2, 1782; Jan. 4, 1783)
See also **Elizabeth.**

A party under Captain Baker Hendricks (1756–1789) sailed to Newark Bay in a whaleboat (see Photo NJ-1) on Thursday, November 29, 1781. They boarded two boats and stripped them and took one man prisoner.[461]

★ Captain Peter Sanford's New Jersey militiamen attacked a Loyalist force under Captain McMichael in Newark Bay on Wednesday, May 29, 1782. They killed one and captured three and lost only one wounded.

★ The following Sunday, June 2, Captain Peter Sanford (ca. 1755–1812) captured Captain McMichael and two others in Newark Bay.[462]

★ Some people from Staten Island captured two whaleboats from Woodbridge and New Brunswick in or near Newark Bay on Saturday, January 4, 1783.

★ The same day, Captain Isaac Burton's privateer *Fair American* brought Captain Samuel Mansfield's (1757–1810) brig *Speedwell* into New York. The *Speedwell* was bound from Nantes to Baltimore with a cargo of dry goods. She was six weeks out of port when she was captured on Monday, December 30, 1782. The HMS *Lion* also brought in a brig bound from Amsterdam to Philadelphia the same day.[463]

Elizabeth

Elizabethtown (July 2, 1776; July 4, 1776; July 13, 1776; July 24, 1776; Aug. 25, 1776; Sept. 24, 1776; Jan. 6, 1777; Jan. 8, 1777; Feb. 24, 1777; Feb. 27, 1777; Mar. 6, 1777; Aug. 19, 1777; Aug. 21, 22, 1777; Sept. 11-12, 1777; Sept. 14, 1777; Sept. 15, 1777; Oct. 12, 1777; Mar. 1778; Sept. 28, 1778; Feb. 24, 25, 1779; Feb. 27, 1779; June 6, 1779; Aug. 16, 1779; Oct. 14, 1779; Jan. 25, 1780; Jan. 30, 1780; Feb. 10, 1780;

Mar. 24, 1780; June 7, 8, 1780; June 14, 15, 1780; June 23, 1780; Nov. 4, 1780; Nov. 14, 1780; Dec. 14, 1780; Jan. 21, 1781; Jan. 25, 1781; Feb. 23, 1781; Mar. 26, 1781; June 2, 1781; June 29, 1781; July 21, 1781; Sept. 17, 1781; Nov. 24, 1781; Nov. 29, 1781; Dec. 6, 1781; Dec. 14, 1781; Feb. 1, 1782; Feb. 23, 1782)

Trembley Point (Mar. 1778; June 26 or 29, 1781)

Halstead's Point (Feb. 13, 1780; June 19, 1779; Apr. 23, 1780; Apr. 21, 1781; Dec. 1, 1781; Dec. 15, 1781)

Elizabethtown Point (June 13, 1777; Aug. 14, 1777; June 6, 1780; May 4, 1781 Mar. 10, 1782)

Elizabethtown was in Essex County during the American War for Independence. It is now in Union County, created in 1857. During the 18th century, Elizabethtown included nearly the whole of present Union County. The towns of Union, Springfield, New Providence, Westfield, Plainfield, Rahway, Linden, and Clark were organized later.

The Minuteman Monument (Elizabeth Avenue at Bank Square) (see Photo NJ-31) commemorates the Battles of Connecticut Farms and Springfield that took place in Union County between June 7 and 23, 1780. It supposedly occupies the site where the first shots were fired at daybreak on June 7 and where British General Sterling (d. 1780) fell. Brigadier General Edward Hand (1744–1802) attacked the 22nd Regiment here after their retreat from Springfield and drove them back to their main position. Many skirmishes occurred in this area as the Crown forces retreated to Staten Island on June 23, 1780.

The First Presbyterian Church (Broad Street and Caldwell Place) was Reverend James Caldwell's (1734–1781) church. He became known as the "high priest of the Revolution" by the Loyalists and as the "fighting parson" by the Whigs. A small iron plaque topped by a man on horseback, on the grounds of the current church, marks the site of the Old Academy. Aaron Burr (1756–1836) and Alexander Hamilton (1755–1804) both attended the Academy here. Lieutenant Colonel Francis Barber 1750–1783), of the 3rd New Jersey Regiment, started his career here as the school master. He was New Jersey's soldier most mentioned in dispatches. He died accidentally at the New Windsor Cantonment, New York, when a wood cutting party felled a tree on him and his horse.

The cemetery next to the church has a monument to Rev. James Caldwell and his wife Hannah (see Photo NJ-22). Her death is depicted on the Union County seal. The Union County Courthouse is adjacent to the cemetery at 2 Broad Street. It occupies the site of the old courthouse which the Crown forces burned and is supposedly haunted by the ghost of Hannah Caldwell (d. 1780).

The Caldwell parsonage is located at 909 Caldwell Ave. in Union. The Presbyterian Church was constructed in 1782 on the grounds of the original 1730 parsonage that was burned by the Crown forces.

Other historic figures from Elizabeth include William Livingston (1723–1790) who, as governor of New Jersey (1776–1790), lived at Liberty Hall, now known as Ursino; and General Winfield Scott (1786–1866), the 1852 Whig presidential candidate.

Although the city suffered many attacks and skirmishes during the American War for Independence, nearly two dozen pre-Revolutionary buildings remain. Identified by plaques, several of these are in the 1000 and 1100 blocks of East Jersey Street.

Photo NJ-31. *Minuteman Monument, Elizabeth commemorates the Battles of Connecticut Farms and Springfield that took place in Union County between June 7 and 23, 1780. It supposedly occupies the site where the first shots were fired at daybreak on June 7 and where British General Sterling fell. Brigadier General Edward Hand (1744–1802) attacked the 22nd Regiment here after their retreat from Springfield and drove them back to their main position.*

The Bonnell House, at 1045 East Jersey Street, dates from about 1682 and is one of the oldest structures in Elizabeth.

Boxwood Hall (1073 East Jersey Street) (see Photo NJ-32) was the home of Elias Boudinot, Jr. (1740–1821), president of the Continental Congress from 1772 to 1795 and signer of the Treaty of Peace with Great Britain. It was built in the 1750s. Alexander Hamilton also stayed here while attending the Academy. Boudinot entertained George Washington in the mansion on April 23, 1789, en route to his presidential inauguration in New York City.

Trembley's Point was about 3 miles from Elizabethtown, now Elizabeth.

When the British occupied Staten Island without opposition on Tuesday, July 2, 1776, the island became a nest for Loyalists and Elizabethtown was brought into the forefront of the field of conflict. The day after their landing, some troops appeared on the western shore of the island opposite Elizabethtown Point. When an alarm brought out the countrymen, the troops retreated, took up the floor of the drawbridge in the salt meadows, and immediately began constructing defenses.[464]

★ Between 10 and 11 AM on July 2, 1776, four British men-of-war, including the HMS *Phoenix, Greyhound,* and *Rose,* and several tenders came through the Narrows and anchored near the Watering Place on Staten Island. That afternoon, they fired several shots at Whigs on shore.[465]

★ About daybreak on Thursday, July 4, 1776, some Rebels attacked a British sloop of eight carriage guns as she lay in the river which separates Staten Island from the

Photo NJ-32. Boxwood Hall, home of Elias Boudinot, president of the Continental Congress from 1772 to 1795 and signer of the Treaty of Peace with Great Britain

mainland. They placed two 9-pounders on Bergen Point and soon forced the crew to abandon ship. The sloop was disabled and, judging by the shrieks, several crewmen must have been killed or wounded.[466]

★ Two young men from Elizabethtown crossed the river in a canoe and fired at the Regulars on July 4, 1776. This drew other troops from the woods, forcing the men to cross the river again. Around midnight, a British armed sloop of 14 guns approached Elizabethtown Point. Two 12-pounders on shore fired on her, killing a great number of men, setting her on fire, and completely destroying her. This occurred only a few hours after the adoption of the Declaration of Independence. Ten cannon were brought to Elizabethtown to prevent the Crown forces from landing and pillaging the town.[467]

★ The British attempted to cross from Staten Island to Elizabethtown on Wednesday, July 10, 1776, but withdrew when the militia assembled.[468]

★ About 5:30 PM on Saturday, July 13, 1776, Lieutenant Blenerhasset, of the 10th Regiment, was sent near Elizabethtown Point, to try to cut off one of the Rebel boats. He came too near and was fired upon with small arms and cannon from the redoubt and breastwork. The lieutenant was seriously wounded in the head, and one man slightly wounded in the leg and thigh.[469]

★ A lone rifleman crossed the river at Elizabethtown on Wednesday, July 24, 1776. He got within 15 yards of the British outpost and demanded them to surrender. He was shot in the head and died instantly.[470]

★ On Sunday afternoon, August 25, 1776, both sides cannonaded each other without doing any damage except disturbing the congregations at worship.

★ On Tuesday, September 24, 1776, four transports arrived at Elizabethtown with 420 Continental soldiers taken prisoners at Quebec the previous winter. They had been liberated on parole.[471]

★ The Continental Army marched from Pluckemin and arrived at Morristown on Monday, January 6, 1777. Brigadier General William Maxwell (1733–1796) marched toward Elizabethtown with a large body of Continental troops and militiamen and requested reinforcements. When two regiments from Woodbridge and Amboy arrived, they advanced and took possession of Elizabethtown and captured 150 prisoners, including 50 Waldeckers and 40 Highlanders quartered there. They also captured 50 baggage wagons fully loaded and a schooner with baggage and blankets on board. In addition, they destroyed all the boats there. About the same time, troops at Spanktown, about 5 miles from Woodbridge, secured 1,000 bushels of salt. When some Continentals attacked the Crown forces there, they sent for reinforcements from Woodbridge; but the Hessians refused to march because they heard the Continentals were very strong in that region. The British troops at Elizabethtown would not allow the Waldeckers to stand sentry at the outposts because several of them deserted.[472]

Captain Eliakim Littell (1744–1805) relates that:

> On the day that the British force abandoned Newark, which they had occupied as a garrison, and marched to Elizabeth Town, a company of Waldeckers was dispatched on some particular service towards the Connecticut Farms. Littell and his followers speedily discovered and followed them. Dividing his small force into two bodies, he placed one ambush in the rear, and appearing in front with the other, demanded an immediate surrender. The Germans wished to retrograde, but meeting with the party expressly concealed to impede their retreat, and briskly assailed in front, surrendered without firing a gun. The British general, exasperated by their capture, ordered out a body of Hessians to revenge the affront; but the superior knowledge of Littell and his associates enabling them to goad the enemy at various points with

spirited attacks, without any great degree of exposure, they were also driven into a swamp and compelled to surrender to inferior numbers. Mortified beyond measure at this second discomfiture, a troop of horse were ordered out; but they in turn were routed, and were only more fortunate than those that preceded them by being able, by the rapid movement of their horses, to escape pursuit. A Tory, to whom a considerable reward was offered for the performance of the service, now led 300 men to the house of Capt. Littell, who, believing he was securely pent up within, commenced a heavy discharge of musketry upon it from all sides. The captain, however, was not to be so easily entrapped, and while they were making preparations to storm the deserted dwelling they were attacked in the rear, being previously joined by another body of volunteers, and driven with precipitation from the field. Littell in the interim, with a part of his force had formed an ambuscade along a fence side, and perceiving the enemy slowly approaching, leveled and discharged his piece, and the commander fell. The British, unable, from the darkness of the night, to make any calculation with regard to the number of their opposers were intimidated, and sought safety in flight.[473]

While the numbers are somewhat exaggerated, this account is typical of the type of warfare conducted by the militia in this area.

★ The following day, the Continentals moved closer to the Crown troops to take advantage of a solar eclipse to attack the Hessians as soon as it began.[474]

★ Congressional forces retook Elizabethtown on Wednesday, January 8, 1777 at the end of the Jersey campaign.[475]

★ British Lieutenant Colonel Thomas Stirling (d. 1808) led a raid on Elizabethtown on Monday, February 24, 1777.[476]

★ Three days later, on the 27th, Major Robert Timpany (1742–1844) and 60 men raided Elizabethtown again. A body of militiamen attacked him. The Loyalists killed two or three men on the spot and captured four or five. Major Carl Leopold Baurmeister (1734–1803) claims they captured 30 prisoners. The raiders returned safely with 10 head of cattle and no casualties.[477]

★ A party of about 12 men went from Staten Island to Elizabethtown Point on Friday, June 13, 1777. A band of Whigs fired at them but were soon dispersed with one man dead and three wounded. The raiders took a new flat-bottomed boat capable of holding 100 men. One of the muskets went off accidentally and shot Peter Kingsland (1712–1777) in the head, killing him instantly.[478]

★ A party of New Jersey Volunteers raided Crane's Ferry near Elizabethtown Point on Thursday evening, August 14, 1777. They captured three militiamen without firing a gun.[479]

★ Colonel Edward Vaughan Dongan (1748–1777), Major Robert Drummond and a detachment of 60 men of the 3rd Battalion of New Jersey Royal Volunteers came over from Staten Island on Tuesday evening, August 19, 1777. They marched about 27 miles into the interior of the colony and captured 14 prisoners, 62 head of cattle, 9 horses, and 30 stand of arms. They destroyed some powder and shot, salt, rum and other articles they could not remove. On his return march to Amboy, Colonel Dongan posted two pickets there with several out sentries to observe enemy movements while the cattle were passing the ferry to Staten Island.

Dr. William Barnet (1728–1790), of Elizabethtown, and his light horsemen appeared on the heights near Amboy; but when they saw that the Loyalists were so well posted, they decided to keep their distance. To their mortification, they watched Colonel Dongan and all his men cross safely to Staten Island with their prisoners and cattle.[480]

★ Colonel Abraham Van Buskirk (1750–1783) was encamped near Decker's Ferry with his regiment of 250 Loyalists in mid-August 1777. Colonel Joseph Barton's regiment of equal number camped near the New Blazing Star Ferry. Colonel Edward Vaughan Dongan (1748–1777) and Lieutenant Colonel Isaac Allen (1741–1806) were camped near Amboy about 2 miles apart, each with about 100 men. The 55th (200 men) and about 100 men of the 27th British Regiments and two regiments of Anspachers (450 men each) and one of the Waldeckers (about 400) were encamped near the Watering Place, by their fortifications. There were also two small detachments of new recruits, one at Richmond, the other at Cuckolds Town.

Major General John Sullivan (1740–1795) intended to land on the west and north sides of Staten Island and to entrap the new recruits in their different camps. He decided that he could not force the other troops from their fortifications without cannon and would probably have to fight all the troops in and around New York which would come as reinforcements.

Sullivan's troops were 20 miles away from Staten Island and would be too tired to march that distance and execute a surprise attack. Moreover, their movements toward the island would alarm the residents of the area around Spanktown who would send messengers to the island. Nevertheless, General Sullivan determined to make as sudden and as fierce a march as possible.

He selected about 1,000 men from General William Smallwood's (1732–1792) and General De Boor's brigade and ordered them to march from Hanover to Elizabethtown at 2 PM on Thursday, August 21, 1777. They arrived at 10 PM and halted a short time to rest. Colonel Matthias Ogden (1754–1791) joined Smallwood and De Boor with his own and Colonel Elias Dayton's (1737–1807) regiment. They moved down to Halstead's Point, near the mouth of Morse's Creek, where they crossed over to Staten Island. Colonel Dayton and Colonel Ogden with their commands, and Colonel Field with the militia, crossed at the Old Blazing Star. The New Jersey Volunteers were posted in small detachments along the shore of the island from Decker's Ferry to the point opposite Amboy, about 15 miles. Colonels Ogden and Dayton fully and successfully carried out their part of the program.

Colonel Frederick Frelinghuysen (1753–1804) and 100 militiamen were to march from Elizabethtown in the evening and cross the river opposite a creek called the Fresh Kills. They would then head up the creek to attack at dawn. The other troops were to cross from Haley's Point. General Smallwood's brigade would attack Lieutenant Colonel Abraham Van Buskirk's (1750–1783) camp and General De Boor's brigade would attack Colonel Barton's regiment. The generals were both instructed to leave one regiment each on the main road to cover their rear and to arrest any fugitives.

General Sullivan managed to collect only six boats to make the crossing. He kept three for his men and sent the other three to Colonel Ogden. General Sullivan's troops crossed before daylight, undiscovered. As they marched, they heard a severe firing from Colonel Ogden's direction. It lasted about two minutes.

General Smallwood proceeded to Decker's Ferry; but his guide deceived him and led him to the wrong side of the enemy. Instead of being in their rear, he was in full front of them. This gave the Crown forces an opportunity to escape to their forts, leaving their colors and their tents standing. General Smallwood took the colors and destroyed the tents and the stores and burned about 35 tons of hay. He burned seven vessels laden with dry goods and killed a few men, wounded others as they ran off, and took two prisoners.

General Sullivan's troops marched briskly to Colonel Barton's quarters where the Loyalists were prepared for the attack.

General Sullivan's main body halted and formed ranks while Lieutenant Colonel Samuel Smith (1752–1839) and his men went around Colonel Barton's rear to prevent any escape. As the main body moved up to charge, the Crown forces threw down their arms and ran away. Colonel Smith's troops killed many of the fugitives but could not prevent them all from escaping, as the fugitives were well-acquainted with the creeks and marshes and eluded the Continentals. Several fugitives got into the boats moored at the ferry and crossed to the Jersey shore. The Continentals captured "a considerable number of arms, blankets, hats, cloaths, &c Col. Barton and about 40 privates were made prisoners."

General Sullivan's men returned to join General Smallwood. Together, they proceeded toward Colonel Ogden's position. As they heard nothing from that direction, General Sullivan concluded that Colonel Ogden routed the Crown forces and waited for General Sullivan who hastened his march as much as possible and sent a boat to order the boats at Halsey's Point to meet him at the Old Blazing Star Ferry. They arrived at the ferry at noon and found that Colonel Ogden had routed the enemy and taken the commander, three captains, one lieutenant, two ensigns and 80 privates prisoners, a large quantity of stores and a loaded sloop as well as a great number of horses and cattle.

Colonel Ogden's troops re-crossed the river. The boats from Halsey's Point had not arrived with the men's packs and provisions because they saw the sloop captured by Colonel Ogden coming up the sound and took her to be a tender. They ran the boats up the river preventing the messenger from finding them. General Sullivan began crossing the river as soon as possible with his three boats. He wanted to cross before the enemy collected their forces and attacked his rear with a superior force and cut off any retreat. The rear guard of 100 men, posted on a hill about 100 yards from the ferry, were just pushing the boats away from shore when Brigadier General John Campbell (d. 1806), commander of the King's troops on the Island, and General Cortlandt Skinner (1728–1799) arrived with a superior number of British troops and Anspachers to attack their rear. They expected no opposition from such a small party and advanced boldly. However, the Continental officers formed their ranks and "gave the enemy so warm a reception, that they were various times driven back in the greatest confusion." The Crown troops took heavy fire and executed a bayonet charge on the Continental flank and put them to flight.

Realizing the Crown forces were about to surround them, the rear guard retired to a hill about 500 feet to their rear. After a while, they retreated to another hill about 50 yards farther. They held their ground until they almost ran out of ammunition. Seeing the boats in the river not coming over and, with no other means of getting off the island, about 40 men surrendered themselves prisoners of war. Some of the remainder swam the river and landed safely on the Jersey shore. The others went to Amboy where some troops were sent to take them across.

If the boatmen had done their duty, not a man would have been lost. However, the Crown troops brought a field piece and a howitzer to play upon the water, frightening the boatmen so much that they refused to put ashore on either side of the river. General Sullivan ordered his men to fire upon them to force them over, but the boatmen rowed toward Amboy. The Crown forces picked up some stragglers and either took them prisoners or killed them. General Sullivan captured three colonels [Lieutenant Colonel Isaac Allen (1741–1806), Colonel Joseph Barton, Colonel Edward Vaughan Dongan

(1748–1777)], two majors, three captains, two lieutenants, two ensigns, one surgeon, one sergeant major, four sergeants, two corporals, two musicians, and about 130 privates and 28 Loyalists along with a British shallop in which the prisoners were sent over to the Jersey side. He estimated killing and wounding at least 400, destroyed their forts and vessels, and captured their arms, baggage, and a great number of cattle. General Sullivan reported 10 men killed and 15 wounded, two seriously. However, because of the deception of his guide, his rear detachments did not get the boats to return by the Old Star Ferry. These losses more than compensated for the advantages obtained by Colonels Ogden and Dayton. General Sullivan was ordered to join the main army at Wilmington, Delaware immediately afterward, leaving only a small force to guard the long New Jersey coastline.[481]

★ General Henry Clinton (1730–1795) led a foraging party into New Jersey on Thursday and Friday, September 11–12, 1777. The raid was intended to act as a diversion for General William Howe's (1732–1786) Philadelphia campaign.

★ The British killed Private Stephen Ward (d. 1777) in a raid at Elizabethtown on Sunday, September 14, 1777. The following day, they killed Captain Francis Locke (d. 1777) "shot through the body" during a skirmish. He was stripped to his shirt when his men came to get his body for burial the next day.[482]

★ The newspaper reported "smart firing" at a sloop in His Majesty's service stationed near Elizabethtown on Sunday, October 12, 1777.[483]

★ The British raided a guard post opposite Staten Island in March 1778. They killed one man, wounded another and captured eight.[484]

★ Some British ships off Elizabethtown exchanged fire with troops on shore on Monday September 28, 1778.

★ Lieutenant Colonel Thomas Stirling (d. 1808) and a British force of between 1,000 and 2,500 men from the 33rd and 42nd Regiments with the light infantry of the Guards embarked at Red Hook, Long Island at 9 PM on Wednesday, February 24, 1779 in an attempt to surprise the troops and inhabitants at Elizabethtown the following morning. They crossed the bay to the Bergen shore, landed and marched overland across the hill to Brown's Ferry, at Newark Bay, where they re-embarked in boats sent from New York to take them around by the Kill von Kull. They landed between 2 and 3 AM on the 25th at the salt meadows about 1 mile north of Crane's Ferry.

Guided by Captain William Luce, Cornelius Hatfield or Hetfield, Jr., and John Smith Hatfield or Hetfield, the 42nd Regiment advanced immediately and took the hill, while the remainder of the force, through a misunderstanding, waited at the landing place for further orders. Colonel Stirling sent one of the guides back to order them forward; but the commanding officer refused to take orders from the guide. The guide returned to Colonel Stirling for an official order. This blunder delayed them by an hour and a half.

Colonel Stirling sent one of the guides with six soldiers to capture one of the residents to gain further intelligence. They entered Mr. Lewis Woodruff's (1754–1816) house, which was directly to the left of the town, and began to plunder while Mr. Woodruff escaped to notify Colonel Matthias Ogden (1754–1791), the officer of the day. Brigadier General William Maxwell (1733–1796) immediately called the troops to arms and marched them to the rear of the town.

The guard at Crane's Ferry discovered the landing and immediately sent the intelligence to town where the alarm was sounded and the militia assembled. The troops marched to the rear of the town where the Whig inhabitants had also gathered, doubtful of the number and movements of the attackers because of the darkness.

Another guide took a detachment along the shortest route to Liberty Hall, Governor William Livingston's (1723–1790) residence, to capture him while the main force advanced to the edge of town. They surrounded the house but the governor had left several hours earlier to spend the night at a friend's house a few miles away.

General Maxwell's troops began to move at dawn and were joined by the militia of Elizabethtown and Newark. The Crown forces retreated, abandoning the considerable number of horses and horned cattle they had collected. They set fire to the barracks, the school (which stored some provisions) and a blacksmith's shop before returning to the salt marsh where they arrived. General Maxwell's militiamen pursued the Crown troops from the rear and attacked their flanks along the route. About half way between the town and the ferry, the Crown forces faced about and paraded as if for action. A few well-directed artillery shots killed two men and induced them to renew their retreat.

The marsh was considered quite inaccessible and hazardous for an embarkation; so the boats were moved more than 1 mile up Newark Bay. Colonel Stirling's troops marched along the meadow's edge, waded a considerable distance waist-deep in mud in many places while a galley and two or three gunboats covered their retreat and re-embarkation. One of the boats grounded and was captured with all hands on board. The British lost four to six killed and about 40 wounded. They captured about 20 elderly men who were soon released. Brigade-Major Aaron Ogden (1756–1839) received a bayonet wound in his right side but escaped capture. Five other men were wounded, a private killed and seven privates missing. Rev. Mr. Hunter, the brigade chaplain, was also captured when he returned to the governor's house where he had been to give the alarm, but he escaped a short while later.[485]

★ General Henry Clinton (1730–1795) led a raid on Elizabethtown on Saturday, February 27, 1779. He captured 30 prisoners.[486]

★ British forces raided Elizabethtown in February 1779 in search of Brigadier General William Maxwell's (1733–1796) corps which was often headquartered in the town. However, they were stationed at Morristown at this time; so the Crown forces plundered many houses.[487]

★ Cornelius Hatfield or Hetfield, Jr. and a band of five Loyalists crossed to the mainland from Staten Island and went to the house of Lieutenant John Haviland's father to get information about the lieutenant's whereabouts on Saturday, June 6, 1779. They then raided Lieutenant Haviland and took him and a captain of a guardboat prisoners.[488]

★ Cornelius Hatfield led a band of Loyalists and about a dozen British soldiers on a plundering and reconnaissance raid a few nights after Friday, June 18, 1779. They landed at Halstead's Point and proceeded in small parties to the guard at Halstead's house. They attacked about dawn, but the guard escaped (except for one man killed) and alarmed the town while the raiders plundered the house, taking Mr. Halstead's sedan chair (see Photo NJ-33) and making him a prisoner. Mr. Halstead surprised his captors by firing a gun and escaped. The raiders had two men wounded, one of them mortally.[489]

★ Some New Jersey militiamen, commanded by two captains, were going from Monmouth County to Elizabethtown in mid-August 1779 when a few "people unknown" fired upon them at Blazing Star Landing. The commanding officer was wounded in the thigh and the rest were routed, several of them having been wounded.[490]

★ Captain James Henry Craig (1748–1812), adjutant Nixon, and eight privates boarded and captured the sloop *Neptune* shortly after midnight on Wednesday, October 14, 1779. As they brought the sloop to the Jersey shore, she ran aground. The men removed

Photo NJ-33. Sedan chair, a chair or windowed cabin suitable for a single occupant. It is borne on poles or wooden rails that pass through brackets on the sides of the chair. The two or more porters who bear the chair are called "chairmen."

beef, pork and rice, some powder and shot, two cohorns, four swivels (see Photo NJ-1), 19 stand of arms, and a considerable quantity of spare rigging (sails, ropes, etc.). They also took the 21 crewmen, the captain, his two mates, and the captain's wife prisoners. The British sent a number of armed boats to retake her. They arrived shortly after Captain Craig's men had stripped the rigging and before they could set her on fire. The Crown troops boarded the sloop and took her away at high tide.[491]

★ Lieutenant General Wilhelm von Knyphausen (1716–1800) sent a small command under Major Charles Lumm, of the 44th Regiment, across the frozen North River in sleighs to Paulus Hook on Tuesday, January 25, 1780 in retaliation for an attack by Brigadier General William Alexander (Earl of Stirling, 1726–1783) against Staten Island during the night of January 14. A large number of New Jersey citizens pretending to be militiamen plundered the settlements on the island and the angry farmers demanded retaliation. Crown forces marched from Paulus Hook about 8 PM with the flank companies of the 44th Regiment and detachments from the 42nd Anspach and Hessian corps and went through Bergen, the nearest way to Newark. They passed Whig patrols along the banks of the Passaic and reached Newark undiscovered about 10:15 or 11:15 PM. Major Lumm posted small parties to cover the principal avenues of the town.

They proceeded to the Academy at Elizabethtown, which now served as a barracks. They surprised and captured about 15 men, all the troops on duty in town, and killed seven or eight men in a brief skirmish. They captured the remaining 34 noncommissioned officers and privates. The lieutenant in command had been captured once before and managed to escape. He was later killed. The raiders then set fire to the Academy building and, as it burned, a party plundered several of the inhabitants' houses. They took any valuables and destroyed anything that was not portable.[492]

★ A second raiding party of about 120 men from the 1st and 4th battalions of Brigadier General Cortlandt Skinner's (1728–1799) brigade, together with 12 dragoons, all commanded by Lieutenant Colonel Abraham Van Buskirk (1750–1783) crossed from Staten Island to Trembley's Point, about 3 miles from Elizabethtown, in the night of Tuesday, January 25, 1780, one of the coldest days of the winter. (Newspaper accounts say this force was about 400 men: 300 infantrymen, about 60 dragoons, and several Loyalists.) Cornelius Hatfield or Hetfield, Jr., Job Hatfield or Hetfield (1754–1825), and John Smith Hatfield or Hetfield guided them to Elizabethtown by the most direct route. They entered the town in two divisions between 10 and 11 AM without being discovered before the alarm was sounded.

The 60 troops stationed in town retreated. The raiders, however, captured the picket guard at Elizabethtown along with two majors, including the commandant of the place, three captains and 47 privates, including five dragoons with their horses, arms, and accoutrements. They killed a few Whigs and the dragoons wounded several who later escaped. They also burned the Presbyterian church of Rev. James Caldwell (1734–1781), then chaplain in Colonel Elias Dayton's (1737–1807) regiment, and the courthouse. They plundered, and took 10 or 12 nonmilitary prisoners, including Belcher Peartree Smith (d. 1787) who was "imprisoned" in a comfortable house on Long Island where he spent most of his time reading.

They dragged 52-year-old Justice Joseph Hedden, Jr. (1728–1780), who was ill in bed, out of his house on Broad Street and bayoneted his wife in the face and breast when she tried to stop them. They marched Mr. Hedden, in sub-zero temperatures, barefoot and clad only in a nightshirt to the British outpost on Paulus Hook and then across the frozen Hudson to New York where he was imprisoned in the Sugar House on Manhattan Island. His frostbitten feet soon turned gangrenous. His captors sent word, under a flag of truce, to his brothers in Newark that they were freeing him. He died a few months later in September. Hedden was "Commissioner for the County of Essex for Signing and Inventorying the Estates and Effects of Persons Gone Over to the Enemy." It was his job to have the houses and lands of Loyalists seized and sold at auction. This raid was their opportunity to get revenge. They stayed in town about 15 or 18 minutes. A few militiamen pursued their rear and captured five, two of whom died from the intense cold a short time later. Justice Hedden was so frost-bitten, that he lost both his legs. The raiders retreated by way of De Hart's Point, after burning Justice Hedden's house.[493]

See **Newark** (summer of 1777).

★ Sunday evening, January 30, 1780, a party of 13 mounted Loyalists went from Staten Island to Rahway near Elizabethtown where they surprised Lieutenant Elias Wynants (1742–1789) and eight privates as they were "merry-making with a party of lasses." They were taken prisoners to Staten Island, along with three handsome sleighs and 10 horses.[494]

★ Brigadier General Thomas Stirling (d. 1808) and General Cortlandt Skinner (1728–1799) led a plundering party to Elizabethtown on Thursday night, February 10, 1780.

They plundered the houses of Doctor William Barnet (1728–1790), Messrs. William P. Smith, William Herriman, Mathias Halstead (1736–1822), and Doctor William Winans (1726–1826), among others. They searched Mr. Smith's house thoroughly for Elisha Boudinot who they believed was hiding there. However, both Mr. Boudinot and Mrs. Smith were out of town. The plunderers frightened the women and children and returned to Staten Island with their plunder and five or six prisoners.[495]

★ A Loyalist plundering party visited Halstead's Point on Sunday morning, February 13, 1780. They plundered a very considerable amount from Mr. Caleb Halstead, Sr. (1721–1824).[496]

★ A party of unidentified Loyalists from Staten Island went to Elizabethtown on Friday night, March 24, 1780. They captured Mathias Halstead.[497]

★ About 30 men from Staten Island attempted to surprise a small guard at Halstead's Point on Sunday night, April 23, 1780. They were spotted by the sentinels and killed one of them. They plundered Mr. Halstead's house, taking his beds and bedding, the family's clothing, and seven or eight head of cattle.[498]

★ On Tuesday, June 6, 1780, Lieutenant General Wilhelm von Knyphausen (1716–1800) crossed from Staten Island to Elizabethtown Point with Generals Edward Mathew (1729–1805), William Tryon (1729–1788), and Sterling (d. 1780), and 5,000 troops. They intended to put on a display of strength that might induce Continental soldiers to desert in large numbers. They also wanted to influence the state's civilian population to return to allegiance to the King. They also considered an attack on Morristown where General George Washington (1732–1799) was too weak to attack them in force. General Sterling advanced toward Elizabethtown before daylight and encountered a party of 12 militiamen. A sentry fired a shot into the advancing column before dawn, striking General Sterling in the thigh. Sterling was carried to the rear and later died of his wound. General Knyphausen took his place at the front.

The Crown forces quickly overcame these militiamen; but Colonel Elias Dayton (1737–1807) began to assemble his regiment around sunrise and harried the advancing column. More militiamen continued to appear, and riflemen kept up a steady fire from behind fences, thickets, orchards, houses, and trees, inflicting many casualties. As the column marched the 7 miles toward the village of Connecticut Farms in Union, it was "annoyed by parties of militia the whole way."

★ After the Battle of Connecticut Farms, Lieutenant General Wilhelm von Knyphausen (1716–1800) realized that "the information upon which the expedition had been undertaken was not to be depended upon." He turned about and returned to Elizabethtown. As the Crown forces marched back from Springfield, on their way to New York, on Wednesday, June 7, 1780, they were annoyed almost constantly by musket fire. General Knyphausen decided to "remain some days longer in New Jersey, lest their precipitate retreat should be represented as a flight." The Crown forces encamped in the form of a square in front of Elizabethtown just before daybreak while the Congressional troops made attacks all night.

The following morning, the 22nd British Regiment "was sent out to check the Rebels." They fired twice without hitting anything and suffered many killed, wounded, and captured. The Crown forces sent out the von Bose regiment and the chasseurs against "an astonishing number of Rebels, nearly all in the bushes." Brigadier General Edward Hand (1744–1802) attacked them near where the Minuteman Monument stands. The conflict lasted several hours. The chasseurs had three men slightly wounded before being driven back to their main position.[499]

★ The Crown forces attacked a picket Wednesday night, June 14, 1780 and were beaten back with severe losses. The following day, a small detachment from Lieutenant General Wilhelm von Knyphausen's (1716–1800) force was caught outside the lines and had one man killed and five captured.

★ General von Knyphausen with 13 regiments, consisting of about 5,000 regular troops plus new levies, advanced Friday morning, June 23, 1780. He headed to the right of the Continental Army commanded by Major General Nathanael Greene (1742–1786). They were on the march to Springfield, a march that took them six hours. A few Continentals and some militiamen met them at Elizabethtown and gave them a warm reception. After the Battle of Springfield, the Crown forces returned through Elizabethtown about 6 PM.[500]

★ November 4, 1780 see **Springfield (Connecticut Farms).**

★ Loyalist Captain Cornelius Hatfield or Hetfield, Jr. raided the Jonathans in New Jersey on Tuesday, November 14, 1780. He captured a lieutenant and five or six others.[501]

★ Mr. Elias Mann (d. 1781) and a party of men under his command attacked the Whig picket at Elizabethtown on Thursday evening, December 14, 1780. They killed two and took six prisoners. Only one escaped. The prisoners were taken to New York on Saturday along with two others captured a few days earlier.[502]

★ Captain Jonathan Dayton (1760–1824) ambushed seven Loyalists from Staten Island at Elizabethtown on Sunday, January 21, 1781. He killed one, mortally wounded another and took three prisoners.[503]

★ Captain Cornelius Hatfield and four other Loyalists, formerly from Elizabethtown, arrested Rahway resident Stephen Ball (1750–1781), a London trader [someone who trades with the British] on Staten Island on Thursday, January 25, 1781. They took him to Brigadier General James Pattison (1724–1805) and then to General Cortlandt Skinner (1728–1799). Both of them refused to take action against him on the charge that he had aided in the execution of Thomas Long (d. 1779), a New Jersey Loyalist, in 1779. They took him over to Bergen Point and hanged him as a spy.[504]

★ Loyalist Cornelius Hatfield or Hetfield, Jr. captured Captain Craig and four inhabitants in a raid on Elizabethtown on Friday, February 23, 1781.[505]

★ On Monday night, March 26, 1781, Major George Beckwith (1763–1823) of the 37th Regiment and about 200 Regulars and Loyalists from Staten Island took circuitous routes to avoid patrols on their way to Elizabethtown. They entered the town in four divisions, plundered the house of Mr. Joseph Crane (1732–1789), and captured 10 inhabitants, one lieutenant and three privates of the New Jersey Militia, and two Continental soldiers. They stayed in town about an hour and a half and lost only one man killed and another taken prisoner.[506]

★ Captain Cornelius Hatfield or Hetfield, Jr. and a party of 70 Loyalists landed at Halstead's Point on Saturday evening, April 21, 1781, and began marching toward town when Captain Baker Hendricks (1756–1789) and a patrol of about 10 or 12 men discovered them. The militiamen kept up a smart fire on the Loyalists, preventing them from entering the town. They gathered a few horses and other cattle, fired through the windows of Doctor Winans's (1726–1826) house, wounding a boy in the arm. They then burned the houses of Mr. Ephraim Marsh (d. 1784) before returning to their boats. John Smith Hatfield or Hetfield was wounded in two places.[507]

★ A party of about 70 Loyalists from the post at Bergen Point came over to Elizabethtown Point on Friday night, May 4, 1781. They collected about 50 head of cattle before the alarm was sounded. They drove their plunder on the great meadows and took it on board their boats while some armed vessels and a field piece covered them. A retaliatory visit to Staten Island followed four days later.[508]

See **Staten Island** in *The Guide to the American Revolution in New York.*

★ On Saturday night, June 2, 1781, David Woodruff (1746–1804) and Philip McCrea (1757–1781) were walking together along one of the town streets when the sentinel hailed them. They did not answer; so the sentinel fired and killed McCrea on the spot.

★ Lieutenant William Hutchison (1745–1826), Ensign Henry L. Barton (ca. 1761–?), of the first Battalion New Jersey Volunteers, and about 34 refugees and militiamen under the command of Captain Durham and Captain Moses Roberts landed at Trembley's Point, near the mouth of the Rahway River on Thursday, June 28, 1781. They surrounded Tairil's tavern to capture three Congressional light horsemen who were patrolling the Sound to give notice of any troops coming from Staten Island. However, the light horsemen had gone to Westfield.

The Loyalists then proceeded to Captain Amos Morse, Jr.'s (1742–1824) house. They surprised him and four other Whigs before dawn on Friday, took them out of bed, and stole between 30 and 40 head of cattle, including six good oxen, and about 80 sheep which they drove to Trembley's Point. About 40 militiamen gathered to harass their rear. Lieutenant Hutchison formed an ambuscade. As 15 militiamen passed, shouting, "Damn the refugees! Cut them down!" the Loyalists sprang from their hiding place. They surprised the militiamen who threw down their arms and were taken prisoners.

★ Some time later, about 20 militiamen gathered near Trembley's Point. The Loyalists charged them and took some prisoners. The Loyalists then embarked with all their cattle and sheep and returned safely to Staten Island. Their only injury resulted when a spent musket ball struck one of the Loyalists on the thigh and left its mark. They believed to have killed some militiamen and wounded several others. They captured 20, two of whom were wounded.

The *New Jersey Journal* dated the event on June 26, 1781 and reported that the Loyalists lost at least two dead on the field and probably several more killed and wounded which they carried off.[509]

★ A band of New Jersey Volunteers took 20 prisoners and some sheep and cattle in a skirmish with local militiamen at Elizabethtown on Friday, June 29, 1781. There were no injuries.[510]

★ Captain Cornelius Hatfield or Hetfield, Jr. and a party of Loyalists captured Lieutenant Obadiah Meeker (1752–1835) and 14 privates of the New Jersey Militia between Newark and Elizabethtown on Saturday night, July 21, 1781. The prisoners were taken from Staten Island to New York the following day.[511]

★ A party of Colonel Stephen Moylan's (1734–1811) light horsemen were at Elizabethtown to collect cattle for the Continental Army on Monday, September 17, 1781. They "took a pair of fat Oxen out of a Team on the Road, and gave the Driver a receipt for them." They then proceeded to the Point Meadows and took all the cattle there but were forced to relinquish their forage.[512]

★ Rev. James Caldwell (1734–1781) was informed that a young lady from New York had arrived at Elizabethtown Point under a flag of truce. She was the daughter of a lady who had cared for Congressional prisoners in New York. He went to the point to bring the young lady up to the town. When he arrived there, the officer commanding the post at Elizabethtown was on board the flag-sloop and asked Rev. Caldwell to go on board. When Rev. Caldwell boarded the sloop, he was informed the young lady had already gone to the town. As he prepared to return, a person in the sloop asked him whether he would take a small parcel tied up in a handkerchief. Rev. Caldwell consented and put the bundle into a chair-box. As he drove off, a soldier approached and demanded to search his chair to search for contraband goods. Rev. Caldwell, thinking it imprudent to take any further risk, asked the soldier if he would allow him to return the bundle to the sloop. The soldier agreed and Rev. Caldwell took the bundle out of the chair-box. As he stepped on board the sloop to return it, a soldier belonging to the state troops who was on the quarterdeck and less than 10 yards away ordered him to stop. Rev. Caldwell stopped and the soldier, an Irishman named Morgan, presented his musket and shot him, killing him instantly on Saturday, November 24, 1781. Rev. Caldwell left nine children, ranging in age from 17 to 2.[513]

★ Captain Baker Hendricks (1756–1789) and a party of men in whaleboats went down Newark Bay near the Kills on Thursday, November 29 or December 6, 1781. They boarded and stripped two wood boats and took one prisoner. They landed a small party of men on Bergen Neck near the Loyalist post and captured two prisoners. On their way back, they captured three other prisoners with all kinds of provisions.[514]

★ Captain Jonathan Dayton (1760–1824), a member of the 2nd New Jersey Regiment, ambushed 10 Loyalists at Halstead's Point on Saturday, December 1, 1781. He captured six, killed one, mortally wounded another, and took three prisoners.[515]

★ Mr. Elias Mann (d. 1781) and a party of men attacked Congressional pickets at Elizabethtown on Friday, December 14, 1781. They killed two and captured six guards while only one escaped.[516]

★ Seven Refugees from Staten Island landed at Halstead's Point Saturday night, December 15, 1781, expecting to meet some of their friends with fat cattle. Captain Jonathan Dayton was informed of their intentions and gathered a party of men. Knowing the route they were to take, he laid an ambush for them. A muddy place in the road made them conceal themselves farther away from the road, obliging them to fire through two fences. They killed one, mortally wounded another, and took three prisoners. The other two escaped in the darkness. Three Refugees who remained with the gunboat heard a boat coming down the creek and headed to the Staten Island shore. Lieutenant David Randall (1739–1820) captured the vessel and crew. Their leader, Swain Parsel (1760–), a deserter from the Continental Army, devised the plan to bring over 20 men "in order to obtain forgiveness, and make some atonement for his crime."[517]

★ Captain Cornelius Hatfield or Hetfield, Jr. and a party of 30 Refugees crossed from Staten Island to Elizabethtown on Friday night, February 1, 1782. They took nine prisoners, including a Whig contractor called Mr. Reed. The prisoners were brought to Staten Island and imprisoned as hostages, awaiting the release of John Smith Hatfield or Hetfield who was captured at Westfield and imprisoned at Burlington.[518]

★ On Friday, February 23, 1782, the same party came to Elizabethtown by night and captured Captain Craig of the State Regiment and four other inhabitants.[519]

★ Lieutenant Blanchard and a party of men in a whaleboat (see Photo NJ-1) sailed to Elizabethtown Point on Sunday, March 10, 1782. They captured a whaleboat off the Point which carried Mr. Lewis Woodruff (1754–1816) and four other New Jersey Whigs.[520]

Chatham (Apr. 3, 1780)

Chatham is about 6 miles southeast of Morristown.

A possible accidental shooting at Chatham on Monday, April 3, 1780 wounded William Cravell (d. 1780), a Whig, who died four days later.[521]

Colt's Neck (June 9, 1780; Aug. 1780; Oct. 15, 1781; Mar. 6, 1782)

> Colt's Neck is 5 miles from Freehold, on a neck of land formed by two branches of the Swimming River. It was the home of Joshua Huddy whose house was attacked by a party of Loyalists in 1780.

A party of African Americans and white Loyalists under Colonel Tye (ca. 1753–1780), an African American, attacked the house of Captain Joshua Huddy (1735–1782) at Colt's Neck on Friday, June 9, 1780. A band of militiamen killed six attackers and wounded several others while having only one man wounded.

See also **Toms River.**

★ Colonel Tye, a mulatto slave named Titus, and a band of 70 Loyalists attacked the home of Joshua Huddy again in August 1780. Huddy defended his house for several hours. When it was riddled with musket balls and in flames, Huddy refused to submit until he obtained safe and honorable terms from the assailants. Colonel Tye was killed and Huddy escaped.[522]

★ A band of Loyalists from Sandy Hook captured six prisoners at Colt's Neck on Monday, October 15, 1781.[523]

★ Captain Joseph Ryerson (1760–1854) and a party of more than 100 Loyalists raided Colt's Neck on Wednesday, March 6, 1782. They supposedly surprised some of the inhabitants in their beds and took great numbers of sheep and calves.[524]

Near Pleasant Valley (June 28, 1778; Feb. 8, 1781; June 21, 1781; Feb. 8, 1782)

> Pleasant Valley is on NJ 34 about 4 miles north of Colt's Neck and about 7 miles west of Shrewsbury.

A skirmish occurred at Pleasant Valley on Sunday, June 28, 1778 at the time of the Battle of Monmouth. Captain John Schenk (1740–1794 or 1745–1834 or 1750–1823) and a party of militiamen skirmished with some Loyalists under Lieutenant Stevenson near Pleasant Valley on Thursday, February 8, 1781. They wounded three and took 12 prisoners while losing one man killed and one wounded.[525]

★ Loyalist General Cortlandt Skinner (1728–1799) and a force of 1,000 new levies, British and foreign troops tried to plunder Pleasant Valley about 11 AM on Thursday, June 21, 1781. The inhabitants succeeded in frustrating them by driving off their stock. The militiamen engaged the raiders in a pretty smart skirmish through the remainder of the day. The Crown forces began their retreat about sundown and did not stop until they got to Garret's Hill where they spent the night. An officer descended upon them during the night and rescued a number of stolen sheep.

The Crown forces embarked the next day, taking with them about 40 cattle and 60 sheep. They lost one man killed, several deserters, and an unknown number of wounded. They killed one man and wounded three or four and burned two houses but did not molest any people.[526]

★ About 40 Loyalists from Sandy Hook, commanded by Lieutenant Stevenson, plundered Pleasant Valley on Friday evening, February 8, 1782. They visited the houses of several people in the neighborhood and seized more than 20 horses, five sleighs which they loaded with plunder, and eight or nine prisoners. The noise woke two young men who slept in the second story of one of the houses. They hid themselves until the raiders went to the barn to take the horses and sleigh, and then came down, escaped and went to the house of Captain John Schenck, of Colonel Asher Holmes's (1740–1808) regiment. They alerted him about an hour and a half before dawn. Captain Schenck mustered a small party and pursued the plunderers. He arrived at the Gut just as they had gotten the prisoners, two or three of the horses, and a small quantity of their plunder carried over.

Captain Schenck immediately attacked the men who were with the remainder of the horses and plunder. His men fired a few volleys that killed one of them and wounded another. They captured 12 Loyalists, three of whom were wounded. Captain Schenck lacked vessels to cross the water and was unable to pursue; so he returned through Middletown with 19 horses, five sleighs with the plunder which had been taken from the inhabitants, and one with prisoners on Saturday morning. He met Lieutenant Stevenson and 16 others who had remained behind to secure the retreat. Both sides immediately began firing. Captain Schenck ordered his men to fix bayonets and charge, but they threw down their arms and surrendered. Eight of Captain Schenck's prisoners took the opportunity to escape.[527]

Conascung (June 21, 1780)

Conascung Point is south of Perth Amboy at Laurence Harbor.

Colonel Tye (ca. 1753–1780) and about 30 African Americans and 30 Loyalists and 36 Queen's Rangers landed at Conascung on Friday, June 21, 1780. The militia skirmished with them as they returned. The Loyalists wounded a captain slightly, broke the arm of a lieutenant, and mortally wounded two privates. They captured two officers and six privates, 10 civilians, several African Americans, and plundered their homes and took their prisoners to New York. All but one of the African Americans, the horses, horned cattle, and sheep were retaken. The Loyalists acknowledged the loss of seven men.[528]

Madison
Bottle Hill (Sept. 12, 1782)

Bottle Hill is now Madison, southeast of Morristown.

An early-rising resident of Bottle Hill, near the Great Swamp, discovered two armed men passing by on Thursday morning, September 12, 1782. One of them, thought to be Caleb Swezy, Jr. (d. 1782), had a reward of $200 for his capture for committing several atrocious robberies. Captain Benjamin Carter and his officers and 10 men set out to capture them. They sent a person to lay in ambush near Isaac Badgley's house. Swezy was good friends with Badgley's wife. When the man saw Badgley's wife carry victuals into the swamp twice, the party entered the swamp a few miles from Badgley's house to avoid being detected. They posted sentinels at the roads they thought they would use for their escape and got within a few rods of the house.

The party caught Swezy and his companion by surprise. Unprepared to defend themselves because the flints were out of their muskets, they tried to flee. One of the sentinels shot Swezey who died a few minutes later. The other man was wounded slightly and taken to jail in Morristown.[529]

Black Point (Sept. 1, 1780; Oct. 16, 1781)

Black Point is on the north shore of the Navesink River, about 2 miles northeast of Red Bank.

A party of Loyalists unsuccessfully attempted to capture Captain Joshua Huddy (1735–1782) at Black Point on Friday, September 1, 1780.[530]

★ The six prisoners taken at Colt's Neck on Monday, October 15, 1781, were brought to Black Point. Dr. Nathaniel Scudder (1733–1781) attempted to recapture them the next day and was killed.[531]

Belford
Gravelly Point (Apr. 12, 1782)

> Gravelly Point is in Belford on Sandy Hook Bay about 1.5 miles southeast of Middletown Point.

A party of Loyalists hanged Captain Joshua Huddy (1735–1782) at Middletown Point about 10 AM on Friday, April 12, 1782 for the death of Philip White (d. 1782) on March 30. He wrote his will under the gallows upon the head of the barrel on which he would later stand to be hanged. The executioners pinned the following label to Captain Huddy's breast:

> We the refugees having with grief long beheld the cruel murders of our brethren and finding nothing but such measures daily carrying into execution, We therefore determine not to suffer without taking vengence for the numerous cruelties, and thus began (and I say may those lose their liberty who do not follow on) and have made use of Capt. Huddy as the first object to present to your views, and further determine to this man for man as long as a refugee is left existing, "Up goes Huddy for Philip White."

Huddy's corpse was brought to Freehold the following day.[532]

See **Shrewsbury.**

Matawan (June 3, 1778)

> Matawan is about 6 miles southeast of South Amboy. The Burrows mansion at 94 Main St. is the home of the Matawan Historical Society.

See also **Sandy Hook, Burrows's Mills** and **Conascung.**

General Cortlandt Skinner (1728–1799) received a tip from Colonel William Taylor in early June 1778 that Captain John Burrows, the "Corn King," would be home on leave in Middletown Point (Matawan). Taylor, a Loyalist, was a relative of Captain Burrows whom the British hated because he supplied corn to the Continental Army, allowed the whaleboat navy to hide in his mill pond, and the local militia to train on his property.

General Skinner organized an expedition to capture Captain Burrows on June 3, 1778. He set out from Staten Island with a group of 70 Loyalists. They landed at Conascung Point near Keansburg/Union Beach shortly after midnight. They then proceeded to Holmdel on their way to Matawan. Local Loyalists joined them on their march and their numbers grew to around 200. Some farmers saw the marchers in the early morning and ran through the woods to Middletown Point to sound the alarm.

When the Loyalists entered the town, they were caught between the townspeople and Major Thomas Hunn's (1735–1796) Freneau Militia Company. The Loyalists began to split up into small groups and spread throughout the town. Captain Burrows, warned a few moments earlier, escaped out the back window of his house as the Loyalists arrived. He slid down an embankment, swam the Matawan Creek and escaped into the woods.

When the Loyalists realized he had escaped, they sent mounted patrols to capture local Whigs for prisoners, including Captain Burrows's father and several militia officers.

Other groups began to burn the town including the Episcopal church, mills, stores and boats. A skirmish killed two militiamen and wounded another. Major Hunn was later court-martialed for conduct unbecoming an officer. After the raid, one group of Loyalists returned to Staten Island with the prisoners while another went to Sandy Hook. Colonel Thomas Henderson (1743–1824), of the Monmouth Militia, sent a party to Middletown Village to capture Colonel William Taylor in retaliation for the raid. When General Sir Henry Clinton (1730–1795) learned of Taylor's capture, he made an agreement for a prisoner exchange.[533]

Edison
Raritan Township
Oak Tree (June 25, 1777)

> Oak Tree is now Edison. It was formerly known as Raritan Township which included Woodbridge and Piscataway townships. The local, county and state governments joined with citizens to purchase and preserve the site of this skirmish as a park in 2004. The 4.5 acre site was bulldozed by the potential developers; but it retained enough integrity to continue to qualify for the National Register of Historic Places as part of the Battle of Short Hills. It is now included within the boundaries of New Jersey's proposed "Crossroads of the American Revolution" Heritage Area.
> St. James Episcopal Church served as a hospital for wounded British soldiers during the war. Six British soldiers killed in one of the skirmishes in the area are buried in the church's cemetery.

A considerable number of Continental troops and militiamen pursued General William Howe (1732–1786) from Brunswick toward Amboy at the end of June 1777. The British encountered a party under Brigadier General William Alexander (Earl of Stirling, 1726–1783) as they converged at Oak Tree on Wednesday morning, June 25, 1777. The two sides engaged in a smart skirmish which forced General Stirling back toward New Market. General George Washington (1732–1799) withdrew his troops from New Market to Middlebrook; but, instead of following them, the British doubled back on their right flank and headed toward Westfield. The next morning, they withdrew to Perth Amboy because the woods along the Short Hills, from Oak Tree through Netherwood to Springfield, were full of Jersey militiamen.[534]

Meanwhile other Continental parties attacked the enemy flanks in light skirmishes until they joined the main body which continued to march to Westfield. General Howe's troops plundered and burned property as they headed to Amboy; and several small parties harassed them along the way. The Continentals lost three cannon at Quibbletown.

See **Short Hills.**

Potterstown (Sept. 15, 1777)

> Potterstown is on US 22, 2 miles east of Lebanon, north of the Round Valley Reservoir.

Congressional troops captured a party of Loyalists at Potterstown on Monday, September 15, 1777.[535]

Rocky Point (July 26, 1781; May 25, 1782)

Rocky Point is on the Atlantic Ocean, north of the Navesink River.

Captain Maffet, in command of a Philadelphia whaleboat (see Photo NJ-1), engaged and captured a sloop from New York off Long Beach on Thursday, July 26, 1781. The sloop was loaded with fish. He also captured three Loyalist boats off Shrewsbury Point which had on board 30 plundered sheep and 23 sheep stealers.[536]

★ Captain Adam Hyler (1735–1782) or Huyler and some militiamen, in armed boats, attacked Captain John Schaak and 25 troops of the 57th British Regiment in the Shrewsbury River on Saturday, May 25, 1782. Captain Schaak and his men had been sent to intercept Hyler in passing through the Gut. As soon as Captain Hyler discovered them, he landed 13 of his men with orders to charge. They killed or wounded four and captured Captain Schaak and eight of his men. Several others may have been killed by fire from the gunboat.[537]

Ringoes (Dec. 14, 1776)

Ringoes is on US 202 about 12 miles northwest of Princeton and 8.5 miles north of Washington Crossing State Park in Titusville.

British Cornet Francis Geary (1752–1776) and a party were ordered to advance into the country to procure intelligence of enemy positions in December 1776. As they returned, a party of Whigs concealed on each side of the road ambushed them at Ringoes on Saturday, December 14, 1776. They fired and killed Cornet Geary.[538]

Secaucus (Feb. 21, 1777; Apr. 2, 1777; Apr. 11, 1777; Sept. 16, 1780)

Secaucus is in Bergen County, north of Bergen and west of Hoboken.

A lieutenant of the Highlanders, a captain and nine recruits of General Cortlandt Skinner's (1728–1799) regiment, two valuable horses, a quantity of Irish linen, eggs, butter, etc. were captured at Secaucus on their way to New York on Friday, February 21, 1777.

A deserter of the 40th Regiment reported that General William Howe (1732–1786) had arrived in Amboy and given orders to the British Army that they should be ready to march at a moment's notice. A sergeant and nine privates were caught trying to depart. They were punished and three died from the whipping they received.[539]

★ The British frigate *Tartar* chased a large Whig vessel on Wednesday, April 2, 1777. The crew, finding no way to escape, ran the vessel ashore on the Jersey coast. The crew of the *Tartar* burned and destroyed her; but, as she had a very valuable cargo on board, some Whigs came down to Secaucus and carried away all the grain, horses, cows, and sheep they could gather. They had to swim over the Hackensack River because they lacked boats.[540]

★ A small Loyalist foraging party went from Bergen Point to Secaucus, about 15 miles away, on Friday, April 11, 1777. They plundered 40 head of horned cattle, 40 loads of fresh hay and several loads of straw. They were joined by 40 inhabitants who returned with the troops that night and brought their arms with them.[541]

★ Four Loyalists went over to Secaucus on Saturday morning, September 16, 1780 and captured three Congressional officers in a raid.[542]

Clinton
Sidney (June 24, 1776)

Sidney, now Clinton, is about 24 miles east of Bethlehem, Pennsylvania and about 23 miles northwest of New Brunswick.

John Vought and about 25 Loyalists conducted a raid at Jones Tavern near Sidney (Clinton) on Monday, June 24, 1776.[543]

Tennent (June 28, 1778)

Tennent is northwest of Freehold near the Monmouth Battlefield State Park.

Some of General Philemon Dickinson's (1739–1809) New Jersey militiamen skirmished with a British covering party at Tennent on Sunday, June 28, 1778.[544]

Bridgewater
Two Bridges (Dec. 8, 1776)

Two Bridges was in Bridgewater, west of Middlebrook, and southeast of exit 17 off I-287.

A large body of Crown troops advanced within 3 miles of Colonel William Malcom's or Malcolm (1745–1791) detachment to cut him off on Saturday, December 7, 1776. Colonel Malcom formed his men and took post in the gorge of the mountains. He placed his field pieces in the road with the wings of his party extending to the hills on each side. He sent out three small scouting parties to warn him of the enemy's approach. The scouting parties returned after cutting down a liberty pole at Tappan, taking the father of one of Malcom's lieutenants prisoner, and stealing a horse and two oxen.

The following day, Colonel Malcom marched a party within 3 miles of the new bridge at Hackensack. They raised a "terrible uproar among the Tories as well as in the enemy's little camp. They abandoned their houses and guard-houses as the party advanced." They captured a straggler, a Loyalist named Pierson, who was with the party that advanced on Colonel Malcom on Saturday.[545]

Somerset
Van Nest's Mill (Jan. 20, 1777)

Van Nest's Mill was near Somerset Courthouse, west of New Brunswick.

Crown forces skirmished with the Middlesex County Militia at Van Nest's Mill on Monday, January 20, 1777.
See also **Somerset Courthouse.**

Vanderberg (June 28, 1778)

Vanderberg is on Conover Road west of NJ Route 34 N between Colt's Neck and Pleasant Valley.

Local militiamen skirmished with Crown forces at Vanderberg at the time of the Battle of Monmouth on Sunday, June 28, 1778.[546]

Bloomfield
Watsessing (Sept. 15, 1777)

Watsessing is known as Bloomfield today and is north of Newark.

General Henry Clinton (1730–1795) began his invasion of New Jersey on Friday, September 12, 1777, the day after General William Howe (1732–1786) defeated General George Washington (1732–1799) at Brandywine, Pennsylvania.

Major General Israel Putnam (1718–1790), at Peekskill, sent Brigadier General Alexander McDougall (1732–1786), with about 700 Continentals and about 200 New England militiamen and two field pieces. They crossed the Hudson at King's Ferry on Sunday afternoon, September 14, 1777. The following afternoon, McDougall proceeded to a point 4 miles below Tappan, halfway between that village and the British positions to the south. He found that, "by the lowest accounts that can be relied on," the Crown troops probably numbered 2,000. Other reports put them "as high as 3,000, though many have represented them as high as 4,000 and 5,000." McDougall complained the local militiamen would not venture near the enemy lines and he was unable to get accurate intelligence. His scouts returned to camp with reports that "the main body of the enemy were strongly posted between Schraalenburgh Church and the New Bridge, with their plunder on their right flanks and somewhat in the rear." McDougall reported that Sir Henry had carried off "two hundred horned cattle, some of which were very poor." He also took 200 sheep and a good deal of other Jersey Dutch provisions and property as well as several Hackensack Valley Whigs.[547]

See **Elizabeth** and **New Bridge.**

Westfield (June 26, 1777)
See **Somerset, Quibbletown, Short Hills,** and **Scotch Plains.**

3
SOUTHERN NEW JERSEY

See the map of Southern New Jersey.

Cranbury Inlet (Oct. 16, 1775)

> Cranbury Inlet is the entrance to Barnegat Bay north of Barnegat Lighthouse State Park .

Captain John Campbell (d. 1806) and two companions were on their way from Boston to New York to recruit new troops for the King's army when they left their ship in a small boat and went into Cranbury Inlet on Monday, October 16, 1775. They were pursued and captured. Before they left the ship, they supposedly threw overboard several pieces of the ship's cannon, 60 muskets and two and a half barrels of powder.[548]

Brigantine Beach (Oct. 16, 1775; Jan. 21, 1778; Feb. 9, 1779)

> Brigantine Beach is northeast of Atlantic City.

British Captain George Hastings's transport ship *Rebecca & Francis* was bound from Boston to New York with 17 seamen when it ran aground at Brigantine Beach on Monday, October 16, 1775. Members of the Egg Harbor Guard (3rd Regiment Gloucester County Militia), under Colonel Richard Somers (d. 1794), captured the seamen and marines and brought them to Philadelphia where the seamen were freed but the marines were "properly secured." The *Rebecca & Francis* was the first ship destroyed in New Jersey during the war.[549]

★ Captain Henry Stevens of Egg Harbor captured the schooner *Two Friends* from New York on Wednesday, January 21, 1778. He captured 22 prisoners.[550]

★ February 9, 1779 see **Woodbridge,** where the account is dated February 1, 1779.

Egg Harbor (Apr. 1, 1776; June 1776; July 5, 1776; Apr. 26, 1777; June 12, 1777; Mar. 23, 1778; Apr. 1778; June 2, 1778; Aug. 24, 1778; Sept. 29, 1778; May 21, 1779; June 1779; Sept. 10, 1779; Ca. Nov. 4, 1779; Jan., 1780; Mar. 13, 1780; Sept. 7, 1780; Oct. 24, 1782; Apr. 3, 1783)

> A considerable salt works at Egg Harbor and a large depot of naval stores supplied the privateers that usually rendezvoused there and in its vicinity to raid New York harbor. The salt works and storehouses were destroyed and most of the privateers got out before Captain Ferguson arrived in early October 1778.[551]

On Monday, April 1, 1776, the sloop *Endeavour,* under Master Job Trip, was headed from Dartmouth to Philadelphia when it was chased northward of Egg Harbor by a British tender carrying four carriage guns, 10 swivels (see Photo NJ-1), and 35 men. The tender fired a broadside and the *Endeavour* hauled down her sails. When the tender came alongside her, she fired another broadside. Captain Trip received a musket ball in the thigh which broke and shattered badly. His mate also had a ball go through one thigh and lodge in the other. The two men went 36 hours without any dressing to their wounds. The crew of the tender plundered the *Endeavour,* set fire to her and scuttled her.[552]

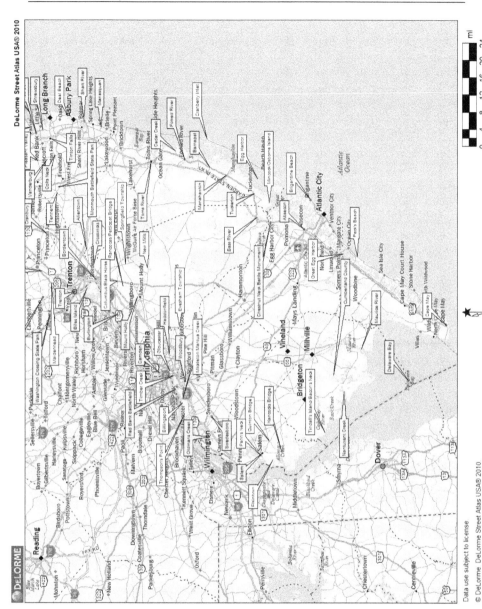

Southern New Jersey: Map for The Guide to the American Revolutionary War in New Jersey © 2011 DeLorme (www.delorme.com) Street Atlas USA®

DeLorme Street Atlas USA® 2010

Data Zoom 7-7

MN (12.2° W)

★ The privateers *Congress* and *Chance* captured the *Lady Julianna, Juno,* and *Reynolds* near Egg Harbor in early June 1776. They seized $22,420, £187 plate, 1052 hogsheads of sugar, 246 bags of pimento, 396 bags of ginger, 568 hides, 25 tons of cocoa, 41 tons of fustic, and one cask of turtle shell.[553]

★ The *General Putnam* engaged a 20-gun ministerial privateer about 400 yards offshore at Egg Harbor on Friday, July 5, 1776. The *General Putnam* received a broadside and ran ashore. Captain Thomas Crieger got all his arms and ammunition on the beach. When the ship anchored about a quarter of a mile away, she began a heavy fire on the *General Putnam* and sent out two barges with about 50 men. As the barges approached the shore, the crew of the *General Putnam* fired at them until they retreated. The ship continued to fire until dark when she weighed anchor. The *General Putnam* had 17 large holes in her mainsail and some shots in the hull.[554]

★ The frigate HMS *Mermaid* destroyed a privateer schooner at Egg Harbor on Saturday, April 26, 1777.[555]

★ The British sloop *Harlem,* Lieutenant John Knight (1748–1831), and the brig tender *Stanley* cut two Continental brigs out of Egg Harbor on Thursday, June 12, 1777. One of them was a privateer, the other was loaded with lumber and tar.[556]

★ Colonel Jehu Eyre and Lieutenant Robert Collings went to join the militia near Egg Harbor with two field pieces on Monday, March 23, 1778. It was decided that Colonel Eyre would join the militia and Lieutenant Collings would go down the bay with four boats. Lieutenant Collings and his men rowed past three tenders anchored near the mouth of Cohansey Creek and got to Ben Davis's Point where he spotted a schooner and a sloop coming up the bay. Lieutenant Collings and his men gave chase and the ships headed down the bay and anchored.

Three other ships appeared but Lieutenant Collings continued his pursuit. He came within gunshot at 3 PM, approached the vessels and hailed them. They responded with three cheers and a gun shot. Lieutenant Collings's crew returned three cheers and attacked them, driving them from their quarters several times. The crew of the sloop abandoned ship and went on board the schooner. When two armed schooners rowed up to assist the two vessels, Lieutenant Collings withdrew and pursued the other ship which was alone. He got close enough to her to create confusion on board. As they headed west, two frigates appeared and all five vessels headed down the bay to get protection.

The frigates anchored and got the other vessels around them to prevent Lieutenant Collings from cutting some of them off. They also seemed determined to block up Lieutenant Collings's vessels if possible.

Three tenders came into the mouth of the Creek, leaving Lieutenant Collings with no retreat, as the Crown forces were coming overland. Lieutenant Collings hid the boat in a gut and sank her. He later raised the boat and captured the two sloops with their cargoes which did not include any grapeshot which Lieutenant Collings needed.[557]

★ A brig from Ireland bound for New York with a large quantity of linen, butter, and supplies was taken off Egg Harbor in April 1778, and brought safely into port with the sailors and several other prisoners.[558]

★ Captain Robert Snell's company of Egg Harbor Guards surprised a party of Loyalists on Tuesday, June 2, 1778.[559]

★ Five privateers attacked the British victuallers *Sybella, Parrot, Hero, Blackie, Baltimore, Longmore; Achilles, Edwards, King George,* and *Redmond* off Egg Harbor on Monday, August 24, 1778. The vessels easily beat off the privateers.[560]

★ A privateer re-captured a sloop with tobacco from the *Amazon*'s tender on Tuesday, September 29, 1778. The prize was brought to Egg Harbor.[561]

★ A 16-gun brig came ashore near Egg Harbor on Friday, May 21, 1779. She was bound for New York from Jamaica with about 160 hogsheads of rum when she ran aground. The crew threw three or four guns overboard to lighten her. They had already thrown overboard about 14 hogsheads of rum when people from the shore boarded her. People from the area boarded her and took proper care of her, refloated her, and landed part of her cargo.[562]

★ Continental forces captured the HMS *True Blue* off Egg Harbor in June 1779.[563]

★ Several armed British boats destroyed a number of vessels and other property in Egg Harbor on Friday, September 10, 1779.[564]

★ Captain Day's sloop *Active* captured Captain Campbell's 8-gun privateer *Mercury* about Thursday, November 4, 1779. The *Mercury* was just out from New York after a cruise. Captain Campbell and four of his men were wounded but not a man aboard the *Active*.[565]

★ Continental forces drove a 40-gun British ship ashore near Egg Harbor in early January 1780.[566]

★ Eleven Loyalist sailors from New York embarked in a whaleboat, named the *Lewis-Town Revenge,* armed with a swivel gun (see Photo NJ-1) in her bow, 11 muskets, and 11 pair of pistols. They passed Sandy Hook and proceeded to Egg Harbor on Monday March 13, 1780. There, they found three privateers ready for sea and a 12-gun letter of marque schooner laden with lumber. As their number was inadequate to take on the force gathered there, they pretended to be Whigs and spent an evening with the local people.

They sailed from Egg Harbor to the Delaware River. When they entered the Maurice River, which flows into the Delaware, they captured a loaded vessel and headed for Reedy Island. Along the way, they fell in with nine outward bound vessels and burned eight of them and took the other. They also captured three vessels carrying produce to Philadelphia. They also released between 50 and 60 prisoners after receiving a parole that a British subject would be exchanged for each of them.[567]

★ HMS *Iris* ran a brig ashore near Egg Harbor on September 7, 1780.

★ Captain Richardson and 12 men aboard the whaleboat *Black Snake* captured Captain Read's 8-gun, 26-man galley *Boston Hero* on Thursday afternoon, October 24, 1782 and brought her to Egg Harbor. Captain Read had sent nine of his men ashore for water near Egg Harbor when the *Black Snake*'s crew captured them in a farm house. They then rowed on board the galley in the night and took her without firing a single shot.

Captain Richardson also brought in with him Captain Dedrick's sloop *Nancy* bound from Egg Harbor for Philadelphia with lumber.[568]

★ After the news of the signing of the peace treaty arrived in Egg Harbor on March 23, 1783, Captain Richard Shreve's (1726–1822) militiamen and a detachment of light horsemen under Cornet Cook surprised Loyalist John Bacon (d. 1783) near Tuckerton and killed him on Thursday, April 3, 1783.

See also **Tuckerton.**

Tindall's Island
Bacon's Neck (May 6, 1776)

> Bacon's Neck is on Tindall's Island on the Delaware River southeast of Wilmington, Delaware.

British ships, anchored at the mouth of Cohansey Creek, landed a foraging party of about 30 men at Bacon's Neck on Tindall's Island (also known as Tindon's, Findle's or Fiddle's Island), on the north bank of the mouth of Cohansey Creek about 10 o'clock on Monday, May 6, 1776. The foragers shot some cattle and took them on board before the Cumberland County Militia arrived. One of the vessels fired a gun to signal the foragers to return to the ship. The militiamen pursued them so closely that they almost took three of them prisoners. One of the foragers left an excellent musket behind, which the militiamen seized along with some cartridges. The foragers hollered to the militiamen to go on board the HMS *Kingfisher* where they would receive payment for the beef. The foragers seized between 20 and 30 head of cattle, left five men dead on the shore and wounded many others.[569]

Delaware River (May 8, 9, 1776; Sept. 26, 1777; Sept. 29, 1777; Oct. 5, 1777; Oct. 7, 8, 9, 1777; Oct. 11, 12, 1777; Nov. 21, 1777; Dec. 31, 1777; Jan. 1, 1778; Jan. 11, 1778)

British ships cannonaded Salem County from the Delaware River for two days—Wednesday and Thursday, May 8, 9, 1776.[570]

★ The vessel named *Lewis's Mill Boat* was employed to carry clothing from Philadelphia to Trenton for the Continental Army in September 1777. Ordered by the commissaries to return to Philadelphia with public stores, the skipper ran her into a dock in Philadelphia on Friday, September 26, 1777, the same day the British occupied the city. An hour or two afterward, a party of Gloucester County militiamen took her and all her cargo which was condemned for the use of the captors. A court of admiralty in the state of New Jersey condemned the vessel to be sold at public auction in the city of Burlington.[571]

★ Continental and British ships battled in the Delaware River off Chester, Pennsylvania on Monday, September 29, 1777.[572]

★ On Sunday, October 5, 1777, Continental troops scuttled two ships in the gap the British made in the chevaux-de-frise (see Photo NJ-34) near Billingsport.[573]

See also **Billingsport.**

★ A skirmish occurred on Province Island in the Delaware River near Fort Mifflin on Tuesday, October 7, 1777. The following day, a naval action took place at the mouth of the Schuylkill River. On Thursday, a floating battery between Little Mud Island and Fort Island fired on the British.[574]

★ Commodore John Hazlewood's (ca. 1726–1800) Pennsylvania Navy galleys cannonaded Carpenter's Island in the Delaware River on Saturday, October 11, 1777 and made another attack the following day.[575]

See also **Billingsport.**

★ After the fall of Billingsport, Fort Mifflin, and Red Bank, the Continental and Pennsylvania navies could no longer count on land support south of Philadelphia. Thirteen row galleys hugged the New Jersey shore and rowed up the Delaware on Wednesday night, November 19, 1777 and passed the British shore batteries without being detected.

Photo NJ-34. Chevaux-de-frise for water defense. The iron-tipped spikes were attached to logs and hidden two or three feet below the water's surface at low tide. Ships striking the chevaux-de-frise had their hulls punctured or damaged.

When a brig, a schooner, and several smaller vessels tried to join the galleys at 3 AM on Friday, November 21, 1777, the shore batteries directed a hot fire at them. The schooner and one of the smaller vessels ran aground on the New Jersey shore and were set on fire by their crews. The rest of the fleet was abandoned near Gloucester and burned as it seemed useless to try to pass Philadelphia.[576]

★ The schooner *Little Hope,* with a cargo of rum, sugar, coffee, tea, and a number of blankets, drifted from Philadelphia with the ice in the Delaware River above Point-no-Point on Tuesday, December 30, 1777. The following day, Major Evan Edwards (1752–1798) and eight men worked their way through the ice with great difficulty and boarded her. The captain of the schooner and five sailors surrendered.

★ The same day, Captain Robert Quigley (1736–1813), of the 1st Regiment Burlington County Militia and 24 militiamen boarded and took the transport brigantine *John* and the armed schooner *Industry* which were among several vessels drifting in the ice between Philadelphia and Gloucester Point. They captured 13 British sailors, including two captains. The *John* had several hogsheads of rum on board while the *Industry* carried tobacco. The militiamen took all the valuable articles and stripped the vessels of their rigging and sails before burning them.

★ The same day, another party of militiamen captured the transport *Lord Howe,* which was also stripped and destroyed.[577]

★ A large brig, bound from New York for Philadelphia, with two field pieces blew ashore in the Delaware River, about 5 miles below Wilmington, Delaware on Wednesday, December 31, 1777. Brigadier General William Smallwood (1732–1792) sent a detachment of Continental troops with two field pieces to fire on her. After a few shots, she struck her colors. The Continentals took her cargo of 350 chests of arms with 25 stand in each, clothing for four regiments, the baggage belonging to the officers of four regiments, and a quantity of wine and spirits. They also captured one captain, three subalterns, and 60 privates, along with about 40 officers' ladies. They also drove three other vessels to the Jersey shore, where inhabitants were "taking proper care of their cargoes."[578]

★ Continental troops captured a sloop in the Delaware River on Thursday, January 1, 1778. She was on her way from Chester to Philadelphia with about 20 barrels of flour on board. They also captured 34 British sailors and soldiers.[579]

★ Captain Andrew Snape Hamond (1738–1828) sent an officer and 17 men in a half galley from the HMS *Roebuck* to reconnoiter the Delaware River down to Mud Island at 4 AM on Sunday, January 11, 1778. They probably went to examine the former Pennsylvania Navy armed boat *Thunder* which deserted to the British in September 1777. The men went ashore on the Jersey shore and destroyed a breastwork and guns at 9 AM. They also destroyed some guns that were left on board the remains of some vessels the Whigs had burned.[580]

Manasquan
Squan (June 8, 1776; Apr. 4, 5, 1778)
Shark River (Apr. 6, 1778)

> Squan is now known as Manasquan, on the Atlantic about 7 miles south of Asbury Park.

After the British captured a Rebel sloop at Manasquan on Saturday, June 8, 1776, the militia fired on a boarding party and forced them from the sloop.[581]

★ Captain James Robertson, of the 35th Regiment, returned from an excursion on the Monmouth coast and reported that Captain Potterfield of the 71st Regiment sailed from New York with a detachment of 150 men in three small vessels on Saturday, April 4, 1778. Under the convoy of the armed sloop *George*, they proceeded to Sandy Hook where they were joined by 40 marines and provincial troops. On the morning of the 5th, they sailed from the Hook, under the command of Captain Collins of the *Fowey* and arrived off Squan at 8 AM the same morning. The troops landed and marched up to a large salt works which the Whigs erected there and completely demolished it along with immense quantities of salt, beef, salted and dried hams, sides of bacon, flour, corn and hay. There were more than 100 houses there, each with six to ten coppers and kettles to boil salt. The raiders captured a sloop belonging to Boston, partly loaded with flour. They re-embarked without opposition at 3 PM.[582]

★ About 135 Crown troops, mostly Loyalists and some Highlanders, landed on the south side of Squan inlet about 10 AM on Sunday, April 5, 1778. They burned all the salt works, broke the kettles, and stripped the beds of some people there. They then crossed the river and burned almost everything except Dirrick Longstreet's house before re-embarking.[583]

★ They landed at Shark River the next day and set fire to two small works. When they saw 15 horsemen coming toward them, they retreated in a hurry, jumping in their flat-bottomed boats in such confusion that they sank one or two of them. One of their pilots was Thomas Oakeson.[584]

Cape May (June 29, 1776; Dec. 18, 1776; July 1, 1777; Aug. 21, 1778)

Cape May is at the mouth of Delaware Bay, south of Atlantic City.

Captain Hugh Montgomery's Rebel brig *Nancy,* hotly pursued by six British men-of-war, ran aground at Cape May on Saturday, June 29, 1776. Local militiamen, under cover of a fog, removed the cargo of powder and arms. Several boats from the men-of-war were seen coming to board the *Nancy* when the fog lifted. Captain Montgomery opened some barrels of gunpowder and wrapped 50 pounds of it in the mainsail. He then set the folds of the sail on fire and abandoned ship. A short while after the boat crews joyously took possession of the brig, "the fire took the desired effect, and blew the pirates forty or fifty yards into the air." The observers on the beach diverted themselves for the next few days by counting the corpses and "the great number of limbs floating and driven ashore." Meanwhile, some local inhabitants and men from two small Rebel vessels mounted a gun on shore and exchanged fire with the sailors. Richard Wickes (d. 1776), an officer of one of the Rebel vessels, was killed and became the first casualty on New Jersey soil. A boy was also wounded.[585]

★ The HM Sloop *Falcon,* near the Cape Henlopen lighthouse, spotted a sloop heading down river on Wednesday morning, December 18, 1776. Captain John Linzee sent his boats after her and ran her ashore under Cape May. The crews of the boats boarded her, but the Whigs fired at them. The boats returned to the *Falcon* without the sloop.[586]

★ A Whig battery fired on Captain Charles Phipps's HMS *Camilla* as it tried unsuccessfully to take a grounded schooner at Cape May on Tuesday, July 1, 1777.

★ One of Admiral Comte Jean-Baptiste-Charles-Henri-Hector d'Estaing's (1729–1794) ships drove the 170-man British cruiser *Mermaid* ashore at Cape May on Friday, August 21, 1778.[587]

Burlington (Dec. 11, 1776; May 8, 1778; May 10, 1778)

Burlington is on the Delaware River south of Trenton and Bordentown.

Pennsylvania galleys in the Delaware River under Commodore Thomas Seymour shelled Burlington on Wednesday, December 11, 1776 when about 400 German troops were observed entering the town and fired on some Continentals.[588]

★ The town was bombarded again on Friday, May 8, 1778, this time by the Royal Navy. Two days later, Captain Edward Pakenham had the HMS *Viper* exchange fire with some Whig Continental dragoons at Burlington on Sunday, May 10, 1778.[589]

Mount Holly (Dec. 21–23, 1776; June 20, 1778)
Rancocas
Petticoat Bridge (Dec. 22, 23, 1776)
Battle of Iron Works Hill

Named after a nearby 183-foot mountain, Mount Holly is a Quaker town dating from 1676. It served as the capitol of the state for two months in 1779. John Woolman (1720–1772), the Quaker abolitionist known for his 1774 "Journal," taught at the Old School House. Other historic buildings include the 18th- and 19th-century county buildings on High Street between Garden and Union streets.

> Petticoat Bridge crossed the Rancocas River to connect Rancocas with Mount Holly south of Bordentown. A marker at Petticoat Bridge Road (1.25 miles south of NJ Route 543 (Mount Pleasant Road) in Mansfield) explains the attack by Colonel Samuel Griffin (1746–1810) and his men on a Hessian outpost. The Hessians used the Springfield Friends Meetinghouse (see Photo NJ-35) as a hospital. To get to the meetinghouse, go south on Petticoat Bridge Road. At the end, go right on Jacksonville-Jobstown Road. Proceed 0.4 miles to the red brick building on the left. It is now privately owned and barely visible from the road. The loft supposedly has a bloody Hessian handprint visible.
>
> The site of the Battle of Iron Works Hill (see Photo NJ-36) is on Pine Street next to St. Andrew's Cemetery in Mount Holly.

General George Washington (1732–1799) ordered Colonel Samuel Griffin (1746–1810) to draw Hessian troops southward, away from support positions near Trenton. He crossed the Delaware River with approximately 600 New Jersey militiamen and Virginia artillery on Saturday, December 21, 1776. He advanced as far as Mount Holly, within 7 miles of Hessian headquarters at Black Horse (Columbus in Burlington County) on Friday, December 22, 1776 and joined several hundred militiamen from southern New Jersey in an attack on Hessian pickets at Petticoat Bridge across the Rancocas Creek.

★ Major General Count Karl Emil Kurt von Donop (1740–1777) set out toward Mount Holly at 5 AM on Saturday, December 23, 1776 with 3,000 Hessians, quartered in Burlington County. They included the 42nd Regiment of Scots, the two grenadier battalions of Linsing and Block, the 12 mounted jaegers under Captain Lorey, and Captain Johann von Ewald's (1744–1813) jaeger company (see Photo NJ-8). They intended

Photo NJ-35. Springfield Friends Meetinghouse, used as a hospital by the Hessians during the Battle of Petticoat Bridge. The loft supposedly has a bloody Hessian handprint visible.

Photo NJ-36. Site of the Battle of Iron Works Hill on Pine Street next to St. Andrew's Cemetery in Mount Holly

to expel the Congressional troops. When the jaegers met a party of militiamen in the wood behind Slabtown, they received a barrage of gunfire.

The militiamen took a new position at a Quaker church on a hill at the end of the wood. The whole militia force was deployed behind this church. The Linsing Battalion attacked the hill while the Block Battalion moved to the left and the jaegers, with four companies of Scots, moved to the right, through the wood, to cut off the enemy from Mount Holly or to gain mastery of the bridge across the Rancocas Creek which intersects this town.

The militiamen withdrew through Mount Holly and across the bridge after the grenadiers occupied the church. Some of them sought refuge in the houses near the bridge; but the jaegers and Scots soon dislodged them with the field pieces. Most of them ran to the woods beyond the town and escaped. The jaegers and Scots pursued them for several miles.

Colonel Griffin and his men retired to the town of Mount Holly and entrenched on Iron Works Hill where another skirmish ensued. The Hessians received reinforcements of an officer and 50 grenadiers (see Photo NJ-7) that afternoon and occupied a post at the Bunting house, a plantation on a hill beyond Black Horse and Bustleton where the roads from Mount Holly and Burlington intersected. No sooner had they taken their position than Colonel Griffin's militiamen appeared in the woods in front of them.

Colonel Griffin hesitated to advance farther with such a small force and requested Colonel John Cadwalader (1742–1786) for two more pieces of artillery and 200–300 reinforcements. Cadwalader's force of about 1500 Pennsylvania militiamen planned to cross the river the next morning to support Griffin in an attack on Black Horse. However, General George Washington (1732–1799) had other plans (to attack the Hessians at Trenton). He advised Colonel Griffin to go to Bristol and stay there two or three days to coordinate matters with Cadwalader.

General Washington instructed Cadwalader to attack one hour before daybreak on the 26th. He sent Colonel Daniel Hitchcock's (1740–1777) New England brigade, numbering about 500 to 600 men, to Bristol to support Colonel Cadwalader. Cadwalader was ordered to provide his men with blankets, which had arrived from Philadelphia a day or two earlier, and cooked provisions for three days. Washington hoped Cadwalader would cross the Delaware near Bristol and, together with Griffin, join him. However, Colonel Griffin became ill by Christmas day and was out of action and had to go to Philadelphia for medical attention.

Shortly after the skirmish at Iron Works Hill ended, heavy small-arms fire mixed with cannon fire was heard in the vicinity of Black Horse or Slabtown (Jacksonville). The jaegers went to investigate and to attack the enemy's rear; but the grenadiers had already driven them back with heavy losses. Colonel Griffin withdrew toward Burlington with the Hessians in pursuit. He lost several dead and wounded while the jaegers had one killed and another severely wounded. The Hessians captured almost 200 men and seized two cannon. Ewald estimated that more than 100 men may have been killed on both sides. *The Pennsylvania Evening Post* reported Griffin's casualties as "only two killed, and seven or eight wounded" in both skirmishes.

General Sir William Howe (1732–1786) decided to keep von Donop in the area. This drew the enemy forces away from Bordentown and reduced the number of forces capable of assisting Colonel Johann Gottlieb Rall (1720–1776) at the Battle of Trenton four days later and assuring victory for General Washington's troops.[590]

★ Another skirmish occurred at Mount Holly on Saturday, June 20, 1778. Crown forces marching through the town came under fire from some Congressional troops. They returned fire, killing five and capturing two.

Bordentown (Dec. 27, 1776; June 14, 1777; May 1, 1778; May 7 or 9, 1778; June 1778)

White Hill (May 7 or 9, 1778)

The reconstructed Borden house (see Photo NJ-37), a private residence, is at 32 Farnsworth Avenue on the corner of Park Street. On the opposite corner of Park Street and Farnsworth Avenue (101 Farnsworth Avenue) is the Hopkinson house (see Photo NJ-38), owned by Francis Hopkinson (1737–1791), a signer of the Declaration of Independence, son-in-law of Colonel Joseph Borden 2nd (1719–1791), and author of *The Battle of the Kegs* and *Chester* which was the closest musical piece we had to a national anthem at that time. Prince Street, which runs off Park Street behind the Borden house, has a statue of Thomas Paine (1737–1809) and, at the end of the street, a marker explaining the events of May 8, 1778. Thomas Paine bought a house farther down Farnsworth Avenue in 1783 and lived in it periodically until his death in 1809.

In the winter of 1776, Major General Count Karl Emil Kurt von Donop (1740–1777) made his headquarters at a colonial tavern (now a private residence at 135 E. Park Street) owned by Colonel Oakly Hoagland (see Photo NJ-39) of the Continental Army. His army of 3,000 Hessians camped nearby. After the battle at Petticoat Bridge, von Donop received reports that a force of 3,000 men was gathering to march north to

Photo NJ-37. Reconstructed Borden house (32 Farnsworth Avenue on the corner of Park Street in Bordentown) was the home of Colonel Joseph Borden

Photo NJ-38. Home of Francis H. Hopkinson, signer of the Declaration of Independence and Colonel Joseph Borden's son-in-law, is across the street from Colonel Borden's house in Bordentown

Photo NJ-39. This building in Bordentown was owned by Colonel Oakly Hoagland of the Continental Army. He operated it as a tavern during the American War for Independence. General von Donop made it his headquarters in the winter of 1776 after the battle at Petticoat Bridge.

Mount Holly. He marched his men there to retaliate for the battle at Petticoat Bridge, to head off the march of the enemy, and to avoid being trapped against the river fighting a stronger force. He encountered a force of only 600 men in the Battle of Iron Works Hill at Mount Holly.

★ After the victory at Trenton, Captain James Nicholson (1737–1804) thought that the Continentals might have beaten the Crown forces at Bordentown on Friday, December 27, 1776 if Colonel John Cadwalader (1742–1786) had been able to cross the Delaware River. However, the ice and bad weather made it impossible. Captain Nicholson anticipated an attack the following day upon the main body of Hessians at Bordentown.[591]

★ Some militiamen fired on British boats on the Delaware River at Bordentown on Saturday, June 14, 1777 and had one man killed.[592]

★ General Philemon Dickinson (1739–1809) had defense lines constructed at the drawbridge near Bordentown in late April 1778 in anticipation of the arrival of the enemy. "The continental troops and great part of the militia had however been withdrawn, except those of the Colonels Philips [Colonel Joseph Phillips] and Shreve [Colonel William Shreve (1737–1812)], who were previously detached to guard a ford one mile further up the creek, and only the three regiments of Colonels Freelinghuysen [Frederick Frelinghuysen (1753–1804)], Van Dike [Colonel Henry Van Dyke] and Webster [Colonel John Webster] remained, when a party of the enemy appeared" on Friday, May 1, 1778. The Crown forces immediately began to repair the bridge which had been cut down. Congressional troops began to arrive when they received news of the enemy's approach; but a small party from one of the Crown regiments killed four Congressional troops and wounded several others, causing them to retire. The lines were again manned the following morning; but the Crown forces took a different route.[593]

★ On Thursday night, May 7, 1778 (some accounts report this event as occurring on Saturday night, May 9, 1778), General William Howe (1732–1786) sent out a small armada of a Highland regiment and Royal Navy units (between 600 and 800 troops) in four row-galleys, an armed brig, a schooner and 24 flat-bottomed boats. Their objective was to destroy the Continental frigates and a number of vessels that had been lodged in the different creeks. The flotilla proceeded up the Delaware River without molestation, causing havoc along the New Jersey shore above Philadelphia from Thursday through Saturday, May 7–9, 1778.

The Crown forces entered Crosswicks Creek and proceeded to Bordentown where they surprised the Continentals who did not have time to sink some frigates according to their plan for such an emergency. The raiders landed near White Hill on Friday morning where about 50 light-horsemen and 50 militiamen resisted them but were soon dispersed with the loss of 14 men killed and four cannon which were demolished. The Crown forces pursued the fugitives into Bordentown where one Ivins was accidentally killed crossing the street.

Meanwhile, the Continental Navy men set fire to the frigates *Washington* and *Effingham* and several other vessels in Crosswicks Creek to prevent them from falling into the hands of the enemy. They destroyed 44 vessels, including 22 ships burned at Bordentown and four others at White Hill and a number of smaller vessels lying in nearby creeks. They also torched four warehouses and a quantity of naval stores and some thousands of tent-poles, pegs etc. as well as private residences, including the home of Joseph Borden 2nd (1719–1791), one of the most prominent Whigs in town. They also killed three militiamen who fell into their hands. The militia lost about 17 men and four pieces of cannon before dispersing. The raiders then reembarked and headed to Biles Island where General Dickinson assembled the militia and artillery.[594]

See **Biles Island.**

General George Washington (1732–1799) pointed out that the blow was avoidable. The loss, however, was not serious, as the frigates were pretty useless as long as the Howe brothers had the lower river bottled up. The raid further exasperated the inhabitants at the very time Parliament was discussing Lord Frederick North's, 2nd Earl of Guilford (1732–92) conciliatory proposals. His commissioners may have been crossing the Atlantic to negotiate a settlement as the *New Jersey Gazette* commented:

> Thus do these people seek peace; and thus would they conciliate the affections of the Americans!—At the very time that terms are pretended to be offered, and proposals of accommodation, as they say, on the point of being made, fire and sword are carried to our habitations, and these Instruments of violence are committing every species of rapine, plunder and cruelty! This is the application of Lord North's Sermon on the 19th of February last![595]

★ The Crown forces burned and destroyed a very valuable merchant mill near Bordentown on their way through Burlington County in June 1778. They also destroyed the iron-works at Mount Holly and the dwelling-houses and outhouses of Peter Tallman, Esq. (1759–1826) and Colonel William Shreve (1737–1812).[596]

Egg Island (June 28, 1777)

There are two Egg Islands. One is near Absecon, north of Brigantine Beach. The other is in Little Egg Harbor near Beach Haven.

Watering parties from three British ships were fired on by Whigs on shore at Egg Island on Saturday, June 28, 1777. One warship returned fire.[597]

National Park

Red Bank (Sept. 7, 1777; Oct. 22, 1777; Nov. 5, 1777; Feb. 2, 1778)

Fort Mercer

Red Bank Battlefield Park (**www.co.gloucester.nj.us/Government/Departments/ ParksnRec/redbank.cfm**), location of Fort Mercer, is in National Park, New Jersey, at 100 Hessian Avenue, 2 miles west at the Delaware River. This location should not be confused with the Red Bank near Shrewsbury in eastern New Jersey.

Visitors to the reconstructed parts of Fort Mercer enjoy sweeping views of the Delaware River and can appreciate the strength of its position. A nearby exhibit of chevaux-de-frise (see Photo NJ-34) shows a rarely seen underwater obstruction salvaged from the Delaware River after about 170 years of immersion. The logs on display, retrieved in 1936, are about 30 feet long and have attached to them portions of the chain that held them together.

The obstacle, fully assembled, consisted of a large coffer filled with long heavy poles from which two to four heavy timbers, each tipped or sheathed in iron, extend outward at 45-degree angles to impale enemy ships. Each section was about 65 feet long and 20 inches square. The entire obstacle was lined with 30,000 feet of 2-inch plank. It was floated into the river and then sunk by using stones to fill the coffers to weigh it down. Anchors held it in place keeping the points of the protruding timbers about 4 feet below the low-water mark. Ships coming toward the city would get impaled. Those traveling away from the city would depress the timbers with no adverse effect.

The exhibit also includes boxes of grapeshot found around the old breastworks.

The house of James and Ann Whithall (see Photo NJ-40) (**www.whitall.org**), also in Red Bank Battlefield Park, was commandeered by the Continental Army in April 1777. The apple orchard was destroyed to build Fort Mercer, and the house was used as a field hospital during the Battle of Red Bank. Major General Karl von Donop died here. He was interred on the battlefield on October 28, 1777. The house is open to the public.

See also **Billingsport** and **Mantua**.

British shore batteries fired on Captain Charles Alexander's frigate USS *Delaware* off Red Bank until it surrendered on Sunday, September 7, 1777.[598]

★ Fort Mercer was named for Brigadier General Hugh Mercer (1725–1777) who died at Princeton. Together with Fort Mifflin, south of Philadelphia across the Delaware River, it presented a deterrent for any force planning a water approach to that city. The fort occupied a bluff above the river. Colonel Thaddeus Kosciusko (1746–1817) fortified it with nine-foot high earthen walls with sharpened tree trunks or branches (see Photo NJ-41), called fraise, embedded in it. Colonel Christopher Greene (1737–1781) commanded the garrison of 400 of his fellow Rhode Islanders and a few New Jersey militiamen and 14 cannons.

The Crown forces needed to eliminate the fort to open the Delaware River to keep supplies flowing to the army. Major General Count Karl Emil Kurt von Donop (1740–1777) and his four battalions of Hessians, totaling 1,200 men, crossed the Delaware at Cooper's Ferry, now Camden, to the north, on Tuesday, October 21, 1777. They marched to Haddonfield that evening and to Red Bank at 3 AM Wednesday morning. A young apprentice blacksmith named Jonas Cattell ran 5 miles from Haddonfield to Fort

Photo NJ-40. *The house of James and Ann Whitall was commandeered by the Continental Army in April 1777. The apple orchard was destroyed to build Fort Mercer, and the house was used as a field hospital during the Battle of Red Bank. Major General Karl von Donop died here. He was interred on the battlefield on October 28, 1777.*

Photo NJ-41. *Fraise consists of sharpened stakes built into the exterior wall of a fortification to deter attackers*

Mercer during the night to warn Colonel Greene that the Hessians were camped to his north, a lightly protected side of Fort Mercer.

Colonel Greene moved his men away from the river to the northern face. When von Donop arrived, he sent a flag to demand the surrender of Fort Mercer at 4:30 PM, but Greene refused. The Hessians began a brisk cannonade at 4:45 PM and soon advanced in two columns to attack from the north and south. They advanced up the steep slopes twice under heavy fire from the smaller Continental force. They passed the abatis and entered the ditch. A few men got over the pickets, but the fire was so heavy they were soon driven back. They lost one lieutenant colonel, three captains, four lieutenants, and nearly 70 privates killed along with General von Donop, his brigade major, a captain lieutenant and more than 70 men, commissioned officers and privates, wounded and taken prisoners and several wagons captured. Having lost nearly half their men, the Hessians retreated toward Haddonfield, then to Philadelphia. They withdrew in such a hurry that a lieutenant who could not run fast enough returned to give himself up. They left a doctor and a sergeant to take care of 12 men who were so badly wounded that they couldn't escape.

The engagement lasted about 40 minutes. Colonel Christopher Greene's regiment lost two sergeants, one fifer, and four privates killed and one sergeant and three privates wounded. One captain, who was reconnoitering, was taken prisoner. Colonel Israel Angell (1740–1832) had one captain killed and one ensign, three sergeants, and three privates wounded. Two of Captain Dupless's company were slightly wounded. Almost 300 muskets were brought into the fort after the battle. The Continentals captured, court-martialed, and hanged two of their countrymen—one white, one black—who had guided von Donop to Fort Mercer.[599]

Two British warships sent to support von Donop ran aground and had to be abandoned. The Continentals set one of them afire, the 64-gun *Augusta*, with hot shot (heated cannon ball) from Fort Mifflin. The warship blew up on October 23. The British burned the other, the 16-gun frigate *Merlin*. The explosion of the *Augusta* caused Joseph Plumb Martin (1760–1850), a soldier at Fort Mifflin, across the river near Philadelphia, to write that it "seemed to shake the earth to its center." Thomas Paine (1737–1809), who was several miles west of Philadelphia, was "stunned with a report as loud as a peal from a hundred cannon at once."[600]

When the defenders of Fort Mifflin were forced to abandon that fort during the night of Saturday, November 15, Fort Mercer became untenable. Colonel Greene abandoned the fort during the night of November 20 as General Charles Cornwallis advanced with 2,000 troops for another assault.[601]

★ HMS *Isis* and *Pearl* exchanged fire for some time with a battery at Mantua Creek on the New Jersey shore below Red Bank Wednesday morning, November 5, 1777. The small fascine battery (see Photo NJ-42, NJ-2), on the east side of the creek about 1 mile from Billingsport, had one 18- and one 12-pounder commanded by Captain Henry "Light-Horse Harry" Lee (1756–1818). Continental galleys joined in the fray at 11 AM but retreated after firing a few shots. The battery resumed fire at 2 PM along with the galleys. They were joined by 12 other galleys about 4 PM. The firing continued until sunset. The hull and rigging of the *Isis* and the *Pearl* suffered much damage. The *Pearl* reported one man killed and another wounded.[602]

See also **Billingsport** and **Mantua.**

★ West Jersey Loyalists left Philadelphia on Monday, February 2, 1778 to raid the vicinity of Red Bank.[603]

Photo NJ-42. Gabions and fascines. The gabions are the basket-like objects in the background. The fascines are the bundles of sticks in the foreground. Together, they are used to strengthen the walls of earthworks or fortifications.

Woodbury (Sept. 23, 1777; Jan. 3, 1778; Mar. 31, 1778)

Woodbury is 3 miles southeast of the Red Bank Battlefield Park in National Park.

Hessian troops skirmished with Congressional forces at Woodbury on Tuesday, September 23, 1777. They then returned toward Philadelphia.

★ A party of Loyalists and a small party of marines marched toward Woodbury on Saturday, January 3, 1778. When they learned the militia had mustered there, they left after taking a large number of cattle.[604]

★ On Tuesday March 31, 1778, a party of Loyalists and few marines marched toward Woodbury to conduct a foraging raid. The New Jersey militiamen learned about it and mustered at Woodbury. The raiders seized a large number of cattle.[605]

Billingsport (Oct. 1–2, 1777; Oct. 6, 1777; Oct. 11, 1777; Oct. 14, 1777; Oct. 15, 1777; Oct. 23, 1777; Nov. 9, 1777; Nov. 19, 1777; Mar. 6, 1778; Mar. 16–17, 1778; Apr. 17, 1778)

Mickleton (Oct. 2, 1777)

Mantua (Oct. 2, 1777; Nov. 5, 1777; November 11, 1777; November 13, 1777; Nov. 15, 1777; Nov. 20–27, 1777; Feb. 2, 1778; Mar. 12, 1778; Mar. 16, 1778)

Billingsport and Fort Billings, also known as Billingsport Redoubt and the Mantua battery, were named after Edward Byllynge. It was a 15-acre square earthwork on the east side of Mantua Creek with four corner bastions (see Photo NJ-11, NJ-12), barracks, officers' quarters, and a bakehouse. It protected the chevaux-de-frise (see Photo NJ-34), set across the Delaware River. The British captured this defense near Paulsboro in 1777 and destroyed it. The Congressional forces rebuilt the fort after the British left Philadelphia. The site is now an oil tank farm at Mount Royal on Kings Highway.

See also **Fort Mercer.**

Brigadier General Silas Newcomb (1723–1779) took a position inland from Fort Billings Wednesday night, October 1, 1777. Before daybreak the following day, he visited Colonel William Bradford (1719–1791) at the fort and told him that he had a few militiamen with two or three field pieces and planned to engage the enemy. He "drew off what Jersey militia was at the Garrison to join his Body" and headed south with his force of about 300 men.

He engaged Lieutenant Colonel Thomas Stirling (d. 1808) in a "pretty brisk fire" about 9 AM and realized that the enemy strength was "not less than 1500" instead of about 400 men as he had thought. Colonel Stirling sent out strong flanking parties which caused Newcomb to order a slow retreat, keeping up a constant fire to avoid being surrounded. The British pursued him past the turn of the road leading to the fort and up Salem Road to Mantua Creek where he took a position "a little way on this side [north] of Manto Creek."

General Newcomb engaged the British here, killing three or four before they withdrew toward the fort. Colonel Bradford sent a small scouting party to reconnoiter when he heard cannon and musket fire. He reported that "the Jersey [militia] had retreated and the Enemy were advancing to the Fort." Colonel Bradford ordered the fort evacuated immediately. The men proceeded to the guard boats from the Continental brig *Andrea Doria* which were waiting to transfer them to Fort Mifflin, across the river, according to General George Washington's (1732–1799) orders of the 28th.

Colonel Bradford and Captain Isaiah Robinson (d. ca. 1781) of the *Andrea Doria* and a few men remained in the fort briefly to take the ammunition, spike the cannon, and set the barracks and bake house on fire. They were still in the fort about noon when Colonel Bradford saw the enemy coming toward them "thro' a cornfield . . . not more than 30 yards" away. He and his few remaining men exchanged several shots as they boarded the last guard boat and began rowing out to the *Andrea Doria*.

Shortly after the British occupied the fort, Continental row galleys, which had dropped down-river began shelling (see Photo NJ-4, NJ-5) the fort. Four British ships came up river to support Colonel Stirling and fired several volleys inflicting considerable punishment on the row galleys which withdrew up-river while the British ships anchored in five fathoms.

The heavy shelling of the galleys caused two whole crews, including the officers, to desert to the enemy after dark. Captain Andrew Snape Hamond (1738–1828,) of the HMS *Roebuck,* took this as a sign of weakness and sent a flag of truce to Commodore John Hazlewood (ca. 1726–1800) the next morning, "desiring him to give up the Fleet, and he should with his men Have his Majesty's Pardon and be treated kindly. The Commodore sent him Word he should defend the Fleet to the last and not give them up, and was not afraid of all the Ships they could bring, and desired they would send no more such flags."

The British replaced the fort's spiked cannon with two 12-pounders and began work to open up the lower chevaux-de-frise early in the morning of the 4th. The work was suddenly stopped on October 6th to evacuate the men in the fort because the British had received intelligence that the Congressional forces were strong in the area and might attack the fort.

Colonel Stirling had taken most of his men on the 4th and gone on a foraging expedition, leaving only 300 men to defend the fort. A company of New Jersey militiamen attacked the foraging party, killing or wounding some men. They retook several cattle. Fearing an attack by the same force, the British evacuated the fort at 6 PM on the 5th deeming it unsafe to remain there with only 300 men.

Continental sailors scuttled two vessels, the brig *Vesuvius* and the ship *Strumbello*, to close the gap where the chevaux-de-frise had been removed.[606]

★ Brigadier General Silas Newcomb (1723–1779) and about 300 New Jersey militiamen tried to block Lieutenant Colonel Thomas Stirling's (d. 1808) advance on Billingsport on Friday morning, October 2, 1777. The British soon routed them and Colonel William Bradford (1719–1791) realized that his 100 Pennsylvania militiamen could not defend the fort against a vastly superior force. He ordered the redoubt abandoned. The defenders spiked the artillery they could not take with them, removed the ammunition and set fire to the barracks and bake house. Boats of the Pennsylvania State Navy transported them to Fort Mifflin. The British occupied the fort shortly after noon without any casualties.[607]

★ Six row galleys came down the river at 11 AM on Monday the 6th and anchored below Hog Island. They fired several shots at the Billingsport fort which returned fire and drove the galleys up the river.[608]

★ Congressional troops completed a second battery of two guns, a 24-pounder and another gun, near Tench Francis's (1731–1800) house near Mantua Creek on Saturday morning, October 11, 1777. The farm consisted of 750 acres between Mantua and Little Mantua Creeks and extended out to the Delaware. There were two houses on the property: one a few hundred feet from the Delaware, the other a considerable distance farther back. The battery was located at the house closer to the river, near the end of what is now Leonard Lane, and was called the Mantua Creek battery.

The Continental fleet of more than 40 miscellaneous vessels moved into position to engage the *HMS Isis* and *Somerset* in the early afternoon. The *Cornwallis, Liverpool, Pearl,* and *Roebuck* came up-river to assist. They came under fire from the two shore batteries at Mantua Creek. The engagement continued for about two hours, with the shore batteries maintaining a steady fire on the British ships, compelling them to divide their fire between the shore batteries and the Continental fleet.

Meanwhile, the British batteries on Province and Carpenter's Island on the Pennsylvania side of the river fired on Fort Mifflin along with the *Vigilant* and *Fury.* The *Somerset* signaled the ships to retreat at 5 PM. All the ships, except the *Vigilant* and *Fury,* weighed anchor, proceeded down-river, and anchored off Billingsport. Every ship was severely damaged. The *Isis* "received 34 shells that went right through it." Many were killed or wounded.

★ The Continentals sent five fire rafts chained together down the Delaware River at 2 AM on Tuesday, October 14, 1777 under cover of their galleys. The HMS *Liverpool* kept up a constant fire on the Continentals who sent four more rafts at 3 o'clock. The *Liverpool* sent her boats to tow them ashore. As the galleys approached Commander John Henry's armed ship *Vigilant* at 5 AM, he fired several shots at them and they retreated. The *Vigilant* proceeded near the chevaux-de-frise at 11 AM to cover the *Liverpool.* She also assisted in moving the chevaux-de-frise off Billingsport and in destroying the platforms of the fort at Billingsport.[609]

★ Captain Henry Bellew sent a landing party from the HMS *Liverpool* to destroy the fort at Billingsport on Wednesday, October 15, 1777. Two days later, men from Captain James Wallace's (1731–1803) HMS *Experiment* captured about eight Congressional troops and supplies at Billingsport.[610]

★ British Major General Thomas Wilson landed at Billingsport at 8 AM on Wednesday, October 18, 1777, along with Brigadier General Alexander Leslie's (1740–1794) infantry and Brigadier General James Pattison's (1724–1805) artillery. The approximately 4,000 troops consisted of "the 7th, 26th, 63rd Regiments, two Battalions of Anspack, about 300 Jaegers, 400 to 500 convalescents and recruits, and the 17th regiment Light Dragoons and 70 of the Guards." Recently arrived from New York, the men were coming for their first action of the campaign.

Meanwhile, Lieutenant General Charles Cornwallis (1738–1805) and Brigadier General William Erskine (1728–1795) marched from Philadelphia at 2 AM with about 3,000 men from the "1st Battalion Grenadiers, 1st Battalion Light Infantry, one Battalion Hessian Grenadiers, 50 Jaegers and the 33d and 27th Regiments, plus the "1st Regiment artillery." They crossed the bridge over the Schuylkill and marched to Chester. The British Delaware squadron began transporting them across the Delaware River at 10 AM on the 19th and completed the task by sunset.

The small British garrison stationed at Billingsport to guard the passage through the lower chevaux-de-frise was now reinforced by the 7,000 troops who arrived without any opposition. General William Howe (1732–1786) also sent the 42nd Regiment across the Delaware to New Jersey. They landed at Cooper's Ferry to protect General Cornwallis's return route to Philadelphia after he took Fort Mercer.

★ The Crown forces began a heavy fire from their batteries and from the vessels which had passed the Billingsport chevaux-de-frise on Thursday morning, October 23, 1777. They kept up a cannonade part of the morning.[611]

★ A battery near the mouth of Mantua Creek fired on British ships in the Delaware River on Wednesday, November 5, 1777.[612]

★ The HMS *Roebuck*, anchored near Fort Billingsport, sent the stream anchor to assist the HMS *Somerset* through the chevaux-de-frise at 11 AM on Sunday, November 9, 1777.[613]

★ The HM Galley *Cornwallis* and the HM Sloop tender *Elk*, belonging to the *Eagle*, fired on a battery near Little Mantua Creek Tuesday afternoon, November 11, 1777 as the Continental soldiers were engaged in constructing it.[614]

★ Brigadier General James Mitchell Varnum (1748–1789) received intelligence that the British in New Jersey numbered close to 8,000 men. He had only about 1,800 Continentals and 200 to 300 New Jersey militiamen under Brigadier General Silas Newcomb (1723–1779) to defend the area. General George Washington (1732–1799), aware of his army's weakness, and having to defend both Pennsylvania and New Jersey, had been urging Major General Horatio Gates (1728–1806), commander of the northern army, for weeks to send a sizable body of troops to the main army. Gates waited until after the victory at Saratoga, New York, on October 17th, before sending Colonel Daniel Morgan (1736–1802) south with his corps. Three weeks later, Brigadier General John Glover's (1732–1797) and General John Paterson's (1744–1808) brigades marched south on November 10.

Morgan's corps of "552 officers and men present and fit for duty" headed for Washington's headquarters at Whitemarsh, Pennsylvania. Paterson's and Glover's brigades of "963 and 1176 men present and fit for duty," also headed for Whitemarsh; but, along the route, they received orders to support General Varnum in New Jersey. When General Cornwallis landed in New Jersey, Paterson's brigade was still in the Hudson Highlands and Glover's brigade had not yet reached Morristown.

General Washington ordered General Jedediah Huntington (1743–1818) and his brigade of 1,200 men to march to assist General Varnum on the 19th. Major General Nathanael Greene's (1742–1786) division of 2,000 men from Brigadier General John Peter Gabriel Muhlenberg's (1746–1807) and Brigadier General George Weedon's (1734–1793) brigades was sent to New Jersey the following day. Morgan's corps had arrived at headquarters a day or two earlier and were badly in need of shoes because of their long march. Washington sent them, under the command of Lieutenant Colonel Richard Butler (1743–1791), to assist General Varnum in New Jersey, on the 21st even though only 170 of them were fit to march.

Meanwhile, General Washington sent word to Colonel Christopher Greene (1737–1781) to hold Fort Mercer "til the relief arrives" if possible. Washington then went to Crooked Billet, now Hatboro, Pennsylvania, to be closer to the action. Varnum's force of 2,000, reinforced by Huntington's brigade of 1,200 and Greene's division of 2,000 plus Morgan's 150 riflemen, now totaling 5,350, was still outnumbered by 2,650 men.

★ The HMS *Liverpool* and *Isis* weighed anchor at 9 AM on Thursday, November 13, 1777 and sailed up the Delaware River to anchor abreast of a small battery the Continental soldiers were constructing near Little Mantua Creek to impede British ships. Captain Henry Bellew dropped a small anchor to steady the ship and began to fire at the Continentals. The cannonade continued until 1 PM.[615]

★ A second battery near the mouth of Mantua Creek opened fire on British ships in the Delaware River on Saturday, November 15, 1777.[616]

★ The British main force kept close to Billingsport on November 19th, as they were "employ'd in getting Waggons for the march" north. A scouting party reconnoitered the Mantua Creek gun emplacements during the day and other scouting parties did some further reconnaissance in the afternoon and evening. "Two Companies Light Infantry were landed on the other side of the mouth of Manto [Mantua] Creek to see if the Battery was evacuated. . . . They were fired on by a Sentry from a Small Guard and return'd." Two more companies were sent over in the morning "and found the Battery evacuated and a 24 pounder unspiked."

Brigadier General James Mitchell Varnum (1748–1789) went to Fort Mercer "at 5 p.m. on the 19th" and found it being evacuated. "Powder . . . was already strewed over the Fort," ready to be lit. The main body of troops was already outside the fort, ready to march after Colonel Christopher Greene (1737–1781) had received erroneous intelligence "that the Enemy were actually crossing the Ford" over Mantua Creek. The main force actually remained at Billingsport and only advance patrols and scouting parties crossed Mantua Creek on the 19th.

General Varnum conferred with Colonel Greene and told him that General Washington "might make a great Effort to save the Garrison [if the troops] agreed to remain; Hoping to take up the scattered Powder by Day Light. Immediately they were alarmed by the rowing of many Boats near the Shore. This changed the Scene and induced us to bring off the Men . . . [because] the firing a single Musket in the Garrison would blow it up, or the bursting of a single shell was concluded to take away the Men, leaving a small Number to set Fire in Case of Necessity, & trust to their Fate."

However, the sound of rowing boats was another false alarm. Instead of British boats coming to attack, they were Continental row galleys being moved "into Lads Cove," between Red Bank and Timber Creek, in preparation for the next day's movement up the east channel past Cooper's Ferry.

Meanwhile, Colonel Greene evacuated his garrison to Haddonfield. When he learned the following morning that the Crown forces had not yet taken Fort Mercer, he decided to make some attempt to comply with General Washington's wishes to hold the fort until relief arrived. Colonel Greene mustered his men and asked that "50 men properly officered . . . turn out" to return to the fort. He indicated they would "go by way of Gloucester Point and there will be supplied with boats to go to the fort." If the enemy approached and they found it necessary to retreat, they should return along the same route. "A Number of large Waggons" were sent to the fort after it was reoccupied. The men spent most of the day removing supplies.

The British light infantry sent to take Fort Mercer received intelligence "that the Rebels had evacuated Red Bank." They were confident that they could take the fort easily, unaware that 50 men had returned to the fort. Instead of waiting for the British to arrive, the Continentals inside the fort ignited the powder at 6 AM on Friday, November 21st. A short while later, the entire countryside "saw the Fort at Red Bank in flames." The 50 Continentals then escaped by water, as planned.

★ About 4,000 or 5,000 Crown troops landed at Billingsport, 7 miles from Red Bank on Wednesday, November 19, 1777. The Continentals left Fort Mercer and went to Haddonfield about 9 miles away. They left about 200 men behind to hold the fort until reinforcements arrived from headquarters.[617]

★ The officers of the Continental Navy met in council late Friday evening, November 19, 1777 aboard the sloop *Speedwell* off Red Bank. Informed of the evacuation of Fort Mercer, they decided unanimously that the larger ships of the fleet be prepared "in the Morning flood . . . of the 20th . . . to go up the Western Channel, [but] be prepared with combustible matter so as to be set instantly on fire and consumed, should the wind on the said Morning flood not be such as to render their passage practicable . . . other smaller vessels destined for the Eastern Channel the same preparation be made for burning."

Commodore John Hazlewood (ca. 1726–1800) ordered "the 13 Gallies to go close up under Cooper's Ferry, it being quite calm" at 3 AM on the 20th. The galleys, propelled by oars, arrived at their destination without incident; but the sound of their oars had precipitated the premature evacuation of Fort Mercer. The rest of the fleet remained in port as there was "no wind blowing." British batteries at Fort Mifflin annoyed them with a few cannon shots during the day.

★ Before dawn on Thursday, November 20, 1777, while it was still calm, Captain John Rice's brig *Convention*, Captain Richard Eyres's schooner *Delaware,* and six shallops set out to pass the British land and sea batteries. They heard and saw the explosion and fire at Fort Mercer shortly after daybreak and were especially anxious to get up-river.

"Being seasonably discovered, they were opposed with so much effect by Lieutenant [James] Watt of the *Roebuck*" who captured the *Delaware*. A "very hot fire of shot and shell from the Town" joined in as the Continental ships attempted to run the blockade. The vessels made it up the western channel under an "exceedingly hot fire . . . except the [schooner] *Delaware* and one shallop, which were ran aground and set on fire. The continental vessels finding . . . no wind to carry them by . . . the brig *Andria Doria, Xebecks Repulse* and *Champion*, the sloops *Race-horse* and *Champion*, with two floating batteries and three fire-ships were accordingly set on fire and destroyed" near League Island. Some of the vessels drifted within 2 miles of Philadelphia before the ebb tide carried them back. They burned nearly five hours; and four of them blew up.

★ General Cornwallis sent the 1st Light Infantry from Billingsport to repair "the bridge at Sand Town [Mt. Royal or Berkeley] over Manto Creek about 4.5 miles in front" on Thursday, November 20, 1777. The main army "march'd by the Bridge over Manto Creek" and proceeded north the next morning. The 7th and 63rd Regiments remained at the bridge to protect it and to "keep up the communications with Billingsport and to Collect Cattle."

Crown forces skirmished with Congressional forces at a ford in Mantua Creek on Thursday, November 20, 1777. The ford was 5 miles above a bridge the Continentals had destroyed.[618]

★ General Charles Cornwallis (1738–1805) burned the barracks at Mantua Creek between November 20 and 27, 1777 as he marched from Billingsport to Gloucester.[619]

When the Crown troops arrived at Woodbury, they encamped "on very advantageous ground round the Village." The 1st Light Infantry marched to Red Bank and Fort Mercer while a detail went to take possession of the "Bridge over Timber Creek which was Broke up."

★ Brigadier General James Mitchell Varnum (1748–1789) remained helpless with 3,000 men on Friday, November 21st. His troops were deployed as follows: "at the Fort and at Woodbury at least 1800 men," plus the militia, which now consisted of "Twelve Hundred, Three Hundred here [at Mt. Holly] Seven Hundred at Haddonfield . . . Two Hundred at Cooper's Ferry and Gloucester." These 3,000 scattered troops, outnumbered by almost three to one, could accomplish very little against an army of 8,000 men, even though Colonel Jedediah Huntington (1743–1818) would arrive before the end of the day with 5,489 men.

Major General Nathanael Greene (1742–1786) had just crossed the Delaware and was at Burlington, New Jersey. General John Glover's (1732–1797) men "were advancing down the Road from Morristown" while General John Paterson (1744–1808) was still farther behind, and Colonel Daniel Morgan's (1736–1802) corps was just leaving Whitemarsh, Pennsylvania.

★ General Greene had assembled a substantial army in New Jersey by Wednesday, November 26, 1777. It consisted of his 2,000 men, Varnum's 1,800, Huntington's 1,200, Morgan's 150, Glover's 1,176, and 1,200 New Jersey militiamen. Paterson and his 963 men were still en route. Greene decided not to wait any longer and prepared to engage Cornwallis's 8,000-man army with his force of 7,526 on the 26th. General Greene set his order of battle as follows:

> General Varnum's and General Huntington's brigade form the right wing, General Varnum's on the right of the wing, Huntington's on the left. The right wing to be commanded by General Varnum. General Muhlenberg's and General Weedon's brigades form the left wing, General Muhlenberg's the left of the wing and General Weedon's the right of the wing. General Muhlenberg commands the left wing.
>
> General Glover's brigade forms the second line. Colonel Hait's [Joseph Haight (1739–1795)] and Colonel [Benoni] Hathaway's [1743–1823] [New Jersey] militia form upon the right flank. Colonel Joseph Ellis' [New Jersey] militia and Morgan's light corps cover the left flank. . . . In marching into action, the Brigades are to march in regimental columns. . . . The artillery to be immediately under the direction of the commanding officer of the brigades.

The battle never occurred because General Washington, on the 25th, had "Accounts from the City [that] say Lord Cornwallis was expected back today or tomorrow." Washington was "suspicious that they mean to collect their whole force while ours is divided, and make an attack on the Army on this side." He wrote General Greene that "I therefore desire (except you have a plan or prospect of doing some thing to advantage) that you will rejoin me with your whole force as quick as possible."[620]

★ About 20 West Jersey Loyalists crossed the Delaware from Philadelphia on Monday, February 2, 1778 to assist some of their friends who had expressed a desire to take refuge in Philadelphia. They fell into an ambuscade with a party of Whigs at the mouth of Mantua Creek. The Loyalists repulsed the militiamen and advanced 4 miles into the country. They captured a man by the name of Wilson who was a committee man who annoyed the Loyalists. They returned to Philadelphia with their friends and their prisoner who was held in confinement.[621]

★ A small party of Loyalist Captain Wigstaff's company went to Billingsport on Friday, March 6, 1778. They marched 10 miles into the country, surrounded the house of Captain John Cozens, captain of the First Battalion of Gloucester Militia, and took him and his guard prisoners. Captain Cozens was exchanged as a prisoner of war on December 8, 1780.[622]

See also **Penn's Neck.**

★ Gloucester County militiamen skirmished with Lieutenant Colonel Charles Mawhood's (d. 1780) foraging party at Mantua Creek on Thursday, March 12, 1778.[623]

★ Lieutenant Colonel Charles Mawhood's Regulars marched up Salem Road to Mantua Creek Bridge, the only place they could cross Mantua Creek on Monday, March 16, 1778. There, they met Captain Samuel Hugg with artillery and other militia and engaged in a brief skirmish.[624]

★ Captain Edward Pakenham of *HMS Viper* exchanged fire with Whigs on shore erecting a breastwork at Billingsport on Monday and Tuesday, March 16–17, 1778.

★ Men from Captain James Wallace's (1731–1803) HMS *Experiment* seized some Whigs and stores at Billingsport on Friday, April 17, 1778. They captured about eight men.[625]

Haddonfield (Oct. 21, 1777; Nov. 24, 1777; Feb. 28, 1778; early Mar. 1778; Apr. 4, 5, 1778; June 18, 1778)

> Haddonfield is east of Philadelphia. The Indian King Tavern Museum (223 Kings Highway E.) (**www.levins.com/tavern.html**) was a meeting place for New Jersey's legislature during the war.

Local militiamen harassed British troops at Haddonfield on Tuesday, October 21, 1777 as they headed to Red Bank.

★ On Monday, November 24, 1777 before the Battle of Gloucester, Congressional troops bivouacked at Haddonfield. A British foraging party harassed them.[626]

See also **Gloucester.**

★ Brigadier General "Mad Anthony" Wayne (1745–1796) was on a foraging expedition for cattle in southern New Jersey at the end of February 1778. General William Howe (1732–1786) sent Lieutenant Colonel Robert Abercromby or Abercrombie (1740–1827) down the Delaware to attack him. He also sent Lieutenant Colonel Thomas Stirling (d. 1808) with the 42nd Regiment and the Queen's Rangers to Haddonfield on Saturday, February 28, 1778 to intercept him while Colonel Enoch Markham's detachment took their post at Cooper's Ferry to forage in its vicinity. The party captured a few militiamen who mistook them for Wayne's rear guard.[627]

★ Two divisions of Crown troops landed and marched into Haddonfield with more than 2,000 men in early March 1778. The Continentals had no more than 500 men in arms in that part of the country at that time. Brigadier General "Mad Anthony" Wayne (1745–1796) secured and sent to camp all the cattle and horses the troops came to steal and set fire to part of the forage that lay along the river bank to draw their attention toward the river and to elude their search.

Although they knew they outnumbered the Continentals, the Crown forces feared an attack by Brigadier General Casimir Pulaski's (1747–1779) light horsemen. They retreated to Cooper's Ferry in a hurry, leaving their baggage, behind. Pulaski's Legion attacked the middle of the force at Cooper's Ferry. Pulaski soon found himself surrounded and the Crown forces closed in on him. However, the militiamen were in their way and gave them a few volleys causing the Crown troops to flee.

The following morning, Count Pulaski was determined to push them into the Delaware, but found they had re-crossed to Philadelphia.[628]

★ Lieutenant Colonel Robert Abercromby or Abercrombie (1740–1827) of the 37th Regiment received information that a body of about 300 Congressional troops and two field pieces were assembled at Haddonfield. He led a detachment of 500 British grenadiers (see Photo NJ-10) and a party of light infantrymen down the Delaware River in flatboats on Saturday night, April 4, 1778. They landed at Gloucester Point and marched to Haddonfield where they intended to surprise a strong enemy post at Haddonfield Meetinghouse the following morning. Scouting dragoons and two deserted sailors informed the militiamen of their danger. They left the meetinghouse and withdrew to Woodbury, 5 miles behind Haddonfield. They left six men behind in a house who fired on the British troops who soon forced their way into the house and bayoneted them.

The grenadiers surprised a picket of only 50 officers and men, killed eight and captured 37, including Major William Ellis (1730–1785). On his return, Lieutenant Colonel Abercromby learned that about 40 Congressional troops were lodged near Cooper's Ferry; so he marched his men to the ferry and surrounded it and had another skirmish there.[629]

See **Gloucester** and **Camden, Cooper's Ferry.**

★ A party of Colonel George Turnbull's (1752–1807) New York Volunteers captured four Congressional troops near Bergen, probably Haddonfield, during the first week in April 1778. The Loyalists brought in more than 30 prisoners from New Jersey on Sunday, April 5, 1778, including Major William Ellis (1730–1785). The troops were stationed to prevent the country people from going to market.[630]

★ Brigadier General William Maxwell's (1733–1796) brigade harassed the British at Haddonfield on Thursday, June 18, 1778, as they evacuated Philadelphia.[631]

Timber Creek (Oct. 21, 1777; Nov. 20, 1777; Nov. 25, 1777)

> Timber Creek empties into the Delaware River south of Gloucester and north of the Red Bank Battlefield in National Park.

Major General Count Karl Emil Kurt von Donop (1740–1777) landed at Cooper's Ferry with four battalions of Hessians totaling 1,200 men on Tuesday, October 21, 1777. They marched to Haddonfield that evening and to Red Bank at 3 AM, Wednesday morning. The guards at Timber Creek bridge were informed of their approach and took up the bridge. When the Hessians arrived, they filed off to the left and crossed at a bridge 4 miles above. Their advance parties were discovered within a quarter of a mile of the fort at noon. The Hessians sent a flag to demand the surrender of Fort Mercer at 4:30 PM and were told that the fort would never surrender.

The Hessians began a brisk cannonade at 4:45 PM and soon advanced in two columns to attack. They passed the abatis, entered the ditch, and a few got over the pickets, but the fire was so heavy they were soon driven back with the loss of one lieutenant colonel, three captains, four lieutenants, and nearly 70 privates killed along with General von Donop, his brigade major, a captain lieutenant and more than 70 men, commissioned officers and privates, wounded and taken prisoners and several wagons captured. Almost 300 muskets were brought into the fort after the battle. The Hessians then retreated quickly toward Haddonfield.

The engagement lasted about 40 minutes. Colonel Christopher Greene's (1737–1781) regiment lost two sergeants, one fifer, and four privates killed and one sergeant and three privates wounded. One captain, who was reconnoitering, was taken prisoner. Colonel Israel Angell (1740–1832) had one captain killed and one ensign, three sergeants, and three privates wounded. Two of Captain Dupless's company were slightly wounded.[632]

★ New Jersey militiamen fired on Crown troops at a bridge over Timber Creek on Thursday, November 20, 1777.[633]

★ A tender belonging to the HMS *Roebuck* arrived at Timber Creek on Tuesday, November 25, 1777 with news of the capture of the forts at Red Bank and Mud Island and the destruction of many Continental vessels. A few of their galleys sought shelter in Timber Creek, upon the river, between Gloucester Point and Red Bank.[634]

Camden
Cooper's Ferry (Pluckemin) (Dec. 16, 1776; Oct. 21, 1777; Dec. 15, 1777; Feb. 28, 1778; Mar. 1, 1778; Apr. 5, 1778)

> Cooper's Ferry crossed the Delaware River between Philadelphia, Pennsylvania and Camden, New Jersey. It was also known as Pluckemin and simply as the Ferry. It consisted of only a few houses until after the war. It was located on the main colonial road through Philadelphia.

British Brigadier General Edward Mathew (often misspelled Matthews) (1729–1805) with part of the Brigade of Guards engaged a small body of Congressional troops at Pluckemin on Monday, December 16, 1776. They wounded two.[635]

★ Congressional troops sniped at British troops at Cooper's Ferry on their way from Philadelphia to Red Bank on Tuesday, October 21, 1777.[636]

★ On their return from a raid at Haddonfield, Lieutenant Colonel Robert Abercromby or Abercrombie (1740–1827) learned that about 40 Congressional troops were lodged near Cooper's Ferry; so he marched to the ferry and surrounded it on Sunday, April 5, 1778. A light horseman had been dispatched to warn the guard at Cooper's Ferry but he was killed along the way; so the guard at the ferry had no notion that the enemy were approaching. After a brief skirmish in which several were wounded, the British captured 36 prisoners, including Major William Ellis (1730–1785) of the Gloucester militia and Lieutenant Abraham Stout (1754–1821) and Lieutenant Thomas Machin (1744–1816) of Colonel Israel Shreve's (1739–1799) 2nd New Jersey Regiment, all of whom were imprisoned in the provost Sunday morning. The British suffered no injuries in this excursion and returned to Philadelphia the same evening after burning several dwelling houses.[637]

★ The New Jersey militia captured 20 British sailors at Cooper's Ferry on Monday, December 15, 1777.[638]

★ Brigadier General "Mad Anthony" Wayne (1745–1796) was on a foraging expedition for cattle in southern Jersey at the end of February 1778. General William Howe (1732–1786) sent Lieutenant Colonel Robert Abercromby or Abercrombie (1740–1827) down the Delaware to attack him. He also sent Lieutenant Colonel Thomas Stirling (d. 1808) with the 42nd Regiment and the Queen's Rangers to Haddonfield to intercept him while Colonel Enoch Markham's detachment took their post at Cooper's Ferry to forage in its vicinity.

Major John Graves Simcoe (1752–1806) was detached early the next morning to destroy the boats and stores that were brought to Timber Creek after the naval armaments on the Delaware were burned. Some Loyalists wanted to bring the boats to Philadelphia; so they were sent down the creek to receive them. The boats were laden with 150 barrels of tar which they found and which the fleet needed. The tar was sent to Captain Andrew Snape Hamond (1738–1828) who commanded the navy in the Delaware.

The party captured a few militiamen who mistook them for Wayne's rear guard. Colonel Stirling, about midnight, ordered Major Simcoe to march as early as possible to quell any militia in the area, as they had attacked the Loyalists who were to receive the boats.

★ Major Simcoe surrounded the house of militia lieutenant Tew with the hussars before daybreak on Sunday, March 1, 1778. They waited in silence for the infantry to arrive; but the only people in the house were Tew's wife and other women. The troops returned to Haddonfield and made an excursion on the road to Egg Harbor early the next morning to get what cattle and rum they might find.

The advanced part of the corps and the hussars procured a few hogsheads of rum and some cattle about 20 miles from Haddonfield and destroyed some tobacco. That night, a man arrived at the outpost with information that Wayne was on his march from Mount Holly to attack the troops at Haddonfield. Colonel Stirling understood that Wayne's force had been so considerably augmented that it would be imprudent to remain at Haddonfield. The whole detachment prepared to march immediately.

A cold sleet fell the whole way from Haddonfield to Cooper's Ferry. When the troops arrived, they had to pass the night without fires, as the area had several barns and forage. The weather cleared up by dawn. Captain James Kerr (1766–1840) was sent with 50 men of the 42nd Regiment and the rangers to escort the wagons that went for some forage about 3.5 miles from Cooper's Ferry and 0.5 miles within the direct road to Haddonfield. Lieutenant Wickham and 10 hussars on patrol in the front toward Haddonfield met Brigadier General Casimir Pulaski (1747–1779) and about 200 dragoons a few miles away.

As the road led through thick woods, Lieutenant Wickham shouted orders to an imaginary infantry to deceive the dragoons into thinking they were entering an ambush. This stratagem gave time to Captain Kerr to retreat. The hussars then joined him and returned to camp. Colonel Markham's detachment followed the dragoons and were barely half way over the Delaware when his pickets were attacked. The 42nd Regiment marched forward and the Queen's Rangers advanced in column, by companies, while Cooper's Creek secured its left flank. When some of the dragoons appeared on the opposite bank of Cooper Creek, Captain Armstrong and the grenadiers took position along a dike. The

42nd kept up a heavy fire on the right. As the Queen's Rangers advanced rapidly to occupy a hill in front, the dragoons, who observed their movements, fled into the wood.

A few straggling shots were fired in the front; and the light infantry company and the Highlanders were sent there to clear the front. A few cannon shots were fired at some of the dragoons who were near the bridge over Cooper Creek until the artillery realized that they were busy destroying the bridge. The firing ceased and the dragoons retreated. A few of the Rangers were wounded. Pulaski's horse was wounded and he might have been captured or killed had not the hussars been sent over the Delaware before the attack.[639]

★ As Lieutenant Colonel Robert Abercromby or Abercrombie (1740–1827) returned to Philadelphia from a raid at Haddonfield on Sunday, April 5, 1778, he went by way of Cooper's Ferry. There, he encountered an outpost of one major, two captains, three subalterns, and 40 soldiers. The major, the captains, and two of the subalterns did not belong to the detachment but had come to reconnoiter the bank, the ships, and the city of Philadelphia. Abercrombie's troops killed one captain and nine men and captured the rest.[640]

Gloucester (Nov. 25, 27, 1777; Apr. 4, 1778; June 11, 18, 1778; Dec. 29, 1778)

Gloucester is on the Delaware River south of Camden.

Major General Marie Jean Paul Joseph du Motier Marquis de Lafayette (1757–1834) led a reconnaissance force consisting of Colonel Jedediah Huntington's (1743–1818) brigade, 170 of Colonel Daniel Morgan's (1736–1802) riflemen, and New Jersey militiamen. They skirmished with and beat a larger force of German troops at Gloucester on Tuesday, November 25, 1777. The Congressional troops lost one man killed and five wounded.[641]

★ General Charles Cornwallis (1738–1805) returned to Philadelphia two days later, after clearing the east bank of the Delaware River of Congressional troops. He took 800 men and was harassed by local militiamen who killed the sergeant-major of the 33rd Regiment and three privates of the 5th Regiment.[642]

★ Having received intelligence that a party of about 300 Whigs had gathered at Haddonfield with two field pieces, the Crown forces sent their light artillery down the river to Gloucester Point on Saturday, April 4, 1778. They then marched to Haddonfield. The Whigs were apprised of their danger and withdrew, leaving six men behind in a house. They fired on the troops who forced the door and bayoneted them. On their return, the Crown forces learned that about 40 Whigs were lodged near Cooper's Ferry; so they headed there. They surrounded the camp and wounded several men and captured 36 in a brief skirmish.[642a]

★ Foraging parties skirmished at Gloucester on Saturday, April 4, 1778.[643]

★ Some Whig cavalrymen skirmished with a band of New Jersey Loyalists and captured them at Gloucester Point on Thursday, June 11, 1778. As the British evacuated Philadelphia a week later, they crossed at Gloucester Point on their way to New York after transporting their supplies and most of their artillery into New Jersey. Some light horsemen pursued them very closely and attacked them as they crossed at Gloucester Point on Thursday morning, June 18, 1778. The dragoons took many prisoners, including some Refugees (Loyalists).[644]

★ Whigs burned three British ships on a foraging expedition on Tuesday, December 29, 1778. The vessels were caught in the ice at Gloucester Point.

Toms River (Dec. 25, 1777; Apr. 15, 1778; Sept. 19, 1778; Jan. 1779; ca. Aug. 9, 1779; Dec. 12–18, 1779; May 14, 1780; Mar. 24, 1782; Apr. 12, 1782; early May 1782; Ca. Aug. 21, 1782; Aug. 23, 1782)

Founded in the early 18th century, the village of Toms River in Dover Township was a haven from which privateers wreaked havoc on British shipping early in the American War for Independence. Toms River was destroyed in March 1782 when more than 100 Loyalists attacked the settlement shortly after dawn in an attempt to seize the highly prized local salt works and warehouses. They burned the houses, the gristmill, and the sawmill in retaliation for privateer attacks initiated from the town. They also stole the only two boats in the port at the time and burned the blockhouse, killing its defenders, and hanging its commander, Captain Joshua Huddy (1735–1782). Huddy Park and a replica of the original blockhouse, both near the waterfront in downtown Toms River, commemorate this event. The Joshua Huddy Monument is at the Colts Neck Town Hall, on Cedar Drive, Colts Neck. The blockhouse that Huddy defended and surrendered was located on the knoll where the Ocean County Courthouse was built on Washington Street in 1850.

See **Colts Neck.**

Linked to the sea and bay, the town primarily relied upon the whaling, shipping and seafood industries. The first tourists reputedly arrived aboard seafood carts that were empty after the morning's deliveries to Philadelphia. The revitalized downtown area contains shops, restaurants and coffee houses. Winding River Park, north on Main Street to NJ Route 37 then 1 mile west, straddles the Toms River.

Colonel John Morris's Second Battalion of New Jersey Loyalists threatened Toms River on Thursday, December 25, 1777; but he inflicted little damage.

★ The Crown forces raided Toms River on Wednesday, April 15, 1778 and destroyed the salt works.[645]

★ Two British armed ships and two brigs anchored close to the bar off Toms River Inlet the night of Thursday, September 18, 1778. Between 7 and 8 the following morning, they sent into the inlet seven armed boats with between 20 and 30 men in each. They retook the ship *Washington*, formerly called the *Love and Unity*, and two sloops, which were near the bar, along with most of their crews. The *Washington's* captain, his mate, boatswain, and three sailors escaped in one of the sloop's boats. Shortly after they reached shore, a certain Robert McMullen, who was condemned to be hanged for burglary and later reprieved, boarded the ship, took the boat, and escaped to join the British.[646]

★ John Gilbertson (d. 1779), a member of the Pine-Banditti, was killed by a party of militiamen near Toms River in early January 1779.[647]

★ A colonel and a major of militia who had been very zealous in persecuting the Loyalists went to Toms River to purchase some goods around August 9, 1779. A party of Loyalists ambushed them on their way home and killed them.[648]

★ Lieutenant Joshua Studson (d. 1780), of Monmouth, was shot during the week of December 12–18, 1779, as he tried to board a trading vessel off Toms River.[649]

★ Militia Major John Van Emburgh (1736–1803) of Bordentown was on a fishing party at Toms River with eight or nine men. While they were in bed on Sunday morning, May 14, 1780, a number of armed Loyalists captured the fishing party and put them on board a vessel bound for New York; but they escaped the next day.[650]

★ On Wednesday, March 20, 1782, Lieutenant Blanchard of the armed Loyalist whale-boats and about 80 seamen along with Captain Evan Thomas (1745–1835) and Lieutenant Roberts, both of the late Buck's County Volunteers, and between 30 and 40 other Loyalists proceeded to Sandy Hook under convoy of Captain Stewart Ross, in the armed brig *Arrogant.* They were detained there until the 23rd by unfavorable winds. About midnight, the party landed near the mouth of Toms River and marched to the blockhouse at the town of Dover. They reached it just at daylight. On the way, they were challenged and fired upon.

When they came to the works at Toms River on Sunday morning, March 24, 1782, they found Captain Joshua Huddy (1735–1782), captain of the Monmouth County Militia, and 25 or 26 twelve-months men and militiamen, apprised of their coming and ready to defend their post which was about six or seven feet high, made of large logs with loopholes (see Photo NJ-15) between and a number of brass swivels (see Photo NJ-1) on the top. The only way to enter was to climb over it. Besides swivels, the militiamen had long pikes and muskets with bayonets.

Captain Huddy and some of the inhabitants took refuge in the blockhouse while others remained outside to defend the house. Lieutenant Blanchard summoned the militiamen to surrender. Not only did they refuse, but they defied the Loyalists. Lieutenant Blanchard immediately ordered his men to storm the place which was defended obstinately. When the defenders ran out of ammunition, around noon, they surrendered. The Loyalists killed nine men in the assault, wounded four, and captured 12 prisoners, two of whom were wounded. The rest made their escape in the confusion. Among the killed was a major of the militia, two captains and one lieutenant. The captain of the 12 months men stationed there was taken prisoner as was Captain Huddy who was hanged later. The Loyalists had two killed, Lieutenant Iredell (d. 1782) of the armed boatmen and Lieutenant Inslee (d. 1782). Lieutenant Roberts and five others were wounded but none seriously.

The Loyalists burned the town, which consisted of about a dozen houses, a grist mill and saw mill, the salt works, and the blockhouse. An iron cannon was spiked and thrown into the river. A fine large barge (called Hyler's barge) and another boat were taken. Bad weather and the condition of the wounded, with no surgeon or medicines, induced the party to return to New York the next day with their prisoners without making any further attempts. They arrived there on Monday, March 25, 1782.

As Huddy had been captured twice before and escaped, his guards took no chances this time. Huddy was jailed briefly near the waterfront in lower Manhattan and was transferred in irons to the British prison ship *Britannia*, at anchor off Sandy Hook, when the Loyalists heard reports that a rescue party might try to free him.[651]

★ About this time, a Loyalist from Monmouth County by the name of Philip White (d. 1782), left New York to visit his wife in New Jersey. Huddy's few remaining men captured White and, a few hours later, he was dead. The militiamen insisted he was shot trying to escape. The Loyalists claimed he "had been brutally murdered, his body mutilated almost beyond recognition, and his corpse shoveled into a makeshift grave before his wife could give him decent burial."

★ The Loyalists planned to avenge his death. Captain Richard Lippincott (1745–1826), one of Huddy's neighbors, and other members of the Board of Associated Loyalists rowed out to the *Britannia* about 10 AM on Friday, April 12, 1782. Without General Henry Clinton's (1730–1795) knowledge, they took Huddy from his guards on the pretext that he was to be exchanged for a Loyalist. Huddy was brought in handcuffs to

Gravelly Point on the bank of the Navesink River on the Jersey shore. There, the Loyalists erected a gallows, using three rails, a barrel, and a rope. They gave Huddy, with the noose already around his neck, a few minutes to write his will.

Huddy was found hanging from the rope in the late afternoon with the overturned barrel at his feet. His will was in his shirt pocket and a roughly printed placard was pinned to his coat. It read:

> We the Refugees, have with grief long beheld the cruel murders of our brethren, and finding nothing but such measures daily carrying into execution; we, therefore, determine not to suffer without taking vengeance for the numerous cruelties, and thus begin, having made use of Captain Huddy as the first object to present to your view, and further determine to hang man for man, as long as a refugee [Loyalist] is left existing, UP GOES HUDDY FOR PHILIP WHITE.[652]

After Huddy's burial at Tennent Church, the people of Monmouth assembled and sent General George Washington (1732–1799) an ultimatum demanding a suitable reprisal for Huddy's death or they would take matters into their own hands and "open to view a scene at which humanity itself may shudder." Washington sent a brief note to General Clinton on Sunday, April 21st, demanding the surrender of Captain Lippincott, the leader of the hanging party. Instead of surrendering Captain Lippincott, it was decided to select someone by lottery.

★ Captain Adam Hyler or Huyler (1735–1782), commander of the privateer armed boat *Revenge*, captured Robert White's British cutter *Alert* at sea on her voyage from New York to Bermuda in April 1782. The *Alert* was brought to New Jersey and auctioned off along with a variety of goods, wares and merchandise as well as several African Americans: John Holland, Charles Jackson, Harry Jackson, John Brown, Plato Williams, Samuel Creighton, Francis Chambers, John Richards, John White, Peter Peters and Frank Oatman.[653]

★ Captain John Dimsey, master of the British schooner *Sukey* captured the 22-ton schooner *Speedwell* off the Virginia Capes near the Chesapeake Bay in early May 1782. Captain Adam Hyler or Huyler (1735–1782) re-captured the *Speedwell* in May 1782 and brought her to Toms River. The *Speedwell* was auctioned off along with her tackle, apparel, furniture and cargo at Raritan Landing on June 20, 1782.[654]

★ A major and 13 young British captains rode through the streets of Lancaster, Pennsylvania, up to the Black Bear Inn, shortly before 9 AM on Sunday, May 26. They entered the tavern and drew lots to settle the reprisal for the hanging of Captain Joshua Huddy (1735–1782). Two drummer boys each carried a hat containing slips of paper. One hat contained 13 names; the other had 12 blanks and a slip marked "Unfortunate." The boys drew 10 blanks before 19-year old Captain Charles Asgill's (1762 or 1763–1823) name was drawn with the "Unfortunate" slip. Asgill, who was captured at Yorktown, blanched and whispered, "I knew it would be so. I never won so much as a bet of backgammon in my life." The lottery condemned Asgill to death for the murder of a man he had never seen.[655]

General Washington, against capital punishment of an innocent man, found a suitable political solution when Asgill's mother wrote an impassioned plea to the French for his release. The Comte de Vergennes (1719–1787) asked King Louis XVI (1754–1793) and his queen to write letters requesting Asgill's release to General Washington. Congress voted unanimously, on November 7, that Asgill's life "should be given as a compliment to the King of France." He was set free and sent home. Partisan warfare continued in New Jersey—mostly in Monmouth County—until Governor William (1723–1790) ordered an end to all hostilities on April 14, 1783.

★ Captain Willis, in a boat from Egg Harbor, captured a Loyalist boat commanded by a man named Perry around August 21, 1782. The boat had 20 African Americans and seven white men on board.[656]

See also **Little Egg Harbor.**

★ Loyalists attacked the blockhouse at Toms River on Friday, August 23, 1782.

Salem (Dec. 11, 1777; Dec. 14, 1777; Feb. 26, 1778; Mar. 17, 1778; between May 7 and May 9, 1779)

Alloway's Bridge (Mar. 17, 1778)

Quinton's (Quintin's, Quintan's) Bridge (Mar. 18, 1778)

Hancock's Bridge (Mar. 21, 1778)

Alloways Creek (Mar. 23, 1778)

> Salem is in southwestern New Jersey near the Delaware River. There were three bridges over Alewas or Alloways Creek south of Salem. Hancock's Bridge was the lower, Quinton's Bridge in the center, and Thompson's Bridge further up. The Redcoats were to forage on the peninsula between Salem Creek and Alloways Creek. The peninsula ranged from 4 miles to 7 miles wide. Congressional forces held positions at Hancock's and Quinton's bridges where they had breastworks.
>
> A historic plaque on NJ Route 49 in Quinton, Salem County, marks the site of the Quinton's Bridge battle. St. John's Episcopal Church (corner of Market and Grant streets in Salem), built in 1728, was badly damaged in the raid. Crown forces camped in and around the Salem Friends Meetinghouse on East Broadway. After the war, local Loyalists were put on trial here and many had their property confiscated.
>
> A monument to the memory of Colonel Benjamin Holme, Colonel Elijah Hand, Captain William Smith, Andrew Bacon and the others who defended Quinton's Bridge stands on the site of the Smith homestead near the house of Judge William Hancock (see Photo NJ-43).

Colonel Charles Mawhood (d. 1780) and some British troops left Philadelphia on Friday, December 11, 1777 and landed at Salem where only a few people gathered to prevent them from gathering forage. On Monday, December 14, a small party mustered under arms but they were too few and were easily crushed with all of them killed or taken prisoners.

★ A few days later, a party of Whigs gathered at Hancock's Bridge. The Queen's Rangers were sent off in boats and landed in back of them. They killed and wounded a few and captured the rest. The Whigs never again appeared in any force; so the British gathered their forage without interruption. The inhabitants brought whatever cattle, provisions and supplies they could spare and received a generous price. They greatly lamented that the army was to depart, leaving them to the tyranny of the Whigs.[658]

★ Captain John Barry (1745–1803), under the direction of Brigadier General "Mad Anthony" Wayne (1745–1796), destroyed a large quantity of hay at Salem on Thursday, February 26, 1778, before British boats arrived to stop him.[659]

★ In the spring of 1778, General William Howe's (1732–1786) army needed to forage for food and supplies which became increasingly scarce as General George Washington's (1732–1799) army also foraged in the same areas. The fertile fields in southern New

Photo NJ-43. House of Judge William Hancock near Quinton's Bridge. A monument to the memory of the defenders of Quinton's Bridge is located on the site of the Smith homestead nearby.

Jersey provided excellent opportunities. There are still many farms operating in the area today. Lieutenant Colonel Charles Mawhood (d. 1780) commanded one of these foraging parties comprising the 17th, 27th, and 46th British Regiments, Lieutenant Colonel John Graves Simcoe's (1752–1806) Queen's Rangers (a mixed force of 270 Loyalist infantrymen and 30 dragoons), and the Loyalist New Jersey Volunteers.

The detachment of 1,200 to 1,300 men set out from Philadelphia, Pennsylvania and crossed the Delaware River to Salem on Thursday, March 12, 1778, to collect forage and cattle and to destroy salt works. They brought with them four cannon, two howitzers, and provisions for two weeks. Captain Charles Phipps's frigate *Camilla* provided security for six transports anchored in the Delaware River close to Salem which Lieutenant Colonel Mawhood expected to fill with cattle, horses, and forage.

Mawhood's party landed about 6 miles from Salem at 3 AM on Tuesday, March 17, and destroyed James Smith's (ca. 1757–1779) house at Alloway's Bridge. James Smith (son of Claudius Smith (1736–1779), "a notorious offender") and one Benson of Long Island had all committed many daring robberies. They were captured at the house of Nathan Miller in Smith's Clove (now Monroe, New York) on Saturday night, February 6, 1779 and jailed.

Colonel Elijah Hand (1730–1790) hastily assembled local Jersey militia units to oppose the raiders. One group of 300 New Jersey militiamen under Colonel Asher Holmes (1740–1808) guarded Quinton's Bridge 3 miles southeast of Salem. This was the middle of three bridges in Salem County that crossed Alloways (Alewas, Aloes) Creek, on the road that ran from Salem to the Maurice River and Millville in 1778. The bridge, which was a wooden drawbridge made of rough-hewn planks, was named after Tobias Quinton (Quintin, Quintan), the first English settler along Alloways Creek.[660]

The militiamen were positioned on the eastern side of the creek in some slight earthworks. They had taken up the planks of the bridge for further security. Mawhood sent a detachment of 70 men from the 17th Regiment to the two-storied Wetherby's Tavern on the west bank of Alloways Creek on March 18th to screen the bridge and allow the foraging party to proceed unmolested. He also concealed the Queen's Rangers to strengthen this party. He placed part of the Rangers under Captain Charles Stephenson in the tavern. Captain John Saunders (1753–1834) commanded another group behind a fence in back of the tavern, while Lieutenant Colonel Simcoe commanded the rest in the woods farther back.

Mawhood and Simcoe stationed the troops of the 17th Regiment in the open while the other units secretly took their positions to create a trap. Mawhood then ordered the 17th to retreat from their exposed location. The militiamen fired their muskets at the departing Crown forces, re-laid the bridge planks, and crossed the creek in pursuit. About 100 militiamen occupied the high ground near the bridge, while Captain William Smith (1728–1814) led the other 200 in pursuit, unaware that the Rangers lay in wait. The militiamen passed Wetherby's Tavern and proceeded up the road from the bridge when a French officer heard someone stifle a laugh behind the fence. He looked down, saw the rangers, and galloped off. He was fired at, wounded, and captured.

Captain Smith ordered a retreat. The militiamen began running back up the road toward the creek when Captain Stephenson's company came out of the tavern to block their escape. The militiamen were caught between two fires and panicked. They fled south, off the road and across the fields to cross the stream above the bridge. Captain Stephenson drove them across the fields. Captain Saunders pursued them. The hussars were let loose upon them, followed by Colonel Mawhood's battalion.

Colonel Simcoe sent the 30 mounted hussars of the rangers to harass the retreating militiamen. Several were taken prisoners. Mawhood and the 17th Regiment joined the rout, accompanied by Simcoe's rangers from the woods. The hussars of the rangers cut down many of the militiamen and shot or drove more into the creek where they drowned. Captain Smith was wounded twice, had his horse shot from under him, and was captured. The rangers had one hussar mortally wounded by a man whom he had passed and not disarmed in his eagerness to pursue. The man was killed by another hussar.

The 100 militiamen who had remained near the bridge managed to recross before Mawhood sprung his trap. Andrew Bacon (1736–1834) grabbed an axe and cut away the drawbridge section of the bridge to keep the Redcoats from crossing. He was severely wounded and crippled for life. Colonel Elijah Hand and a company of Cumberland County militiamen arrived at the eastern bank of the creek with two cannon at this time. They stopped the British advance and provided cover for the survivors.

There is no official count of casualties incurred by Congressional troops, but the death toll was heavy—30 to 40 killed and an unknown number of drowned. The Crown forces lost one hussar, mortally wounded. The affair was called a massacre in New Jersey, but it was a well-planned and well-executed trap sprung on unsuspecting and militarily naive militiamen. The engagement aroused strong feelings against the New Jersey Loyalists for their participation in the ruthless pursuit and slaughter of their countrymen.

★ Three days later, on Saturday, March 21, Lieutenant Colonel John Graves Simcoe (1752–1806) and Lieutenant Colonel Charles Mawhood (d. 1780) struck the New Jersey militia again at Hancock's Bridge, 5 miles south of Salem. Simcoe's Rangers and the New Jersey Volunteers proceeded in boats down the Delaware to an inlet 7 miles south of the mouth of the Alloway during the night of March 20th. They marched 2 miles through knee-deep swamps before they got near Hancock's Bridge while the 27th Regiment approached the bridge in front. Mawhood and Simcoe hoped to trap 400 militiamen at the bridge. They sent troops to occupy different houses in the village, including William Abbott's farm and Judge William Hancock's (d. 1778) house near the bridge where they thought the Whigs were quartered. Hancock's house (see Photo NJ-43) was a large brick house with many store houses and a few cottages around it.[661]

Captain John Saunders (1754–1834) was detached to set up an ambuscade at the dike that led to Quinton's Bridge, about 0.5 miles from the houses. He took up a small bridge that the militiamen would probably use for a retreat. Captain James Dunlop (1759–1832) was sent to the rear of Hancock's house to force it open, occupy it, and barricade it, as it commanded the bridge.

Most of the militiamen holding the bridge had been withdrawn the day before, leaving only a detachment of 20 to 30 men to guard it. A party of Rangers was sent to relay the bridge. As they approached, they discovered two sentries. Two light infantrymen with the party turned about and bayoneted them. The Rangers found a patrol of seven militiamen and shot six of them, taking no prisoners.

The Rangers then entered Hancock's house which was supposed to be the militia headquarters. They found the few remaining militiamen sleeping here. The militiamen made no opposition but offered to shake hands with some of the New Jersey Volunteers when they recognized them. They too were bayoneted as was every occupant of the house, including Judge Hancock and his brother, both Loyalists, held prisoners. Unlike the engagement at Quinton's Bridge three days earlier, the event at Hancock's Bridge was a true "massacre," typical of the ruthlessness of Simcoe's operations.

The roads leading to the country were immediately ambuscaded. Lieutenant Whitlock was sent to surprise a patrol of seven men coming down the creek. When they refused to surrender, he fired on them. Only one escaped. When a Congressional patrol passed where an ambuscade had been and discovered the corps, they galloped back.[662]

★ Some militiamen who had been posted at Thompson's Bridge were alarmed when a cow approached during the night of Sunday, March 22, 1778. They fired at it, wounded it, and then fled. The militiamen also abandoned Quinton's Bridge and retired to a creek 16 miles from Alloway Creek. Lieutenant Colonel Simcoe led a patrol with the hussars the following day, Monday. They took a circuitous route toward the rear of one of the parties sent to protect the foragers. A party of militiamen had been watching them the whole day. Having completed the forage, the Regulars had just begun to return when they met the patrol which pursued them. The hussars captured one of the militiamen who was pursued into a bog which the hussars attempted to cross in vain.[663]

★ Thirteen Loyalists went from Philadelphia, Pennsylvania to Salem between Thursday, May 7 and Saturday, May 9, 1779 to capture a Whig colonel there. They went ashore without any arms and captured him; but before they could take him away, a party of armed Whigs, who had been informed of the affair by some neighbors, came upon them and rescued the colonel and captured the Loyalists. The prisoners were sent to headquarters under a guard of seven men with fixed bayonets. Along the way, about 10 miles from Billingsport, the Loyalists overpowered the guards and disarmed them, taking five of them prisoners. The Loyalists took their prisoners first to Billingsport and then to the provost in Philadelphia.[664]

Swedesboro [Jan. 2, 1778; Mar. 22, 1778 (or Elsinboro, Mar. 24, 1778); Mar. 27, 1778; Apr. 4, 1778]

Wrangletown
Spicer's Ferry (Apr. 4, 1778)

> Swedesboro, also known as Wrangletown, due to the frequent quarrels and fighting which took place at elections, sales, or after paydays, is south of Billingsport and east of Wilmington, Delaware.
> Spicer's Ferry was in Swedesboro.
> Elsinboro Township is on the eastern shore of the Delaware River and runs from the area of Hancock's Bridge to north of Salem.

A party of Loyalists from Billingsport who had suffered at the hands of the Whigs marched south to Wrangletown and surrounded the house of a Captain Brown of the militia on Friday, January 2, 1778. Captain Brown somehow got information of their coming and escaped, leaving two other captains behind. They were captured along with a calico printer and militia lieutenant named Huston and taken to Billingsport.[665]

★ Three militiamen captured a wagon and three horses with baggage and stores belonging to Daniel Cozen, a well-known Loyalist, in a foraging raid at Swedesboro on Sunday, March 22, 1778. Joseph Sheppard Sickler says this event occurred at Elsinboro on Tuesday, March 24, 1778.[666]

★ A band of 60 Loyalists and marines under a man named Cox captured Lieutenant Bateman Lloyd (1765–1814), of the 4th New Jersey Regiment, and two recruits at Swedesboro on Friday, March 27, 1778. They also plundered the house of Captain Robert Brown (1744–1823).[667]

★ A party of 300 Loyalist and British troops arrived at Swedesboro in three divisions on Saturday, April 4, 1778. They surrounded the militiamen who escaped with great difficulty. The Crown troops then burned the schoolhouse where some of their friends had been kept prisoners. The officers could not maintain proper military discipline. The militiamen returned after a while and took their position on a wooded hill nearby and began to fire on the Crown troops.[668]

Congressional and Crown foraging parties skirmished at the bridge at Spicer's Ferry on Saturday, April 4, 1778.[669]

Penn's Neck (Mar. 6, 1778)

> Penn's Neck is on the Salem River, in the southern part of what is now Pennsville, about 2 miles east of the Delaware River.

On Friday, March 6, 1778, Captain Wigstaff (Loyalist) went down to Penn's Neck with part of his New Jersey Independent Volunteers. There, they were attacked by two armed boats from Christeen. As they only had muskets aboard their sloop, they were forced to run her ashore after exchanging several shots. After Captain Wigstaff abandoned the sloop, the Whigs removed the provisions and burned her. Captain Wigstaff and his men traveled 9 miles into the country to Raccoon Creek where they boarded another sloop and returned to Philadelphia with a quantity of provisions.[670]

Biles's Island (May 10, 1778)

> Biles's Island is about 3 miles south of Trenton.

★ Two British row galleys, three armed vessels and 24 flat-bottomed boats carrying between 600 and 800 British troops proceeded up the Delaware River to Biles's Island on Saturday morning, May 10, 1778. Their crews set several frigates on fire while the boats went up to Watson's Creek where they found the Whig galleys with only their masts above water. The Whigs saluted the boats with a number of cannon shots which did no damage. The two galleys had run aground and exchanged shots with the Congressional troops from the lower point of the island. It took several hours before the galleys could be refloated. General Philemon Dickinson (1739–1809) ordered the artillery to fire at the boats and the militia quickly assembled in large numbers. They fired a few shots and the British decided not to proceed any further.

In the meantime, the exasperated sailors set fire to Mr. Kirkbride's house and other buildings and to the ferry house. General Dickinson had sent a detachment of militiamen down the river to protect the inhabitants from small parties. They captured an enemy sloop with six men on board which had been loaded with plunder.

As soon as the galleys were refloated, the troops marched across the country and halted at Bristol until the vessels came down the river. They burned two frigates at Bristol and several below Burlington, including two privateers, one of 14 guns, the other of 10; one large ship pierced for 24 guns; nine other ships; and 14 or 15 smaller vessels. They then re-embarked and proceeded down the river. The troops and vessels employed on this excursion returned to the town on Sunday without losing a man.[671]

Allentown (Dec. 27, 1776; Mar. 31, 1778; June 24, 1778; Aug. 7, 1782)

> Allentown is east of Bordentown and Crosswicks.

Major General Count Karl Emil Kurt von Donop (1740–1777) commanded the Hessian forces at Burlington in December 1776. He learned of the battle of Trenton on Thursday, December 27 from fleeing Hessians who had escaped. They estimated the size of General George Washington's (1732–1799) force to be considerably larger than it really was. Spies reported a variety of possible enemy plans. Rumors of possible attacks were widespread and worried Crown forces all across the state. Von Donop moved his troops first to Allentown on the 27th, then to Princeton, to avoid the rumored attacks.[672]

★ Some Congressional troops clashed with a body of Loyalists at Allentown on Tuesday, March 31, 1778. The Congressional troops had one man wounded.[673]

★ After a skirmish at Crosswicks on Tuesday, June 23, 1778, the Crown forces proceeded to Allentown where they camped that evening on the other side of the village. The Queen's Rangers headed the column and the jaeger corps (see Photo NJ-8) was placed opposite the Maidenhead pass to cover the army's left flank and then to form the rear guard.

The bridge over a small rivulet at Allentown had the boards taken up. Lieutenant Colonel John Graves Simcoe (1752–1806) had two or three cannon shots fired to drive away a small party of the enemy. He then crossed his men over and encountered a patrol from the Cranberry road. The patrol retired into a wood which a party of Rangers scoured without finding them.[674]

See also **Crosswicks.**

★ Militiaman Richard Wilgus (d. 1782) was shot on Wednesday, August 7, 1782, while keeping guard near Allentown to prevent contraband trade with the Crown forces.[675]

Shark River (July 22, 1776; Apr. 7, 1778)

> The Shark River is south of Asbury Park.

The HM Brig *Halifax* and her sloop consort were cruising along the New Jersey coast as far south as Shark River between the present Bradley Beach and Belmar in mid-July 1776. Her master saw some people on the shore at 7 AM on Monday, July 22, 1776. He sent his yawl and whaleboats (see Photo NJ-1) to them, thinking they were Loyalists. When the boats got close to shore about 9 AM, the Whigs began a heavy fire of small arms at them. The *Halifax* fired several 4-pound shots at them at noon and got the boats on board safely.

★ At 3 PM, at the mouth of the Shark River, some people were spotted on shore. The *Halifax* sent her whaleboat to them about 5 PM which returned with some Loyalists.[676]

★ About 135 Crown troops—mostly Loyalists and some Highlanders—landed at Shark River on Tuesday, April 7, 1778 and set fire to two small works. When they saw 15 horsemen come into view, they hurried to escape. They jumped into their flat-bottomed boats in such confusion that they sank one or two of them.[677]

Crosswicks (May 5, 1778; June 23, 1778)

> Crosswicks is 8 miles southeast of Trenton and 3.5 miles east of Bordentown. The place figured in the Trenton raid and the Monmouth campaign. The action probably occurred at a point on Crosswicks Creek, 4 miles from Trenton.

See **Bordentown.**

The British galleys *Hussar, Cornwallis, Ferret,* and *Philadelphia* proceeded up the Delaware River from Philadelphia at 10 PM on Tuesday, May 5, 1778. They were accompanied by the armed schooners *Viper* and *Pembroke*, four gun boats, and 18 flat boats containing the 2nd battalion of light infantry and two field pieces. The expedition proceeded 12 miles and anchored because of the adverse wind, heavy rain, and ebbing tide. They remained at anchor until 5 AM the following morning when they got under weigh and sailed up the river. They were opposite White Hill at noon where the galleys, armed vessels, and gunboats were stationed to cover the troop landing which occurred without opposition.

The troops torched the Continental frigates *Washington* (pierced for 32 guns) and *Effingham* (pierced for 28 guns) together with a brig and a sloop. They then marched, took possession of Bordentown, and destroyed a battery of three 6-pounders. The galleys and armed vessels proceeded to Bordentown where the crews burned two new ships, one of which was pierced for 18 guns. They also burned a 10-gun privateer sloop and 10 brigs, schooners and sloops. They set fire to several storehouses containing provisions, artillery stores, camp equipage, and some tobacco. The boats then proceeded up Crosswicks Creek to burn the privateer *Sturdy Beggar*, pierced for 18 guns, and eight brigs, sloops and schooners. The troops then reembarked and landed on the Pennsylvania side where they rested that night.

The galleys *Hussar* and *Ferret* rowed up to Biles Island Creek with the gunboats and other vessels at 5 AM on Saturday morning. They burned a new schooner pierced for 14 guns, a new sloop for 16 guns, an old schooner for 10 guns, an old large sloop for 16 guns, and two large new sloops. They discovered some Continental galleys sunk and hidden at low water in Watson's Creek on the Jersey shore. The troops then marched to Bristol, Pennsylvania at noon and arrived at Philadelphia at 6 AM on Sunday morning. This expedition up the Delaware destroyed 44 vessels and some houses.[678]

See also **Biles's Island.**

★ On Tuesday, June 23, 1778, before dawn, the Crown forces marched to Crosswicks, with no difficulty except for a bridge, the boards of which had been taken up. As the boards lay only a few yards away, they were easily replaced. As they approached Crosswicks, they met a body of Congressional troops. The Queen's Rangers, leading the left column, tried to cut off the Whigs before they could pass the creek. The rangers were too late for that, but in time to prevent them from cutting down the trees near the bridge and throwing them across it. The Congressional troops took up the planks and took shelter behind a wood on the opposite bank.

When the Queen's Rangers returned, Lieutenant Colonel John Graves Simcoe (1752–1806) formed his corps behind the meetinghouse, ready to pass the bridge. The dragoons arrived, dismounted, and lined the fences on the right. The Congressional troops left the woods and escaped. Captain Charles Stephenson was wounded by a Quaker who fired at him with a long fowling-piece. The Queen's Rangers remained posted beyond the creek with some other troops, but the army did not cross the bridge.

A hot skirmish occurred a short while later and Colonel Elias Dayton (1737–1807), of the 3rd New Jersey Regiment, had his horse shot out from under him. The militia lost one man killed, one wounded and another captured. The Crown forces then proceeded to Allentown.[679]

See **Allentown.**

Oldman's Creek (June 12, 1778)

> Oldman's Creek is about halfway between the Delaware River and Swedesboro.

A skirmish occurred at the Moravian Church at Oldman's Creek on Friday, June 12, 1778.[680]

Cranberry Inlet (June 15, 1778; Sept. 19–20, 1778; Jan. 20, 1782; Sept. 1, 1782)
Egg Harbor

> Cranberry Inlet is the entrance to Barnegat Bay at Barnegat Light. Little Egg Harbor is about 15 miles south.

Three four-gun galleys from New London arrived at Cranberry Inlet on Monday, June 15, 1778, with several captured vessels. The prizes included a schooner from Cork, Ireland with provisions and a vessel from the West Indies with rum and sugar.[681]

★ The boats of the HMS *Delaware* and the armed brig *Halifax* entered Cranberry Inlet and burned a ship of about 200 tons and a small sloop on Saturday, September 19, 1778. The following day, they captured a sloop with 96 barrels of flour.[682]

★ On Sunday, January 20, 1782, Captain (Richard?) Gray pursued a British brig but was captured himself.[683]

★ On Sunday, September 1, 1782, Captain Douglass and some Gloucester militiamen attacked a boat containing 18 Loyalists, 14 of whom were killed or drowned. The others escaped.[684]

Evesham Township

Evesham (June 19, 1778)

Evesham is east of Haddonfield.

General Alexander Leslie's (1740–1794) division began marching an hour before daylight on Friday, June 19, 1778. They headed toward Evesham by way of Fostertown and arrived on the left bank of Belly Bridge Creek (Southwest branch of the Ancocas, now Rancocas Creek) about midday. They found that the Congressional troops had destroyed the bridges but left two beams. The advanced guard of 80 jaegers (see Photo NJ-8) crossed over and occupied a hill to protect the workmen who repaired the bridge. Meanwhile, 30 jaegers patrolled the area. After advancing an hour and a half, they saw several roofs of houses in a hollow.

Captain Johann von Ewald (1744–1813) ordered 10 men forward to skirmish. They fired and signaled the captain and the rest of the party forward. They crossed the creek near a mill which people were working to destroy. The mill was occupied by riflemen who fired at the jaegers who took cover in the nearest wood. They occupied the bank of the bridge with 20 men while a corporal and 10 jaegers crossed the beams of the bridge, occupied the mill, and barricaded the entrance.

The main army had crossed Belly Bridge Creek by this time and encamped in a long quadrangle. Captain Ewald received reinforcements of 150 jaegers and orders to maintain the post. As evening approached, the carpenters arrived with the construction wagon and repaired the bridge. Johann Ewald recorded in his journal:

> At midday the army reached the left bank of Moores Creek (Pennsauken Creek). The enemy had ruined the bridges across the creek, but they were soon repaired, whereupon the army crossed them and camped in a long quadrangle in an uninhabited area.
>
> The 19th. The army marched off one hour before daylight, as it had the day before, going by way of Fostertown. Toward midday the army arrived on the left bank of Belly-Bridge Creek, (the South West Branch of the Ancocas (now Rancocas) Creek) where the enemy had destroyed the bridges. There were still two beams left here, and since I had the advanced guard, I immediately tried to cross over with eighty jagers to take post on the other side of the water, by which the workmen on the bridge were protected. I found a very suitable post on a hill, which I occupied. I then took thirty jagers with me to patrol the area ahead. When I had ventured one hour further on, it seemed to me from my map that the terrain in the distance indicated I must not be far from Eayrestown, (Earystown, also known as Airstown, Arystown, and Irestown) where the army was headed according to my idea of the

march. I sent back a jager who was to guide a lieutenant and thirty men to the place I had left, and I continued on my march.

After a half an hour's time, I caught sight of several roofs of houses in a hollow. I ordered 10 men forward to skirmish, who fired in a little while and beckoned to me with their hands. I followed at once and found the creek (the South Branch of the Rancocas Creek at Earystown). There was a bridge over it next to a mill, on which people were working to destroy it. The mill was occupied by riflemen, who boldly fired when they discovered us. But since I let fly in earnest at the windows of the mill, they abandoned the mill and bridge and ran away into the nearest wood. I immediately occupied the bank on this side of the bridge with twenty men. I then ordered a corporal and ten jagers to cross the beams of the bridge, occupy the mill, and barricade the entrance, which I reported instantly to my chief. During this time the army had crossed Belly-Bridge Creek and encamped in a long quadrangle. I received reinforcements of 150 jagers and orders to maintain the post. Toward evening the carpenters arrived with the construction wagon and the bridge was repaired. I received from the Commander in Chief his thanks and the compliment that I had saved the army a longer march by my diligence.

The 20th. At daybreak the army set out, passed the defile of Eayrestown, and toward midday encamped in an irregular quadrangle on the heights of Mount Holly. On this march the head of the queue and both flanks were constantly annoyed by the enemy (Brigadier General William Maxwell (1733–1796) with 1300 New Jersey Continentals in front and General Philemon Dickinson (1739–1809) with 800 New Jersey militiamen on the left flank).[685]

Columbus
Black Horse (Dec. 22, 1776; June 22, 1778)

Black Horse is now Columbus in Burlington County.

Black Horse, near (December 22, 1776) see **Rancocas, Petticoat Bridge.**

A party of Crown forces exchanged shots with Congressional patrols at Blackhorse on Monday, June 22, 1778.[686]

Chestnut Neck (Oct. 6, 1778)
Little Egg Harbor (Oct. 5–15, 1778)
Mincock (also called Osborn's) Island (Oct. 15, 1778)

The Chestnut Neck Battle Monument, at the intersection of US Route 9 and NJ Route 575 in Chestnut Neck–Port Republic, south of exit 48 on the Garden State Parkway, stands 50 feet tall and is topped by a privateer. The site of the village of Chestnut Neck is privately owned. Access is restricted; but it may be developed as a historic landmark.

A historical marker stands in front of the house of Captain Micajah Smith (1742–1807) (The Franklin Inn) on Mill Road just west of Main Street. Smith was a privateer and mill owner who supplied wood to the shipbuilding industry on Nacote Creek (next to the house). Many of the privateer ships were built on the Nacote which flows into the Mullica River. In the burning of Chestnut Neck, innkeeper Daniel Mathis's place was torched. He bought the Smith house and called it the Franklin Inn.

Smith's Meetinghouse and Blackman's Cemetery are about 0.25 miles west of the Franklin Inn on the left of Main Street near the corner of English Creek Road, Port

Republic Road (NJ Route 575), and Indian Cabin Road. The cemetery contains the graves of several soldiers of the American War for Independence, including those of privateers Captain Micajah Smith (1742–1807) and Captain John Van Sant (1726–1820).

The Pulaski Monument (South Pulaski Boulevard and Kosciusko Way in Little Egg Harbor) is on the site of a house where the Crown forces bayoneted the sleeping dragoons. Pulaski's headquarters, the Willets-Andrews farmhouse at the north end of the island, burned down in the 1930s.

Congress commissioned about 450 privateers during the war to prey on British shipping. Many of them operated out of New Jersey, especially out of the Mullica River area which was perfect for maritime guerilla warfare for several reasons. First, there were established boat-building operations in the area. Second, the British strongholds in New York and Philadelphia filled the New Jersey shipping lanes with prospective targets. Third, warships could not navigate the rivers, coves, and inlets in the region. Privateers had natural protection from capture by the Royal Navy. The wagonmen also carried on a thriving business carrying goods from Chestnut Neck to points along the Delaware River.

Some 30 armed sloops operated from Little Egg Harbor which made it probably the chief base for privateering. Toms River was also a thriving center as it enjoyed easy access to the ocean through Island Beach by way of Cranberry Inlet, almost opposite the mouth of the river.[687]

★ The Crown forces planned an expedition against Little Egg Harbor, on the east coast of New Jersey, as it was a noted rendezvous for privateers. The surrounding area was used by vessels and was convenient for annoying shipping. The expedition was intended both to procure forage and to open the country on both sides of the North River.

General Charles Cornwallis (1738–1805) led the first division down the west side of the North River to take a position between the river and New Bridge on the Hackensack. His right extended to the North River and his left to the Hackensack. Lieutenant General Wilhelm von Knyphausen (1716–1800) took the other division of the army to a parallel position on the east side of the North River. His left reached the North River at Wepperham and his right extended to the Bronx.

General George Washington (1732–1799), not having command of the river, made no attempt to draw his troops together, but sent detachments to interrupt and confine the operations of the foragers as much as possible. Colonel George Baylor (1752–1784) headed one of these detachments at Old and New Tappan.

See **River Vale/Westwood (Old Tappan, New Jersey).**

After Baylor's detachment was annihilated, a squadron under the direction of Captain John Collins of the *Zebra* set sail from New York for Little Egg Harbor on Wednesday, September 30, 1778. The squadron of nine vessels, under the command of Captain Patrick Ferguson (1744–1780), consisted of the sloops *Zebra*, *Vigilant*, and *Nautilus*, two galleys and four other armed boats and transports which carried 350 infantrymen from the 5th Regiment and 100 New Jersey Loyalists. It didn't arrive off Little Egg Harbor until the evening of Monday, October 5, due to contrary winds. This gave the inhabitants time to learn of its destination and to prepare for their defense.

Governor William Livingston (1723–1790) received information about the intended attack on Tuesday evening September 29 and convened a meeting of the Council of Safety at 3 AM. General George Washington (1732–1799) also received immediate notice of the fleet's destination and sent Brigadier General Count Casimir Pulaski (1747–1779) and his legion to Egg Harbor. The *Pennsylvania Packet* of October 10 announced "the arrival of Count Pulaski with his legion of horse and foot from Pennsylvania, who, hearing of the descent of the enemy on the coast at Egg Harbor, immediately marched to the assistance of that place with the troops in high spirits, and with great alacrity."

Four privateers put to sea and escaped while the other vessels were brought up the river as far as their draught of water would permit. Captain Collins's squadron arrived at an inlet about 1 mile above Brigantine inlet late Monday afternoon, October 5, 1778. They could not enter the harbor the following morning because of ill winds. Captain Ferguson decided not to wait until he could get the sloops into the inlet. He had his troops board the galleys and armed boats and proceeded about 20 miles up the Mullica River toward Chestnut Neck where he had been informed there was a wharf and storehouse for prize vessels and their goods.

The village of Chestnut Neck was obscured by thick fog on Tuesday morning, October 6. Ferguson prepared to land and attack. As his men reached the shore at Chestnut Neck and the neighboring hamlet of Bass River, they came under fire from a small body of local militiamen firing from behind a breastwork and from another nearby battery. One of the two batteries was level with the water and the other on high ground, but neither of them had any artillery. The militia put up "a formidable shew of resistance" behind these batteries and a breastwork.

The fire from the galleys covered the landing of the troops and only one man was wounded. The soldiers charged the militiamen, drove them back, and forced them to take refuge in the adjoining woods where the women and children had preceded them. The troops immediately demolished the batteries, plundered and destroyed the 12 houses in the village and several barns, and stripped the storehouse near the wharf of all its goods and burned it. Meanwhile the seamen returned to the shore where they found two large prize ships scuttled and dismantled. They burned these ships, eight other sloops and schooners, some large whaleboats (see Photo NJ-1) and smaller boats—30 ships in all.

The expedition intended to head up the same river to a place called the Forks, about 35 miles from Philadelphia. However, as the militia there had been reinforced by a detachment of infantrymen, a small train of artillery, and a corps of light-horsemen and as the row-galleys could not accompany the troops any farther because of the shallow water, this part of the expedition was abandoned as impracticable.[688]

★ The troops re-embarked and proceeded down the river. They landed twice along the way to destroy three salt works, including the salt works at the mouth of the Bass River. They also destroyed some houses and stores belonging to people who either outfitted privateers or who persecuted Loyalists. Captain Patrick Ferguson's (1744–1780) troops returned to the harbor the following day, Wednesday, October 7th. The *Zebra* and the *Vigilant* were still stuck on the sandbar but were floated the following morning.

Contrary winds prevented the vessels from putting to sea for several days. During this time, Lieutenant Gustav Juliet, who had deserted from the Hessian army to join Brigadier General Casimir Pulaski's (1747–1779) American Legion the year before, organized a fishing party on Tuesday, October 13th. He got three of the men intoxicated while in the bay and forced two others to comply with him. He gave a signal and the men were taken aboard one of the sloops. Juliet then apprised Captain Ferguson of the strength and location of General Pulaski's corps only 12 miles up the river. He also falsely reported that Pulaski had given orders to give no quarter to prisoners taken in battle. Lieutenant Colonel the Baron de Bosen, Pulaski's second in command, had no respect for deserters and plainly showed it in his treatment of Juliet who sought the first opportunity for revenge.

Captain Ferguson decided to surprise General Pulaski's corps of three companies of light infantrymen, three troops of horse, and a detachment of artillery with one brass field piece quartered about 1 mile beyond a bridge. They were encamped at James Willets's (1716–1792) farm down the Island Road in the village of Tuckerton on the evening of October 8th. The location gave Pulaski a good view of the harbor and the fleet at anchor. He posted a picket of about 50 infantrymen, a detachment of artillerymen, and some field pieces about 2 miles farther down the road.

Some 250 Regulars and New Jersey Volunteers and a number of marines embarked in the boats at 11 PM on October 14. They rowed 10 miles up the river to Osborn's or Mincock Island where they landed at 3 or 4 AM on Thursday, October 15, and immediately secured the bridge where they posted a guard of 50 men.

Captain Ferguson sent a party to the home of Richard Osborn, Jr. (1714–1792) to guard the occupants and to force Osborn's son Thomas (1755–1781) at the point of a sword to guide them to Pulaski's picket on the mainland. After crossing the island, Ferguson left 50 men at a bridge over Big Creek to secure his retreat. His troops then traveled about 1 mile over rough road until they found a single sentinel and captured him before he could fire his weapon. (Some accounts say this man was killed.)

The troops then rushed and surrounded the three buildings housing the sleeping infantrymen and bayoneted them and then burned the buildings. Thomas Osborn had hid in the meadow grass and heard the cries of the legionnaires as they were being massacred. Lieutenant Colonel de Bosen unsuccessfully tried to get his men to break through Captain Ferguson's perimeter. Juliet spotted him and called out, "This is the Colonel; kill him." De Bosen was immediately bayoneted several times and his men's appeal for quarter went unheeded. The raiders killed 50 men, including three officers, and only took five prisoners. Very few escaped. Ferguson later reported that the casualties were "almost entirely cut to pieces."

General Pulaski heard the first shots at his headquarters more than 1 mile away and rallied his dragoons "mounting in hot haste." They rushed down the road to help de Bosen but arrived too late. Captain Ferguson's men made a hasty retreat and removed the planking at the bridge, preventing Pulaski's pursuit.

Ferguson's men re-embarked without any loss other than two men missing and one officer and two privates wounded. As they crossed the island, a Loyalist told them that Colonel Thomas Proctor (1739–1806) had come from The Forks of the Mullica with a detachment of artillery. They had two brass 12-pounders and one 3-pounder and were only about 2 miles away. Ferguson had no artillery to oppose them and decided not to engage them. He and his men sailed back to New York in the middle of the afternoon of October 16, as soon as the wind became favorable. The flagship *Zebra* ran aground again passing over the bar. Captain John Collins tried in vain to free her. He transferred the troops to the *Vigilant* and the *Nautilus* and ordered the *Zebra* to be torched. Fragments of the wreck were visible in the vicinity of Chestnut Neck for many years after the war.

Judge Jones, a Loyalist historian, said that "they (the British) plundered the inhabitants, burnt their houses, their churches and their barns; ruined their farms; stole their cattle, hogs, horses, and sheep, and then triumphantly returned to New York." Just as after the Battles of Herringtown and Paoli Tavern, the attackers were charged with massacring their victims.[689]

Barnegat

Barnegat Beach (Dec. 9, 1778; Mar. 22, 1779; Mar. 24, 1779; July 28, 1779; Nov. 18, 1779; Mar. 9, 1780; Aug. 18, 1781; June 1, 1782; Oct. 26, 1782)

The Barnegat Historical Society's Heritage Village, at 575 E. Bay Ave., (**www .barnegathistoricalsociety.com**) has some historic houses and barber and butcher shops.

A British armed vessel, bound from Halifax to New York, ran aground near Barnegat a few days before Wednesday, December 9, 1778. The crew of about 60 surrendered to the militiamen; and the people took the cargo which amounted to about £5,000.[690]

★ The British frigate *Delaware*, bound from Baltimore to Amsterdam, captured the Boston scow *Molly* 25 leagues north of Cape Charles on Monday, March 22, 1779. William Hornor says the crew and cargo were taken and brought in. The newspaper account says the crew escaped in their boats when *Molly* struck her colors and that her mate, named Coop, was the only person to remain on board "to take care of her and save the cargo."[691]

★ The sloop *Success* came ashore at Barnegat Beach on Wednesday, March 24, 1779. She had been taken previously by the brig *Diligence*. The Monmouth County militia took her cargo and sent her crew to Princeton.[692]

★ The cutter *Intrepid* (formerly the *Dublin*), with 12 4-pounders and 50 men, sailed on a cruise on Tuesday, July 27, 1779. The following day, she fell in with two Continental sloops off Barnegat. One sloop had 14 guns, the other eight. The *Intrepid* beat off the sloops in an engagement that lasted three and a half hours. She had her boom shot away and sails greatly damaged, preventing her from pursuing the sloops. The *Intrepid* lost her lieutenant and another man killed and seven wounded, some of them mortally.[693]

★ Captain Davidson's schooner, on its way from Gothenburg to Boston, ran aground at Barnegat a few days before Thursday, November 18, 1779. The vessel and most of the cargo were lost.[694]

★ A whaleboat attacked British privateers off Barnegat Inlet on Thursday, March 9, 1780.[695]

★ Captain Thompson's Loyalist whaleboat *Surprize* and her consort fought a severe action off Little Barnegat about 3 PM on Tuesday, August 18, 1781. The crews, consisting of a total of 26 men fought two Philadelphia whaleboats within pistol range in a conflict that lasted more than an hour. Captain Thompson received a dangerous pistol shot in the groin. Yet, he continued the fight. He discharged his fusil twice. When the pain prevented him from participating in the fight, he continued giving orders in the supine position, exhorting his men not to strike their colors. The Whigs eventually took to their oars after throwing four of their dead overboard, including one of their captains named Eeler (d. 1781).[696]

★ A Loyalist raid at Forked River resulted in a skirmish at Barnegat on Saturday, June 1, 1782.[697]

★ New Jersey militiamen took a beached British ship at Barnegat on Saturday, October 26, 1782. John Bacon (d. 1783) led a Loyalist raid that same night and killed the militiamen.[698]

Peck's Beach (Apr. 29, 1779)

> Peck's Beach is about 13 miles south/southwest of Atlantic City.

The privateer brig *Delight* ran aground at Peck's Beach in Cape May County on Thursday, April 29, 1779. Militiamen seized the crew and vessel which was sold at public auction on Monday, June 7 at the house of Colonel Nicholas Stillwill (1742–1792). The cargo, which was also auctioned, consisted of "80 puncheons of good West-India rum, about one ton of gun-powder, a number of small arms, and two or three tons of cannon ball; together with the great guns, cables, anchors, sails, rigging and furniture of said brig."[699]

Absecon (Oct. 1779)

> Absecon is on Absecon Bay near the Atlantic City International Airport.

Some Loyalists skirmished with the Egg Harbor Guards (3rd Regiment, Gloucester County Militia) at Absecon salt works in October 1779.[700]

Delaware Bay (Oct. 13, 1779; Dec. 4, 1779)

Crown privateers captured Captain Caleb Armitage's (1737–1832) Philadelphia brig *Sally* in Delaware Bay on Wednesday, October 13, 1779. The 66-man *Sally* mounted fourteen 3-pounders and was only one day out from the Delaware Capes. The same day, the Crown privateers captured the 12-gun schooner *Hawk,* belonging to Egg Harbor, with 70 men aboard.[701]

★ Captain Andrew Snape Hamond's *HMS Roebuck* captured Captain Samuel Young's ship *Lady Washington* and the brig *Three Sisters* in Delaware Bay on Saturday, December 4, 1779. Both vessels were bound from Philadelphia for Old France. The *Lady Washington* mounted 18 guns and had a crew of 58 men and a cargo of 220 hogsheads of tobacco, naval stores, and other supplies.[702]

Cumberland County
Downe County (Mar. 22, 1780; Aug. 20, 1781)
Maurice River

> Downe County is now Cumberland County on the Delaware Bay, in southwestern New Jersey, south of Millville. The Maurice River runs through Millville and flows south to empty into Delaware Bay.

Loyalists in whaleboats captured many fishermen in Delaware Bay on Wednesday, March 22, 1780. The same day, privateers captured prizes in the Maurice (Morris's) River and Delaware Bay and about 400 Crown troops from New York advanced to Paramus where they took some prisoners and plundered several houses.[703]

See **Hopperstown.**

★ A band of 15 Loyalists tried to board a shallop near the bridge in the Maurice River on Monday, August 20, 1781. Some New Jersey militiamen engaged them in "a sharp contest" in which four Loyalists were killed and four wounded. When the Captain (who was very badly wounded) called out that he would give no quarter, the action became desperate. The remaining seven Loyalists were captured and taken to Philadelphia. Only one militiaman received a slight wound.[704]

Deal Beach (Apr. 15, 1780)

> Deal Beach is on the Atlantic Ocean less than 2 miles north of Asbury Park.

Captain Sutherland, of the HMS *Vulture*, drove the privateer brig *Black Snake* ashore at Deal Beach, 12 miles from Sandy Hook on Saturday, April 15, 1780.[705]

Cumberland County
Nantuxent Creek (Aug. 30, 1780)

> Nantuxent Creek empties into Delaware Bay west of Newport.

New Jersey militiamen under Colonel Pope captured eight Loyalists at Nantuxent Creek in Cumberland County on Wednesday, August 30, 1780. They brought their prisoners to the Cumberland County jail but they later escaped.[706]

Burlington County
Springfield Township (Aug. 1780; Sept. 22, 1782)
New Mills, Springfield Township (Sept. 22, 1782)

> Springfield Township is in Burlington County near Fort Dix. It should not be confused with the town of Springfield, near Union, where the Battle of Connecticut Farms occurred.

More than 6,000 Crown troops, headed by the "Queen's Own" marched to Springfield Township in August 1780. General George Washington (1732–1799) kept his 3,000 Continentals at Morristown. Brigadier General William Maxwell (1733–1796) opposed the Crown forces with his Jersey militia. He recorded: "In the latter part of the day the militia flocked from all quarters and gave the enemy no respite till the day closed the scene." By evening, the Crown forces were on the shore of Arthur Kill waiting to cross to Staten Island.[707]

★ Around 8 PM on Sunday, September 22, 1782, a man wrapped up in a great coat and armed with pistols passed through New Mills, arousing the curiosity of some boys who were playing in the road. When they asked him where he was going, he knocked one of the boys down. The others dispersed and the man escaped to the pines. The neighbors were alarmed and assembled but decided not to pursue him through woods in the dark. They posted sentinels.

Around midnight, two of the sentinels, who stood together, spotted a man coming from the woods. It was the same man who had been in the town in the evening. They hailed him seven or eight times, but he refused to answer. As the man kept advancing toward them, one of the sentinels tried to fire, but his musket did not go off. The man rushed toward them as fast as he could run. The other sentinel, who was not discovered by him, fired and wounded him in the thigh. He died the following morning, refusing to identify himself other than saying he was one of General Charles Cornwallis's (1738–1805) men who had escaped from Lancaster, Pennsylvania.[708]

Fairfield County (Aug. 30, 1780)

> Fairfield Township is south of Elsinboro Township.

See **Nantuxent Creek.**

Manahawkin (Dec. 31, 1781)

Manahawkin is at the junction of NJ 72 (Route 72 E) and US 9 (N Main Street) east of exit 63 off the Garden State Parkway.

Jersey militiamen clashed with Loyalists under Captain John Bacon (1738–1820) at Manahawkin on Monday, December 31, 1781. Lines Pangborn (d. 1781), of the militia, was killed during the action.[709]

Off Great Egg Harbor (May 18, 1782)

Great Egg Harbor is located south of Atlantic City.

Two boats from Cape May drove the Loyalist boat *Old Ranger* on shore near Egg Harbor on Saturday, May 18, 1782. The two boats also captured two coasting schooners carrying on an illicit trade.[710]

Cedar Creek Bridge (Dec. 27, 1782)

Cedar Creek empties into Barnegat Bay south of Toms River and north of Forked River.

Captain Richard Shreve (1726–1822), of the Burlington County light-horse, and Captain Edward Thomas (1750–1797), of the Mansfield militia, received information that a band of robbers were in the neighborhood of Cedar Creek on Friday, December 27, 1782. They gathered a party of men and immediately went in pursuit of them. They met the robbers at Cedar Creek Bridge. Even though the Loyalists held an advantageous position on the south side, Captains Shreve and Thomas decided to charge them.

The militiamen made a furious attack and the Loyalists resisted them with great firmness for a considerable time. Several of them had committed such enormous crimes that they had no expectation of mercy should they surrender. At the point the militiamen were going to seal their victory, some of the inhabitants began firing on them, causing some confusion and giving the Loyalists time to escape. The militiamen had one man killed and another wounded. The Loyalists had one killed on the spot and three wounded. The militiamen pursued the Loyalists and took seven inhabitants prisoners as well as a considerable quantity of contraband and stolen goods when they searched some suspected houses and cabins on the shore.[711]

Forked River (June 1, 1782)

Forked River empties into Barnegat Bay south of Toms River.

A Loyalist by the name of Davenport landed at Forked River on Saturday, June 1, 1782 with about 40 whites and 40 African Americans. They burned Samuel Brown's (1740–) salt works and plundered him. They then proceeded southward toward Barnegat to burn the salt works along the shore between those places.[712]

Tuckerton (Apr. 3, 1783)

Tuckerton is on Little Egg Harbor north of Atlantic City.

Captain John Stewart (1749–1823) and several militiamen discovered Captain John Bacon (d. 1783), a notorious Loyalist, near Tuckerton on Thursday, April 3, 1783. Captain Stewart shot Bacon as he tried to escape.[713]

NOTES

ABBREVIATION

NDAR: United States. Naval History Division. *Naval Documents of the American Revolution*.William Bell Clark, editor; with a foreword by President John F. Kennedy and an introd. by Ernest McNeill Eller. Washington: Naval History Division, Dept. of the Navy : For sale by the Supt. of Docs., U.S. G.P.O., 1964–

Preface

1. Desmarais, Norman. *Battlegrounds of Freedom: A Historical Guide to the Battlefields of the War of American Independence*. Busca: Ithaca, N.Y., 2005.

2. Heitman, Francis B. *Historical Register of Officers of the Continental Army during the War of the Revolution, April 1775 to December 1783*. Washington, DC. : The Rare Book Shop Publishing Company, 1914; Baltimore: Genealogical Publishing Company, 1967.

3. Peckham, Howard Henry. *The Toll of Independence: Engagements & Battle Casualties of the American Revolution*. Chicago: University of Chicago Press, 1974.

4. Boatner, Mark Mayo. *Encyclopedia of the American Revolution*. 3d ed., New York: McKay, 1980.

5. Boatner, Mark Mayo. *Landmarks of the American Revolution: A Guide to Locating and Knowing What Happened at the Sites of Independence*. Stackpole Books: Harrisburg, PA., 1973; 2nd ed.—Library of Military History. Detroit: Charles Scribner's Sons, 2007.

6. Selesky Harold E., editor in chief. *Encyclopedia of the American Revolution*, 2nd ed. Detroit: Charles Scribner's Sons, 2007.

7. Fremont-Barnes, Gregory, Richard Alan Ryerson, eds. *The Encyclopedia of the American Revolutionary War: A Political, Social, and Military History*. Santa Barbara, CA: ABC-CLIO, 2006.

8. Anderson, Fred. *A People's Army: Massachusetts Soldiers and Society in the Seven Years' War*. Chapel Hill, N.C. 1984. pp.84–85, 129.

9. Waller, George M. *The American Revolution in the West*. Chicago: Nelson Hall, 1976. pp.30–31.

10. Adams, Charles F., ed. *The Works of John Adams*. Boston: Charles C. Little and James Brown, 1850. vol. 10 p.110.

11. Ibid., pp.192–93.

12. Raphael, Ray. *A People's History of the American Revolution: How Common People Shaped the Fight for Independence*. New York: New Press, 2001. pp.145, 342.

New Jersey

1. *New York Gazette and Weekly Mercury*. (March 17, 1777). *Documents Relating to the Revolutionary History, State of New Jersey*. Edited by William S. Stryker. Trenton: The John L. Murphy Publishing Co., 1901. Series 2. 1:316. Nelson, William. *History of the City of Paterson and the County of Passaic*. Paterson: Press Print and Publishing Co. 1901. p.402.

2. *New York Gazette and Weekly Mercury*. (January 27,1777). *Documents Relating to the Revolutionary History, State of New Jersey*. Edited by William S. Stryker. Trenton: The John L. Murphy Publishing Co., 1901. Series 2. 1:271–272.

3. David Marinus's Pension Record, W385. *New York Gazette and Weekly Mercury*. (May 19, 1777). *Documents Relating to the Revolutionary History, State of New Jersey*. Edited by William S. Stryker. Trenton: The John L. Murphy Publishing Co., 1901. Series 2. 1:379. Washington, George. *The writings of George Washington from the original manuscript sources, 1745–1799*; prepared under the direction of the United States George Washington Bicentennial Commission and published by authority of Congress; John C. Fitzpatrick, editor. Washington, U.S. Govt. Print. Off. [1931–44] 8 p.72. Heard to Washington, May 14, 1777, The Papers of George Washington, Library of Congress. Leiby, Adrian Coulter. *The Revolutionary War in the Hackensack Valley; the Jersey Dutch and the Neutral Ground, 1775–1783*. New Brunswick, N.J.: Rutgers University Press 1962, 117.

4. *The Providence Gazette; And Country Journal*. XV:773 (October 24, 1778) p.2.

5. *The New-York Gazette: and the Weekly Mercury*. 1436 (April 26, 1779). *Documents Relating to the Revolutionary History, State of New Jersey*. Edited by William S. Stryker. Trenton: The John L. Murphy Publishing Co., 1901. Series 2. 3:265–266.

6. Ibid., p.408.

7. *The New-York Gazette: and the Weekly Mercury*. 1513 (October 16, 1780). *Documents Relating to the Revolutionary History, State of New Jersey*. Edited by William S. Stryker. Trenton: The John L. Murphy Publishing Co., 1901. Series 2. 5:40.

8. *The Pennsylvania Packet or the General Advertiser*. XI:876 (April 25, 1782) p.3. *The Freeman's Journal: or, The North-American Intelligencer*. LIII (April 24, 1782) p.2. *The Independent Ledger, and the American Advertiser*. 4:210 (May 13, 1782) p.1. *Connecticut Courant*. 902 (May 7, 1782) p.2.

9. Extract of a letter from an officer in the American army, dated North-Castle, near New York, Oct. 19. *The Norwich Packet and the Connecticut, Massachusetts, New-Hampshire, and Rhode Island Weekly Advertiser.* 4:165 (November 18–25, 1776) p.3.

10. Force, Peter. *American archives: consisting of a collection of authentick records, state papers, debates, and letters and other notices of publick affairs, the whole forming a documentary history of the origin and progress of the North American colonies; of the causes and accomplishment of the American revolution; and of the Constitution of government for the United States, to the final ratification thereof. In six series.* [Washington, 1837–1853]. ser. 2 5:1266. Leiby, Adrian Coulter. *The Revolutionary War in the Hackensack Valley; the Jersey Dutch and the Neutral Ground, 1775–1783.* New Brunswick, N.J.: Rutgers University Press 1962, 52–53. Extract of a letter to Congress, from Fort Lee (formerly Fort Constitution) dated Oct. 28, 1776. *The Norwich Packet and the Connecticut, Massachusetts, New-Hampshire, and Rhode Island Weekly Advertiser.* 4:165 (November 18–25, 1776) p.3. Peckham, Howard Henry. *The Toll of Independence: Engagements & Battle Casualties of the American Revolution.* Chicago: University of Chicago Press, 1974. p.25.

11. Greene, Nathanael. *The Papers of General Nathanael Greene.* Chapel Hill: Published for the Rhode Island Historical Society [by] the University of North Carolina Press, c1976–. 1 pp.327–328.

12. *Encyclopedia of the American Revolution.* Harold E. Selesky, editor in chief.—2nd Ed. Detroit: Charles Scribner's Sons, 2007.1:372–373. *The Encyclopedia of the American Revolutionary War: a political, social, and military history.* Gregory Fremont-Barnes, Richard Alan Ryerson, editors. Santa Barbara, CA: ABC-CLIO, 2006. 2:426–427. Flood, Charles Bracelen. *Rise, and Fight Again: Perilous Times along the Road to Independence.* New York: Dodd, Mead, 1976. Lefkowitz, Arthur. *George Washington's Indispensable Men: The 32 Aides-de-Camp Who Helped Win American Independence.* Mechanicsburg, PA: Stackpole, 2003. Schechter, Barnet. *The Battle for New York: the City at the heart of the American Revolution.* New York: Walker, 2002. Ward, Christopher. *The War of the Revolution.* New York: Macmillan, 1952. 267–284.

13. *The Lee Papers.* New York: New York Historical Society, 1874–1875. 2:295. Muenchhausen, Friedrich von. *At General Howe's Side 1776–1778: The diary of General William Howe's aide de camp.* Captain Friedrich von Muenchhausen. Translated by Ernst Kippling and annotated by Samuel Smith. Monmouth Beach, N.J.: Philip Freneau Press, 1974. p.5. Kemble, Stephen. *Journals of Lieut.-Col. Stephen Kemble, 1773–1789; and British Army Orders: Gen. Sir William Howe, 1775–1778; Gen. Sir Henry Clinton, 1778; and Gen. Daniel Jones, 1778.* Prepared by New York Historical Society; Boston: Gregg Press, 1972. p.101.

14. *The Providence Gazette; And Country Journal.* XIV:690 (March 22,1777) p.2.

15. Peckham, Howard Henry. *The Toll of Independence: Engagements & Battle Casualties of the American Revolution.* Chicago: University of Chicago Press, 1974. p.86.

16. *The New-York Gazette; and The Weekly Mercury.* 15444 (May 21, 1781) p.3.

17. Philadelphia, October 23. Extract of a letter from Fort Lee dated October 20, 1776. *Pennsylvania Journal and Weekly Advertiser.* (October 23, 1776). *Documents Relating to the Revolutionary History, State of New Jersey.* Edited by William S. Stryker. Trenton: The John L. Murphy Publishing Co., 1901. Series 2. 1:216–217.

18. Force, Peter. *American archives: consisting of a collection of authentick records, state papers, debates, and letters and other notices of publick affairs, the whole forming a documentary history of the origin and progress of the North American colonies; of the causes and accomplishment of the American revolution; and of the Constitution of government for the United States, to the final ratification thereof. In six series.* [Washington, 1837–1853]. ser. 3 5:780. Leiby, Adrian Coulter. *The Revolutionary War in the Hackensack Valley; the Jersey Dutch and the Neutral Ground, 1775–1783.* New Brunswick, N.J.: Rutgers University Press 1962. p.64.

19. Heath,William. *Memoirs Major-General William Heath By Himself.* New Edition, With Illustrations And Notes. Edited By William Abbatt. New York: William Abbatt, 1901. pp.71– 73.

20. Extract of a letter from Fort Lee, November 10. *Pennsylvania Journal and Weekly Advertiser.* (November 13,1776). *Documents Relating to the Revolutionary History, State of New Jersey.* Edited by William S. Stryker. Trenton: The John L. Murphy Publishing Co., 1901. Series 2. 1:223.

21. Lettter to the Honorable Abraham Tenbroeck Esqr. Pyramus, 21st Dec'r 1776. Clinton, George. *Public Papers of George Clinton, first Governor of New York, 1777–1795, 1801–1804.* Hugh Hastings, ed. New York and Albany: Pub. by the State of New York,1900. V. 1, No. 276, pp.477–478. Leiby, Adrian Coulter. *The Revolutionary War in the Hackensack Valley; the Jersey Dutch and the Neutral Ground, 1775–1783.* New Brunswick, N.J.: Rutgers University Press 1962. pp.95–97.

22. *Documents Relating to the Revolutionary History, State of New Jersey.* Edited by William S. Stryker. Trenton: The John L. Murphy Publishing Co., 1901. Series 1. 2:322, 326, 354; Serle, Ambrose. *The American Journal of Ambrose Serle, Secretary to Lord Howe, 1776–1778.* edited by Edward H. Tatum, Jr., San Marino, California, 1940; Eyewitness accounts of the American Revolution). [New York]: New York Times ; Arno Press, c1969. p.200. Clinton, George. *Public Papers of George Clinton, first Governor of New York, 1777–1795, 1801–1804.* Pub. by the State of New York. New York, Albany, 1899–1914. 1:677. Leiby, Adrian Coulter. *The Revolutionary War in the Hackensack Valley; the Jersey Dutch and the Neutral Ground, 1775–1783.* New Brunswick, N.J.: Rutgers University Press, 1962. pp.116–117.

23. Lobdell, Jared C. Paramus in the War of the Revolution. *Proceedings of the New Jersey Historical Society: A Magazine of New Jersey History.* 78, 1960. pp.162–177. *New Jersey History.* 78:165–166.

24. *New Jersey History.* First Series. 7:96.

25. *New York Gazette and Weekly Mercury.* (July 21, 1777). *Documents Relating to the Revolutionary History, State of New Jersey.* Edited by William S. Stryker. Trenton: The John L. Murphy Publishing Co., 1901. Series 2. 1:429.

26. *New Jersey History.* First Series. 7:109.

27. *New York Gazette and Weekly Mercury.* (November 3, 1777). *Documents Relating to the Revolutionary History, State of New Jersey.* Edited by William S. Stryker. Trenton: The John L. Murphy Publishing Co., 1901. Series 2. 1:481.

28. *Documents Relating to the Revolutionary History, State of New Jersey.* Edited by William S. Stryker. Trenton: The John L. Murphy Publishing Co., 1901. Series 2. 2:47. Winfield, Charles H. *History of the County of Hudson, New Jersey.* New York: Kennard & Hay, 1874. pp.434–35.

29. Jones, Thomas. *History of New York During the Revolutionary War.* Edited by Edward Floyd De Lancey. New York: New York Historical Society, 1879. p.280. Leiby, Adrian Coulter. *The Revolutionary War in the Hackensack Valley.* New Brunswick: Rutgers University Press, 1962. p.145–147.

30. *New York Gazette and Weekly Mercury.* (March 30, 1778). *Documents Relating to the Revolutionary History, State of New Jersey.* Edited by William S. Stryker. Trenton: The John L. Murphy Publishing Co., 1901. Series 2. 2:134.

31. *New York Gazette and Weekly Mercury.* (March 30, 1778). *Documents Relating to the Revolutionary History, State of New Jersey.* Edited by William S. Stryker. Trenton: The John L. Murphy Publishing Co., 1901. Series 2. 2:134; 3:458.

32. *New York Gazette and Weekly Mercury.* (May 18, 1778). *Documents Relating to the Revolutionary History, State of New Jersey.* Edited by William S. Stryker. Trenton: The John L. Murphy Publishing Co., 1901. Series 2. 2:218. Winfield, Charles Hardenburg. *History of the County of Hudson, New Jersey.* New York: Kennard & Hay Printing Co. 1874. p.149.

33. Affidavits of John House, Pension Records, S1022; John A. Haring, Pension Records, S6980; John G. Ryerson, S1099; Samuel Vervalen, W16774. Robertson, Archibald. *Archibald Robertson, His Diaries and Sketches in America, 1762–80*, edited by Harry Miller Lydenberg, New York, 1930; (Eyewitness accounts of the American Revolution). [New York] New York Public Library [1971] p.182. Leiby, Adrian Coulter. *The Revolutionary War in the Hackensack Valley; the Jersey Dutch and the Neutral Ground, 1775–1783.* New Brunswick, N.J.: Rutgers University Press 1962, 160. *Revolution in America: Confidential Letters and Journals 1776–1784 of Adjutant General Major Baurmeister of the Hessian Forces.* Translated and annotated by Berhard A. Uhlendorf. New Brunswick, N.J.: Rutgers University Press, 1957. p.216.

34. Leiby, Adrian Coulter. *The Revolutionary War in the Hackensack Valley; the Jersey Dutch and the Neutral Ground, 1775–1783.* New Brunswick, N.J.: Rutgers University Press 1962. p.160.

35. *The Pennsylvania Packet.* (October 6, 1778). *Documents Relating to the Revolutionary History, State of New Jersey.* Edited by William S. Stryker. Trenton: The John L. Murphy Publishing Co., 1901. Series 2. 3:458.

36. Peckham, Howard Henry. *The Toll of Independence: Engagements & Battle Casualties of the American Revolution.* Chicago: University of Chicago Press, 1974. p.59. *Documents Relating to the Revolutionary History, State of New Jersey.* Edited by William S. Stryker. Trenton: The John L. Murphy Publishing Co., 1901. Series 2. 3:359, 369–370.

37. *The New York Gazette and the Weekly Mercury.* 1442 (June 7, 1779). *Documents Relating to the Revolutionary History, State of New Jersey.* Edited by William S. Stryker. Trenton: The John L. Murphy Publishing Co., 1901. Series 2. 3:401–402.

38. *The New York Gazette: and the Weekly Mercury.* 1444 (June 21, 1779). *Documents Relating to the Revolutionary History, State of New Jersey.* Edited by William S. Stryker. Trenton: The John L. Murphy Publishing Co., 1901. Series 2. 3:458.

39. Ewald, Johann. *Diary of the American War: A Hessian Journal.* Translated and edited by Joseph P. Tustin. New Haven and London: Yale University Press, 1979. p.175. Leiby, Adrian Coulter. *The Revolutionary War in the Hackensack Valley; the Jersey Dutch and the Neutral Ground, 1775–178*3. New Brunswick, N.J.: Rutgers University Press, 1962. p.221.

40. Ewald, Johann. *Diary of the American War: A Hessian Journal.* Translated and edited by Joseph P. Tustin. New Haven and London: Yale University Press, 1979. p.175.

41. Extract of a letter from an officer at Paramus, August 21, in the *New Hampshire Gazette.* (September 7, 1779). *Pennsylvania Packet.* (September 2, 1779). Moore, Frank. *Diary of the American Revolution: from Newspapers and Original Documents.* New York: Charles Scribner; London: Sampson Low, Son & Co., 1890. 2 pp.206–212.

42. *The New-York Gazette: and the Weekly Mercury.* 1501 (July 24, 1780). *Documents Relating to the Revolutionary History, State of New Jersey.* Edited by William S. Stryker. Trenton: The John L. Murphy Publishing Co., 1901. Series 2. 4:523.

43. Peckham, Howard Henry. *The Toll of Independence: Engagements & Battle Casualties of the American Revolution.* Chicago: University of Chicago Press, 1974. p.74. *Documents Relating to the Revolutionary History, State of New Jersey.* Edited by William S. Stryker. Trenton: The John L. Murphy Publishing Co., 1901. Series 2. 4:570.

44. *The New-York Gazette: and the Weekly Mercury.* 1506 (August 28,1780). *Documents Relating to the Revolutionary History, State of New Jersey.* Edited by William S. Stryker. Trenton: The John L. Murphy Publishing Co., 1901. Series 2 4:605.

45. Military Pension Records, #W20525 (John Lozier). Shanahan, Robert J., Jr, Esq. *Captain John Outwater and his Militia: Bergen County, New Jersey 1776–1781.* Unpublished Work © 1987.

46. *The Pennsylvania Evening Post and Public Advertiser.* 7:761 (August 6, 1781) p.122.

47. Affidavit of John Blauvelt, Pension records W20721.

48. *Pennsylvania Gazette* (April 2, 1777).

49. Extract of a letter from Morristown, dated April 28. *The Independent Chronicle and the Universal Advertiser.* IX:457 (May 22, 1777) p.2.

50. Ward, Harry M. *General William Maxwell and the New Jersey Continentals.* Westport, CT; London: Greenwood Press, 1997. p.144. Abner Prior to Washington, March 23, 1780. *Washington Papers*—Library of Congress; St Clair to Washington. February 11 & 20, 1780. William H. Smith. *The St. Clair Papers: the Life and Public Services of Arthur St. Clair.* 1:499–500, 502. *New Jersey Gazette.* (February 9, 1780). *New York Gazette and Weekly Mercury.* (February 7, 1780). Weig, Melvin J. *Morristown National Historical Park, New Jersey: a military capital of the American Revolution.* by Melvin J. Weig; with assistance from Vera B. Craig. Washington, D.C.: National Park Service, 1950, p.19. Freeman, Douglas Southall. *George Washington, a biography.* New York: Scribner, 1948–1957. 5:144.

51. *New Jersey History.* 1st Ser., 7, 95.

52. Lobdell, Jared C. Paramus in the War of the Revolution. *Proceedings of the New Jersey Historical Society: A Magazine of New Jersey History.* 78, 1960. pp.162–177.

53. Clayton, W. Woodford. *History of Bergen and Passaic Counties, New Jersey, with biographical sketches of many of its pioneers and prominent men.* Philadelphia: Everts & Peck, 1882. p.53. *The Massachusetts Spy: or American Oracle of Liberty.* VII:336 (October 9, 1777) p.1.

54. *Bergen County Court Indictments, January Term, 1784.* Lenk, Jr. Richard William. Hackensack. *New Jersey from Settlement to Suburb 1686–1804.* Ph.D. dissertation. New York University, 1968. p.92.

55. *Proceedings of the New Jersey Historical Society: A Magazine of New Jersey History. New Jersey History.* 1 Ser., 7:109. Ward, Harry M. *Charles Scott and the "Spirit of '76."* Charlottesville: University Press of Virginia, 1988. p.59.

56. Extract of a letter from Springfield, New-Jersey, dated Oct. 6, 1778. *The Pennsylvania Evening Post.* (October 9, 1778). *New-York Gazette and Weekly Mercury.* (October 19, 1778). Extract of a letter from an officer in Jersey, dated Aquakanock, October 4, 1778. *Documents Relating to the Revolutionary History, State of New Jersey.* Edited by William S. Stryker. Trenton: The John L. Murphy Publishing Co., 1901. Series 2. 2:454, 462–63, 471–72, 484–85.

57. Krafft, John Charles Philip von. *Journal of Lieutenant John Charles Philip von Krafft.* Collections of the New-York Historical Society for the year 1882. New York: the Society, 1883;—Eyewitness Accounts of the American Revolution.—New York: The New York Times & Arno Press, 1968. pp.62–65.

58. Munn, David C. *Battles and Skirmishes of the American Revolution in New Jersey.* [Trenton]: Bureau of Geology and Topography, Department of Environmental Protection, c. 1976. p.43. *New Jersey History.* 78 p.164. Ward, Harry M. *Charles Scott and the "spirit of '76".* Charlottesville: University Press of Virginia, 1988 p.59. Washington to Scott, Sept. 29, 1778, to Greene and to Gates, Oct. I, 1778, Tallmadge to Gates, Sept. 29, 1778, Scott to Washington, Sept. 29, 30 (letters nos. 1,2), 1778, ibid.; David Griffith to Stirling, Oct. 20, 1778, Virginia State Library photostat; G. D. Scull, ed. *The Montresor Journals.* New-York Historical Society Collections. 14 (1881), Sept. 28, 1778, 513; Ritchie, Carson I. A. A New York Diary of the Revolutionary War. Edited, with an introduction by Carson I. A. Ritchie. *The New York Historical Society Quarterly.* 50 (1966), 221–280, 441–446. *Narratives of the Revolution in New York: A Collection of Articles from the New-York Historical Society Quarterly.* New York: The New York Historical Society, 1975. pp.243. 279; Thomas Jones, *History of New York during the Revolutionary War.* (New York, 1879), 2:286; Stedman. *History of the American War.* 2:41–42; Burt G. Loescher, *Washington's Eyes: The Continental Light Dragoons.* Ft. Collins, Colo., 1977, pp.69–76. David H. Murdoch, ed., *Rebellion in America. . .* [Excerpts from the Annual Register]: Santa Barbara. Calif., 1979), 1779, 666. Thomas H. Edsall, ed., *"Journal of Lieutenant John Charles Philip von Kraft."* New-York Historical Society, Collections. 15 (1882): Sept. 30. 1778,62; John C. Fitzpatrick, ed. *The Writings of George Washington, 1745–99 ·* 39 vols. Washington, D.C., 1931–44, 13:4n.

59. *Documents Relating to the Revolutionary History, State of New Jersey.* Edited By William S. Stryker. Trenton: The John L. Murphy Publishing Co., 1901. Series 2. 3:369–370.

60. Freeman, Douglas Southall. *George Washington, a biography.* New York: Scribner, 1948–1957. 5:147. Smith, William. *Historical Memoirs of William Smith, 1778–1783.* New York, 1781; New York: 1971. pp.218 ff. Fleming, Thomas J. *The forgotten victory; the battle for New Jersey–1780.* [New York] Reader's Digest Press; distributed by Dutton, 1973. p.38.

61. *The American Journal and General Advertiser.* 2:92 (December 30,1780) p.3. *The Pennsylvania Journal.* (December 20, 1780). *Documents Relating to the Revolutionary History, State of New Jersey.* Edited by William S. Stryker. Trenton: The John L. Murphy Publishing Co., 1901. Series 2. 5:44.

62. Chatham, Sept. 5. *The Pennsylvania Evening Post, and Public Advertiser.* VII:771 (September 10, 1781) p.146. *New Jersey Journal* (September 5, 1781). Winfield, Charles H. *History of the County of Hudson, New Jersey.* New York: Kennard & Hay, 1874. pp.195–196.

63. Leiby, Adrian Coulter. *The Revolutionary War in the Hackensack Valley; the Jersey Dutch and the Neutral Ground, 1775–1783.* New Brunswick, N.J.: Rutgers University Press 1962, 116–117. *New York Gazette and Weekly Mercury.* (April 28, 1777). *Documents Relating to the Revolutionary History, State of New Jersey.* Edited by William S. Stryker. Trenton: The John L. Murphy Publishing Co., 1901. Series 1. 1:344, 354.

64. *Documents Relating to the Revolutionary History, State of New Jersey.* Edited by William S. Stryker. Trenton: The John L. Murphy Publishing Co., 1901. Series 3. 2:251, 265, 292–293, 358, 369, 391. *The Pennsylvania Evening Post.* 5:594 (April 30, 1779) p.106.

65. Affidavits of Catherine Lozier, Pension Records, R936; James I. Blauvelt, Pension Records, W5828; and John Huyler, Pension Records, W1775.

66. Affidavit of Abraham Haring, Pension Records, W20728. Leiby, Adrian Coulter. *The Revolutionary War in the Hackensack Valley; the Jersey Dutch and the Neutral Ground, 1775–1783.* New Brunswick, N.J.: Rutgers University Press, 1962. pp.201–202. *The New Jersey Gazette.* 2:73 (April 28, 1779) p.2. *The Pennsylvania Evening Post.* 2:594 (April 30, 1779) p.106.

67. Affidavit of John Huyler, Pension Records, W1775. Leiby, Adrian Coulter. *The Revolutionary War in the Hackensack Valley; the Jersey Dutch and the Neutral Ground, 1775–1783.* New Brunswick, N.J.: Rutgers University Press 1962 pp.209–210.

68. Clayton, W. Woodford. *History of Bergen and Passaic Counties, New Jersey, with biographical sketches of many of its pioneers and prominent men.* Philadelphia: Everts & Peck, 1882. pp.56, 66. Westervelt, Frances A. Johnson, ed. *History of Bergen County, New Jersey, 1630–1923.* New York: Lewis Historical Pub. Co., 1923. 1:114.

69. Kemble, Stephen. *Journals of Lieut.-Col. Stephen Kemble, 1773–1789; and British Army Orders: Gen. Sir William Howe, 1775–1778; Gen. Sir Henry Clinton, 1778; and Gen. Daniel Jones, 1778.* Prepared by New York Historical Society; Boston: Gregg Press, 1972. 1:177, 178.

70. Wemyss to Lord Rawdon (undated letter), Papers of Sir Henry Clinton, Clements Library, Ann Arbor, MI.

71. Ibid.

72. Leiby, Adrian Coulter. *The Revolutionary War in the Hackensack Valley; the Jersey Dutch and the Neutral Ground, 1775–1783*. New Brunswick, N.J.: Rutgers University Press, 1962. pp.210–212.

73. Extract of a Letter from New-Barbadoes, July 22, 1779. *The New Jersey Gazette*. 2:83 (July 28, 1779) p.3. *The Independent Ledger, and the American Advertiser*. 2:62 (Aug. 16,1779) p.2. Clayton, W. Woodford. *History of Bergen and Passaic Counties, New Jersey, with biographical sketches of many of its pioneers and prominent men*. Philadelphia: Everts & Peck, 1882. p.66. *Documents Relating to the Revolutionary History, State of New Jersey*. Edited by William S. Stryker. Trenton: The John L. Murphy Publishing Co., 1901. Series 2. 3:518–519.

74. Clayton, W. Woodford. *History of Bergen and Passaic Counties, New Jersey, with biographical sketches of many of its pioneers and prominent men*. Philadelphia: Everts & Peck, 1882. p.56. Westervelt, Frances A. Johnson, ed. *History of Bergen County, New Jersey, 1630–1923*. New York: Lewis Historical Pub. Co., 1923. 1:113–114. Lenk, Jr. Richard William. *Hackensack, New Jersey from Settlement to Suburb 1686–1804*. Ph.D. dissertation. New York University, 1968. pp.101–102.

75. *The New Jersey Gazette*. 3:129 (June 14, 1780) p.3.

76. Blanch to Livingston, June 8, 1780, Livingston Papers. New York Public Library. Blanch to Livingston, June 10, 1780, Livingston Papers New York Public Library. Leiby, Adrian Coulter. *The Revolutionary War in the Hackensack Valley*. New Brunswick: Rutgers University Press, 1962. p.255. *Documents Relating to the Revolutionary History, State of New Jersey*. Edited by William S. Stryker. Trenton: The John L. Murphy Publishing Co., 1901. Series 2. 4:434.

77. Blanch to Livingston, June 10, 1780, Livingston Papers. New York Public Library. affidavits of James Riker and Peter S. Van Orden pension Records, W15877. Captain Blanch was wounded shortly afterward. See affidavit of Peter S. Van Orden. Id. Leiby, Adrian Coulter. *The Revolutionary War in the Hackensack Valley*. New Brunswick: Rutgers University Press, 1962. p.255.

78. *Documents Relating to the Revolutionary History, State of New Jersey*. Edited by William S. Stryker. Trenton: The John L. Murphy Publishing Co., 1901. Series 2. 4:443.

79. Heath to Washington, March 14, 1781, George Washington Papers, Library of Congress. Damages by British, New Jersey State Library, Harrington Precinct Nos. 39, 47, 48. Isaac Siscoe, British Intelligence, March 25, 1781, Emmet Collection, New York Public Library. Leiby, Adrian Coulter. *The Revolutionary War in the Hackensack Valley*. New Brunswick: Rutgers University Press, 1962. pp.296–297.

80. *New York Mercury*. (September 17, 1781). Winfield, Charles H. *History of the County of Hudson, New Jersey*. New York: Kennard & Hay, 1874. p.196.

81. Heath Papers. Massachusetts Historical Society. 91, 94. Clinton, George. *Public Papers of George Clinton, first Governor of New York, 1777–1795, 1801–1804*. Pub. by the State of New York. New York, Albany, 1899–1914. 1:468, 469. Force, Peter. *American archives: consisting of a collection of authentick records, state papers, debates, and letters and other notices of publick affairs, the whole forming a documentary history of the origin and progress of the North American colonies; of the causes and accomplishment of the American revolution; and of the Constitution of government for the United States, to the final ratification thereof*. In six series. Washington, 1837–1853]. ser. 3 5:1261.

82. George Clinton to the President of the Convention of the state of New York. Ramepough, 28th Dec'r 1776. Clinton, George. *Public Papers of George Clinton, First Governor of New York, 1777–1795, 1801–1804*. Hugh Hastings, ed. New York and Albany: Pub. by the State of New York, 1900. 1:496–497.

83. Clinton, George. *Public Papers of George Clinton, first Governor of New York, 1777–1795, 1801–1804*. Pub. by the State of New York. New York, Albany, 1899–1914. 1 p.216. Leiby, Adrian Coulter. *The Revolutionary War in the Hackensack Valley; the Jersey Dutch and the Neutral Ground, 1775–1783*. New Brunswick, N.J.: Rutgers University Press, 1962. pp.98–99.

84. Clinton, George. *Public Papers of George Clinton, first Governor of New York, 1777–1795, 1801–1804*. Pub. by the State of New York. New York, Albany, 1899–1914 1 pp.740–741. Leiby, Adrian Coulter. *The Revolutionary War in the Hackensack Valley; the Jersey Dutch and the Neutral Ground, 1775–1783*. New Brunswick, N.J.: Rutgers University Press 1962, 117.

85. *New York Gazette and Weekly Mercury*. (May 19, 1777). *Documents Relating to the Revolutionary History, State of New Jersey*. Edited By William S. Stryker. Trenton: The John L. Murphy Publishing Co., 1901. Series 2. 1:378–379.

86. *The Providence Gazette; And Country Journal*. XIV:701(June 7,1777) p.2. *The Norwich Packet and the Connecticut, Massachusetts, New-Hampshire, and Rhode Island Weekly Advertiser*. 4:195 (June 16 to June 23, 1777) p.3. *New York Gazette and Weekly Mercury* (May 19, 1777). *Documents Relating to the Revolutionary History, State of New Jersey*. Edited by William S. Stryker. Trenton: The John L. Murphy Publishing Co., 1901. Series 2. 1:379. Heard to Washington, May 14, 1777. George Washington Papers, Presidential Papers Microfilm (Washington: Library of Congress, 1961). Washington, George. *The writings of George Washington from the original manuscript sources, 1745–1799*; prepared under the direction of the United States George Washington Bicentennial Commission and published by authority of Congress; John C. Fitzpatrick, editor. Washington, U.S. Govt. Print. Off. [1931–44] 8 p.72. Leiby, Adrian Coulter. *The Revolutionary War in the Hackensack Valley; the Jersey Dutch and the Neutral Ground, 1775–1783*. New Brunswick, N.J.: Rutgers University Press, 1962. p.117.

87. *New York Gazette and Weekly Mercury* (June 16, 1777). *Documents Relating to the Revolutionary History, State of New Jersey*. Edited by William S. Stryker. Trenton: The John L. Murphy Publishing Co., 1901. Series 2. 1:398.

88. *Documents Relating to the Revolutionary History, State of New Jersey*. Edited by William S. Stryker. Trenton: The John L. Murphy Publishing Co., 1901. Series 2. 3:345, 358–359. Leiby, Adrian Coulter. *The Revolutionary War in the Hackensack Valley*. New Brunswick: Rutgers University Press, 1962. p.204–205. Nelson, William. *History of the city of Paterson and the County of Passaic, New Jersey*. Paterson: Press Print. and Pub. Co., 1901. pp.345–346.

89. *The Royal Gazette*. 365 (March 29, 1780). *Documents Relating to the Revolutionary History, State of New Jersey*. Edited by William S. Stryker. Trenton: The John L. Murphy Publishing Co., 1901. Series 2. 4:251–253; 280. Bernhard Uhlendorf ed. *Revolution in America: Confidential Letters and Journals 1776–1784 of Adjutant General Major Baurmeister of the Hessian Forces* (New Brunswick, 1957) p.346. Lobdell, Jared C. Paramus in the War of the Revolution. *Proceedings of the New Jersey Historical Society: A Magazine of New Jersey History*. 78 (July 1960) pp.171–172. Rees, John U. "The Enemy was in Hackansack last night Burning & Destroing. . ." British Incursions into Bergen County, Spring 1780. Part I. "'So much for a Scotch Prize.': Paramus, New Jersey, 23 March 1780." (www.continentalline.org/articles/article .php?date=0502&article=050201).

90. Döhla, Johann Conrad. A *Hessian Diary Of the American Revolution*. By Johann Conrad Döhla translated, edited, and with an introduction by Bruce E. Burgoyne. Norman and London: University of Oklahoma Press, 1990. pp.121–122.

91. *The Royal Gazette*. 371 (April 19, 1780). *Documents Relating to the Revolutionary History, State of New Jersey*. Edited by William S. Stryker. Trenton: The John L. Murphy Publishing Co., 1901. Series 2. 1:227; 4:306–307. *New Jersey Journal*. (April 19, 1780; May 17, 1780). *Royal American Gazette*. (April 18, 1780). *Pennsylvania Packet*. (May 23, 1780). *Continental Journal*. CCXIX (May 11, 1780) p.4. *The New York Packet, and the American Advertiser*. 169 (April 20, 1780). Moore, Frank. *Diary of the American Revolution: from Newspapers and Original Documents*. New York: Charles Scribner; London: Sampson Low, Son & Co., 1890. 2 pp.265–266. *Documents Relating to the Revolutionary History, State of New Jersey*. Edited by William S. Stryker. Trenton: The John L. Murphy Publishing Co., 1901. Series 2. 4:252, 253, 257, 308; 321, 324, 350. Lobdell, Jared C. Paramus in the War of the Revolution. *Proceedings of the New Jersey Historical Society: A Magazine of New Jersey History*. 78, (July 1960) pp.172–173. Israel Shreve Papers, New Jersey Room. Rutgers University. Fleming, Thomas J. *The forgotten victory; the battle for New Jersey–1780*. [New York] Reader's Digest Press; distributed by Dutton, 1973. pp.86–7. Leiby, Adrian Coulter. *The Revolutionary War in the Hackensack Valley; the Jersey Dutch and the Neutral Ground, 1775–1783*. New Brunswick, N.J.: Rutgers University Press 1962 pp.239–243; 246–249. Jonathan Hallett to George Washington, 16 April 1780, George Washington Papers, Presidential Papers Microfilm (Washington: Library of Congress, 1961), series 4. Rees, John U. "The Enemy was in Hackansack last night Burning & Destroing. . ." British Incursions into Bergen County, Spring 1780 Part II. "Had all the Cavalry been in the front. I believe not one man could have escaped.': Hopperstown, New Jersey, 16 April 1780". (www.continentalline.org/articles/article .php?date=0502&article=050201).

91a. Nelson, William. *History of the City of Paterson and the County of Passaic*. Paterson: Press Print and Publishing Co., 1901. p.424.

92. *Minutes of the Council of Safety of the State of New Jersey*. Jersey City, 1872. pp.352–53, 359–60. Leiby, Adrian Coulter. *The Revolutionary War in the Hackensack Valley; the Jersey Dutch and the Neutral Ground, 1775–1783*. New Brunswick, N.J.: Rutgers University Press, 1962. pp.119–120.

93. *New-York Gazette and Weekly Mercury*. (October 5, 1778). *Documents Relating to the Revolutionary History, State of New Jersey*. Edited by William S. Stryker. Trenton: The John L. Murphy Publishing Co., 1901. Series 2. 2:457–459. Mazur, D. Bennett and Wayne Daniels. *Baylor's Dragoons Massacre, September 28. 1778*. s.l. s.n., 1968.

94. *The New Jersey Gazette*. 2:73 (April 28, 1779) p.2. *Documents Relating to the Revolutionary History, State of New Jersey*. Edited by William S. Stryker. Trenton: The John L. Murphy Publishing Co., 1901. Series 2. 2:293, 359. Return of Prisoners, April 13, 1779, Papers of Sir Henry Clinton, Clements Library, Ann Arbor, MI. *New York Gazette and the Weekly Mercury*.1435 (April 19, 1779) p.3. *The Pennsylvania Evening Post*. 5:594 (April 30,1779) p.106.

95. *Documents Relating to the Revolutionary History, State of New Jersey*. Edited by William S. Stryker. Trenton: The John L. Murphy Publishing Co., 1901. Series 2. 3:251, 265, 292, 293, 358, 369, 391. Leiby, Adrian Coulter. *The Revolutionary War in the Hackensack Valley; the Jersey Dutch and the Neutral Ground, 1775–1783*. New Brunswick, N.J.: Rutgers University Press, 1962. p.200.

96. Affidavit of John Lozier, Pension Records, W20525. Abraham Vanderbeek, Pension Records, S1130. Leiby, Adrian Coulter. *The Revolutionary War in the Hackensack Valley*. New Brunswick: Rutgers University Press, 1962. pp.297.

97. *Documents Relating to the Revolutionary History, State of New Jersey*. Edited by William S. Stryker. Trenton: The John L. Murphy Publishing Co., 1901. Series 2. 3:347.

98. Affidavits of Garrett C. Oblenis and Harmanus Blauvelt, Pension Records, S22653. Leiby, Adrian Coulter. *The Revolutionary War in the Hackensack Valley*. New Brunswick: Rutgers University Press, 1962. 143 n36.

99. *The Pennsylvania Evening Post*. 5:594 (April 30, 1779) p.106. *The New Jersey Gazette*. 2:73 (April 28, 1779) p.2.

100. Dawson, Henry B. *Battles of the United States by Sea and Land*. New York: Johnson, Fry, & Company, 1858. I 548–549. Peckham, Howard Henry. *The Toll of Independence: Engagements & Battle Casualties of the American Revolution*. Chicago: University of Chicago Press, 1974. p.59.

101. Force, Peter. *American archives: consisting of a collection of authentick records, state papers, debates, and letters and other notices of publick affairs, the whole forming a documentary history of the origin and progress of the North American colonies; of the causes and accomplishment of the American revolution; and of the Constitution of government for the United States, to the final ratification thereof. In six series*. [Washington, 1837–1853]. ser. 5, 3:1139.

102. George Clinton to the President of the Convention of the state of New York. Ramepough, 28th Dec'r 1776. Clinton, George. *Public Papers of George Clinton, First Governor of New York, 1777–1795, 1801–1804*. Hugh Hastings, ed. New York and Albany: Pub. by the State of New York,1900.1:496.

103. *The Independent Chronicle and the Universal Advertiser*. 10:476 (October 2, 1777) p.3. *Boston Gazette*. 1205 (October 6, 1777) p.2.

104. Letter from lieutenant-general Sir Henry Clinton, to Gen. Sir William Howe, dated Kingsbridge, Sept, 23, 1777. *Pennsylvania Gazette*. (March 3, 1778). *Documents Relating to the Revolutionary History, State of New Jersey*. Edited by

William S. Stryker. Trenton: The John L. Murphy Publishing Co., 1901. Series 2. 2:42–44. *Pennsylvania Gazette.* (March 3, 1778). *Pennsylvania Evening Post.* (March 6, 1778). Clinton, Henry. *The American Rebellion: Sir Henry Clinton's Narrative of His Campaigns, 1775–1782,* with an appendix of original documents. Edited by William B. Willcox. New Haven: Yale University Press, 1954 p.71. *Kemble's Journals, 1773–1789,* New York Historical Society Collections, 1883–1884. 1 p.132. *The Massachusetts Spy: or American Oracle of Liberty.* VII: 336 (October 9, 1777) p.1. Clayton, W. Woodford. *History of Bergen and Passaic Counties, New Jersey, with biographical sketches of many of its pioneers and prominent men.* Philadelphia: Everts & Peck, 1882. pp.53–54. Leiby, Adrian Coulter. *The Revolutionary War in the Hackensack Valley; the Jersey Dutch and the Neutral Ground, 1775–1783.* New Brunswick, N.J.: Rutgers University Press 1962 pp.134–135. *Documents Relating to the Revolutionary History, State of New Jersey.* Edited by William S. Stryker. Trenton: The John L. Murphy Publishing Co., 1901. Series 2. 2:42–44.

105. Bergen Historical Society, 1906–1907, 49.

106. *New York Gazette and Weekly Mercury.* (February 9, 1778). *Documents Relating to the Revolutionary History, State of New Jersey.* Edited by William S. Stryker. Trenton: The John L. Murphy Publishing Co., 1901. Series 2. 2:47.

107. *Pennsylvania Packet.* (May 23, 1780). Moore, Frank. *Diary of the American Revolution: from Newspapers and Original Documents.* New York: Charles Scribner; London: Sampson Low, Son & Co., 1890. 2 pp.265–266.

108. *Documents Relating to the Revolutionary History, State of New Jersey.* Edited by William S. Stryker. Trenton: The John L. Murphy Publishing Co., 1901. Series 2. 4:433–434. Leiby, Adrian Coulter. *The Revolutionary War in the Hackensack Valley.* New Brunswick: Rutgers University Press, 1962. pp.254–255. Extract of a letter from New-Barbados, Bergen County, dated May 30, 1780. *The New Jersey Gazette.* 3:129 (June 14, 1780) p.3; *The Pennsylvania Evening Post.*VI:673 (June 16, 1780) p.68. *The Pennsylvania Packet or the General Advertiser.* (June 17, 1780) p.2. *The Norwich Packet and the Weekly Advertiser.* 351 (June 22, 1780) p.2; *The American Journal And General Advertiser.* 2:68 (June 28, 1780) p.3.

109. *The Pennsylvania Evening Post and Public Advertiser.*7:761 (August 6, 1781) p.122.

110. *The Pennsylvania Evening Post.* 6:682 (July 28, 1780) p.86. Leiby, Adrian Coulter. *The Revolutionary War in the Hackensack Valley; the Jersey Dutch and the Neutral Ground, 1775–1783.* New Brunswick, N.J.: Rutgers University Press 1962 pp.253–255. Library of Congress, George Washington Papers, Series 4, General Correspondence, 3 April 1780–6 June 1780. Munn, David C. *Battles and Skirmishes of the American Revolution in New Jersey.* [Trenton]: Bureau of Geology and Topography, Department of Environmental Protection, c. 1976. New York Public Library, Box— Miscellaneous New Jersey Manuscripts, "New Jersey–Bergen County" folder. Keesey, Ruth M. *Loyalty and Reprisal: The Loyalists of Bergen County, New Jersey and their Estates.* Ph.D. Dissertation, Columbia University, 1957 p.22. New Jersey Legislature. *Votes and Proceedings of the General Assembly of the State of New Jersey, 1776–1810,* 1780.

111. *The Norwich Packet and the Weekly Advertiser.* 358 (August 10, 1780) p.3. *Documents Relating to the Revolutionary History, State of New Jersey.* Edited by William S. Stryker. Trenton: The John L. Murphy Publishing Co., 1901. Series 2. 4:538; 546; 553; 556; 577; 581. Winfield, Charles H. *History of the County of Hudson, New Jersey.* New York: Kennard & Hay, 1874. p.167–169. Clinton, Henry. *The American Rebellion: Sir Henry Clinton's Narrative of His Campaigns, 1775–1782, with an appendix of original documents.* Edited by William B. Willcox. New Haven: Yale University Press, 1954 p.200. Leiby, Adrian Coulter. *The Revolutionary War in the Hackensack Valley; the Jersey Dutch and the Neutral Ground, 1775–1783.* New Brunswick, N.J.: Rutgers University Press, 1962. pp.257–259.

112. *History Address of Francis J. Swayze.* Sesqui-Centennial Sussex County, N.J.: Newton, N.J., 1903. p.38.

113. *Documents Relating to the Revolutionary History, State of New Jersey.* Edited by William S. Stryker. Trenton: The John L. Murphy Publishing Co., 1901. Series 2. 3:515–516.

114. Ibid., 5:296.

115. Clayton, W. Woodford. *History of Bergen and Passaic Counties, New Jersey, with biographical sketches of many of its pioneers and prominent men.* Philadelphia: Everts & Peck, 1882. p.74.

116. *New York Gazette and Weekly Mercury.* (May 19, 1777). *Documents Relating to the Revolutionary History, State of New Jersey.* Edited By William S. Stryker. Trenton: The John L. Murphy Publishing Co., 1901. Series 2. 1:378–379.

117. *Documents Relating to the Revolutionary History, State of New Jersey.* Edited by William S. Stryker. Trenton: The John L. Murphy Publishing Co., 1901. Series 2. 3:226.

118. Ibid., pp.215–216. See 9 p.451 for a sketch of Robert Ogden.

119. *The Royal Gazette.* 306 (September 4, 1779). *Documents Relating to the Revolutionary History, State of New Jersey.* Edited by William S. Stryker. Trenton: The John L. Murphy Publishing Co., 1901. Series 2. 1:55, 456; 3:592–593.

120. *The Royal Gazette.* 306 (September 4, 1779). *Documents Relating to the Revolutionary History, State of New Jersey.* Edited by William S. Stryker. Trenton: The John L. Murphy Publishing Co., 1901. Series 2. 3:593.

121. *Pennsylvania Evening Post.* 6:673 (June 16, 1780) p.68. *New Jersey Gazette.* (June 14, 1780) p.3.

122. *Documents Relating to the Revolutionary History, State of New Jersey.* Edited by William S. Stryker. Trenton: The John L. Murphy Publishing Co., 1901. Series 2. 4:476. Lundin, Leonard. *Cockpit of the Revolution.* Princeton: Princeton University Press, 1940. 83–85. Moody, James. *Narrative of the Exertions and Sufferings of Lieut. James Moody, in the Cause of Government since the Year 1776.* New York: 1865. pp.10–11, 13–14, 55.

123. New Jersey Department of Defense Manuscripts; Pension #20104.

124. Barber, John Warner. *Historical Collections of New Jersey.* New York: S. Tuttle, 1844. pp.484–485.

125. *The Massachusetts Spy: Or, American Oracle of Liberty.* IX:422 (June 3, 1779) p.3. *The Independent Chronicle and the Universal Advertiser.* XI:563 (June 3,1779) p.2.

126. John Huyler and Thomas Blanch to WL, May 26/27, 1780 (NN), Thomas Blanch to WL, June 8 and June 18, 1780 (NN), and www.doublegv.com/ggv/militia.html. David Van Bussam, John Huyler, and William Logan to WL, June 9, 1780 (NN).

127. Pension Records, S11160. Leiby, Adrian Coulter. *The Revolutionary War in the Hackensack Valley; the Jersey Dutch and the Neutral Ground, 1775–1783.* New Brunswick, N.J.: Rutgers University Press 1962 p.204. Peckham, Howard Henry. *The Toll of Independence: Engagements & Battle Casualties of the American Revolution.* Chicago: University of Chicago Press, 1974. p.96.

128. Peckham, Howard Henry. *The Toll of Independence: Engagements & Battle Casualties of the American Revolution.* Chicago: University of Chicago Press, 1974. p.96.

129. *The Pennsylvania Evening Post.* 2:192 (April 13, 1776) p.186. *Connecticut Journal.* 444 (April 17, 1776) p.3.

130. Farrier, George H. *Memorial of the centennial celebration of the battle of Paulus Hook, August 19th, 1879: with a history of the early settlement and present condition of Jersey City, N.J.* Jersey City: M. Mullone, printer, 1879. p.27.

131. Master's Log of HM Brig *Halifax.* British National Archives, Admiralty 52/1775; NDAR 5:1191.

132. *The Pennsylvania Evening Post.* (September 12,1776). *Documents Relating to the Revolutionary History, State of New Jersey.* Edited by William S. Stryker. Trenton: The John L. Murphy Publishing Co., 1901. Series 2. 1:185–186.

133. Mackenzie, Frederick. *The Diary of Frederick Mackenzie.* Cambridge, MA: Harvard University Press, 1930 p.57. *The Pennsylvania Evening Post.* (October 1, 1776). *Documents Relating to the Revolutionary History, State of New Jersey.* Edited by William S. Stryker. Trenton: The John L. Murphy Publishing Co., 1901. Series 2. 1:227.

134. Clayton, W. Woodford. *History of Bergen and Passaic Counties, New Jersey, with biographical sketches of many of its pioneers and prominent men.* Philadelphia: Everts & Peck, 1882. p.51. *The Pennsylvania Evening Post.* (October 1, 1776). *Documents Relating to the Revolutionary History, State of New Jersey.* Edited by William S. Stryker. Trenton: The John L. Murphy Publishing Co., 1901. Series 2. 1:199, 227.

135. Journal of HMS *Renown,* Captain Francis Banks. British National Archives, Admiralty 51/776. NDAR 6:861.

136. Serle, Ambrose. *The American Journal of Ambrose Serle Secretary To Lord Howe 1776–1778.* Edited with an introduction by Edward H. Tatum, Jr. San Marino, CA: The Huntington Library, 1940, pp.107–108.

137. *Documents Relating to the Revolutionary History, State of New Jersey.* Edited by William S. Stryker. Trenton: The John L. Murphy Publishing Co., 1901. Series 2. 1:204. NDAR 6:965. Lundin, Leonard. *Cockpit of the Revolution.* Princeton: Princeton University Press, 1940. p.136. *Documents Relating to the Revolutionary History, State of New Jersey.* Edited by William S. Stryker. Trenton: The John L. Murphy Publishing Co., 1901. Series 2. 1:204, 227–229. Heath, William. *Memoirs of Major General William Heath.* (Eyewitness accounts of the American Revolution). [New York] New York Times [1968, c1901] 55–58. NDAR 6:962–964.

138. Journal of HM Galley *Dependence.* British National Archives, Admiralty 51/4159. NDAR 7:1258.

139. *Encyclopedia of the American Revolution.* Harold E. Selesky, editor in chief.—2nd Ed. Detroit: Charles Scribner's Sons, 2007. 2:876–879. *The Encyclopedia of the American Revolutionary War: a political, social, and military history.* Gregory Fremont-Barnes, Richard Alan Ryerson, editors. Santa Barbara, CA: ABC-CLIO, 2006. 3:958–961. Extract of a letter from an officer at Paramus, August 21, in the *New Hampshire Gazette.* (September 7, 1779). *Pennsylvania Packet.* (September 2, 1779). Boyd, Thomas. *Light-Horse Harry Lee.* New York: Scribner, 1931. Dornfest, Walter T. "British, Hessian, and Provincial Troops at Paulus Hook, 18th–19th August, 1779." *Journal of the Society for Army Historical Research.* 45 (1967): 177–183. Gerson, Noel B. *Light-Horse Harry: A Biography of Washington's Great Cavalryman, General Henry Lee.* Garden City, N.Y.: Doubleday, 1966. Greene, Francis V. *The Revolutionary War and the Military Policy of the United States.* New York: Scribner, 1911. Hartley, Cecil B. *Life of Major General Henry Lee, Commander of Lee's Legion in the Revolutionary War, and Subsequently Governor of Virginia.* New York: Derby and Jackson, 1859. Kemble, Stephen. *Journals of Lieut.-Col. Stephen Kemble, 1773–1789; and British Army Orders: Gen. Sir William Howe, 1775–1778; Gen. Sir Henry Clinton, 1778; and Gen. Daniel Jones, 1778.* Prepared by New York Historical Society; Boston: Gregg Press, 1972. pp.182–183. Koke, Richard J. "The Britons Who Fought at Stony Point: Uniforms of the American Revolution." *New York Historical Society Quarterly.* 44 (1960): 443–471. Lee, Henry, *Memoirs of the War in the Southern Department of the United States.* New York: University Publishing Co., 1869. Nelson, Paul David. *William Alexander, Lord Stirling.* University of Alabama Press, 1987. Richardson, William H. and Walter P. Gardner. *Washington and "The Enterprise against Powles Hook": A New Study of the Surprise and Capture of the Fort Thursday, August 19, 1779.* Jersey City: New Jersey Title Guarantee and Trust, 1938. Royster, Charles. *Light-Horse Harry Lee and the Legacy of the American Revolution.* New York: Knopf, 1981. Templin, Thomas E. "Henry 'Light-Horse Harry' Lee: A Biography." PhD. Diss., University of Kentucky, 1975. Ward, Christopher. *The War of the Revolution.* New York: Macmillan, 1952. pp.604–610. Letter of Captain Levin Handy to George Handy. Paramus 22 July 1779 in Farrier, George H. *Memorial of the centennial celebration of the battle of Paulus Hook, August 19th, 1879: with a history of the early settlement and present condition of Jersey City, N.J.* Jersey City: M. Mullone, printer, 1879. pp.72–73. Westervelt, Frances A. Johnson, ed. *History of Bergen County, New Jersey, 1630–1923.* New York: Lewis Historical Pub. Co. 1923. 1:109–110.

139a. *The New York Gazette: and the Weekly Mercury,* December 27, 1779. No. 1471. *Documents Relating to the Revolutionary History, State of New Jersey.* Edited by William S. Stryker. Trenton: The John L. Murphy Publishing Co., 1901. Series 2. 4:114.

140. Clinton, George. *Public Papers of George Clinton, first Governor of New York, 1777–1795, 1801–1804.* Hugh Hastings, ed. New York and Albany: Pub. by the State of New York, 1900. 1:531–2.

141. Wall, John P. *The Chronicles of New Brunswick, New Jersey 1667–1931.* New Brunswick: Thatcher-Anderson Company, 1931. pp.207, 217–220.

142. *The Pennsylvania Evening Post.* (July 26, 1777). *Documents Relating to the Revolutionary History, State of New Jersey.* Edited by William S. Stryker. Trenton: The John L. Murphy Publishing Co., 1901. Series 2. 1:433.

143. Wall, John P. *The Chronicles of New Brunswick, New Jersey 1667–1931.* New Brunswick: Thatcher-Anderson Company, 1931. p.220.

144. *The Pennsylvania Evening Post.* (January 23, 1777).

145. *New York Gazette and Weekly Mercury.* January 27,1777. *Documents Relating to the Revolutionary History, State of New Jersey.* Edited by William S. Stryker. Trenton: The John L. Murphy Publishing Co., 1901. Series 2. 1:271–272.

146. *The Pennsylvania Gazette.* (February 5, 1777). *Documents Relating to the Revolutionary History, State of New Jersey.* Edited by William S. Stryker. Trenton: The John L. Murphy Publishing Co., 1901. Series 2. 1:279. Somerset County Historical Society 4:167.

147. Whitehead, William Adee. *Contributions to the Early History of Perth Amboy.* New York: D. Appleton & Co., 1856. p.341.

148. *Connecticut Journal.* 492 (March 19, 1777) p.2. Wall, John P. *The Chronicles of New Brunswick, New Jersey 1667–1931.* New Brunswick: Thatcher-Anderson Company, 1931. pp.217–18. Clayton, W. Woodford, ed. *History of Union and Middlesex Counties, New Jersey, with Biographical Sketches of Many of their Pioneers and Prominent Men.* Philadelphia: Everts & Peck, 1882. pp.647, 469. *Documents Relating to the Revolutionary History, State of New Jersey.* Edited by William S. Stryker. Trenton: The John L. Murphy Publishing Co., 1901. Series 2. 4:402n. New Jersey Department of Defense Manuscripts.

149. Muenchhausen, Friedrich von. *At General Howe's Side 1776–1778: The diary of General William Howe's aide de camp.* Captain Friedrich von Muenchhausen. Translated by Ernst Kipping and annotated by Samuel Smith. Monmouth Beach, N.J.: Philip Freneau Press, 1974. pp.9–10.

150. Peebles, John. *John Peebles' American War: the Diary of a Scottish Grenadier, 1776–1782.* edited by Ira D. Gruber. Mechanicsburg, PA: Stackpole Books, 1998. p.101.

151. Sabine, Lorenzo. *Biographical sketches of Loyalists of the American Revolution.* Port Washington, N.Y.: Kennikat Press [1966]. 2:356. *The New York Gazette and Weekly Mercury.* (March 17,1777). *Documents Relating to the Revolutionary History, State of New Jersey.* Edited by William S. Stryker. Trenton: The John L. Murphy Publishing Co., 1901. Series 2. 1:316.

152. *The Pennsylvania Journal.* (March 26, 1777). *Documents Relating to the Revolutionary History, State of New Jersey.* Edited by William S. Stryker. Trenton: The John L. Murphy Publishing Co., 1901. Series 2. 1:323.

153. *The Pennsylvania Evening Post.* 3:339 (April 15, 1777) p.206.

154. Pension record #22373.

155. Peckham, Howard Henry. *The Toll of Independence: Engagements & Battle Casualties of the American Revolution.* Chicago: University of Chicago Press, 1974. p.35. General William Howe's letter dated New York July 5, 1777. *Documents Relating to the Revolutionary History, State of New Jersey.* Edited by William S. Stryker. Trenton: The John L. Murphy Publishing Co., 1901. Series 2. 1:428, 477. Clayton, W. Woodford. *History of Union and Middlesex Counties.* Philadelphia: Everts and Peck, 1882. pp.78–79.

156. General William Howe's letter dated New York July 5, 1777. *Documents Relating to the Revolutionary History, State of New Jersey.* Edited by William S. Stryker. Trenton: The John L. Murphy Publishing Co., 1901. Series 2. 1:428, 477. Clayton, W. Woodford. *History of Union and Middlesex Counties.* Philadelphia: Everts and Peck, 1882. pp.78–79.

157. New York Historical Society *Collections*, 1881, 423.

158. Cresswell, Nicholas. *The Journal of Nicholas Cresswell, 1774–1777.* New York, 1924. p.242.

159. Wall, John P. *The Chronicles of New Brunswick, New Jersey 1667–1931.* New Brunswick: Thatcher-Anderson Company, 1931. p.226. Muenchhausen, Friedrich von. *At General Howe's Side 1776–1778: The diary of General William Howe's aide de camp, Captain Friedrich von Muenchhausen.* Translated by Ernst Kippling and annotated by Samuel Smith. Monmouth Beach, N.J.: Philip Freneau Press, 1974. June 20, 21, 22. Lundin, Leonard. *Cockpit of the Revolution.* Princeton: Princeton University Press, 1940. p.321.

160. *Royal Gazette.* 322 (October 30, 1779) p.3. *New-York Gazette, and Weekly Mercury.* 1463:2 .

161. *The Pennsylvania Evening Post.* 5:636 (November 6, 1779) p.246. General William Howe's letter dated New York July 5, 1777. *Documents Relating to the Revolutionary History, State of New Jersey.* Edited by William S. Stryker. Trenton: The John L. Murphy Publishing Co., 1901. Series 2. 1:428, 477. Clayton, W. Woodford. *History of Union and Middlesex Counties.* Philadelphia: Everts and Peck, 1882. pp.78–79.

162. *Documents Relating to the Revolutionary History, State of New Jersey.* Edited by William S. Stryker. Trenton: The John L. Murphy Publishing Co., 1901. Series 2. 5:285.

163. Letter of Lieut. Colonel John Taylor, Commandant 2d. Batt. Middlesex Militia, to Mr. Collins January 10, 1782. *Documents Relating to the Revolutionary History, State of New Jersey.* Edited by William S. Stryker. Trenton: The John L. Murphy Publishing Co., 1901. Series 2. 5:358. *The Pennsylvania Packet of the General Advertiser.* 11:386 (January 22, 1782) p.3. Whitehead, William A. *Contributions to the Early History of Perth Amboy and Adjoining Country.* New York: D. Appleton & Company, 1856. p.353.

164. *The Freeman's Journal: or, The North-American Intelligencer.* XL (January 23, 1782) p.3. *Connecticut Courant.* 889 (February 5, 1782) p.2. *The Independent Chronicle and the Universal Advertiser.* XIV:702 (Febuary 7, 1782) p.3. *The Pennsylvania Packet or the General Advertiser.* XI:838 (January 26, 1782) p.3. Wall, John P. *History of Middlesex County, New Jersey, 1664–1920.* New York, Chicago, Lewis historical publishing company, inc. 1921. 1:285. *Annals of Staten Island, from its discovery to the present time.* J. J. Clute. New York: Press of C. Vogt, 1877. p.112.

165. Extract of a letter from New Jersey, June 19, 1782. *The Freeman's Journal: or, the North-American Intelligencer.* II:LXII (June 26, 1782) p.3.

166. *Continental Journal.* 35 (January 32, 1777) p.2.

167. Extract of a letter from Rariton, (New-Jersey) Jan. 23. *Pennsylvania Journal and Weekly Advertiser.* (January 29, 1777). *Documents Relating to the Revolutionary History, State of New Jersey.* Edited by William S. Stryker. Trenton: The John L. Murphy Publishing Co., 1901. Series 2. 1:276–277.

168. *Pennsylvania Journal and Weekly Advertiser.* (January 29, 1777). *Documents Relating to the Revolutionary History, State of New Jersey.* Edited by William S. Stryker. Trenton: The John L. Murphy Publishing Co., 1901. Series 2. 1:276–277.

169. *Connecticut Journal.* 492 (March 19, 1777) p.2.

170. Whitehead, William A. *Contributions to the Early History of Perth Amboy and Adjoining Country.* New York: D. Appleton & Company, 1856. pp.341. *The Pennsylvania Journal.* (March 19, 1777). *Documents Relating to the Revolutionary History, State of New Jersey.* Edited by William S. Stryker. Trenton: The John L. Murphy Publishing Co., 1901. Series 2. 1:318–320. Extract of a letter from Haddonfield, New Jersey, in *Pennsylvania Journal.* (March 19, 1777). Moore, Frank. *Diary of the American Revolution: from Newspapers and Original Documents.* New York: Charles Scribner; London: Sampson Low, Son & Co., 1890. 1:405–406. Kemble, Stephen. *Journals of Lieut.-Col. Stephen Kemble, 1773–1789; and British Army Orders: Gen. Sir William Howe, 1775–1778; Gen. Sir Henry Clinton, 1778; and Gen. Daniel Jones, 1778.* Prepared by New York Historical Society; Boston: Gregg Press, 1972. p.111. Dally, Joseph W. *Woodbridge and vicinity: the story of a New Jersey township, embracing the history of Woodbridge, Piscataway, Metuchen, and contiguous places, from the earliest times; the history of the different ecclesiastical bodies ; important official documents relating to the township, etc.* Madison, N.J.: Hunterdon House, 1967, 1873. p.272.

171. Extract of a Letter from an Officer at Camp, near Bonhamtown, Dated April 15, 1777. *The Pennsylvania Evening Post.* 3:342 (April 22, 1777) p.226. *The Maryland Journal And Baltimore Advertiser.* 4:181 (April 29, 1777) p.3.

172. *Connecticut Journal.* 500 (May 14, 1777) p.1. *New York Gazette and Weekly Mercury.* (April 28, 1777). *The Pennsylvania Packet.* (April 29, 1777). *Documents Relating to the Revolutionary History, State of New Jersey.* Edited by William S. Stryker. Trenton: The John L. Murphy Publishing Co., 1901. Series 2. 1:344, 354.

173. *Connecticut Journal.* 500 (May 14, 1777) p.1.

174. Extract of Letter from a General Officer at Post near Bonham-Town Dated May 11. *The Maryland Journal And Baltimore Advertiser.* 4:185 (May 20, 1777) p.3.

175. Ewald, Johann. *Diary of the American War: A Hessian Journal.* Translated and edited by Joseph P. Tustin. New Haven and London: Yale University Press, 1979. pp.65–68. *Narratives of the Revolution In New York: A Collection of Articles From The New-York Historical Society Quarterly.* New York: The New York Historical Society, 1975. p.238.

176. Vermeule, Cornelius C. *The Revolutionary Camp Ground at Plainfield.* New York: The Evening Post Job Printing Office, Inc., 1923. p.17. Boatner, Mark M. *Encyclopedia of the American Revolution.* McKay: New York, 3d ed., 1980. p.872. Serle, Ambrose. *The American Journal of Ambrose Serle.* [New York]: New York Times ; Arno Press, c1969. p.222.

177. The following Exaggerated Account is Taken from a New-York Paper of July 3. *The Pennsylvania Evening Post.* 3:377 (July 12, 1777) p.371. *The Virginia Gazette.* 1354 (July 25,1777) p.2.

178. *Royal Gazette.* 322 (October 30, 1779) p.3. *New-York Gazette, and Weekly Mercury.* 1463:2. *Documents Relating to the Revolutionary History, State of New Jersey.* Edited by William S. Stryker. Trenton: The John L. Murphy Publishing Co., 1901. Series 2. 3:719–720. Washington, George. *Papers of George Washington.* Dorothy Twohig, ed.—Revolutionary War Series.—Charlottesville and London: University Press of Virginia. 17:38. Leiby, Adrian Coulter. *The Revolutionary War in the Hackensack Valley.* New Brunswick: Rutgers University Press, 1962. pp.223–224.

179. Ward, Harry M. *Charles Scott and the "Spirit of '76".* Charlottesville: University Press of Virginia, 1988. pp.28–30. Bostwick, Elisha. *A Connecticut Soldier Under Washington: Elisha Bostwick's Memoirs of the First Years of the Revolution.* William S. Powell, ed. *The William and Mary Quarterly*, 3rd Ser., 6, No. 1. (January 1949) pp.105–106. Harry M. Lydenberg, ed. *Archibald Robertson: His Diaries and Sketches in America, 1762–80.* New York, 1930, Feb. 3, 1777. *Pennsylvania Gazette.* (March 5, 1777) in *Documents Relating to the Revolutionary History, State of New Jersey.* Edited by William S. Stryker. Trenton: The John L. Murphy Publishing Co., 1901. Series 2. 1:306. Lobdell, Jared C. "Journal of McCarty," *Proceedings of the New Jersey Historical Society.* 82 (1964): Jan.–Feb. 1777, 44–45. Lobdell, Jared C. Two Forgotten Battles in the Revolutionary War. *New Jersey History.* 85:3 & 4 (Fall and Winter, 1967) pp.226–230. James Taylor's version of Scott's entreaty, recorded for Daniel Drake in the 19th century: "Shin them (shoot low) Shin the d - - d rascals twill take two Well ones to carry off one crippled one, Shin them, G.D - - them" (Draper Coll., 8CC 166:5). *The Pennsylvania Evening Post.* 3:320 (February 27, 1777) p.110. www.westJerseyhistory.org/books/battlesmunn/partfive.shtml.

180. *The Pennsylvania Evening Post.* (May 24, 1777). 1:384. *Documents Relating to the Revolutionary History, State of New Jersey.* Edited by William S. Stryker. Trenton: The John L. Murphy Publishing Co., 1901. Series 2. 1:384.

181. *Pennsylvania Gazette.* (February 5, 1777) p.3.

182. Washington, George. *The writings of George Washington from the original manuscript sources, 1745–1799;* prepared under the direction of the United States George Washington Bicentennial Commission and published by authority of Congress; John C. Fitzpatrick, editor. Washington, U.S. Govt. Print. Off. [1931–44] Volume 7. To The President of Congress January 26, 1777. http://128.143.22.16/etcbin/toccer-new2?id=WasFi07.xml&images=images/modeng&data=/texts/english/modeng/parsed&tag=public&part=all.

183. *The Pennsylvania Journal.* (February 5, 1777). *Documents Relating to the Revolutionary History, State of New Jersey.* Edited by William S. Stryker. Trenton: The John L. Murphy Publishing Co., 1901. Series 2. 1:565–567.

184. Whitehead, William A. *Contributions to the Early History of Perth Amboy and Adjoining Country.* New York: D. Appleton & Company, 1856. pp.340–341.

185. Ewald, Johann. *Diary of the American War: A Hessian Journal.* Translated and edited by Joseph P. Tustin. New Haven and London: Yale University Press, 1979. pp.53– 55. Lobdell, Jared C. Two Forgotten Battles in the Revolutionary War. *New Jersey History.* 85:3 & 4 (Fall and Winter, 1967) p.228. Wall, John P. *The Chronicles of New Brunswick, New Jersey 1667–1931.* New Brunswick: Thatcher-Anderson Company, 1931. p.221. *New York Gazette and Weekly Mercury.* (February 17, 1777). *Documents Relating to the Revolutionary History, State of New Jersey.* Edited by William S. Stryker. Trenton: The John L. Murphy Publishing Co., 1901. Series 2. 1:287.

186. Lobdell, Jared C. Two Forgotten Battles in the Revolutionary War. *New Jersey History.* 85:3 & 4 (Fall and Winter, 1967) p.230. *Pennsylvania Gazette.* (February 27, 1777).

187. *Connecticut Journal.* 492 (March 19, 1777) p.2.

188. *Pennsylvania Gazette.* (March 20, 1777). *Continental Journal.* 46 (April 10, 1777) p.1. *Dunlap's Pennsylvania Packet or the General Advertiser.* 6:279 (March 18, 1777) p.4.

189. Extract of a letter from Morristown, dated March 10. *Pennsylvania Gazette.* (March 20, 1777). *Dunlap's Pennsylvania Packet or the General Advertiser.* 6:279 (March 18, 1777) p.4.

190. *The Pennsylvania Gazette.* (March 12, 1777). Letter from Morristown, dated March 10. *Documents Relating to the Revolutionary History, State of New Jersey.* Edited by William S. Stryker. Trenton: The John L. Murphy Publishing Co., 1901. Series 2. 1:313.

191. *Connecticut Journal.* 496 (April 16, 1777) p.496. *New York Gazette, and Weekly Mercury.* (April 14, 1777). *Documents Relating to the Revolutionary History, State of New Jersey.* Edited by William S. Stryker. Trenton: The John L. Murphy Publishing Co., 1901. Series 2. 1:338.

192. *New York Gazette and Weekly Mercury.* (May 19, 1777). *Documents Relating to the Revolutionary History, State of New Jersey.* Edited By William S. Stryker. Trenton: The John L. Murphy Publishing Co., 1901. Series 2.1:378–379.

193. Whitehead, William A. *Contributions to the Early History of Perth Amboy and Adjoining Country.* New York: D. Appleton & Company, 1856. p.344. This account appears to be a variation of the previous one.

194. Vermeule, Cornelius C. *The Revolutionary Camp Ground at Plainfield.* New York: The Evening Post Job Printing Office, Inc., 1923. p.17. Boatner, Mark M. *Encyclopedia of the American Revolution.* McKay: New York, 3d ed., 1980. p.872. Serle, Ambrose. *The American Journal of Ambrose Serle.* [New York]: New York Times ; Arno Press, c1969. p.222. *The Pennsylvania Gazette.* (May 28, 1777). Extract of a letter from the Jersies, dated Chatham, May 19. *Documents Relating to the Revolutionary History, State of New Jersey.* Edited by William S. Stryker. Trenton: The John L. Murphy Publishing Co., 1901. Series 2. 1:386. Wall, John P. *The Chronicles of New Brunswick, New Jersey 1667–1931.* New Brunswick: Thatcher-Anderson Company, 1931. pp.224–225. Extract of Letter from Morristown Dated May 13, 1777. *The Maryland Journal And Baltimore Advertiser.* 4:185 (May 20,1777) p.3.

195. General William Howe's letter dated New York July 5, 1777. *Documents Relating to the Revolutionary History, State of New Jersey.* Edited by William S. Stryker. Trenton: The John L. Murphy Publishing Co., 1901. Series 2. 1:428, 477. Clayton, W. Woodford. *History of Union and Middlesex Counties.* Philadelphia: Everts and Peck, 1882. pp.78–79.

196. NJ Supreme Court Records 36122, 36989.

197. Lundin, Leonard. *Cockpit of the Revolution.* Princeton: Princeton University Press, 1940. p.185. Sullivan, John. *Letters and papers of Major-General John Sullivan, Continental Army.* Concord, N.H.: New Hampshire Historical Society, 1930–39. 1 p.303.

198. *Connecticut Journal.* 496 (April 16, 1777) p.1.

199. *The Pennsylvania Evening Post.* (December 28, 1776). *Documents Relating to the Revolutionary History, State of New Jersey.* Edited By William S. Stryker. Trenton: The John L. Murphy Publishing Co., 1901. Series 2. 1:245–247.

200. Extract of a letter from an officer of distinction, dated at Chatham (between Morristown and Elizabethtown, New Jersey) February 3, 1777. *The Pennsylvania Packet.* 277 (March 4, 1777). *Documents Relating to the Revolutionary History, State of New Jersey.* Edited by William S. Stryker. Trenton: The John L. Murphy Publishing Co., 1901. Series 2. 1:305.

201. Smith, William. *Historical Memoirs of William Smith, 1778–1783.* New York, 1781 pp.218 ff. Fleming, Thomas J. *The forgotten victory; the battle for New Jersey–1780.* [New York] Reader's Digest Press; distributed by Dutton, 1973. p.38.

202. Extract of Letter from Ash Swamp, Dated February 26, 1777. *The Pennsylvania Evening Post.* 3:323 (March 6,1777) p.124. *Continental Journal.* XLIV (March 27, 1777) p.2. *The Providence Gazette; And Country Journal.* XIV:691 (March 29, 1777) p.2. Fish-Kill, March 6 Extract of a Letter from Morris Town March 2. *The Providence Gazette; And Country Journal.* XIV:690 (March 22,1777) p.2. *Connecticut Courant.* 633 (March 10, 1777) p.2. *Virginia Gazette.* 1336 (March 14, 1777) p.2. *The Norwich Packet and the Connecticut, Massachusetts, New-Hampshire, and Rhode-Island Weekly Advertiser.* 4:181 (From Monday, March 10, to Monday, March 17, 1777) p.3.

203. Ward, Harry M. *General William Maxwell and the New Jersey Continentals.* Westport, CT; London: Greenwood Press, 1997. pp.54–55. Whitehead, William A. *Contributions to the Early History of Perth Amboy and Adjoining Country.* New York: D. Appleton & Company, 1856. p.341. *The Pennsylvania Journal.* (March 19, 1777). *Documents Relating to the Revolutionary History, State of New Jersey.* Edited by William S. Stryker. Trenton: The John L. Murphy Publishing Co., 1901. Series 2. 1:318–320. Extract of a letter from Haddonfield, New Jersey, in *Pennsylvania Journal.* (March 19). Moore, Frank. *Diary of the American Revolution: from Newspapers and Original Documents.* New York: Charles Scribner; London: Sampson Low, Son & Co., 1890. 1:405–406. Kemble, Stephen. *Journals of Lieut.-Col. Stephen Kemble, 1773–1789; and British Army Orders: Gen. Sir William Howe, 1775–1778; Gen. Sir Henry Clinton, 1778; and Gen. Daniel Jones, 1778.* Prepared by New York Historical Society; Boston: Gregg Press, 1972. p.111. Vermeule, Cornelius C. *The Revolutionary Camp Ground at Plainfield.* New York: The Evening Post Job Printing Office, Inc., 1923. p.16.

204. *Freeman's Journal.* (April 26) Moore, Frank. *Diary of the American Revolution: from Newspapers and Original Documents.* New York: Charles Scribner; London: Sampson Low, Son & Co., 1890. 1:409. *Documents Relating to the Revolutionary*

History, State of New Jersey. Edited by William S. Stryker. Trenton: The John L. Murphy Publishing Co., 1901. Series 2. 1:328. Wolk, Ruth. *The History of Woodbridge, New Jersey.* Woodbridge: Printed privately, 1970. p.29.

205. Clayton, W. Woodford, ed. *History of Union and Middlesex Counties, New Jersey, with Biographical Sketches of Many of their Pioneers and Prominent Men.* Philadelphia: Everts & Peck, 1882. p.479.

206. Peckham, Howard Henry. *The Toll of Independence: Engagements & Battle Casualties of the American Revolution.* Chicago: University of Chicago Press, 1974. p.52.

207. Ibid., p.53.

208. Extract of a letter from a Correspondent at Woodbridge, dated February 10, 1779. *The New Jersey Gazette.* 2:63 (February 17, 1779) p.2. *The New-York Gazette: and the Weekly Mercury.* 1446 (July 5, 1779). *Documents Relating to the Revolutionary History, State of New Jersey.* Edited by William S. Stryker. Trenton: The John L. Murphy Publishing Co., 1901. Series 2. 3:65, 76–77, 81, 491. *The Pennsylvania Evening Post.* 5:575 (February 22, 1779) p.46. *La Prensa.* VI:284 (March 2,1779) p.2. *The Royal Gazette.* 247 (February 10,1779).

209. *The New Jersey Gazette.* 2:63 (February 17, 1779) p.2.

210. Extract of a Letter from Hampstead, Long-Island, Dated June 29, 1779. *The New-York Gazette; and The Weekly Mercury.* 1446 (July 5, 1779) p.3. *Documents Relating to the Revolutionary History, State of New Jersey.* Edited By William S. Stryker. Trenton: The John L. Murphy Publishing Co., 1901. Series 2. 3:491, 493. New Jersey Department of Defense Manuscripts #10301.

211. *The New-York Gazette: and the Weekly Mercury.* 1:1452 (August 16, 1779). *Documents Relating to the Revolutionary History, State of New Jersey.* Edited by William S. Stryker. Trenton: The John L. Murphy Publishing Co., 1901. Series 2. 3:555.

212. Simcoe, John Graves. *Simcoe's Military Journal. A History of the Operations of a Partisan Corps, Called The Queen's Rangers, Commanded by Lieut. Col. J. G. Simcoe.* New-York: Bartlett & Welford, 1844. pp.132–134.

213. *Documents Relating to the Revolutionary History, State of New Jersey.* Edited by William S. Stryker. Trenton: The John L. Murphy Publishing Co., 1901. Series 2. 4:406. Wolk, Ruth. *The History of Woodbridge, New Jersey.* Woodbridge: Printed privately, 1970. p.31. *The New Jersey Gazette.* (June 7, 1780) p.3.

214. *Documents Relating to the Revolutionary History, State of New Jersey.* Edited by William S. Stryker. Trenton: The John L. Murphy Publishing Co., 1901. Series 2. 4:569, 580.

215. *The Pennsylvania Journal.* (September 27, 1780). *Documents Relating to the Revolutionary History, State of New Jersey.* Edited by William S. Stryker. Trenton: The John L. Murphy Publishing Co., 1901. Series 2. 4:655, 660.

216. Hatfield, Edwin F. *History of Elizabeth, New Jersey: including the early history of Union County.* New York: Carlton & Lanahan, 1868. p.502. Dally, Joseph W. *Woodbridge and vicinity: the story of New Jersey township, embracing the history of Woodbridge, Piscataway, Metuchen, and contiguous places, from the earliest times ; the history of the different ecclesiastical bodies ; important official documents relating to the township, etc.* Madison, N.J.: Hunterdon House, 1967, 1873. p.278.

217. Extract of a letter from New Jersey, June 19, 1782. *The Freeman's Journal: or, the North-American Intelligencer.* II:LXII (June 26, 1782) p.3. *Connecticut Journal.* 767 (July 11, 1782) p.2.

218. Smith, Samuel Stelle. *The Battle of Princeton.* Monmouth Beach, N.J.: Philip Freneau Press, 1967. p.6.

219. Ewald, Johann. *Diary of the American War: A Hessian Journal.* Translated and edited by Joseph P. Tustin. New Haven and London: Yale University Press, 1979. pp.27, 30.

220. Ibid., p.30. Stryker, William Scudder. *The Battles of Trenton and Princeton.* Boston: Houghton, Mifflin, & Co., 1898. p.28.

221. Extract of a letter from an officer of distinction in the American army. Philadelphia, December 28, 1776. *The Pennsylvania Evening Post.* 2:295 (December 28, 1776) p.613.

222. *Pennsylvania Evening Post.* (July 26, 1777). *Documents Relating to the Revolutionary History, State of New Jersey.* Edited by William S. Stryker. Trenton: The John L. Murphy Publishing Co., 1901. Series 2. 1:433. Smith, Samuel Stelle. *The Battle of Princeton.* Monmouth Beach, N.J.: Philip Freneau Press, 1967. p.13. Fischer, David Hackett. *Washington's Crossing.* Oxford: Oxford University Press, 2004. p.193. message from Von Donop to General Grant, December 17, 1776 in Fast, Howard. *The Crossing.* New York: Ibooks, 1971, 1999. pp.81–82.

223. Message from Von Donop to General Grant December 17, 1776 in Fast, Howard. *The Crossing.* New York: Ibooks, 1971, 1999. pp.81–82.

224. Smith, Samuel Stelle. *The Battle of Trenton.* Monmouth Beach, N.J.: Philip Freneau Press, 1965. p.13.

225. Fischer, David Hackett. *Washington's Crossing.* Oxford: Oxford University Press, 2004. p.193.

226. Smith, Samuel Stelle. *The Battle of Princeton.* Monmouth Beach, N.J.: Philip Freneau Press, 1967. p.13.

227. Fischer, David Hackett. *Washington's Crossing.* Oxford: Oxford University Press, 2004. p.193. Smith, Samuel Stelle. *The Battle of Princeton.* Monmouth Beach, N.J.: Philip Freneau Press, 1967. p.13.

228. Fischer, David Hackett. *Washington's Crossing.* Oxford: Oxford University Press, 2004. p.193. See Col. David Chambers to Washington 16 December 1776 and Philemon Dickinson to Washington, 21 December, *Writings of George Washington.* 7:350, 394; correspondence of Rall, Donop, and Grant, 17–23 December 1776, Donop Papers, Marburg Hessian Transcripts, Library of Congress. Smith, Samuel Stelle. *The Battle of Trenton.* Monmouth Beach, N.J.: Philip Freneau Press, 1965. pp.13–14.

229. Ewald, Johann. *Diary of the American War: A Hessian Journal.* Translated and edited by Joseph P. Tustin. New Haven and London: Yale University Press, 1979. p.35.

230. Smith, Samuel Stelle. *The Battle of Princeton.* Monmouth Beach, N.J.: Philip Freneau Press, 1967. pp.17–18.

231. Bostwick, Elisha. A Connecticut Soldier Under Washington: Elisha Bostwick's Memoirs of the First Years of the Revolution. William S. Powell, ed. *The William and Mary Quarterly,* 3rd Ser., 6, No. 1. (January 1949) pp.102–103.

232. *The Pennsylvania Evening Post.* (December 28, 1776). *Documents Relating to the Revolutionary History, State of New Jersey.* Edited By William S. Stryker. Trenton: The John L. Murphy Publishing Co., 1901. Series 2. 1:245–247.

233. *Encyclopedia of the American Revolution.* Harold E. Selesky, editor in chief.—2nd ed. Detroit: Charles Scribner's Sons, 2007.2:1161–1164. *The Encyclopedia of the American Revolutionary War: a political, social, and military history.* Gregory Fremont-Barnes, Richard Alan Ryerson, editors. Santa Barbara, CA: ABC-CLIO, 2006. 4:1257–1261. Billias, George Allen. *General John Glover and his Marblehead Mariners.* New York: Henry Holt, 1960. Blanco, Richard L., ed. *The War of the Revolution, 1775–1783: an encyclopedia.* New York: Garland Pub., 1993. Carrington, Henry B. *Battles of the American Revolution 1775–1781, including battle maps and charts of the American Revolution.* New York: Promontory Press (1974), originally published in 1877 and 1881. Dwyer, William M. *The Day is Ours! An Inside View of the Battles of Trenton and Princeton, November 1776–January 1777.* New Brunswick, N.J.: Rutgers University Press, 1998. Fischer, David Hackett. *Washington's Crossing.* Oxford: Oxford University Press, 2004. Fleming, Thomas J. *1776: Year of Illusions.* New York: Norton, 1975. Flexner, James Thomas. *George Washington in the American Revolution.* Boston: Little Brown, 1968. Freeman, Douglas Southall. *George Washington, a biography.* New York: Scribner, 1948–1957. 4: Leader of the Revolution, 1951. Ketchum, Richard M. *The Winter Soldiers.* Garden City, N.Y.: Doubleday, 1973. McPhillips, Martin. *The Battle of Trenton.* Morristown, N.J.: Silver Burdett, 1985. Nelson, Paul David. *General James Grant: Scottish Soldier and Royal Governor of East Florida.* Gainesville: University Press of Florida, 1993. Nelson, Paul David. *William Alexander, Lord Stirling.* University of Alabama Press, 1987. Stryker, William Scudder. *The Battles of Trenton and Princeton.* Boston: Houghton, Mifflin, & Co., 1898. Thayer, Theodore. *Nathanael Greene: Strategist of the American Revolution.* New York: Twayne, 1960. Ward, Christopher. *The War of the Revolution.* New York: Macmillan, 1952. pp.291–305. Ward, Harry M. *Major General Adam Stephen and the Cause of American Liberty.* Charlottesville: University of Virginia Press. 1952. Whittemore, Charles P. *A General of the Revolution: John Sullivan of New Hampshire.* New York: Columbia University Press, 1961. Wood, W. J. *Battles of the Revolutionary War, 1775–1781.* Chapel Hill, NC: Algonquin, 1990.

233a. Smith, Samuel Stelle. *The Battle of Princeton.* Monmouth Beach, N.J.: Philip Freneau Press, 1967. pp.13–18.

233b. Wilkinson, James. *Memoirs of My Own Time.* Philadelphia, 1816. 1:140–141.

233c. Smith, Samuel Stelle. *The Battle of Princeton.* Monmouth Beach, N.J.: Philip Freneau Press, 1967. pp.13–18.

234. Smith, Samuel Stelle. *The Battle of Princeton.* Monmouth Beach, N.J.: Philip Freneau Press, 1967. pp.13–18. Ewald, Johann. *Diary of the American War: A Hessian Journal.* Translated and edited by Joseph P. Tustin. New Haven and London: Yale University Press, 1979. pp.48–49. *The Norwich Packet and the Connecticut, Massachusetts, New-Hampshire, and Rhode-Island Weekly Advertiser.* 4:174 (January 27, 1777) p.3.

235. *New York Gazette and Weekly Mercury. Documents Relating to the Revolutionary History, State of New Jersey.* Edited by William S. Stryker. Trenton: The John L. Murphy Publishing Co., 1901. Series 2. 2:97–98.

236. *New York Gazette and Weekly Mercury.* (April 6, 1778). *Documents Relating to the Revolutionary History, State of New Jersey.* Edited by William S. Stryker. Trenton: The John L. Murphy Publishing Co., 1901. Series 2. 2:147.

237. Trenton, March 29 Extract of a Letter from Hackensack, Dated March 24. *La Prensa.* VII:342 (April 11–1780) p.2. Extract of a Letter from Hackinsack, Dated March 24. *The New Jersey Gazette.* 3:118 (March 29,1780) p.3. *The Pennsylvania Packet or the General Advertiser.* (April 4, 1780) p.3. *The Norwich Packet and the Weekly Advertiser.* 341 (April 18, 1780) p.2.

238. Smith, Samuel Stelle. *The Battle of Trenton.* Monmouth Beach, N.J.: Philip Freneau Press, 1965. pp.13–14.

239. Ibid., p.13–15.

240. Lundin, Leonard. *Cockpit of the Revolution.* Princeton: Princeton University Press, 1940. p.202. Smith, Samuel Stelle. *The Battle of Princeton.* Monmouth Beach, N.J.: Philip Freneau Press, 1967. p.11. Collins, Varnum Lansing. *A Brief narrative of the ravages of the British and Hessians at Princeton in 1776–1777.* [New York] New York Times 1968, ©1906. p.30.

241. *Encyclopedia of the American Revolution.* Harold E. Selesky, editor in chief.—2nd Ed. Detroit: Charles Scribner's Sons, 2007. 2:933–937. *The Encyclopedia of the American Revolutionary War: a political, social, and military history.* Gregory Fremont-Barnes, Richard Alan Ryerson, editors. Santa Barbara, CA: ABC-CLIO, 2006. 3:1012–1016. Bill, Alfred Hoyt. *The Campaign of Princeton, 1776–1777.* Princeton, N.J.: Princeton University Press, 1948. Dwyer, William M. *The Day is Ours! An Inside View of the Battles of Trenton and Princeton, November 1776–January 1777.* New Brunswick, N.J.: Rutgers University Press, 1998. English, Frederick. *General Hugh Mercer: Forgotten Hero of the American Revolution.* New York: Vantage, 1975. Fischer, David Hackett. *Washington's Crossing.* Oxford: Oxford University Press, 2004. Fleming, Thomas J. *1776: Year of Illusions.* New York: Norton, 1975. Ketchum, Richard M. *The Winter Soldiers.* Garden City, N.Y.: Doubleday, 1973. Lundin, Leonard. *Cockpit of the Revolution.* Princeton: Princeton University Press, 1940. Nelson, Paul David. *General James Grant: Scottish Soldier and Royal Governor of East Florida.* Gainesville: University Press of Florida, 1993. Smith, Samuel Stelle. *The Battle of Princeton.* Monmouth Beach, N.J.: Philip Freneau Press, 1967. Stryker, William Scudder. *The Battles of Trenton and Princeton.* Boston: Houghton, Mifflin, & Co., 1898. Ward, Christopher. *The War of the Revolution.* New York: Macmillan, 1952. Wood, W. J. *Battles of the Revolutionary War, 1775–1781.* Chapel Hill, NC: Algonquin, 1990.

242. Extract of a Letter from a Gentleman of Great worth in the American Army, to the Printer of This Paper. *The Virginia Gazette.* 1329 (January 24, 1777) p.3. Extract of a letter from General Sir William Howe, to Lord George. Germaine, dated New-York, January 5,1777. *New York Gazette and Weekly Mercury.* (May 12, 1777). *Documents Relating to the Revolutionary History, State of New Jersey.* Edited By William S. Stryker. Trenton: The John L. Murphy Publishing Co., 1901. Series 2. 1:369–71.

243. *The Pennsylvania Packet.* (January 22, 1777). *Documents Relating to the Revolutionary History, State of New Jersey.* Edited by William S. Stryker. Trenton: The John L. Murphy Publishing Co., 1901. Series 2. 1:268. Vermeule, Cornelius C. *The Revolutionary Camp Ground at Plainfield.* New York: The Evening Post Job Printing Office, Inc. 1923. p.16.

244. Smith, Samuel Stelle. *The Battle of Trenton.* Monmouth Beach, N.J.: Philip Freneau Press, 1965. p.13.

245. Extract of a Letter from a Gentleman of Great worth in the American Army, to the Printer of This Paper. *The Virginia Gazette.* 1329 (January 24, 1777) p.3.

246. Marshall, Christopher. *Extracts From the Diary of Christopher Marshall, Kept In Philadelphia And Lancaster, During The American Revolution, 1774–1781.* Edited By William Duane. Albany: Joel Munsell, 1877. pp.110–111.

247. *Documents Relating to the Revolutionary History, State of New Jersey.* Edited by William S. Stryker. Trenton: The John L. Murphy Publishing Co., 1901. Series 2. 3:697.

248. Fischer, David Hackett. *Washington's Crossing.* Oxford: Oxford University Press, 2004. p.193.

249. *Pennsylvania Post.* (January 23, 1777) p.36. Kemble, Stephen. *Journals of Lieut.-Col. Stephen Kemble, 1773–1789; and British Army Orders: Gen. Sir William Howe, 1775–1778; Gen. Sir Henry Clinton, 1778; and Gen. Daniel Jones, 1778.* Prepared by New York Historical Society; Boston: Gregg Press, 1972. pp.105–106.

250. *The Pennsylvania Evening Post.* (January 23, 1777). *Documents Relating to the Revolutionary History, State of New Jersey.* Edited by William S. Stryker. Trenton: The John L. Murphy Publishing Co., 1901. Series 2. 1:270.

251. *New York Gazette and Weekly Mercury.* (February 10, 1777). *Documents Relating to the Revolutionary History, State of New Jersey.* Edited by William S. Stryker. Trenton: The John L. Murphy Publishing Co., 1901. Series 2. 1:280–281.

252. *Encyclopedia of the American Revolution.* Harold E. Selesky, editor in chief.—2nd Ed. Detroit: Charles Scribner's Sons, 2007.2:1100–1102. The *Encyclopedia of the American Revolutionary War: a political, social, and military history.* Gregory Fremont-Barnes, Richard Alan Ryerson, editors. Santa Barbara, CA: ABC-CLIO, 2006. 4:1187–1189. Atwood, R. *The Hessians.* Cambridge: Cambridge University Press, 2002. Diedrich, M.C. *The Battle of Springfield, June 1780.* Hillside, N.J.: Enslow, 1980. Fleming, Thomas J. *The Battle of Springfield.* Trenton: New Jersey Historical Commission, 1976. Fleming, Thomas J. *The Forgotten Victory; The Battle for New Jersey–1780.* [New York]: Reader's Digest Press; distributed by Dutton, 1973. Freeman, Douglas Southall. *George Washington, a biography.* New York: Scribner, 1948–1957. Lundin, Leonard. *Cockpit of the Revolution.* Princeton: Princeton University Press, 1940. Nelson, Paul David. *William Tryon and the Course of Empire: A Life in British Imperial Service.* Chapel Hill: University of North Carolina Press, 1990. Ward, Christopher. *The War of the Revolution.* New York: Macmillan, 1952. Ward, Harry M. *General William Maxwell and the New Jersey Continentals.* Westport, CT; London: Greenwood Press, 1997.

252a. Lossing, Benson. *Pictorial Field Book of the Revolution* I, 325 n.

253. *Documents Relating to the Revolutionary History, State of New Jersey.* Edited by William S. Stryker. Trenton: The John L. Murphy Publishing Co., 1901. Series 2. 4:597–598.

254. *Documents Relating to the Revolutionary History, State of New Jersey.* Edited by William S. Stryker. Trenton: The John L. Murphy Publishing Co., 1901. Series 2. 5:92.

255. *Pennsylvania Ledger.* (Saturday August 3, 1776); NDAR 5:1214. *The Pennsylvania Evening Post.* 2:235 (July 23, 1776) p.363. *Documents Relating to the Revolutionary History, State of New Jersey.* Edited by William S. Stryker. Trenton: The John L. Murphy Publishing Co., 1901. Series 2. 1:148. Winfield, Charles Hardenburg. *History of the County of Hudson, New Jersey.* New York: Kennard & Hay Printing Co. 1874. p.142; American Archives p.5. *Documents Relating to the Revolutionary History, State of New Jersey.* Edited by William S. Stryker. Trenton: The John L. Murphy Publishing Co., 1901. Series 2. 1:148.

256. Heath, William. *Memoirs Major-General William Heath By Himself.* New Edition, with Illustrations and Notes. Edited By William Abbatt. New York: William Abbatt, 1901. pp.93–94.

257. *Documents Relating to the Revolutionary History, State of New Jersey.* Edited by William S. Stryker. Trenton: The John L. Murphy Publishing Co., 1901. Series 1. 2:12, 54n, 456n. Diary Entries of John Fell in E. C. Burnett, *Letters of Members of the Continental Congress.* Washington, 1921–1936. Leiby, Adrian Coulter. *The Revolutionary War in the Hackensack Valley; the Jersey Dutch and the Neutral Ground, 1775–1783.* New Brunswick, N.J.: Rutgers University Press 1962. pp.119–120.

258. *New York Gazette and Weekly Mercury.* (May 19, 1777). *Documents Relating to the Revolutionary History, State of New Jersey.* Edited by William S. Stryker. Trenton: The John L. Murphy Publishing Co., 1901. Series 2. 1:377–378. *A History of the 3rd Battalion, New Jersey Volunteers* www.royalprovincial.com/military/rhist/njv/3njvhist.htm. New Jersey Volunteers - 3rd Battalion in *The American Revolution in South Carolina* www.carolana.com/SC/Revolution/loyalist_militia_nj_volunteers.html.

259. *The Pennsylvania Evening Post.* (July 15, 1777) p.375.

260. Clayton, W. Woodford. *History of Bergen and Passaic Counties, New Jersey, with biographical sketches of many of its pioneers and prominent men.* Philadelphia: Everts & Peck, 1882. p.54.

261. *New York Gazette and Weekly Mercury.* (September 22, 1777). *Documents Relating to the Revolutionary History, State of New Jersey.* Edited by William S. Stryker. Trenton: The John L. Murphy Publishing Co., 1901. Series 2. 1:473.

262. *New York Gazette and Weekly Mercury.* (November 24, 1777). *Documents Relating to the Revolutionary History, State of New Jersey.* Edited by William S. Stryker. Trenton: The John L. Murphy Publishing Co., 1901. Series 2. 1:486.

263. *Pennsylvania Evening Post.* (December 18, 1777). *Documents Relating to the Revolutionary History, State of New Jersey.* Edited by William S. Stryker. Trenton: The John L. Murphy Publishing Co., 1901. Series 2. 1:505.

264. *Documents Relating to the Revolutionary History, State of New Jersey.* Edited by William S. Stryker. Trenton: The John L. Murphy Publishing Co., 1901. Series 2. 2:147. *New York Gazette and Weekly Mercury,* April 6, 1778.

265. *Revolution in America: Confidential Letters and Journals 1776–1784 of Adjutant General Major Baurmeister of the Hessian Forces.* Translated and annotated by Berhard A. Uhlendorf. New Brunswick, N.J.: Rutgers University Press, 1957. pp.220–221.

266. Leiby, Adrian Coulter. *The Revolutionary War in the Hackensack Valley.* New Brunswick: Rutgers University Press, 1962. p.191n.

267. *Documents Relating to the Revolutionary History, State of New Jersey.* Edited by William S. Stryker. Trenton: The John L. Murphy Publishing Co., 1901. Series 2. 3:40. *The Royal Gazette.* 241 (January 20, 1779).

268. *Rivington's Gazette.* (March 17, 1770). Winfield, Charles H. *History of the County of Hudson, New Jersey.* New York: Kennard & Hay, 1874. p.152.

269. *The Independent Chronicle and the Universal Advertiser.* 11:558 (April 29, 1779) p.2. *The Royal Gazette.* 263 (April 7, 1779). *Documents Relating to the Revolutionary History, State of New Jersey.* Edited by William S. Stryker. Trenton: The John L. Murphy Publishing Co., 1901. Series 2. 3:224.

270. *Documents Relating to the Revolutionary History, State of New Jersey.* Edited by William S. Stryker. Trenton: The John L. Murphy Publishing Co., 1901. Series 2. 3:359.

271. Ibid., pp.391–392.

272. Ibid., p.514.

273. Johnston to Wayne, Oct. 29, 1779, Wayne Papers, Historical Society of Pennsylvania. Leiby, Adrian Coulter. *The Revolutionary War in the Hackensack Valley.* New Brunswick: Rutgers University Press, 1962. p.224.

274. *Rivington's Gazette.* No. 511. Winfield, Charles H. *History of the County of Hudson, New Jersey.* New York: Kennard & Hay, 1874. p.195.

275. *New Jersey Gazette.* 3:147 (October 18, 1780). *The New York Gazette and the Weekly Mercury.* 1513 (October 16, 1780). *Documents Relating to the Revolutionary History, State of New Jersey.* Edited by William S. Stryker. Trenton: The John L. Murphy Publishing Co., 1901. Series 2. 5:40–41, 49–50.

276. *New York Mercury.* (April 2, 1781). New York Packet. (Aug. 30, 1781).

277. *Royal Gazette.* 481:3 (May 9, 1781) p.3.

278. *New Jersey Journal.* (December 12, 1781).

279. *The Massachusetts Spy: Or, American Oracle of Liberty.* XI:555 (December 27, 1781) p.3. *New Jersey Journal.* (December 12,1781). Clayton, W. Woodford. *History of Union and Middlesex Counties.* Philadelphia: Everts and Peck, 1882. p.95. Winfield, Charles H. *History of the County of Hudson, New Jersey.* New York: Kennard & Hay, 1874. p.197.

280. *New Jersey Journal.* (February 13, 1782). *New York Mercury.* (February 11, 1782). Winfield, Charles H. *History of the County of Hudson, New Jersey.* New York: Kennard & Hay, 1874. p.197.

281. *Rivington's Gazette,* No. 573. Winfield, Charles H. *History of the County of Hudson, New Jersey.* New York: Kennard & Hay, 1874. p.198. New Jersey Department of Defense Manuscripts #3773.

282. *The Boston Evening-Post and the General Advertiser.* I:XXXVII (June 29, 1782) p.2.

283. *New Jersey Journal.* (September 11, 1782); (October 9, 1782). Winfield, Charles H. *History of the County of Hudson, New Jersey.* New York: Kennard & Hay, 1874. p.198. Clayton, W. Woodford. *History of Bergen and Passaic Counties, New Jersey, with biographical sketches of many of its pioneers and prominent men.* Philadelphia: Everts & Peck, 1882. pp.66–67.

284. Peckham, Howard Henry. *The Toll of Independence: Engagements & Battle Casualties of the American Revolution.* Chicago: University of Chicago Press, 1974. p.22.

285. Whitehead, William A. *Contributions to the Early History of Perth Amboy and Adjoining Country.* New York: D. Appleton & Company, 1856. pp.339. Vermeule, Cornelius C. *The Revolutionary Camp Ground at Plainfield.* New York: The Evening Post Job Printing Office, Inc., 1923. p.12. *New York Gazette and Weekly Mercury.* (January 13, 1777). *Documents Relating to the Revolutionary History, State of New Jersey.* Edited By William S. Stryker. Trenton: The John L. Murphy Publishing Co., 1901. Series 2. 1:253–255. Fleming, Thomas J. *The forgotten victory; the battle for New Jersey–1780.* [New York] Reader's Digest Press; distributed by Dutton, 1973. *Virginia Gazette.* 1330 (January 31, 1777) p.3. Hatfield, Edwin F. *History of Elizabeth, New Jersey: including the early history of Union County.* New York: Carlton & Lanahan, 1868. p.455. Dally, Joseph W. *Woodbridge and vicinity: the story of a New Jersey township, embracing the history of Woodbridge, Piscataway, Metuchen, and contiguous places, from the earliest times; the history of the different ecclesiastical bodies ; important official documents relating to the township, etc.* Madison, N.J.: Hunterdon House, 1967, 1873. p.270.

286. Clayton, W. Woodford, ed. *History of Union and Middlesex Counties, New Jersey, with Biographical Sketches of Many of their Pioneers and Prominent Men.* Philadelphia: Everts & Peck, 1882. p.246.

287. Clayton, W. Woodford. *History of Union and Middlesex Counties.* Philadelphia: Everts and Peck, 1882. p.77.

288. Hall, William Cornwallis.; Hall, John. *History of the civil war in America: I, comprehending the campaigns of 1775, 1776 and 1777.* London: Printed for T. Payne and Sons, 1780. p.262. Dally, Joseph W. *Woodbridge and vicinity: the story of a New Jersey township, embracing the history of Woodbridge, Piscataway, Metuchen, and contiguous places, from the earliest times; the history of the different ecclesiastical bodies ; important official documents relating to the township, etc.* Madison, N.J.: Hunterdon House, 1967, 1873. p.272.

289. Whitehead, William A. *Contributions to the Early History of Perth Amboy and Adjoining Country.* New York: D. Appleton & Company, 1856. p.343. Lobdell, Jared C. Two Forgotten Battles in the Revolutionary War. *New Jersey History.* 85:3 & 4 (Fall and Winter, 1967) pp.226–234 ; James Murray to Mrs. Smith, February 25, 1777, Eric Robson, ed. *Letters from America, 1773–1780. . .Sir James Murray, to his home during the War of American Independence.* New York, 1951. pp.39–41. *New York Gazette and Weekly Mercury.* (March 3, 1777). "Active Operations between February 8 and

23, 1777." Clinton, George. *Public Papers of George Clinton, first Governor of New York, 1777–1795, 1801–1804.* Pub. by the State of New York. New York, Albany, 1899–1914. 1:623. Ward, Harry M. *General William Maxwell and the New Jersey Continentals.* Westport, CT; London: Greenwood Press, 1997. pp.55–56.

290. *Pennsylvania Gazette.* (March 20, 1777). Extract from a letter from an officer in New-Jersey. Philadelphia, March 15. *Pennsylvania Evening Post.* (March 15, 1777). *Documents Relating to the Revolutionary History, State of New Jersey.* Edited By William S. Stryker. Trenton: The John L. Murphy Publishing Co., 1901. Series 2. 1:314. Wall, John P. *The Chronicles of New Brunswick, New Jersey 1667–1931.* New Brunswick: Thatcher-Anderson Company, 1931. p.221.

291. *The Pennsylvania Gazette.* (March 19, 1777; March 20, 1777). *Dunlap's Pennsylvania Packet or the General Advertiser.* 6:279 (March 18, 1777) p.4. *Documents Relating to the Revolutionary History, State of New Jersey.* Edited by William S. Stryker. Trenton: The John L. Murphy Publishing Co., 1901. Series 2. 1:320.

292. *The Pennsylvania Gazette.* (March 26, 1777). *New York Gazette and Weekly Mercury.* (March 24, 1777). *Documents Relating to the Revolutionary History, State of New Jersey.* Edited by William S. Stryker. Trenton: The John L. Murphy Publishing Co., 1901. Series 2. 1:316, 321–322.

293. *The Pennsylvania Journal.* (April 9, 1777). *Documents Relating to the Revolutionary History, State of New Jersey.* Edited by William S. Stryker. Trenton: The John L. Murphy Publishing Co., 1901. Series 2. 1:334.

294. Clayton, W. Woodford. *History of Union and Middlesex Counties.* Philadelphia: Everts and Peck, 1882. pp.78–79.

295. Clayton, W. Woodford. *History of Union and Middlesex Counties.* Philadelphia: Everts and Peck, 1882. p.79.

296. *Documents Relating to the Revolutionary History, State of New Jersey.* Edited by William S. Stryker. Trenton: The John L. Murphy Publishing Co., 1901. Series 2. 4:167; Clayton, W. Woodford. *History of Union and Middlesex Counties.* Philadelphia: Everts and Peck, 1882. p.87.

297. *The Newport Mercury.* 964 (March 1, 1780) p.2. *The Pennsylvania Evening Post.* VI:654 (March 10,1780) p.30. *The Massachusetts Spy: Or, American Oracle of Liberty.* IX:468 (April 27, 1780) p.4.

298. *New Jersey Journal.* 106, 107. *Rivington's Gazette.* 461. *The New-York Gazette; and The Weekly Mercury.* no. 1532, 1633. Clayton, W. Woodford, ed. *History of Union and Middlesex Counties, New Jersey, with Biographical Sketches of Many of their Pioneers and Prominent Men.* Philadelphia: Everts & Peck, 1882. p.92.

299. *New Jersey Journal.* (March 29, 1781). Clayton, W. Woodford, ed. *History of Union and Middlesex Counties, New Jersey, with Biographical Sketches of Many of their Pioneers and Prominent Men.* Philadelphia: Everts & Peck, 1882. p.92.

300. New Jersey Department of Defense Manuscripts 9867.

301. Clayton, W. Woodford. *History of Union and Middlesex Counties.* Philadelphia: Everts and Peck, 1882. p.95.

302. Somerset County Historical Society. 3:250.

303. New Jersey Department of Defense Manuscripts #10301.

304. Serle, Ambrose. *The American Journal of Ambrose Serle Secretary To Lord Howe 1776–1778.* Edited with an introduction by Edward H. Tatum, Jr. San Marino, CA: The Huntington Library, 1940. p.211. Letter of Nathanael Greene to John Adams, April 13, 1777 and Letter of Nathanael Greene to Catherine Greene, April 19, 1777. Greene, Nathanael. *The Papers of General Nathanael Greene.* Published for the Rhode Island Historical Society [by] the University of North Carolina Press, c1976–. 2:55–57. Van Horn, J. H. comp. *Historic Somerset.* New Brunswick: Published by the compiler, 1965. pp.40–41. Wall, John P. *The Chronicles of New Brunswick, New Jersey 1667–1931.* New Brunswick: Thatcher-Anderson Company, 1931. pp.221–222. Vermeule, Cornelius C. *The Revolutionary Camp Ground at Plainfield.* New York: The Evening Post Job Printing Office, Inc., 1923. p.17. *The Pennsylvania Evening Post.* 3:339 (April 15, 1777) p.206. *Continental Journal.* 48 (April 24, 1777) p.3. *The Royal American Gazette.* XIV (April 17, 1777) p.3.

305. Extract of a letter dated camp near Bound-Brook, May 31, 1777. *Documents Relating to the Revolutionary History, State of New Jersey.* Edited by William S. Stryker. Trenton: The John L. Murphy Publishing Co., 1901. Series 2. 1:389–390, 392. *The Pennsylvania Gazette.* (June 4, 1777).

306. Extract of a letter from Middle Brook, June 7. *The Pennsylvania Evening Post.* (June 12, 1777).

307. *Narratives of the Revolution In New York: A Collection Of Articles From The New-York Historical Society Quarterly.* New York: The New York Historical Society, 1975. pp.130–134.

308. *The Providence Gazette.* XVI:805 p.2.

310. Extract of a letter from Elizabeth-Town, May 30. *The Boston Gazette, and Country Journal.* 1312 (October 18, 1779) p.4. Extract of a letter from Elizabeth-Town, May 30. *The New Jersey Gazette.* 2:79 (June 9, 1779) p.3.

312. *Royal Gazette.* 322 (October 30, 1779) p.3. *New-York Gazette, and Weekly Mercury.* 1463:2. *Documents Relating to the Revolutionary History, State of New Jersey.* Edited by William S. Stryker. Trenton: The John L. Murphy Publishing Co., 1901. Series 2. 3:719–720.

313. *The Pennsylvania Evening Post.* 5:636 (November 6, 1779) p.246.

314. *The New-York-Gazette: and the Weekly Mercury.* 1463 (November 1, 1779). *Documents Relating to the Revolutionary History, State of New Jersey.* Edited by William S. Stryker. Trenton: The John L. Murphy Publishing Co., 1901. Series 2. 3:719–720. Leiby, Adrian Coulter. *The Revolutionary War in the Hackensack Valley.* New Brunswick: Rutgers University Press, 1962. pp.223–224.

315. Wall, John P. *The Chronicles of New Brunswick, New Jersey 1667–1931.* New Brunswick: Thatcher-Anderson Company, 1931. pp.232–235. *The Pennsylvania Evening Post.* 5:636 (November 6, 1779) p.246. *Documents Relating to the Revolutionary History, State of New Jersey.* Edited by William S. Stryker. Trenton: The John L. Murphy Publishing Co., 1901. Series 2. 3:719–720. New Jersey Department of Defense Manuscripts #2244.

316. New Jersey Department of Defense Manuscripts #1145, 10301.

317. *Documents Relating to the Revolutionary History, State of New Jersey.* Edited by William S. Stryker. Trenton: The John L. Murphy Publishing Co., 1901. Series 2. 5:211.

318. Fischer, David Hackett. *Washington's Crossing.* Oxford: Oxford University Press, 2004. p.349. *Pennsylvania Journal and Weekly Advertiser.* (January 29, 1777). *Documents Relating to the Revolutionary History, State of New Jersey.* Edited by William S. Stryker. Trenton: The John L. Murphy Publishing Co., 1901. Series 2. 1:276–277.

319. *Freeman's Journal.* 1:40 (February 25,1777) p.1. *The Providence Gazette; And Country Journal.* XIV:683 (February 1, 1777) p.2. *Continental Journal.* XXXVI (January 30, 1777) p.3. *The Massachusetts Spy: Or, American Oracle of Liberty.* VI:300 (January 30, 1777) p.2.

320. *Freeman's Journal.* 1:40 (February 25, 1777) p.1. *The Providence Gazette; And Country Journal.* XIV:683 (February 1,1777) p.2. *Continental Journal.* XXXVI (January 30, 1777) p.3. *The Massachusetts Spy: Or, American Oracle of Liberty.* VI:300 (January 30, 1777) p.2.

321. *The Royal American Gazette.* XIV (April 17, 1777) p.3.

322. Extract of a Letter from Freehold, June 24, 1777. *The Pennsylvania Evening Post.* 3:370 (June 26, 1777) p.339. *Virginia Gazette.* 1352 (July 11, 1777) p.1. *Virginia Gazette.* 128 (July 11, 1777) p.3. Watson, John Fanning. *Annals of Philadelphia and Pennsylvania.* 2nd ed. Philadelphia: the author, 1844. II 294–295. Smith, Samuel Stelle. *The Battle of Monmouth.* Monmouth Beach: Philip Freneau Press, 1964. p.7. *The Pennsylvania Evening Post.* (June 26, 1777). *Documents Relating to the Revolutionary History, State of New Jersey.* Edited by William S. Stryker. Trenton: The John L. Murphy Publishing Co., 1901. Series 2. 1:410.

323. Martin, Joseph Plumb. *Private Yankee Doodle; being a narrative of some of the adventures, dangers, and sufferings of a Revolutionary Soldier,* edited by George F. Scheer, originally published in Hallowell, Me., 1830, anonymously. (Republished, Boston, 1962). *A narrative of some of the adventures, dangers and sufferings of a Revolutionary soldier.* (Eyewitness accounts of the American Revolution). [New York] New York Times [1968] pp.132–133.

324. *Encyclopedia of the American Revolution.* Harold E. Selesky, editor in chief.—2nd Ed. Detroit: Charles Scribner's Sons, 2007. 2:733–740. *An Account of the Action from Brandywine to Monmouth: A Seminar on the Impact of the Revolutionary War on the Delaware Valley.* Philadelphia: Council of American Revolutionary Sites, 1997. *The Encyclopedia of the American Revolutionary War: a political, social, and military history.* Gregory Fremont-Barnes, Richard Alan Ryerson, editors. Santa Barbara, CA: ABC-CLIO, 2006. 3:806–810. André, Major John, *Major Andre's Journal: Operations of the British Army under Lieutenant Generals Sir William Howe, and Sir Henry Clinton, June 1777, to November 1778,* edited by Henry Cabot Lodge, Boston, 1902; Tarrytown, N.Y.: William Abbatt, 1930. Black, Jeremy. *War for America: the fight for independence.* Stroud, UK: Alan Sutton, 1991. Blanco, Richard L., ed. *The War of the Revolution, 1775–1783: an encyclopedia.* New York: Garland Pub., 1993. Carrington, Henry B. *Battles of the American Revolution 1775–1781, including battle maps and charts of the American Revolution.* New York: Promontory Press, (1974), originally published in 1877 and 1881. Clinton, Henry. *The American Rebellion: Sir Henry Clinton's Narrative of His Campaigns, 1775–1782, with an appendix of original documents.* Edited by William B. Willcox. New Haven: Yale University Press, 1954. Conway, Stephen. *The War of American Independence, 1775–1783.* London: Arnold, 1995. Ewald, Johann. *Diary of the American War: A Hessian Journal.* Translated and edited by Joseph P. Tustin. New Haven and London: Yale University Press, 1979. Higginbotham, Don. *The War of American Independence: Military Attitudes, Policies, and Practice, 1763–1789.* New York: Macmillan, 1971. Lengel, Edward G. *General George Washington, A Military Life.* New York: Random House, 2005. Lundin, Leonard. *Cockpit of the Revolution.* Princeton: Princeton University Press, 1940. Mackesy, Piers. *The War for America, 1775–1783.* Lincoln: University of Nebraska Press, 1993. Smith, Samuel Stelle. *The Battle of Monmouth.* Monmouth Beach, N.J.: Philip Freneau Press, 1964. Stryker, William Scudder. *The Battle of Monmouth.* Port Washington, N.Y.: Kennikat Press, (1927), 1970. Ward, Christopher. *The War of the Revolution.* New York: Macmillan, 1952. pp.576–586. Wood, W. J. *Battles of the Revolutionary War, 1775–1781.* Chapel Hill, NC: Algonquin, 1990.

324a. New Jersey Department of Defense Manuscripts #5114.

325. *New Jersey Gazette.* (February 23, 1780) p.3. *Documents Relating to the Revolutionary History, State of New Jersey.* Edited by William S. Stryker. Trenton: The John L. Murphy Publishing Co., 1901. Series 2. 4:190–191.

326. Extract of a letter from Monmouth County, June 12. *New Jersey Gazette.* (June 14, 1780) p.3. *Pennsylvania Evening Post.* 6:673 (June 16, 1780) p.68. *Documents Relating to the Revolutionary History, State of New Jersey.* Edited by William S. Stryker. Trenton: The John L. Murphy Publishing Co., 1901. Series 2. 4:434–435.

327. *Documents Relating to the Revolutionary History, State of New Jersey.* Edited By William S. Stryker. Trenton: The John L. Murphy Publishing Co., 1901. Series 2. 4:603.

328. *Massachusetts Spy.* 715 (July 12, 1781) p.1. *The Massachusetts Spy: Or, American Oracle of Liberty.* 9:531 (July 12, 1781) p.3. *Documents Relating to the Revolutionary History, State of New Jersey.* Edited by William S. Stryker. Trenton: The John L. Murphy Publishing Co., 1901. Series 2. 5:264–265.

329. *Freeman's Journal.* 1:40 (February 25, 1777) p.1. *The Providence Gazette; And Country Journal.* XIV:683 (February 1,1777) p.2. *Continental Journal.* XXXVI (January 30, 1777) p.3. *The Massachusetts Spy: Or, American Oracle of Liberty.* VI:300 (January 30,1777) p.2. *John Chilton Diary, Jan.–Feb., 1777,* VHS. Ward, Christopher. *The War of the Revolution.* New York: Macmillan, 1952. 1:319. Marshall, Christopher. *Extracts from the Diary of Christopher Marshall, Kept in Philadelphia and Lancaster, during the American Revolution, 1774–1781.* Edited by William Duane, Albany, N.Y., 1877; (Eyewitness accounts of the American Revolution). [New York]: New York Times ; Arno Press, c1969. (January 10, 1777) p.111. Lobdell, Jared C. "Journal of McCarty" *New Jersey Historical Society Publications.* 82 (1964): Jan. 13–29, 1777, 42–44. Vanderpoel, Ambrose E. *History of Chatham, New Jersey.* Chatham, 1959. p.184.

330. *Documents Relating to the Revolutionary History, State of New Jersey.* Edited by William S. Stryker. Trenton: The John L. Murphy Publishing Co., 1901. Series 2. 1:296–297.

331. Extract of a letter from Morristown, dated April 28, 1777. *Documents Relating to the Revolutionary History, State of New Jersey.* Edited by William S. Stryker. Trenton: The John L. Murphy Publishing Co., 1901. Series 2. 1:360–361.

332. Adam Stephen to Angus McDonald, March 15, 1777. Adam Stephen Papers, Library of Congress.

333. *The Pennsylvania Evening Post.* (January 23, 1777. *Documents Relating to the Revolutionary History, State of New Jersey.* Edited by William S. Stryker. Trenton: The John L. Murphy Publishing Co., 1901. Series 2. 1:268. Whitehead, William A. *Contributions to the Early History of Perth Amboy and Adjoining Country.* New York: D. Appleton & Company, 1856. p.340.

334. Whitehead, William A. *Contributions to the Early History of Perth Amboy and Adjoining Country.* New York: D. Appleton & Company, 1856. pp.340.

335. Wall, John P. *The Chronicles of New Brunswick, New Jersey 1667–1931.* New Brunswick: Thatcher-Anderson Company, 1931. p.222. Boatner, Mark M. *Encyclopedia of the American Revolution.* McKay: New York, 3d ed., 1980. p.1017. New Jersey Department of Defense Manuscripts. Ward, Harry M. *General William Maxwell and the New Jersey Continentals.* Westport, CT; London: Greenwood Press, 1997. pp.54–55. Lobdell, Jared C. Two Forgotten Battles in the Revolutionary War. *New Jersey History.* 85:3 & 4 (Fall and Winter, 1967) pp.230–34. Washington to William Livingston 3 Feb. 1777. Washington to John Hancock 5 Feb. 1777. Washington, George. *The writings of George Washington from the original manuscript sources, 1745–1799*; prepared under the direction of the United States George Washington Bicentennial Commission and published by authority of Congress; John C. Fitzpatrick, editor. Washington, U.S. Govt. Print. Off. [1931–44]. 8:234–35, 250. *New York Gazette and Weekly Mercury.* (January 13,1777). *Documents Relating to the Revolutionary History, State of New Jersey.* Edited by William S. Stryker. Trenton: The John L. Murphy Publishing Co., 1901. Series 2. 1:253–255. Fleming, Thomas J. *The forgotten victory; the battle for New Jersey–1780.* [New York] Reader's Digest Press; distributed by Dutton, 1973. For British accounts, see *Kemble Papers.* 1:109 (February 1, 1777).

336. New York Historical Society *Collections*, 1881, 423.

337. Ibid. *Documents Relating to the Revolutionary History, State of New Jersey.* Edited by William S. Stryker. Trenton: The John L. Murphy Publishing Co., 1901. Series 2. 1:405.

338. *The Pennsylvania Packet.* (June 24, 1777). *Documents Relating to the Revolutionary History, State of New Jersey.* Edited by William S. Stryker. Trenton: The John L. Murphy Publishing Co., 1901. Series 2. 1:400. For Lord Howe's official dispatch of July 5, 1777, see Washington, George. *The writings of George Washington from the original manuscript sources, 1745–1799*; prepared under the direction of the United States George Washington Bicentennial Commission and published by authority of Congress; John C. Fitzpatrick, editor. Washington, U.S. Govt. Print. Off. [1931–44] 4 p.481. Whitehead, William A. *Contributions to the Early History of Perth Amboy and Adjoining Country.* New York: D. Appleton & Company, 1856. pp.345.

339. *The New Jersey Gazette.* 5:212 (January 16, 1782) p.3. Wall, John P. *The Chronicles of New Brunswick, New Jersey 1667–1931.* New Brunswick: Thatcher-Anderson Company, 1931. pp.229–230.

340. *New York Gazette and Weekly Mercury.* (June 10, 1776). *Documents Relating to the Revolutionary History, State of New Jersey.* Edited by William S. Stryker. Trenton: The John L. Murphy Publishing Co., 1901. Series 2. 1:110–111.

341. Jones, William Northey. *The history of St. Peter's Church in Perth Amboy, New Jersey, the oldest congregation of the church in the state of New Jersey, from its organization in 1698 to the year of our Lord 1923, and the celebration of the 225th anniversary of the parish, also a genealogy of the families buried in the churchyard.* New York: Patterson Press, 1924. p.76.

342. Whitehead, William A. *Contributions to the Early History of Perth Amboy and Adjoining Country.* New York: D. Appleton & Company, 1856. pp.330–331.

343. *New York Gazette and Weekly Mercury.* (July 29, 1776). *Documents Relating to the Revolutionary History, State of New Jersey.* Edited by William S. Stryker. Trenton: The John L. Murphy Publishing Co., 1901. Series 2. 1:154.

344. *The Pennsylvania Gazette.* (July 29, 1776). Whitehead, William A. *Contributions to the Early History of Perth Amboy and Adjoining Country.* New York: D. Appleton & Company, 1856. pp.332–33.

345. Journal of HM Sloop *Tamar*, Lieutenant Christopher Mason. British National Archives, Admiralty 51/968. NDAR 6:875.

346. Journal of HM Sloop *Senegal.* British National Archives, Admiralty 51/885. NDAR 6:1024.

347. *Documents Relating to the Revolutionary History, State of New Jersey.* Edited By William S. Stryker. Trenton: The John L. Murphy Publishing Co., 1901. Series 2. 1:232.

348. *The Independent Chronicle and the Universal Advertiser.* IX:447 (March 13, 1777) p.3.

349. Ibid.

350. *The New-York Gazette; and the Weekly Mercury.* 1324 (March 10, 1777) p.3. *Documents Relating to the Revolutionary History, State of New Jersey.* Edited By William S. Stryker. Trenton: The John L. Murphy Publishing Co., 1901. Series 2. 1:310.

351. Whitehead, William A. *Contributions to the Early History of Perth Amboy and Adjoining Country.* New York: D. Appleton & Company, 1856. pp.341.

352. *Virginia Gazette.* 1336 (March 14, 1777) p.2.

353. Scull, G. D. (Gideon Delaplaine) *The Montresor journals*; ed. and annotated by G.D. Scull: [New York, Printed for the Society, 1882]; July 1, 1777, to July 1, 1778. p.421.

354. Whitehead, William A. *Contributions to the Early History of Perth Amboy and Adjoining Country.* New York: D. Appleton & Company, 1856. p.344. Dalley, Joseph W. *Woodbridge and Vicinity.* New Brunswick: A. E. Gordon, 1873. p.273. *New York Gazette and Weekly Mercury.* (April 28, 1777). *Documents Relating to the Revolutionary History, State of New Jersey.* Edited by William S. Stryker. Trenton: The John L. Murphy Publishing Co., 1901. Series 2. 1:354. Clayton, W. Woodford, ed. *History of Union and Middlesex Counties, New Jersey, with Biographical Sketches of Many of their Pioneers and Prominent Men.* Philadelphia: Everts & Peck, 1882. pp.93–94.

355. Cresswell, Nicholas. *The Journal of Nicholas Cresswell, 1774–1777.* New York, 1924. p.242. Ward, Christopher. *The War of the Revolution.* New York: Macmillan, 1952. p.327.

356. Ewald, Johann. *Diary of the American War: A Hessian Journal.* Translated and edited by Joseph P. Tustin. New Haven and London: Yale University Press, 1979. p.68.

357. *The Providence Gazette; and Country Journal.* XIV:705 (July 5, 1777) p.3.

358. *Documents Relating to the Revolutionary History, State of New Jersey.* Edited by William S. Stryker. Trenton: The John L. Murphy Publishing Co., 1901. Series 2. 2:255–256.

359. *The Pennsylvania Evening Post.* 5:635 (October 26, 1779) p.244. Whitehead, William A. *Contributions to the Early History of Perth Amboy and Adjoining Country.* New York: D. Appleton & Company, 1856. p.348. *Documents Relating to the Revolutionary History, State of New Jersey.* Edited by William S. Stryker. Trenton: The John L. Murphy Publishing Co., 1901. Series 2. 3:698.

360. *Royal Gazette.* 322 (October 30, 1779) p.3. *New-York Gazette, and Weekly Mercury.* 1463:2.

361. *The Pennsylvania Evening Post.* 9:715 (January 25, 1781) p.18. *New Jersey Gazette.* 4:160 (January 17, 1781) p.3.

362. *The Boston Gazette and Country Journal.* 1182 (May 5, 1777) p.1. *The Providence Gazette and Country Journal.* 18:894 (February 17, 1781) p.1. New Jersey Department of Defense Manuscripts 848.

363. *The Pennsylvania Packet.* (January 29, 1776). *Documents Relating to the Revolutionary History, State of New Jersey.* Edited by William S. Stryker. Trenton: The John L. Murphy Publishing Co., 1901. Series 2. 1:25–26. Force, Peter. *American archives: consisting of a collection of authentick records, state papers, debates, and letters and other notices of publick affairs, the whole forming a documentary history of the origin and progress of the North American colonies; of the causes and accomplishment of the American revolution; and of the Constitution of government for the United States, to the final ratification thereof. In six series.* [Washington, 1837–1853]. 4 Ser. 4:987–989.

364. New York Provincial Congress 1:340, 341, 342, 353, 354, 355. Captain Hyde Parker, Jr., RN. To Vice Admiral Molyneux Shuldham 29th April 1776. British National Archives, Admiralty 1/484. NDAR 4:195, 310, 1312.

365. Letter from Governor Tryon to the Mayor. *Pennsylvania Journal and Weekly Advertiser.* (May 1, 1776). *Constitutional Gazette.* 79 (May 1, 1776) p.2. *Connecticut Courant.* 589 (May 6, 1776) p.3. *Documents Relating to the Revolutionary History, State of New Jersey.* Edited by William S. Stryker. Trenton: The John L. Murphy Publishing Co., 1901. Series 2. 1:92–93.

366. *The Newport Mercury.* 923 (May 13, 1776) p.1.

367. Journal of HMS *Phoenix.* British National Archives, Admiralty 51/693; NDAR 5:78.

368. Journal of HMS *Asia,* Captain George Vandeput. British National Archives, Admiralty 51/67. NDAR 5:203.

369. Journal Of HMS *Orpheus,* Captain Charles Hudson. British National Archives, Admiralty 51/4297. Howe's Prize List. British National Archives, Admiralty 1/487.

370. Lieutenant Colonel Benjamin Tupper to George Washington, Washington Papers, Library of Congress. NDAR 5:663. Extract of a Letter from Philadelphia, Dated 25th June, 1776. *The New-York Journal; or, The General Advertiser.* 1747 (June 27, 1776) p.3. *Norwich Packet and the Connecticut, Massachusetts, New Hampshire, and Rhode-Island Weekly Advertiser.* 3:144 (June 24–July 1, 1776) p.2. *The New-Hampshire Gazette, and Historical Chronicle.* 1:8 (July 13, 1776) p.2. *New York Gazette and Weekly Mercury.* (June 24, 1776). *The Pennsylvania Ledger: or the Virginia, Maryland, Pennsylvania, & New-Jersey Weekly Advertiser.* LXXV (June 29, 1776) p.3. *The Providence Gazette; And Country Journal.* XIII:652 (June 29, 1776) p.2. *The Norwich Packet and the Connecticut, Massachusetts, New-Hampshire, and Rhode-Island Weekly Advertiser.* 3:144 (From Monday, June 24, to Monday, July 1, 1776) p.2. *New York Gazette and Weekly Mercury.* (June 24, 1776). *Documents Relating to the Revolutionary History, State of New Jersey.* Edited by William S. Stryker. Trenton: The John L. Murphy Publishing Co., 1901. Series 2. 1:132. Bangs, Isaac. *Journal Of Lieutenant Isaac Bangs, April 1 To July 29, 1776.* Edited by Edward Bangs. Cambridge: John Wilson and Son. University Press, 1890. pp.45–46.

370a. NDAR 5:962–963.

371. Journal of HMS *Perseus.* British National Archives, Admiralty 51/688. NDAR 7:120.

372. Journal of HMS *Syren.* British National Archives, Admiralty 41/930. NDAR 7:475.

373. Extract of a Letter from an Officer at Amboy, Feb. 16. *Documents Relating to the Revolutionary History, State of New Jersey.* Edited by William S. Stryker. Trenton: The John L. Murphy Publishing Co., 1901. Series 2. 1:291–292. New Jersey Department of Defense Manuscripts.

374. *The New-York Gazette; and the Weekly Mercury.* 1324 (March 10, 1777) p.3. *New Jersey Gazette.* 1:42 (September 23, 1778). *Documents Relating to the Revolutionary History, State of New Jersey.* Edited by William S. Stryker. Trenton: The John L. Murphy Publishing Co., 1901. Series 2. 1:310.

375. *Documents Relating to the Revolutionary History, State of New Jersey.* Edited by William S. Stryker. Trenton: The John L. Murphy Publishing Co., 1901. Series 2. 2:237, 759.

376. *York Gazette and Weekly Mercury.* (September 28, 1778). *Documents Relating to the Revolutionary History, State of New Jersey.* Edited by William S. Stryker. Trenton: The John L. Murphy Publishing Co., 1901. Series 2. 2:445.

377. *The Pennsylvania Evening Post.* (January 21, 1779). *Documents Relating to the Revolutionary History, State of New Jersey.* Edited by William S. Stryker. Trenton: The John L. Murphy Publishing Co., 1901. Series 2. 3:41.

378. *Documents Relating to the Revolutionary History, State of New Jersey.* Edited by William S. Stryker. Trenton: The John L. Murphy Publishing Co., 1901. Series 2. 4:134–135. *New Jersey Gazette* (January 19, 1780) p.3.

379. *The Pennsylvania Evening Post.* VI:647 p.11. *Documents Relating to the Revolutionary History, State of New Jersey.* Edited by William S. Stryker. Trenton: The John L. Murphy Publishing Co., 1901. Series 2. 4:154–155.

380. Journal of HMS *Swift.* British National Archives, Admiralty 51/C log 964 part 6 (1780) p.51. Peckham, Howard Henry. *The Toll of Independence: Engagements & Battle Casualties of the American Revolution.* Chicago: University of Chicago Press, 1974. p.70.

381. Extract of a Letter from New Brunswick, Oct. 7, 1781. *The Pennsylvania Evening Post, and Public Advertiser.* VII:784 (October 15, 1781) p.172. *New Jersey Gazette.* 4:198 (October 10, 1781) p.2. *Documents Relating to the Revolutionary History, State of New Jersey.* Edited by William S. Stryker. Trenton: The John L. Murphy Publishing Co., 1901. Series 2. 5:306.

382. *Connecticut Courant.* 902 (May 7, 1782) p.2. *The Freeman's Journal: or, the North-American Intelligencer.* II:LXIII (April 24, 1782) p.3. Extract of a letter from New Jersey, June 19, 1782. *The Freeman's Journal: or, the North-American Intelligencer.* II:LXII (June 26, 1782) p.3. Sandy Hook June 1776 see *George* and *Annabella* NDAR 5:563, 376–577, 579, 581–584, 618–621, 635; 7:103–104.

383. New Jersey Department of Defense Manuscripts #3782.

384. Extract of a letter from New Jersey, June 19, 1782. *The Freeman's Journal: or, the North-American Intelligencer.* II:LXII (June 26, 1782) p.3. Near Sandy Hook between April 17 and 24, 1782.

385. Extract of a Letter from Philadelphia, Dated 25th June, 1776. *The New-York Journal; or, The General Advertiser.* 1747 (June 27, 1776) p.3.

386. Nash, Solomon. *Journal of Solomon Nash, a Soldier of the Revolution, 1776–1777.* New York: privately printed, 1861. p.22.

387. *New York Gazette and Weekly Mercury.* (August 18, 1777). *Documents Relating to the Revolutionary History, State of New Jersey.* Edited by William S. Stryker. Trenton: The John L. Murphy Publishing Co., 1901. Series 2. 1:449. Trevett, John. "Journal of John Trevett," *Rhode Island Historical Magazine,* 6, 72–74, 106–11; 6, 194–99, 271–78. August 31, 1777. NDAR 9:765, 853–854.

388. *New-York Gazette and Weekly Mercury.* (May 18, 1778). *Documents Relating to the Revolutionary History, State of New Jersey.* Edited by William S. Stryker. Trenton: The John L. Murphy Publishing Co., 1901. Series 2. 2:219.

389. Baurmeister, Carl Leopold. *Revolution in America: Confidential Letters and Journals, 1776–1784.* trans. and annotated by Bernhard A. Uhlendorf. New Brunswick: Rutgers University Press, 1957. p.189. *Documents Relating to the Revolutionary History, State of New Jersey.* Edited by William S. Stryker. Trenton: The John L. Murphy Publishing Co., 1901. Series 2. 2:318.

390. *The New Jersey Gazette.* 2:82 (June 30, 1779) p.2.

391. Ibid., pp. 2–3.

392. Ibid.

393. *The New York Gazette: and the Weekly Mercury.* 1:1452 (August 16, 1779). *Documents Relating to the Revolutionary History, State of New Jersey.* Edited by William S. Stryker. Trenton: The John L. Murphy Publishing Co., 1901. Series 2. 3:556.

394. Ibid., p.616. New Jersey Department of Defense Manuscripts.

395. Hornor, William S. *This Old Monmouth of Ours.* Freehold: Moreau Brothers, 1932. p.65.

396. *The New Jersey Gazette.* 2:102 (December 8, 1779) p.3.

397. *Documents Relating to the Revolutionary History, State of New Jersey.* Edited by William S. Stryker. Trenton: The John L. Murphy Publishing Co., 1901. Series 2. 4:121.

398. *New Jersey Gazette.* 4:158. *Documents Relating to the Revolutionary History, State of New Jersey.* Edited by William S. Stryker. Trenton: The John L. Murphy Publishing Co., 1901. Series 2. 5:167.

399. *The Royal Gazette.* 358 (March 4, 1780). *Documents Relating to the Revolutionary History, State of New Jersey.* Edited by William S. Stryker. Trenton: The John L. Murphy Publishing Co., 1901. Series 2. 4:207. Hornor,William S. *This Old Monmouth of Ours.* Freehold: Moreau Brothers, 1932. p.69.

400. *The Royal Gazette.* 371 (April 19, 1780). *Documents Relating to the Revolutionary History, State of New Jersey.* Edited by William S. Stryker. Trenton: The John L. Murphy Publishing Co., 1901. Series 2. 4:308.

401. *The Royal Gazette.* 371 (April 19, 1780). *Documents Relating to the Revolutionary History, State of New Jersey.* Edited by William S. Stryker. Trenton: The John L. Murphy Publishing Co., 1901. Series 2. 4:308.

402. *New Jersey Gazette.* (May 3, 1780) p.3. *Connecticut Journal.* 654 (May 11, 1780) p.3. *Documents Relating to the Revolutionary History, State of New Jersey.* Edited by William S. Stryker. Trenton: The John L. Murphy Publishing Co., 1901. Series 2. 4:351–352.

403. *The New-York Gazette and the Weekly Mercury.* 1498 (July 3, 1780). *Documents Relating to the Revolutionary History, State of New Jersey.* Edited by William S. Stryker. Trenton: The John L. Murphy Publishing Co., 1901. Series 2. 4:472.

404. *Documents Relating to the Revolutionary History, State of New Jersey.* Edited by William S. Stryker. Trenton: The John L. Murphy Publishing Co., 1901. Series 2. 4:490.

405. *The New-York Gazette: and the Weekly Mercury.* 1499 (July 10, 1780). *Documents Relating to the Revolutionary History, State of New Jersey.* Edited by William S. Stryker. Trenton: The John L. Murphy Publishing Co., 1901. Series 2. 4:491.

406. Hornor, William S. *This Old Monmouth of Ours.* Freehold: Moreau Brothers, 1932. p.75.

407. Extract of a letter from New-Brunswick, dated October 29, 1781. *Documents Relating to the Revolutionary History, State of New Jersey.* Edited by William S. Stryker. Trenton: The John L. Murphy Publishing Co., 1901. Series 2. 5:320. Extract of a Letter from New-Brunswick, Dated October 29, 1781. *The New Jersey Gazette.* 4:202 (November 7, 1781) p.3. *The Pennsylvania Evening Post, and Public Advertiser.* VII:793 (November 12, 1781) p.186.

408. *The New Jersey Gazette.* 5:210 (January 2, 1782) p.3.

409. Mackenzie, Frederick. *The Diary of Frederick Mackenzie.* Cambridge, MA: Harvard University Press, 1930. 2 p.705.

410. *New Jersey Gazette* (January 2, 1782) p.3. *The New-York Gazette: and the Weekly Mercury.* 1472 (January 3, 1780). *Documents Relating to the Revolutionary History, State of New Jersey.* Edited by William S. Stryker. Trenton: The John L. Murphy Publishing Co., 1901. Series 2. 4:121.

411. *The New Jersey Gazette.* 5:232 (June 5, 1782) p.4. *The Pennsylvania Packet or the General Advertiser.* XI:896 (June 11, 1782) p.3. *The Newport Mercury.* 1082 (June 22, 1782) p.2. *Salem Gazette.* 1:37 (June 27, 1782) p.3. *The New-Hampshire Gazette; or State Journal, and General Advertiser.* XXVI:1339 (June 29, 1782) p.2.

412. New Jersey Department Of Defense Manuscripts #3782. *Connecticut Journal.* 764 (June 20, 1782) p.2. *The Providence Gazette and Country Journal.* XIX:964 (June 22, 1782) p.2. Hornor, William S. *This Old Monmouth of Ours.* Freehold: Moreau Brothers, 1932. pp.53–54.

413. Extract of a Letter from Elizabeth-Town, Dated July 9. *The Independent Gazetteer.* 14 (July 13,1782) p.3. *Connecticut Courant.* 914 (July 30, 1782) p.2. *Connecticut Journal.* 770 (August 1, 1782) p.2. *The Massachusetts Spy: Or, American Oracle of Liberty.* XII:587 (August 1, 1782) p.3. *The Pennsylvania Packet or the General Advertiser.* XI:911 (July 16, 1782) p.3. *The New Jersey Gazette.* 5:238 (July 17, 1782) p.4. *The New-York Gazette; and The Weekly Mercury.* 1603 (July 8, 1782) p.3. Peckham, Howard Henry. *The Toll of Independence: Engagements & Battle Casualties of the American Revolution.* Chicago: University of Chicago Press, 1974. p.96.

414. Peckham, Howard Henry. *The Toll of Independence: Engagements & Battle Casualties of the American Revolution.* Chicago: University of Chicago Press, 1974. p.32. *New York Gazette, and Weekly Mercury.* (April 14, 1777). *Documents Relating to the Revolutionary History, State of New Jersey.* Edited by William S. Stryker. Trenton: The John L. Murphy Publishing Co., 1901. Series 2. 1:338.

415. Vermeule, Cornelius C. *The Revolutionary Camp Ground at Plainfield.* New York: The Evening Post Job Printing Office, Inc. 1923. p.16.

416. *The New Jersey Gazette.* 3:131 (June 28, 1780) p.3. *Documents Relating to the Revolutionary History, State of New Jersey.* Edited by William S. Stryker. Trenton: The John L. Murphy Publishing Co., 1901. Series 2. 4:458. Sir William Howe's report to Lord George Germain dated New York, July 5, 1777 appeared in *The New-Jersey Gazette.* 1:2 (December 10, 1777) p.2.

417. *The Pennsylvania Evening Post.* (July 15, 1777).

418. Gordon, William. *The History . . . of the United States of America.* London: 1788. 2:474 in Ward, Christopher. *The War of the Revolution.* New York: Macmillan, 1952. p.327.

419. Israel Shreve to John Stilley, June 29, to Dr. Bodo Otto, June 29, and to his wife, July 6, 1777, Ward, Harry M. *General William Maxwell and the New Jersey Continentals.* Westport, CT; London: Greenwood Press, 1997. p.197 note 52.

420. Extract of a letter from the Hon. General Sir William Howe to Lord George Germain. New York, July 5, 1777. From the *London Gazette.* Whitehall, August 22, 1777 in *The New-York Gazette; and the Weekly Mercury.* 1356 (October 20, 1777) p.2. Scull, G. D. (Gideon Delaplaine). *The Montresor journals,* ed. and annotated by G.D. Scull: [New York, Printed for the Society, 1882]. p.426. Ward, Christopher. *The War of the Revolution.* New York: Macmillan, 1952. pp.327–328. *Documents Relating to the Revolutionary History, State of New Jersey.* Edited by William S. Stryker. Trenton: The John L. Murphy Publishing Co., 1901. Series 2. 1:428, 477. Clayton, W. Woodford. *History of Union and Middlesex Counties.* Philadelphia: Everts and Peck, 1882. pp.78–79. Stedman, C. (Charles). *The history of the origin, progress, and termination of the American war.* (Eyewitness accounts of the American Revolution) [New York]: New York Times; Arno Press, c1969. 1:285.

421. Ward, Harry M. *General William Maxwell and the New Jersey Continentals.* Westport, CT; London: Greenwood Press, 1997. p.63.

422. *New York Gazette and Weekly Mercury.* (June 30, 1777). *Documents Relating to the Revolutionary History, State of New Jersey.* Edited by William S. Stryker. Trenton: The John L. Murphy Publishing Co., 1901. Series 2. 1:412. Shaw, William H. comp. *History of Essex and Hudson Counties, New Jersey.* Philadelphia: Everts & Peck, 1884. p.954. Winfield, Charles H. *History of the County of Hudson, New Jersey.* New York: Kennard & Hay, 1874. p.318.

423. *The Pennsylvania Evening Post.* 5:594 (April 30, 1779) p.106.

424. *New York Mercury.* (Aug. 3, 1778) p.3.

425. *New-York Gazette and Weekly Mercury.* (September 7, 1778). *Documents Relating to the Revolutionary History, State of New Jersey.* Edited by William S. Stryker. Trenton: The John L. Murphy Publishing Co., 1901. Series 2. 2:405. Winfield, Charles Hardenburg. *History of the County of Hudson, New Jersey.* New York: Kennard & Hay Printing Co. 1874. p.150.

426. Winfield, Charles Hardenburg. *History of the County of Hudson, New Jersey.* New York: Kennard & Hay, 1874. p.153. Shaw, William H. *History of Essex and Hudson Counties, New Jersey.* Philadelphia: Everts & Peck, 1884. p.954.

427. *The New-York Journal, and the General Advertiser* for May 3, 1779 says the event occurred "About three weeks ago" but the article's dateline is Chatham, (New-Jersey) April 13. *The New-York Journal, and the General Advertiser* 1823 (May 3, 1779). *Documents Relating to the Revolutionary History, State of New Jersey.* Edited by William S. Stryker. Trenton: The John L. Murphy Publishing Co., 1901. Series 2. 3:303.

428. *The Royal Gazette.* 409 (August 30, 1780). *New York Gazette and Weekly Mercury.* (June 30, 1777). *Documents Relating to the Revolutionary History, State of New Jersey.* Edited by William S. Stryker. Trenton: The John L. Murphy Publishing Co., 1901. Series 2. 1:412; 4:606, 613.

429. *Documents Relating to the Revolutionary History, State of New Jersey.* Edited by William S. Stryker. Trenton: The John L. Murphy Publishing Co., 1901. Series 2. 5:53.

430. Extract of a letter from Fort Lee (late Fort Constitution but now altered by general orders) dated October 20, 1776 and Extract of a letter from Fort Lee, dated October 22, 1776. *Virginia Gazette.* 1318 (November 8, 1776) p.2.

431. *New York Gazette and Weekly Mercury.* (November 10, 1777). *Documents Relating to the Revolutionary History, State of New Jersey.* Edited by William S. Stryker. Trenton: The John L. Murphy Publishing Co., 1901. Series 2. 1:485. New Jersey Department of Defense Manuscripts.

432. Baurmeister, Carl Leopold. *Revolution in America: Confidential Letters and Journals, 1776–1784.* trans. and annotated by Bernhard A. Uhlendorf. New Brunswick: Rutgers University Press, 1957. p.84.

433. *New York Gazette and Weekly Mercury.* (October 6, 1777). *Documents Relating to the Revolutionary History, State of New Jersey.* Edited by William S. Stryker. Trenton: The John L. Murphy Publishing Co., 1901. Series 2. 1:473–474.

434. Extract of a letter from Monmouth Court-house, January 26, 1779. *New Jersey Gazette.* (February 3, 1779) p.3. *Documents Relating to the Revolutionary History, State of New Jersey.* Edited by William S. Stryker. Trenton: The John L. Murphy Publishing Co., 1901. Series 2. 3:53–54.

435. *New Hampshire Gazette.* (May 25, 1779). *Documents Relating to the Revolutionary History, State of New Jersey.* Edited by William S. Stryker. Trenton: The John L. Murphy Publishing Co., 1901. Series 2. 3:320–321. Washington, George. *The writings of George Washington from the original manuscript sources, 1745–1799;* prepared under the direction of the United States George Washington Bicentennial Commission and published by authority of Congress; John C. Fitzpatrick, editor. Washington, U.S. Govt. Print. Off. [1931–44]. 14:443n. Ewald, Johann. *Diary of the American War: A Hessian Journal.* Translated and edited by Joseph P. Tustin. New Haven and London: Yale University Press, 1979. pp.159, 409n. Mandeville, Ernest W. *The story of Middletown: the oldest settlement in New Jersey.* Middletown, N.J.: Christ Church, 1927. p.64.

436. Letter from Col. Ford to Gen. Washington, April 26, 1779 Near Tenton Falls. Library of Congress, George Washington Papers, Reel 57, Series 4, 25 March 1779–26 April 1779. www.royalprovincial.com/history/battles/njvrep4.shtml. *New Hampshire Gazette.* (May 25, 1779). *Pennsylvania Packet.* (May 1, 1779). Moore, Frank. *Diary of the American Revolution: from Newspapers and Original Documents.* New York: Charles Scribner; London: Sampson Low, Son & Co., 1890. 2:155–157. *The Pennsylvania Evening Post.* (April 30, 1779). *Documents Relating to the Revolutionary History, State of New Jersey.* Edited by William S. Stryker. Trenton: The John L. Murphy Publishing Co., 1901. Series 2. 3:300–301,320–321. Washington, George. *The writings of George Washington from the original manuscript sources, 1745–1799;* prepared under the direction of the United States George Washington Bicentennial Commission and published by authority of Congress; John C. Fitzpatrick, editor. Washington, U.S. Govt. Print. Off. [1931–44]. 14:443n. Ewald, Johann. *Diary of the American War: A Hessian Journal.* Translated and edited by Joseph P. Tustin. New Haven and London: Yale University Press, 1979. pp.159, 409n.

437. *Documents Relating to the Revolutionary History, State of New Jersey.* Edited by William S. Stryker. Trenton: The John L. Murphy Publishing Co., 1901. Series 2. 3:441.

438. Moody, James. *Lieut. James Moody's Narrative Of His Exertions and Sufferings In The Cause of Government, Since the year 1776; Authenticated By Proper Certificates.* Second Edition. London: Richardson and Urquhart, 1783. pp.10–12, 18–19. *The New-York Gazette: and the Weekly Mercury.* 1443 (June 14, 1779) p.3. *Documents Relating to the Revolutionary History, State of New Jersey.* Edited by William S. Stryker. Trenton: The John L. Murphy Publishing Co., 1901. Series 2. 3:441, 456–457. *Collins' Gazette.* (June 1779). Ellis, Franklin. *History of Monmouth County, New Jersey,* Philadelphia: R. T. Peck & Co., 1885. pp.207–208. New Jersey Department of Defense Manuscripts. *Virginia Gazette.* 21 (July 3, 1779) p.2.

439. *The Pennsylvania Evening Post.* 4:520 (August 20, 1778) p.301.

440. *Documents Relating to the Revolutionary History, State of New Jersey.* Edited by William S. Stryker. Trenton: The John L. Murphy Publishing Co., 1901. Series 2. 3:504.

441. *The New-York Gazette: and the Weekly Mercury.* 1452 (August 16, 1779). *Documents Relating to the Revolutionary History, State of New Jersey.* Edited by William S. Stryker. Trenton: The John L. Murphy Publishing Co., 1901. Series 2. 3:556.

443. *The New Jersey Gazette.* 3:119 (April 5, 1780) p.3. *The Pennsylvania Packet or the General Advertiser.* (April 11, 1780) p.3. *Documents Relating to the Revolutionary History, State of New Jersey.* Edited by William S. Stryker. Trenton: The John L. Murphy Publishing Co., 1901. Series 2. 4:285.

444. *The New Jersey Gazette.* 3:120 (April 4, 1780) p.3. *Documents Relating to the Revolutionary History, State of New Jersey.* Edited by William S. Stryker. Trenton: The John L. Murphy Publishing Co., 1901. Series 2. 4:299.

445. *New Jersey Gazette.* (April 12, 1780) p.3. Trenton, May 3; *Connecticut Journal.* 654 (May 11, 1780) p.3.

446. *The American Journal and General Advertiser.* 2:63 (May 24, 1780) p.2.

447. *The New Jersey Gazette.* (Aug. 1, 1781) p.3. *The Providence Gazette and Country Journal.* 18:920 (August 18, 1781) p.3. *Documents Relating to the Revolutionary History, State of New Jersey.* Edited by William S. Stryker. Trenton: The John L. Murphy Publishing Co., 1901. Series 2. 5:279.

448. Extract of a letter from Freehold. Monmouth County, dated April 15, 1782. *Documents Relating to the Revolutionary History, State of New Jersey.* Edited by William S. Stryker. Trenton: The John L. Murphy Publishing Co., 1901. Series 2. 5:424. Barber, John Warner and Howe, Henry. *Historical Collections of New Jersey.* New York: S. Tuttle, 1844. p.366.

449. Clayton, W. Woodford, ed. *History of Union and Middlesex Counties, New Jersey, with Biographical Sketches of Many of their Pioneers and Prominent Men.* Philadelphia: Everts & Peck, 1882. p.77.

450. *The Pennsylvania Evening Post.* (April 17, 1777). *Documents Relating to the Revolutionary History, State of New Jersey.* Edited by William S. Stryker. Trenton: The John L. Murphy Publishing Co., 1901. Series 2. 1:342.

451. *The Royal Gazette.* 362 (March 18, 1780). *Documents Relating to the Revolutionary History, State of New Jersey.* Edited by William S. Stryker. Trenton: The John L. Murphy Publishing Co., 1901. Series 2. 4:235–236.

452. *The Pennsylvania Journal.* (March 15, 1780). *Documents Relating to the Revolutionary History, State of New Jersey.* Edited by William S. Stryker. Trenton: The John L. Murphy Publishing Co., 1901. Series 2. 4:221.

453. *The Royal Gazette.* 382 (May 27, 1780). *Documents Relating to the Revolutionary History, State of New Jersey.* Edited by William S. Stryker. Trenton: The John L. Murphy Publishing Co., 1901. Series 2. 4:394.

454. *New Jersey Gazette.* 3:128 (June 7, 1780) p.2. *The New Jersey Journal.* (May 31, 1780). Extract of a letter from William Maxwell to George Washington, dated one mile from Elizabeth Town, 28 May 1780. Library of Congress, George Washington Papers, Series 4, General Correspondence, 3 April 1780–6 June 1780.

455. *The Royal Gazette.* 397 (July 19, 1780). *Documents Relating to the Revolutionary History, State of New Jersey.* Edited by William S. Stryker. Trenton: The John L. Murphy Publishing Co., 1901. Series 2. 4:519, 537.

456. *Rivington's Gazette.* No. 511. Winfield, Charles Hardenburg. *History of the County of Hudson, New Jersey.* New York: Kennard & Hay, 1874. p.195.

457. *The New-York Gazette; and The Weekly Mercury.* 1519 (November 27, 1780) p.3. *The New Jersey Gazette.* 3:153 (November 29,1780) p.3. *The New-York Gazette; and The Weekly Mercury.* November 27, 1780. Moore, Frank. *Diary of the American Revolution: from Newspapers and Original Documents.* New York: Charles Scribner; London: Sampson Low, Son & Co., 1890. 2:348–349.

458. *Documents Relating to the Revolutionary History, State of New Jersey.* Edited by William S. Stryker. Trenton: The John L. Murphy Publishing Co., 1901. Series 2. 5:223.

459. *The Boston Gazette, and the Country Journal.* 1411(September 10, 1781) p.2.

460. *The Pennsylvania Evening Post, and Public Advertiser.* VII:771 (September 10, 1781) p.146.

461. *New Jersey Journal.* (December 12, 1781). Winfield, Charles Hardenburg. *History of the County of Hudson, New Jersey.* New York: Kennard & Hay Printing Co. 1874. p.197.

462. *The Newport Mercury.* 1082 (June 22, 1782) p.2.

463. *The New-York Gazette; and The Weekly Mercury.* 1629 (January 6, 1783) p.3.

464. Clayton, W. Woodford, ed. *History of Union and Middlesex Counties, New Jersey, with Biographical Sketches of Many of their Pioneers and Prominent Men.* Philadelphia: Everts & Peck, 1882. pp.70–71.

465. Heath, William, *Memoirs of Major-General Heath, Containing Anecdotes, Details of Skirmishes, Battles, and other Military Events, during the American War. Written by Himself.* Boston, 1898. (Edition edited by William Abbott, New York, 1901.) [New York]: New York Times, [1968]. p.41. NDAR 5:873. Journal Of HMS *Phoenix,* Captain Hyde Parker, Jr. British National Archives, Admiralty 51/693. NDAR 5:895.

466. Journal Of Lieutenant Colonel Samuel Blachley Webb Ford, ed., Webb Papers, I, 152. NDAR 5:917.

467. Diary Of Ensign Caleb Clap. *The Historical Magazine,* 3rd series. 3:137. NDAR 5:917. Clayton, W. Woodford, ed. *History of Union and Middlesex Counties, New Jersey, with Biographical Sketches of Many of their Pioneers and Prominent Men.* Philadelphia: Everts & Peck, 1882. p.71.

468. *The Pennsylvania Evening Post.* (July 9, 1776). *Documents Relating to the Revolutionary History, State of New Jersey.* Edited by William S. Stryker. Trenton: The John L. Murphy Publishing Co., 1901. Series 2. 1:137–138.

469. *Journal of Lieutenant Colonel Stephen Kemble,* "The Kemble Papers," *Collections of the New-York Historical Society.* 1:81. NDAR 5:1063.

470. *The New-Hampshire Gazette and Historical Chronicle.* 1:14 (August 24, 1776) p.2.

471. Clayton, W. Woodford, ed. *History of Union and Middlesex Counties, New Jersey, with Biographical Sketches of Many of Their Pioneers and Prominent Men.* Philadelphia: Everts & Peck, 1882. p.73.

472. *Virginia Gazette.* 1330. (January 31, 1777) p.3. *The Pennsylvania Evening Post.* 3:302 (January 16, 1777) p.21. Extract of a Letter from Morris Town, Dated January 7, 1777. *Essex Journal.* 161 (January 30, 1777) p.2. Clayton, W. Woodford, ed. *History of Union and Middlesex Counties, New Jersey, with Biographical Sketches of Many of their Pioneers and Prominent Men.* Philadelphia: Everts & Peck, 1882. p.77

473. Garden, Alexander. *Anecdotes of the American Revolution, Illustrative of the Talents and Virtues of the Heroes and Patriots who Acted the Most Conspicuous Parts Therein.* Second series. Charleston, S.C.: A. E. Miller, 1828. 2d Ser. p.210. Barber, John Warner. *Historical collections of New Jersey, past and present; containing a general collection of the most interesting facts, traditions, biographical sketches, anecdotes, etc., relating to the history and antiquities, with geographical descriptions, of all the important places in the State, and the State census of all the towns in 1865.* Spartanburg, S.C., Reprint Co. 1966, 1868. pp.184–185 in Clayton, W. Woodford, ed. *History of Union and Middlesex Counties, New Jersey, with Biographical Sketches of Many of their Pioneers and Prominent Men.* Philadelphia: Everts & Peck, 1882. p.77.

474. *The Pennsylvania Evening Post.* 3:302 (January 16, 1777) p.21. Extract of a Letter from Morris Town, Dated January 7, 1777. *Essex Journal.* 161 (January 30, 1777) p.2.

475. Clayton, W. Woodford, ed. *History of Union and Middlesex Counties, New Jersey, with Biographical Sketches of Many of their Pioneers and Prominent Men.* Philadelphia: Everts & Peck, 1882. p.77. Boatner, Mark M. *Encyclopedia of the American Revolution.* 3d ed., New York: McKay, 1980. p.345.

476. Drake, J. Madison. *Historical Sketches of the Revolutionary and Civil Wars.* New York: Webster Press, 1908. p.12.

477. *The New-York Gazette; and the Weekly Mercury.* 1324 (March 10, 1777) p.3. *Documents Relating to the Revolutionary History, State of New Jersey.* Edited by William S. Stryker. Trenton: The John L. Murphy Publishing Co., 1901. Series 2. 1:310. Clayton, W. Woodford. *History of Union and Middlesex Counties.* Philadelphia: Everts and Peck, 1882. p.78. Baurmeister, Carl Leopold. *Revolution in America: Confidential Letters and Journals, 1776–1784.* trans. and annotated by Bernhard A. Uhlendorf. New Brunswick, N.J.: Rutgers University Press, 1957. pp.257–258.

478. *New York Gazette and Weekly Mercury.* Nos. 1324, 1338 in Clayton, W. Woodford, ed. *History of Union and Middlesex Counties, New Jersey, with Biographical Sketches of Many of their Pioneers and Prominent Men.* Philadelphia: Everts & Peck, 1882. p.78. *New York Gazette and Weekly Mercury.* (June 16, 1777). *Documents Relating to the Revolutionary*

History, State of New Jersey. Edited by William S. Stryker. Trenton: The John L. Murphy Publishing Co., 1901. Series 2. 1:398.

479. *New York Gazette and Weekly Mercury.* (August 18, 1777). *Documents Relating to the Revolutionary History, State of New Jersey.* Edited by William S. Stryker. Trenton: The John L. Murphy Publishing Co., 1901. Series 2. 1:449.

480. *New-York Gazette and Weekly Mercury.* (August 25, 1777). *The Independent Chronicle and the Universal Advertiser.* 10:473 (September 11, 1777) p.3. *Continental Journal.* LXVIII (September 11, 1777) p.3. *Documents Relating to the Revolutionary History, State of New Jersey.* Edited by William S. Stryker. Trenton: The John L. Murphy Publishing Co., 1901. Series 2. 1:451–452.

481. *Continental Journal.* LXVIII (September 11, 1777) p.3. *Virginia Gazette.* 1380 (September 12, 1777) p.1. *Pennsylvania Journal.* 1806. *The Remembrancer, or impartial repository of public events.* Almon, John, Pownall, Thomas. London: J. Almon, 1775–1784. pp.483–85. Sparks, Jared. *The Life of George Washington.* Boston: Ferdinand Andrews, 1839. v. 47. Moore, Frank. *Diary of the American Revolution: from Newspapers and Original Documents.* New York: Charles Scribner; London: Sampson Low, Son & Co., 1890. pp.482–86. Marshall, John. *The life of George Washington, commander in chief of the American forces, during the war which established the independence of his country, and first president of the United States.* Philadelphia: Printed and published by C.P. Wayne, 1804. 3:135–137 in Clayton, W. Woodford, ed. *History of Union and Middlesex Counties, New Jersey, with Biographical Sketches of Many of their Pioneers and Prominent Men.* Philadelphia: Everts & Peck, 1882. p.79.

482. Pension record #892. Half-Pay to Hunterdon County Families of the Revolution—1780–1796. *Proceedings of the New Jersey Historical Society: A Quarterly Magazine.* New Series, 13:2 (April, 1928) pp.191–192.

483. *Documents Relating to the Revolutionary History, State of New Jersey.* Edited by William S. Stryker. Trenton: The John L. Murphy Publishing Co., 1901. Series 2. 1:474.

484. Peckham, Howard Henry. *The Toll of Independence: Engagements & Battle Casualties of the American Revolution.* Chicago: University of Chicago Press, 1974. p.48.

485. *The New Jersey Gazette.* 2:65 (March 25, 1779) p.13. Clayton, W. Woodford, ed. *History of Union and Middlesex Counties, New Jersey, with Biographical Sketches of Many of their Pioneers and Prominent Men.* Philadelphia: Everts & Peck, 1882. p.83. Extract of a Letter from an Officer at Elizabeth-Town, Dated March 1, 1779. *The New Jersey Gazette.* 2:65 (March 3, 1779) p.2. Extract of a Letter from an Officer at Middle-Brook, Dated March 2, 1779. *The Providence Gazette; And Country Journal.* XVI:793 (March 13, 1779) p.3. Clayton, W. Woodford. *History of Bergen and Passaic Counties, New Jersey, with biographical sketches of many of its pioneers and prominent men.* Philadelphia: Everts & Peck, 1882. p.54.

486. Baurmeister, Carl Leopold. *Revolution in America: Confidential Letters and Journals, 1776–1784.* trans. and annotated by Bernhard A. Uhlendorf. New Brunswick: Rutgers University Press, 1957. pp.257–258.

487. *The Encyclopedia of the American Revolutionary War: a political, social, and military history.* Gregory Fremont-Barnes, Richard Alan Ryerson, editors. Santa Barbara, CA: ABC-CLIO, 2006. 2:381.

488. *The New-York Gazette: and the Weekly Mercury.* 1443 (June 14, 1779) p.3. *Documents Relating to the Revolutionary History, State of New Jersey.* Edited by William S. Stryker. Trenton: The John L. Murphy Publishing Co., 1901. Series 2. 3:441, 458–459.

489. *The New-York Gazette: and the Weekly Mercury.* 1443 (June 14, 1779). *New Jersey Journal.* no. 19. *Documents Relating to the Revolutionary History, State of New Jersey.* Edited by William S. Stryker. Trenton: The John L. Murphy Publishing Co., 1901. Series 2. 3:458.

490. *Documents Relating to the Revolutionary History, State of New Jersey.* Edited by William S. Stryker. Trenton: The John L. Murphy Publishing Co., 1901. Series 2. 3:555.

491. *The Pennsylvania Evening Post.* 5:635 (October 26, 1779) p.244. *Documents Relating to the Revolutionary History, State of New Jersey.* Edited by William S. Stryker. Trenton: The John L. Murphy Publishing Co., 1901. Series 2. 3:698.

492. *Documents Relating to the Revolutionary History, State of New Jersey.* Edited by William S. Stryker. Trenton: The John L. Murphy Publishing Co., 1901. Series 2. 4:151–152. Clayton, W. Woodford, ed. *History of Union and Middlesex Counties, New Jersey, with Biographical Sketches of Many of their Pioneers and Prominent Men.* Philadelphia: Everts & Peck, 1882. p.87. *Encyclopedia of the American Revolutionary War* 2:381.

493. *New Jersey Journal.* 51 (January 27, 1780). *Pensylvania Ledger.* (February 21, 1778). Moore, Frank. *Diary of the American Revolution: from Newspapers and Original Documents.* New York: Charles Scribner; London: Sampson Low, Son & Co., 1890. 2:255–257. *Rivington's Gazette.* 348 (February 16, 1780). *New Jersey Journal.* (February 2, 1780). *Documents Relating to the Revolutionary History, State of New Jersey.* Edited by William S. Stryker. Trenton: The John L. Murphy Publishing Co., 1901. Series 2. 4:166. Clayton, W. Woodford, ed. *History of Union and Middlesex Counties, New Jersey, with Biographical Sketches of Many of their Pioneers and Prominent Men.* Philadelphia: Everts & Peck, 1882. pp.85–86. Shaw, William H. comp. *History of Essex and Hudson Counties, New Jersey.* Philadelphia: Everts & Peck, 1884. pp.38–39. Atkinson, Joseph. *The History of Newark.* Newark, N.J., 1878. pp.98–99.

494. *The New Jersey Gazette.* 3:112 (February 16, 1780) p.3. *Rivington's Gazette* (no. 349). Clayton, W. Woodford, ed. *History of Union and Middlesex Counties, New Jersey, with Biographical Sketches of Many of their Pioneers and Prominent Men.* Philadelphia: Everts & Peck, 1882. p.87. *The New-York Gazette: and the Weekly Mercury.* no. 1477. Moore, Frank. *Diary of the American Revolution: from Newspapers and Original Documents.* New York: Charles Scribner; London: Sampson Low, Son & Co., 1890. 2:257–58.

495. *New Jersey Gazette.* no. 112.

496. *The Newport Mercury.* 964 (March 1, 1780) p.2. *The Pennsylvania Evening Post.* VI:654 (March 10, 1780) p.30. *The Massachusetts Spy: Or, American Oracle of Liberty.* IX:468 (April 27, 1780) p.4.

497. *New Jersey Journal.* 59 (April 26, 1780). *Documents Relating to the Revolutionary History, State of New Jersey.* Edited by William S. Stryker. Trenton: The John L. Murphy Publishing Co., 1901. Series 2. 4:258. Clayton, W. Woodford, ed. *History of Union and Middlesex Counties, New Jersey.* Philadelphia: Everts & Peck, 1882. p.87.

498. *The New Jersey Journal.* 59 (April 26, 1780). Clayton, W. Woodford, ed. *History of Union and Middlesex Counties, New Jersey, with Biographical Sketches of Many of their Pioneers and Prominent Men.* Philadelphia: Everts & Peck, 1882. p.87.

499. Krafft, John Charles Philip von. *Journal of Lieutenant John Charles Philip von Krafft. Collections of the New-York Historical Society for the year 1882.* New York: the Society, 1883;—Eyewitness Accounts of the American Revolution.— New York: The New York Times & Arno Press, 1968. pp.112–113.

500. *The Pennsylvania Gazette.* (June 28, 1780). *Documents Relating to the Revolutionary History, State of New Jersey.* Edited by William S. Stryker. Trenton: The John L. Murphy Publishing Co., 1901. Series 2. 4:455–456.

501. *The New York Gazette: and the Weekly Mercury.* 1519 (November 27, 1780). *Documents Relating to the Revolutionary History, State of New Jersey.* Edited by William S. Stryker. Trenton: The John L. Murphy Publishing Co., 1901. Series 2. 5:127.

502. *New York Gazette and Weekly Mercury.* (December 18, 1780). Hatfield, Edwin F. *History of Elizabeth, New Jersey: including the early history of Union County.* New York: Carlton & Lanahan, 1868 p.501.

503. Clayton, W. Woodford. *History of Union and Middlesex Counties.* Philadelphia: Everts and Peck, 1882. p.95.

504. *Rivington's Gazette.* no. 454. *New Jersey Journal.* no. 105. Clayton, W. Woodford, ed. *History of Union and Middlesex Counties, New Jersey, with Biographical Sketches of Many of their Pioneers and Prominent Men.* Philadelphia: Everts & Peck, 1882. p.92.

505. Clayton, W. Woodford. Ibid.

506. *New Jersey Journal.* no. 111. Clayton, W. Woodford, ed. *History of Union and Middlesex Counties, New Jersey, with Biographical Sketches of Many of their Pioneers and Prominent Men.* Philadelphia: Everts & Peck, 1882. pp.92–3. *Documents Relating to the Revolutionary History, State of New Jersey.* Edited by William S. Stryker. Trenton: The John L. Murphy Publishing Co., 1901. Series 2. 5:229.

507. *The Pennsylvania Evening Post.* VII:735 (April 30, 1781) p.70. *New Jersey Gazette.* no. 176. *New Jersey Journal.* no. 114. *American Journal and General Advertiser.* 3:126 May 12, 1781 p.2. *The Freeman's Journal: or, The North-American Intelligencer.* 2:2 (May 2, 1781) p.2. *Connecticut Journal.* 705 (May 2, 1781) p.3. *Connecticut Courant.* 849 (May 1, 1781) p.2. *The Pennsylvania Evening Post.* VII:35 (April 30, 1781) p.70. *The New York Gazette and the Weekly Mercury.* 1541 (April 30, 1781) p.2. Clayton, W. Woodford, ed. *History of Union and Middlesex Counties, New Jersey, with Biographical Sketches of Many of their Pioneers and Prominent Men.* Philadelphia: Everts & Peck, 1882. p.93. *Documents Relating to the Revolutionary History, State of New Jersey.* Edited by William S. Stryker. Trenton: The John L. Murphy Publishing Co., 1901. Series 2. 5:244.

508. *The New Jersey Journal.* 116 (May 9, 1781). *The New Jersey Gazette.* 4:176 (May 9, 1781) p.3. Clayton, W. Woodford, ed. *History of Union and Middlesex Counties, New Jersey, with Biographical Sketches of Many of their Pioneers and Prominent Men.* Philadelphia: Everts & Peck, 1882. p.93. *Documents Relating to the Revolutionary History, State of New Jersey.* Edited by William S. Stryker. Trenton: The John L. Murphy Publishing Co., 1901. Series 2. 5:244.

509. *Rivington's Gazette.* 496 (June 30, 1781). *The New Jersey Journal.* 123 (June 27, 1781). Clayton, W. Woodford, ed. *History of Union and Middlesex Counties, New Jersey, with Biographical Sketches of Many of their Pioneers and Prominent Men.* Philadelphia: Everts & Peck, 1882. p.93–94.

510. Clayton, W. Woodford. *History of Union and Middlesex Counties.* Philadelphia: Everts and Peck, 1882. p.93.

511. *The New York Gazette and the Weekly Mercury.* 1553 (July 23, 1781).

512. *The New York Gazette and the Weekly Mercury.* (September 23, 1781). Clayton, W. Woodford, ed. *History of Union and Middlesex Counties, New Jersey, with Biographical Sketches of Many of their Pioneers and Prominent Men.* Philadelphia: Everts & Peck, 1882. p.92.

513. *New-York Gazette, and Weekly Mercury.* 1572 (December 3, 1781) p.2. *Documents Relating to the Revolutionary History, State of New Jersey.* Edited by William S. Stryker. Trenton: The John L. Murphy Publishing Co., 1901. Series 2. 5:339–340. Clayton, W. Woodford. *History of Union and Middlesex Counties.* Philadelphia: Everts and Peck, 1882. p.94. Shaw, William H. comp. *History of Essex and Hudson Counties, New Jersey.* Philadelphia: Everts & Peck, 1884. pp.42–44.

514. *The New Jersey Journal.* 147 (December 12, 1781).

515. Harrison, Richard A. *Princetonians 1776–1783: a biographical dictionary.* Princeton: Princeton University Press, 1981 p.32. Clayton, W. Woodford, ed. *History of Union and Middlesex Counties, New Jersey, with Biographical Sketches of Many of their Pioneers and Prominent Men.* Philadelphia: Everts & Peck, 1882. p.95.

516. *The New York Gazette and the Weekly Mercury.* 1510, 1522. *Rivington's Gazette.* no. 417. Clayton, W. Woodford, ed. *History of Union and Middlesex Counties, New Jersey, with Biographical Sketches of Many of their Pioneers and Prominent Men.* Philadelphia: Everts & Peck, 1882. p.92.

517. *The Massachusetts Spy: Or, American Oracle of Liberty.* 11:554 (December 20, 1781) p.3.

518. *New Jersey Journal.* 155. *The New York Gazette and the Weekly Mercury.* 1392 (June 29, 1782). Clayton, W. Woodford, ed. *History of Union and Middlesex Counties, New Jersey, with Biographical Sketches of Many of their Pioneers and Prominent Men.* Philadelphia: Everts & Peck, 1882. p.94.

519. *New Jersey Journal.* nos. 106, 107. *Rivington's Gazette.* no. 461. *The New York Gazette and the Weekly Mercury.* nos. 1532, 1633.

520. *New Jersey Journal.* No. 149. Hatfield, Edwin F. *History of Elizabeth, New Jersey: including the early history of Union County.* New York: Carlton & Lanahan, 1868. p.509.

521. Seely, Sylvanus. *Diary of Sylvanus Seeley.* Morristown: Morristown National Historical Park Library. p.61.

522. Barber, John Warner. *Historical Collections of New Jersey.* New York: S. Tuttle, 1844. p.365. Extract of a letter from Freehold. Monmouth county, dated April 15, 1782. *Documents Relating to the Revolutionary History, State of New Jersey.* Edited by William S. Stryker. Trenton: The John L. Murphy Publishing Co., 1901. Series 2. 5:424.

523. Hornor, William S. *This Old Monmouth of Ours.* Freehold: Moreau Brothers, 1932. p.45.

524. *The New Jersey Gazette.* 5:220 (February 3, 1779) p.3. *New Jersey Gazette.* (March 13, 1782, 3. *Documents Relating to the Revolutionary History, State of New Jersey.* Edited by William S. Stryker. Trenton: The John L. Murphy Publishing Co., 1901. Series 2. 5:397.

525. Smith, Samuel Stelle. *The Battle of Monmouth.* Monmouth Beach, N.J.: Philip Freneau Press, 1964. p.11.

526. *Documents Relating to the Revolutionary History, State of New Jersey.* Edited by William S. Stryker. Trenton: The John L. Murphy Publishing Co., 1901. Series 2. 5:264–265.

527. Ibid., p.372. New Jersey Department of Defense Manuscripts #3782.

528. *Documents Relating to the Revolutionary History, State of New Jersey.* Edited by William S. Stryker. Trenton: The John L. Murphy Publishing Co., 1901. Series 2. 4:456–457.

529. *The Boston Evening-Post and the General Advertiser.* I:LI (October 5, 1782) p.3.

530. *History of Monmouth County, New Jersey, 1664–1920.* New York: Lewis Historical Publishing Company, 1922. p.116.

531. *Documents Relating to the Revolutionary History, State of New Jersey.* Edited by William S. Stryker. Trenton: The John L. Murphy Publishing Co., 1901. Series 2. 1:528n. New Jersey Department of Defense Manuscripts.

532. Extract of a letter from Freehold. Monmouth county, dated April 15, 1782. *Documents Relating to the Revolutionary History, State of New Jersey.* Edited by William S. Stryker. Trenton: The John L. Murphy Publishing Co., 1901. Series 2. 5:424.

533. www.uelac.org/Loyalist-Trails/2007/Loyalist-Trails-2007.php?issue=200722.

534. Vermeule, Cornelius C. Some Revolutionary Incidents in the Raritan Valley. *Proceedings New Jersey Historical Society.* New Series. 6 (1921) pp.73–85. *New Jersey History,* New Series. 6:84. *The Pennsylvania Evening Post.* 3:378 (July 15, 1777) p.375.

535. *New Jersey Supreme Court Records* 36122, 36989.

536. *Documents Relating to the Revolutionary History, State of New Jersey.* Edited by William S. Stryker. Trenton: The John L. Murphy Publishing Co., 1901. Series 2. 5:279.

537. *Salem Gazette.* 1:37 (June 27, 1782) p.3. *The New Jersey Gazette.* 5:232 (June 5, 1782) p.3. Koke, Richard J. *New York Historical Society Quarterly.* 41:301.

538. Force, Peter. *American archives: consisting of a collection of authentick records, state papers, debates, and letters and other notices of publick affairs, the whole forming a documentary history of the origin and progress of the North American colonies; of the causes and accomplishment of the American revolution; and of the Constitution of government for the United States, to the final ratification thereof. In six series.* [Washington, 1837–1853]. 5, 3:1277.

539. *Connecticut Journal.* 492 (March 19, 1777) p.2.

540. *New York Gazette and Weekly Mercury.* (April 7, 1777). Documents Relating to the Revolutionary History, State of New Jersey. Edited by William S. Stryker. Trenton: The John L. Murphy Publishing Co., 1901. Series 2. 1:331.

541. *The Royal American Gazette.* XIV (April 17, 1777) p.3.

542. *The New York Gazette and the Weekly Mercury.* 1509 (September 18, 1780). *Documents Relating to the Revolutionary History, State of New Jersey.* Edited by William S. Stryker. Trenton: The John L. Murphy Publishing Co., 1901. Series 2. 4:646.

543. Hunterdon County. Manuscripts. 5716.

544. Smith, Samuel Stelle. *The Battle of Monmouth.* Monmouth Beach: Philip Freneau Press, 1964. p.10.

545. Col. Malcom to General Heath. December 9, 1776. Force, Peter. *American archives: consisting of a collection of authentick records, state papers, debates, and letters and other notices of publick affairs, the whole forming a documentary history of the origin and progress of the North American colonies; of the causes and accomplishment of the American revolution; and of the Constitution of government for the United States, to the final ratification thereof. In six series.* [Washington, 1837–1853]. 5, III 1139.

546. Smith, Samuel Stelle. *The Battle of Monmouth.* Monmouth Beach: Philip Freneau Press, 1964. p.11.

547. General Putnam to Washington, Sept. 13, 1777, The Papers of George Washington, Library of Congress. McDougall to Washington, Sept. 17, 1777, The Papers of George Washington, Library of Congress. Leiby, Adrian Coulter. *The Revolutionary War in the Hackensack Valley; the Jersey Dutch and the Neutral Ground, 1775–1783.* New Brunswick, N.J.: Rutgers University Press 1962. pp.137–141. McDougall Papers. New York Historical Society. Clinton's figures were exactly double those of McDougall: "about four hundred cattle and the same quantity of sheep." Clinton, Henry. *The American Rebellion: Sir Henry Clinton's Narrative of His Campaigns, 1775–1782, with an appendix of original documents.* Edited by William B. Willcox. New Haven: Yale University Press, 1954. p.71.

548. *Pennsylvania Journal.* 1716 (October 25, 1775). *Archives of the State of New Jersey.* First Series, XXXI. Somerville, 1923. pp.210–211. Force, Peter. *American archives: consisting of a collection of authentick records, state papers, debates, and letters and other notices of publick affairs, the whole forming a documentary history of the origin and progress of the North American colonies; of the causes and accomplishment of the American revolution; and of the Constitution of government for the United States, to the final ratification thereof. In six series.* [Washington, 1837–1853]. 4 Ser. III, 1825.

549. Ibid.

550. Salter, Edwin. *Old Times in Old Monmouth*. Freehold: Monmouth Democrat, 1874. p.202.

551. Clinton, Henry. *The American Rebellion: Sir Henry Clinton's Narrative of His Campaigns, 1775–1782, with an appendix of original documents*. Edited by William B. Willcox. New Haven: Yale University Press, 1954. p.105.

552. *The Providence Gazette; And Country Journal*. 8:642 (April 20, 1776) p.2.

553. *New York Gazette and Weekly Mercury*. (June 10, 1776). *Documents Relating to the Revolutionary History, State of New Jersey*. Edited by William S. Stryker. Trenton: The John L. Murphy Publishing Co., 1901. Series 2. 1:110–111.

554. Captain Thomas Crieger to Thomas Randall. *New York Provincial Congress*. 2:304–305. NDAR 5:991–92.

555. *New York Gazette and Weekly Mercury*. (April 28, 1777). *Documents Relating to the Revolutionary History, State of New Jersey*. Edited by William S. Stryker. Trenton: The John L. Murphy Publishing Co., 1901. Series 2. 1:354.

556. *New York Gazette and Weekly Mercury*. (June 23, 1777). *Documents Relating to the Revolutionary History, State of New Jersey*. Edited by William S. Stryker. Trenton: The John L. Murphy Publishing Co., 1901. Series 2. 1:400.

557. Lieutenant Robert Collings To Pennsylvania Navy Board, Newingland Town 16 Miles up Cohansey creek. March 23, 1778. Historical Society of Pennsylvania. William Bradford Collection 2 in NDAR 11:767–768.

558. *Documents Relating to the Revolutionary History, State of New Jersey*. Edited by William S. Stryker. Trenton: The John L. Murphy Publishing Co., 1901. Series 2. 2:137.

559. New Jersey Department of Defense Manuscripts.

560. *New York Gazette and Weekly Mercury*. (August 31, 1778). *Documents Relating to the Revolutionary History, State of New Jersey*. Edited by William S. Stryker. Trenton: The John L. Murphy Publishing Co., 1901. Series 2. 2:389–90.

561. *Documents Relating to the Revolutionary History, State of New Jersey*. Edited by William S. Stryker. Trenton: The John L. Murphy Publishing Co., 1901. Series 2. 2:458.

562. Ibid., 3:397.

563. New Jersey Department of Defense Manuscripts.

564. *The Pennsylvania, Evening Post*. (September 11, 1779). *Documents Relating to the Revolutionary History, State of New Jersey*. Edited by William S. Stryker. Trenton: The John L. Murphy Publishing Co., 1901. Series 2. 3:616.

565. *Boston Gazette*. (November 4, 1779).

566. *New Jersey Gazette*. (January 12, 1780) p.3.

567. *Documents Relating to the Revolutionary History, State of New Jersey*. Edited by William S. Stryker. Trenton: The John L. Murphy Publishing Co., 1901. Series 2. 4:251.

568. *The Pennsylvania Evening Post, and Public Advertiser*. VIII:869 (October 21, 1782) p.155.

569. *The Pennsylvania Ledger*. (May 11, 1776). *Documents Relating to the Revolutionary History, State of New Jersey*. Edited by William S. Stryker. Trenton: The John L. Murphy Publishing Co., 1901. Series 2. 1:549.

570. Stewart, Frank H. *Salem a Century Ago*. Salem, N.J.: Salem Standard and Jerseyman, 1934. p.11. Sickler, Joseph Sheppard. *The History of Salem County, New Jersey*. Salem, N.J.: Philip Freneau Press, 1970. p.140.

571. *Documents Relating to the Revolutionary History, State of New Jersey*. Edited by William S. Stryker. Trenton: The John L. Murphy Publishing Co., 1901. Series 2. 2:80.

572. Smith, Samuel Stelle. *Fight for the Delaware, 1777*. Monmouth Beach, N.J.: Philip Freneau Press, 1970. p.9.

573. *Pennsylvania Archives*. 1, 5:649–650.

574. Smith, Samuel Stelle. *Fight for the Delaware, 1777*. Monmouth Beach, N.J.: Philip Freneau Press, 1970. p.13.

575. Ibid., p.14.

576. Lundin, Leonard. *Cockpit of the Revolution*. Princeton: Princeton University Press, 1962. p.370.

577. *Documents Relating to the Revolutionary History, State of New Jersey*. Edited by William S. Stryker. Trenton: The John L. Murphy Publishing Co., 1901. Series 2. 2:5.

578. *The Pennsylvania Packet or the General Advertiser*. 3222. (January 7, 1778) p.3.

579. *Documents Relating to the Revolutionary History, State of New Jersey*. Edited by William S. Stryker. Trenton: The John L. Murphy Publishing Co., 1901. Series 2. 2:5.

580. Journal of HMS *Roebuck*, Captain Andrew S. Hamond. British National Archives, Admiralty 51/4311. NDAR 11:96–97.

581. http://nj.gov/dep/njgs/enviroed/oldpubs/battles.pdf.

582. Extract of a letter from, Kildare, Monmouth county, April 9, 1778. *New-York Gazette and Weekly Mercury*. (April 16, 1778). *Documents Relating to the Revolutionary History, State of New Jersey*. Edited by William S. Stryker. Trenton: The John L. Murphy Publishing Co., 1901. Series 2. 1:485; 2:160, 170–71.

583. Extract of a letter from Kildare, Monmouth County, April 9, 1778. *The Pennsylvania Ledger: or the Philadelphia Market-Day Advertiser*. CXLVI (April 22, 1778) p.3.

584. Ibid. *Documents Relating to the Revolutionary History, State of New Jersey*. Edited by William S. Stryker. Trenton: The John L. Murphy Publishing Co., 1901. Series 2. 1:485; 2:160, 170–71.

585. Lundin, Leonard. *Cockpit of the Revolution*. Princeton: Princeton University Press, 1962. p.113. Force, Peter. *American archives: consisting of a collection of authentick records, state papers, debates, and letters and other notices of publick affairs, the whole forming a documentary history of the origin and progress of the North American colonies; of the causes and accomplishment of the American revolution; and of the Constitution of government for the United States, to the final ratification thereof. In six series*. [Washington, 1837–1853]. 5 Ser. I, 14.

586. Journal of HM Sloop *Falcon*. British National Archives, Admiralty 51/336. NDAR 7:514.

587. *Documents Relating to the Revolutionary History, State of New Jersey.* Edited by William S. Stryker. Trenton: The John L. Murphy Publishing Co., 1901. Series 2. 2:380.

588. See Fitzpatrick, John C., ed. *The Writings of George Washington from the Original Manuscript Sources 1745–1799.* Washington: USGPO, VI:355.

589. Schermerhorn, William E. *The History of Burlington, New Jersey.* Burlington, N.J.: Press of Enterprise Publishing Co., 1927. p.78. Peckham, Howard Henry. *The Toll of Independence: Engagements & Battle Casualties of the American Revolution.* Chicago: University of Chicago Press, 1974. p.50.

590. Ewald, Johann. *Diary of the American War: A Hessian Journal.* Translated and edited by Joseph P. Tustin. New Haven and London: Yale University Press, 1979. pp.35–39. *The Pennsylvania Evening Post.* (December 24, 1776). *Documents Relating to the Revolutionary History, State of New Jersey.* Edited by William S. Stryker. Trenton: The John L. Murphy Publishing Co., 1901. Series 2. 1:243. Smith, Samuel Stelle. *The Battle of Trenton.* Monmouth Beach, N.J.: Philip Freneau Press, 1965. pp.15–16. Smith, Samuel Stelle. *The Battle of Princeton.* Monmouth Beach, N.J.: Philip Freneau Press, 1967. pp.115–116.

591. Letter of James Nicholson to Samuel Purviance, Jr. dated Philadelphia Decr. 7th, 1776. NDAR 7:614. *The Virginia Gazette.* 102 (January 10, 1777) p.2.

592. Peckham, Howard Henry. *The Toll of Independence: Engagements & Battle Casualties of the American Revolution.* Chicago: University of Chicago Press, 1974. p.35.

593. *The New Jersey Gazette.* 1:31 (July 8, 1778) p.3.

594. *The Pennsylvania Evening Post.* 4:490 (May 13, 1778 p.194. *The Pennsylvania Ledger: or the Philadelphia Market-Day Advertiser.* CLII (May 13, 1778 p.3. *Connecticut Journal.* 554 (May 27, 1778) p.3. Ward, Harry M. *General William Maxwell and the New Jersey Continentals.* Westport, CT; London: Greenwood Press, 1997. p.95. *Revolution in America: Confidential Letters and Journals 1776–1784 of Adjutant General Major Baurmeister of the Hessian Forces.* Translated and annotated by Berhard A. Uhlendorf. New Brunswick, N.J.: Rutgers University Press, 1957. p.174. Bodle, Wayne K.; Thibaut, Jacqueline. *Valley Forge historical research project.* Valley Forge, Pa.: U.S. Dept. of the Interior, National Park Service, 1980. 1:426–7. Jackson, John W. *With the British Army in Philadelphia, 1777–1778.* San Rafael, Calif.: Presidio Press, 1979. pp.296–297. Wildes, Harry Emerson. *Valley Forge.* New York, Macmillan Co., 1938. pp.235–37. *Documents Relating to the Revolutionary History, State of New Jersey.* Edited by William S. Stryker. Trenton: The John L. Murphy Publishing Co., 1901. Series 2. 2:208, 216–219. Lundin, Leonard. *Cockpit of the Revolution.* Princeton: Princeton University Press, 1940. p.391.

595. *Documents Relating to the Revolutionary History, State of New Jersey.* Edited by William S. Stryker. Trenton: The John L. Murphy Publishing Co., 1901. Series 2. 2:208. Lundin, Leonard. *Cockpit of the Revolution.* Princeton: Princeton University Press, 1940. p.391.

596. *Documents Relating to the Revolutionary History, State of New Jersey.* Edited by William S. Stryker. Trenton: The John L. Murphy Publishing Co., 1901. Series 2. 2:269.

597. Peckham, Howard Henry. *The Toll of Independence: Engagements & Battle Casualties of the American Revolution.* Chicago: University of Chicago Press, 1974. p.36.

598. Peckham, Howard Henry. *The Toll of Independence: Engagements & Battle Casualties of the American Revolution.* Chicago: University of Chicago Press, 1974. p.40. *New York Gazette and Weekly Mercury.* (October 20, 1777). *Documents Relating to the Revolutionary History, State of New Jersey.* Edited by William S. Stryker. Trenton: The John L. Murphy Publishing Co., 1901. Series 2. 1:475–476.

599. General Washington, dated Red-Bank, October 23d, 1777. *Dunlap's Maryland Gazette Or The Baltimore General Advertiser.* III:CXXXII (November 4, 1777) p.1. *The Providence Gazette; And Country Journal.* XIV:724 (November 15, 1777) p.3.

600. Martin, Joseph Plumb. *Private Yankee Doodle; being a narrative of some of the adventures, dangers, and sufferings of a Revolutionary Soldier,* edited by George F. Scheer, originally published in Hallowell, Me., 1830, anonymously. (Republished, Boston, 1962.). *A narrative of some of the adventures, dangers and sufferings of a Revolutionary soldier.* (Eyewitness accounts of the American Revolution). [New York] New York Times [1968]. p.87.

601. *Encyclopedia of the American Revolution.* Harold E. Selesky, editor in chief.—2nd Ed. Detroit: Charles Scribner's Sons, 2007. 1:373–374. *The Encyclopedia of the American Revolutionary War: a political, social, and military history.* Gregory Fremont-Barnes, Richard Alan Ryerson, editors. Santa Barbara, CA: ABC-CLIO, 2006. 2:427–428. Atwood, Rodney. *The Hessians: Mercenaries from Hesse-Kassel in the American Revolution.* New York: Cambridge University Press, 1980. Ford, Worthington. *Defences of Philadelphia in 1777.* Brooklyn, N.Y.: Historical Printing Club, 1897. Jackson, John. *The Pennsylvania Navy, 1775–1781: the Defense of the Delaware.* New Brunswick, N.J.: Rutgers University Press, 1974. McGuire, Thomas J. *The Philadelphia Campaign.* Mechanicsburg, PA: Stackpole Books. Muenchhausen, Friedrich von. *At General Howe's Side 1776–1778: The diary of General William Howe's aide de camp, Captain Friedrich von Muenchhausen.* Translated by Ernst Kipping and annotated by Samuel Smith. Monmouth Beach, N.J.: Philip Freneau Press, 1974. Reed, John F. *Campaign to Valley Forge: July 1, 1777–December 19, 1777.* Philadelphia: University of Pennsylvania Press, 1965. Smith, Samuel Stelle. *Fight for the Delaware, 1777.* Monmouth Beach, N.J.: Philip Freneau Press, 1970. Taaffe, Stephen R. *The Philadelphia Campaign, 1777–1778.* Lawrence, KS: University Press of Kansas, 2003. Ward, Christopher. *The War of the Revolution.* New York: Macmillan, 1952. pp.372–383.

602. Lieutenant's Journal of HMS *Isis,* Captain William Cornwallis, R.N. British National Archives, Admiralty/ L/J/116. NDAR 10:405. Journal of HMS *Pearl,* Captain John Linzee. British National Archives, Admiralty 51/675. NDAR 10:405. Master's Journal of HMS *Roebuck,* Captain Andrew S. Hamond. British National Archives, Admiralty 52/1964. NDAR 10:406.

603. *Documents Relating to the Revolutionary History, State of New Jersey.* Edited by William S. Stryker. Trenton: The John L. Murphy Publishing Co., 1901. Series 2. 2:35.

604. Extract of a Letter from London, Jan. 10, 1778. *The Pennsylvania Evening Post.* 4:474 (April 1, 1778) p.143. *The Pennsylvania Ledger: or the Philadelphia Market-Day Advertiser.* CXL (April 1, 1778) p.3.

605. *Royal Pennsylvania Gazette.* (April 3, 1778). *Documents Relating to the Revolutionary History, State of New Jersey.* Edited by William S. Stryker. Trenton: The John L. Murphy Publishing Co., 1901. Series 2. 2:146.

606. Smith, Samuel Stelle. *Fight for the Delaware, 1777.* Monmouth Beach, N.J.: Philip Freneau Press, 1970. pp.10–11. William Bradford to Thomas Wharton, Jr. Fort Mifflin, October 7, 1777. Pennsylvania Historical and Museum Commission, Division of Archives and Manuscripts. RG 27. In NDAR 10:62–63.

607. *The Encyclopedia of the American Revolutionary War: a political, social, and military history.* Gregory Fremont-Barnes, Richard Alan Ryerson, editors. Santa Barbara, CA: ABC-CLIO, 2006. 1:99–100.

608. Journal Of HMS *Camilla,* Captain Charles Phipps, British National Archives, Admiralty 51/157. NDAR 10:53.

609. Journal of the HMS *Liverpool,* Captain Henry Bellew. British National Archives, Admiralty 51/548. NDAR 10:165. Journal of the HM Armed Ship *Vigilant,* Commander John Henry. British National Archives, Admiralty 51/1037. NDAR 10:166.

610. Smith, Samuel Stelle. *Fight for the Delaware, 1777.* Monmouth Beach, N.J.: Philip Freneau Press, 1970. pp.36–37. Journal Of HMS *Liverpool,* Captain Henry Bellew, British National Archives, Admiralty 51/548. NDAR 10:165. Master's Journal Of HMS *Roebuck,* Captain Andrew S. Hamond, British National Archives, Admiralty. 52/1964. NDAR 10:165. Journal Of HM Armed Ship *Vigilant,* Commander John Henry, British National Archives, Admiralty 51/1037. NDAR 10:166.

611. Extract of a letter from Major Francois Louis Teissedre de Fleury to Lieutenant Colonel Alexander Hamilton. Dated Fort Mifflin, October 28, 1777. NDAR 10:334.

612. Smith, Samuel Stelle. *Fight for the Delaware, 1777.* Monmouth Beach, N.J.: Philip Freneau Press, 1970. p.28.

613. Master's Journal of HMS *Roebuck,* Captain Andrew S. Hamond. British National Archives, Admiralty 51/4311. NDAR 10:448.

614. Journal of HMS *Pearl,* Captain John Linzee. British National Archives, Admiralty 51/675. NDAR 10:467.

615. Journal of the HMS *Liverpool,* Captain Henry Bellew. British National Archives, Admiralty 51/548. Journal of HMS *Roebuck,* Captain Andrew S. Hamond. British National Archives, Admiralty 51/4311. NDAR v10:478 .

616. *Pennsylvania Archives.* I, 6:23.

617. Extract of a Letter from Norwich, Dated Nov. 28. *The Independent Chronicle and the Universal Advertiser.* X:485 (December 4, 1777) p.3. *Continental Journal.* LXXXI (December 11, 1777 p.2.

618. Stewart, Frank H. *History of the Battle of Red Bank.* Woodbury, N.J.: the author, 1927. p.21.

619. Stewart, Frank J. *Salem a Century Ago.* Salem, N.J.: Salem Standard and Jerseyman, 1934. p.32.

620. Smith, Samuel Stelle. *The Battle of Trenton.* Monmouth Beach, N.J.: Philip Freneau Press, 1965. pp.38–41.

621. *The Pennsylvania Evening Post.* 4:452 (February 3, 1778) p.55.

622. *Documents Relating to the Revolutionary History, State of New Jersey.* Edited by William S. Stryker. Trenton: The John L. Murphy Publishing Co., 1901. Series 2. 2:134.

623. Sickler, Joseph Sheppard. *The History of Salem County, New Jersey.* Salem, N.J.: Philip Freneau Press, 1970. p.146.

624. Barber, John Warner and Howe, Henry. *Historical Collections of New Jersey.* New York: S. Tuttle, 1844. p.439.

625. Peckham, Howard Henry. *The Toll of Independence: Engagements & Battle Casualties of the American Revolution.* Chicago: University of Chicago Press, 1974. p.50.

626. Smith, Samuel Stelle. *Fight for the Delaware, 1777.* Monmouth Beach: Philip Freneau Press, 1970. pp.18–19, 39–40.

627. Stewart, Frank H. *Foraging for Valley Forge by General Anthony Wayne in Salem and Gloucester Counties.* Woodbury, N.J.: the author, 1929. p.11.

628. *Documents Relating to the Revolutionary History, State of New Jersey.* Edited By William S. Stryker. Trenton: The John L. Murphy Publishing Co., 1901. Series 2. 2:101–102.

629. *Revolution in America: Confidential Letters and Journals 1776–1784 of Adjutant General Major Baurmeister of the Hessian Forces.* Translated and annotated by Berhard A. Uhlendorf. New Brunswick, N.J.: Rutgers University Press, 1957 p.162. *The Royal Pennsylvania Gazette.* XI (April 7, 1778) p.3. *The Massachusetts Spy: Or, American Oracle of Liberty.* VIII:364 (April 23, 1778) p.2.

630. *The Pennsylvania Evening Post.* (April 6, 1778). *New York Gazette and Weekly Mercury.* (April 6, 1778). *Documents Relating to the Revolutionary History, State of New Jersey.* Edited by William S. Stryker. Trenton: The John L. Murphy Publishing Co., 1901. Series 2. 2:147.

631. Carrington, Henry B. *Battles of the American Revolution 1775–1781, including battle maps and charts of the American Revolution.* New York: Promontory Press, (1974), originally published in 1877 and 1881. pp.414–415.

632. General Washington, dated Red-Bank, October 23d, 1777. *Dunlap's Maryland Gazette or the Baltimore General Advertiser.* III:CXXXII (November 4, 1777) p.1. *The Providence Gazette; And Country Journal.* XIV:724 (November 15, 1777) p.3.

633. Smith, Samuel Stelle. *Fight for the Delaware, 1777.* Monmouth Beach: Philip Freneau Press, 1970. p.39.

634. *The New-York Gazette; and The Weekly Mercury.* (December 1, 1777). *Documents Relating to the Revolutionary History, State of New Jersey.* Edited By William S. Stryker. Trenton: The John L. Murphy Publishing Co., 1901. Series 2. 1:487–488.

635. Smith, Samuel Stelle. *The Battle of Trenton.* Monmouth Beach, N.J.: Philip Freneau Press, 1965. p.15.

636. Smith, Samuel Stelle. *Fight for the Delaware, 1777.* Monmouth Beach, N.J.: Philip Freneau Press, 1970. p.19.

637. *The Royal Pennsylvania Gazette.* XI (April 7, 1778) p.3. *The Massachusetts Spy: Or, American Oracle of Liberty.* VIII:364 (April 23, 1778) p.2.

638. *Documents Relating to the Revolutionary History, State of New Jersey.* Edited by William S. Stryker. Trenton: The John L. Murphy Publishing Co., 1901. Series 2. 1:514 515.

639. Simcoe, John Graves. *Simcoe's Military Journal. A History Of the Operations Of A Partisan Corps, Called The Queen's Rangers, Commanded By Lieut. Col. J. G. Simcoe.* New-York: Bartlett & Welford, 1844. pp.38–46. Stewart, Frank H. *Salem a Century Ago.* Salem, N.J.: Salem Standard and Jerseyman, 1934. p.39.

640. *Revolution in America: Confidential Letters and Journals 1776–1784 of Adjutant General Major Baurmeister of the Hessian Forces.* Translated and annotated by Berhard A. Uhlendorf. New Brunswick, N.J.: Rutgers University Press, 1957. p.162.

641. Boatner, Mark M. *Encyclopedia of the American Revolution.* 3d ed., New York: McKay, 1980. p.437.

642. *New York Gazette and Weekly Mercury.* (December 8, 1777). *Documents Relating to the Revolutionary History, State of New Jersey.* Edited by William S. Stryker. Trenton: The John L. Murphy Publishing Co., 1901. Series 2. 1:505.

642a. *The Royal Pennsylvania Gazette.* XI (April 7, 1778) p.3.

643. Baurmeister, Carl Leopold. *Revolution in America: Confidential Letters and Journals, 1776–1784.* trans. and annotated by Bernhard A. Uhlendorf. New Brunswick: Rutgers University Press, 1957. p.52.

644. *The Pennsylvania Evening Post.* (June 20, 1778). *Documents Relating to the Revolutionary History, State of New Jersey.* Edited by William S. Stryker. Trenton: The John L. Murphy Publishing Co., 1901. Series 2. 2:263.

645. Sabine, Lorenzo. *Biographical sketches of Loyalists of the American Revolution.* Port Washington, N.Y.: Kennikat Press [1966]. 2:107. Horner, William S. *This Old Monmouth of Ours.* Freehold, N.J.: Moreau Brothers, 1932. p.28.

646. *The Pennsylvania Evening Post.* 4:537 (October 7, 1778) p.366. *Documents Relating to the Revolutionary History, State of New Jersey.* Edited by William S. Stryker. Trenton: The John L. Murphy Publishing Co., 1901. Series 2. 2:453.

647. Extract of a letter from Monmouth Court-house, January 26, 1779. *The Pennsylvania Evening Post.* 5:572 (February 15, 1779) p.40. *The New Jersey Gazette.* 2:61 (February 3, 1779) p.3. *Documents Relating to the Revolutionary History, State of New Jersey.* Edited by William S. Stryker. Trenton: The John L. Murphy Publishing Co., 1901. Series 2. 3:53–54.

648. *The New-York Gazette: and the Weekly Mercury.* 1452 (August 16, 1779). *Documents Relating to the Revolutionary History, State of New Jersey.* Edited by William S. Stryker. Trenton: The John L. Murphy Publishing Co., 1901. Series 2. 3:555.

649. *Documents Relating to the Revolutionary History, State of New Jersey.* Edited by William S. Stryker. Trenton: The John L. Murphy Publishing Co., 1901. Series 2. 5:145.

650. *The New Jersey Gazette.* (June 7, 1780) p.3. *Documents Relating to the Revolutionary History, State of New Jersey.* Edited by William S. Stryker. Trenton: The John L. Murphy Publishing Co., 1901. Series 2. 4:407.

651. *Salem Gazette.* 1:26 (April 11, 1782) p.3. *The Royal Gazette.* 573 (March 31, 1782) p.3. Boatner, Mark M. *Encyclopedia of the American Revolution.* McKay: New York, 3d ed., 1980. p.529.

652. Damon, Allan L: "A Melancholy Case." New York. *American Heritage: the magazine of history.* 21:2 (February, 1970) pp.19, 92.

653. *The New Jersey Gazette.* 5:227 (May 1, 1782) p.3.

654. *The New Jersey Gazette.* 5:232 (June 5, 1782) p.4. *The New Jersey Gazette.* 5:233 (June 12, 1782) p.3. Hornor, William S. *This old Monmouth of ours: history, tradition, biography, genealogy, and other anecdotes related to Monmouth County, New Jersey.* Baltimore, MD: Clearfield Co., 1990, 1932 p.52.

655. Damon, Allan L. "A Melancholy Case." New York. *American Heritage: the magazine of history.* 21:2 (February, 1970) p.92–94.

656. *The Freeman's Journal: or, the North-American Intelligencer.* II:LXX (August 21, 1782) p.3.

657. Barber, John Warner. *Historical Collections of New Jersey.* New York: S. Tuttle, 1844. p.328n–329n.

658. Extract of a Letter from London, Jan. 10. *The Pennsylvania Ledger: or the Philadelphia Market-Day Advertiser.* CXLI (April 4, 1778) p.3.

659. Stewart, Frank J. *Salem a Century Ago.* Salem, N.J.: Salem Standard and Jerseyman, 1934. p.37.

660. *Documents Relating to the Revolutionary History, State of New Jersey.* Edited by William S. Stryker. Trenton: The John L. Murphy Publishing Co., 1901. Series 2. 2:129. Stewart, Frank J. *Salem a Century Ago.* Salem, N.J.: Salem Standard and Jerseyman, 1934. p.47; 3:65, 76–77, 81. Sickler, Joseph Sheppard. *The History of Salem County, New Jersey.* Salem, N.J.: Sunbeam Publishing Company, 1937. p.146.

661. Sickler, Joseph Sheppard. *The History of Salem County, New Jersey.* Salem, N.J.: Sunbeam Publishing Company, 1937. 150–151. Stewart, Frank J. *Salem a Century Ago.* Salem, N.J.: Salem Standard and Jerseyman, 1934. p.47.

662. Simcoe, John Graves. *Simcoe's Military Journal. A History Of the Operations Of A Partisan Corps, Called The Queen's Rangers, Commanded By Lieut. Col. J. G. Simcoe.* New-York: Bartlett & Welford, 1844. pp.46–56. *Documents Relating to the Revolutionary History, State of New Jersey.* Edited by William S. Stryker. Trenton: The John L. Murphy Publishing Co., 1901. Series 2. 1:313.

663. Simcoe, John Graves. *Simcoe's Military Journal. A History Of the Operations Of A Partisan Corps, Called The Queen's Rangers, Commanded By Lieut. Col. J. G. Simcoe.* New-York: Bartlett & Welford, 1844. p.54.

664. *The Pennsylvania Evening Post.* 4:490 (May 13,1778) p.194. *The Pennsylvania Ledger: or the Philadelphia Market-Day Advertiser.* CLII (May 13, 1778) p.3. *Documents Relating to the Revolutionary History, State of New Jersey.* Edited By William S. Stryker. Trenton: The John L. Murphy Publishing Co., 1901. Series 2. 2:217–218.

665. Extract of a Letter from London, Jan. 10, 1778. *The Pennsylvania Evening Post.* 4:474 (April 1, 1778) p.143. *The Pennsylvania Ledger: or the Philadelphia Market-Day Advertiser.* CXL (April 1, 1778) p.3. CLI (April 4, 1778) p.3.

666. Stewart, Frank H. *Foraging for Valley Forge by General Anthony Wayne in Salem and Gloucester Counties.* Woodbury, N.J.: the author, 1929. p.29. Sickler, Joseph Sheppard. *The History of Salem County, New Jersey.* Salem, N.J.: Philip Freneau Press, 1970. p.170.

667. Sickler ibid.

668. Johnson, Amandus. *The Journal and Biography of Nicholas Collin, 1746–1831.* Philadelphia: New Jersey Society of Pennsylvania, 1936. p.246.

669. Baurmeister, Carl Leopold. *Revolution in America: Confidential Letters and Journals, 1776–1784.* trans. and annotated by Bernhard A. Uhlendorf. New Brunswick, N.J.: Rutgers University Press, 1957. p.162.

670. *Documents Relating to the Revolutionary History, State of New Jersey.* Edited by William S. Stryker. Trenton: The John L. Murphy Publishing Co., 1901. Series 2. 2:134.

671. *The Pennsylvania Evening Post.* 4:490 (May 13, 1778) p.194. *The Pennsylvania Ledger: or the Philadelphia Market-Day Advertiser.* CLII (May 13, 1778) p.3. *Connecticut Journal.* 554 (May 27, 1778) p.3. *Documents Relating to the Revolutionary History, State of New Jersey.* Edited by William S. Stryker. Trenton: The John L. Murphy Publishing Co., 1901. Series 2. 2:217–218.

672. www.doublegv.com/ggv/battles/Trenton.html.

673. Peckham, Howard Henry. *The Toll of Independence: Engagements & Battle Casualties of the American Revolution.* Chicago: University of Chicago Press, 1974. p.49.

674. Ewald, Johann. *Diary of the American War: A Hessian Journal.* Translated and edited by Joseph P. Tustin. New Haven and London: Yale University Press, 1979. pp.134–135. Simcoe, John Graves. *A Journal of the Operations of the Queen's Rangers.* New York: Bartlett & Welford, 1844; New York: Arno Press, 1968. pp.66–67.

675. Salter, Edwin. *Old Times in Old Monmouth.* Freehold: Monmouth Democrat, 1874. p.88.

676. Master's Log of HM Brig *Halifax.* British National Archives, Admiralty 52/1775. NDAR 5:1190–1.

677. Extract of a letter from Kildare, Monmouth county, April 9, 1778. *Documents Relating to the Revolutionary History, State of New Jersey.* Edited by William S. Stryker. Trenton: The John L. Murphy Publishing Co., 1901. Series 2. 2:170–171.

678. Report of Captain John Henry. *The New-York Gazette and Weekly Mercury.* (Aug. 24, 1778). *Documents Relating to the Revolutionary History, State of New Jersey.* Edited by William S. Stryker. Trenton: The John L. Murphy Publishing Co., 1901. Series 2. 2:375–76.

679. Simcoe, John Graves. *Simcoe's Military Journal. A History Of the Operations Of A Partisan Corps, Called The Queen's Rangers, Commanded By Lieut. Col. J. G. Simcoe.* New-York: Bartlett & Welford, 1844, pp.64–66. Freeman, Douglas Southall. *George Washington, a biography.* New York: Scribner, 1948–1957. 5:15. *Narratives of the Revolution In New York: A Collection Of Articles From The New-York Historical Society Quarterly.* New York: The New York Historical Society, 1975. p.238.

680. Stewart, Frank J. *Salem a Century Ago.* Salem, N.J.: Salem Standard and Jerseyman, 1934. p.90.

681. *New-York Gazette and Weekly Mercury.* (June 15, 1778). *Documents Relating to the Revolutionary History, State of New Jersey.* Edited by William S. Stryker. Trenton: The John L. Murphy Publishing Co., 1901. Series 2. 2:253.

682. *New York Gazette and Weekly Mercury.* (September 28, 1778). *Biographical Cyclopedia of Ocean County, New Jersey.* Philadelphia: A.D. Smith & Co. 1899. p.47. *Documents Relating to the Revolutionary History, State of New Jersey.* Edited by William S. Stryker. Trenton: The John L. Murphy Publishing Co., 1901. Series 2. 2:445.

683. Salter, Edwin, *Old Times in Old Monmouth.* Freehold: Monmouth Democrat, 1874. pp.79–80.

684. Heston, Alfred M. *Absegami.* Camden, N.J., 1904. p.146. *The New Jersey Gazette.* 5:246 (September 11, 1782) p.3.

685. Ewald, Johann. *Diary of the American War: A Hessian Journal.* Translated and edited by Joseph P. Tustin. New Haven and London: Yale University Press, 1979. pp.132–133.

686. Smith, Samuel Stelle. *The Battle of Monmouth.* Monmouth Beach: Philip Freneau Press, 1964. p.6.

687. Lundin, Leonard. *Cockpit of the Revolution.* Princeton: Princeton University Press, 1940. p.404.

688. Heston, Alfred M. *Absegami.* Camden, N.J., 1904. pp.138–46. Livingston to Stirling, Oct. 11, 1778, Washington Papers 87. *The Pennsylvania Evening Post.* (October 9, 1778). *Documents Relating to the Revolutionary History, State of New Jersey.* Edited by William S. Stryker. Trenton: The John L. Murphy Publishing Co., 1901. Series 2. 2:472–473. Kemp, Franklin W. *Nest of Rebel Pirates.*—2nd ed.—Egg Harbor City, N.J.: The Batsto Citizens Committee, The Laureate Press, 1993. p.30.

689. Stedman, C. (Charles). *The history of the origin, progress, and termination of the American war.* London: printed for the author, 1794; (Eyewitness accounts of the American Revolution) [New York]: New York Times ; Arno Press, c1969. 2:41–46. *The Pennsylvania Evening Post.* (October 9, 1778). *The Pennsylvania Packet.* (October 10, 1778). *Documents Relating to the Revolutionary History, State of New Jersey.* Edited by William S. Stryker. Trenton: The John L. Murphy Publishing Co., 1901. Series 2. 2:472–473; 487–88. Kemp, Franklin W. *Nest of Rebel Pirates.* 2nd ed. Egg Harbor

City, N.J.: The Batsto Citizens Committee, The Laureate Press, 1993, pp.30–31, 47–50. Heston, Alfred M. *Absegami*. Camden, N.J., 1904. pp.138–46. Livingston to Stirling, Oct. 11, 1778, Washington Papers 87.

690. *Documents Relating to the Revolutionary History, State of New Jersey*. Edited by William S. Stryker. Trenton: The John L. Murphy Publishing Co., 1901. Series 2. 2:577. Salter, Edwin. *Old Times in Old Monmouth*. Freehold, N.J.: Monmouth Democrat, 1874. p.202.

691. Hornor, William S. *This Old Monmouth of Ours*. Freehold, N.J.: Moreau Brothers, 1932. p.62. *Documents Relating to the Revolutionary History, State of New Jersey*. Edited by William S. Stryker. Trenton: The John L. Murphy Publishing Co., 1901. Series 2. 3:200.

692. *Documents Relating to the Revolutionary History, State of New Jersey*. Edited by William S. Stryker. Trenton: The John L. Murphy Publishing Co., 1901. Series 2. 3:201. Salter, Edwin. *Old Times in Old Monmouth*. Freehold, N.J.: Monmouth Democrat, 1874. p.195.

693. *The Royal Gazette*. 297 (August 4, 1779). *Documents Relating to the Revolutionary History, State of New Jersey*. Edited by William S. Stryker. Trenton: The John L. Murphy Publishing Co., 1901. Series 2. 3:537–538.

694. Extract of a letter dated Boston, November 18. *The New Jersey Gazette*. 2:102 (December 8, 1779) p.3.

695. Burgess, Paul C. *A Colonial Scrapbook, the Southern New Jersey Coast, 1675–1783*. New York: Carlton Press, 1971. p.177.

696. *The New-York Gazette; and The Weekly Mercury*. 1558 (August 27, 1781) p.3.

697. Salter, Edwin. *Old Times in Old Monmouth*. Freehold: Monmouth Democrat, 1874. p.213.

698. Ibid., 209–210; Hornor, William S. *This Old Monmouth of Ours*. Freehold, N.J.: Moreau Brothers, 1932. p.45.

699. *Documents Relating to the Revolutionary History, State of New Jersey*. Edited by William S. Stryker. Trenton: The John L. Murphy Publishing Co., 1901. Series 2. 3:398.

700. New Jersey Department of Defense Manuscripts 636A, Pension #2904, 2361.

701. *The Pennsylvania Packet*. (October 16, 1779). *Documents Relating to the Revolutionary History, State of New Jersey*. Edited by William S. Stryker. Trenton: The John L. Murphy Publishing Co., 1901. Series 2. 3:685.

702. *Documents Relating to the Revolutionary History, State of New Jersey*. Edited by William S. Stryker. Trenton: The John L. Murphy Publishing Co., 1901. Series 2. 4:113.

703. Ibid., pp.251–252; 280. *New Jersey History* 78:171.

704. *New Jersey Gazette*. 4:194 (September 12, 1781). *Documents Relating to the Revolutionary History, State of New Jersey*. Edited by William S. Stryker. Trenton: The John L. Murphy Publishing Co., 1901. Series 2. 5:290–291. Peckham, Howard Henry. *The Toll of Independence: Engagements & Battle Casualties of the American Revolution*. Chicago: University of Chicago Press, 1974. p.90.

705. *The Royal Gazette*. 371 (April 19, 1780). *Documents Relating to the Revolutionary History, State of New Jersey*. Edited by William S. Stryker. Trenton: The John L. Murphy Publishing Co., 1901. Series 2. 4:308.

706. *The Pennsylvania Gazette*. (October 11, 1780). *Documents Relating to the Revolutionary History, State of New Jersey*. Edited by William S. Stryker. Trenton: The John L. Murphy Publishing Co., 1901. Series 2. 5:19.

707. Vermeule, Cornelius C. Some Revolutionary Incidents in the Raritan Valley. *Proceedings New Jersey Historical Society*. New Series 6 (1921) pp.73–85.

708. *The New Jersey Gazette*. 5:248 (September 25, 1782) p.3.

709. Wilson, Harold Fisher. *The Jersey Shore*. New York: Lewis Historical Publishing Co. 1953. p.230. New Jersey Department of Defense Manuscripts.

710. *Connecticut Journal*. 764 (June 20, 1782) p.2.

711. *Royal Gazette*. 656 (January 8, 1783) p.2. *New Jersey Gazette*. 6:263 (January 8, 1783) p.3.

712. *The Newport Mercury*.1082 (June 22, 1782) p.2. *Salem Gazette*. 1:37 (June 27, 1782) p.3. *The New-Hampshire Gazette; or State Journal, and General Advertiser*. XXVI:1339 (June 29, 1782) p.2. *Documents Relating to the Revolutionary History, State of New Jersey*. Edited by William S. Stryker. Trenton: The John L. Murphy Publishing Co., 1901. Series 2. 5:446.

713. Salter, Edwin. *Old Times in Old Monmouth*. Freehold: Monmouth Democrat, 1874. 210–212. New Jersey Department of Defense Manuscripts.

Glossary

1. *Oxford English Dictionary*.

GLOSSARY

Abatis: Sharpened branches pointing out from a fortification at an angle toward the enemy to slow or disrupt an assault.

Accoutrement: Piece of military equipment carried by soldiers in addition to their standard uniform and weapons.

Bar shot: A double shot consisting of two half cannon balls joined by an iron bar, used in sea-warfare to damage masts and rigging (see Photo NJ-5).

Bastion: A fortification with a projecting part of a wall to protect the main walls of the fortification (see Photos NJ-11 and NJ-12).

Battalion: The basic organizational unit of a military force, generally 500 to 800 men. Most regiments consisted of a single battalion which was composed of 10 companies.

Bateau: A light flat-bottomed riverboat with sharply tapering stern and bow.

Battery: Two or more similar artillery pieces that function as a single tactical unit; a prepared position for artillery; an army artillery unit corresponding to a company in an infantry regiment. (See Photo NJ-12.)

Bayonet: A long, slender blade that can be attached to the end of a musket and used for stabbing.

Best bower: The large anchor (about 4,000 pounds) on the starboard side of the bow of a vessel. The other is called the small-bower. Also the cable attached to this anchor.

Blunderbuss: A short musket with a large bore and wide muzzle capable of holding a number of musket or pistol balls, used to fire shot with a scattering effect at close range. It is very effective for clearing a narrow passage, door of a house or staircase, or in boarding a ship.

Bomb: An iron shell, or hollow ball, filled with gunpowder. It has a large touch-hole for a slow-burning fuse which is held in place by pieces of wood and fastened with a cement made of quicklime, ashes, brick dust, and steel filings worked together with glutinous water. A bomb is shot from a mortar mounted on a carriage. It is fired in a high arc over fortifications and often detonates in the air, raining metal fragments with high velocity on the fort's occupants. (See Photo NJ-4.)

Bombproof: A structure built strong enough to protect the inhabitants from exploding bombs and shells.

Brig: A small two-masted sailing vessel with square-rigged sails on both masts.

Brigade: A military unit consisting of about 800 men.

Broadside: 1. The firing of all guns on one side of a vessel as nearly simultaneously as possible. 2. A large piece of paper printed on one side for advertisements or public notices.

Canister or Cannister shot: A kind of case-shot consisting of a number of small iron balls packed in sawdust in a cylindrical tin or canvas case. They were packed in four tiers between iron plates. (See Photo NJ-5.)

Carronade: A short, stubby piece of artillery, usually of large caliber, having a chamber for the powder like a mortar. It is chiefly used on shipboard.

Chain shot: A kind of shot formed of two balls, or half-balls, connected by a chain, chiefly used in naval warfare to destroy masts, rigging, and sails (see Photo NJ-5).

Chandeliers: Large and strong wooden frames used instead of a parapet. Fascines are piled on top of each other against it to cover workmen digging trenches. Sometimes they are only strong planks with two pieces of wood perpendicular to hold the fascines.

Chevaux-de-frise: Obstacles consisting of horizontal poles with projecting spikes to block a passageway. They were used on land and modified to block rivers to enemy ships. (See Photo NJ-34.)

Cohorn or coehorn: A short, small-barreled mortar for throwing grenades.

Company: The smallest military unit of the army consisting of about 45 to 110 men commanded by a captain, a lieutenant, and an ensign, and sometimes by a second lieutenant. A company usually has two sergeants, three or four corporals and two drums.

Crown forces: The allied forces supporting King George III. They consisted primarily of the British army, Hessian mercenaries, Loyalists, and Native Americans.

Cutter: 1. A single-masted sailing vessel similar to a sloop but having its mast positioned further aft. 2. A ship's boat, usually equipped with both sails and oars. In the 18th century, the terms sloop and cutter seem to have been used almost interchangeably.

Demilune: Fortification similar to a bastion but shaped as a crescent or half-moon rather than as an arrow.

Dragoon: A soldier who rode on horseback like cavalry. Dragoons generally fought dismounted in the 17th and 18th centuries.

Earthworks: A fortification made of earth (see Photos NJ-3, NJ-41).

Embrasure: A slanted opening in the wall or parapet of a fortification designed for the defender to fire through it on attackers (see Photos NJ-2, NJ-3).

Envelopment: An assault directed against an enemy's flank. An attack against two flanks is a double envelopment.

Espontoon: See **Spontoon.**

Fascine: A long bundle of sticks tied together, used in building earthworks and in strengthening ramparts (see Photo NJ-42).

Fraise: Sharpened stakes built into the exterior wall of a fortification to deter attackers (see Photo NJ-41).

Gabion: A cylindrical basket made of wicker and filled with earth for use in building fortifications (see Photo NJ-42).

Galley: A long boat propelled by oars. These boats had a shallow draft and were particularly useful in rivers, lakes, and other shallow bodies of water.

General engagement: An encounter, conflict, or battle in which the majority of a force is involved.

Grapeshot: A number of small iron balls tied together to resemble a cluster of grapes. When fired simultaneously from a cannon, the balls separate into multiple projectiles. The shot usually consisted of nine balls placed between two iron plates (see Photo NJ-5).

Grenadier: A soldier armed with grenades; a specially selected foot soldier in an elite unit selected on the basis of exceptional height and ability (see Photos NJ-7, NJ-10).

Gun: A cannon. Guns were referred to by the size of the shot they fired. A 3-pounder fired a 3-pound ball, a 6-pounder fired a 6-pound ball.

Gundalow: An open, flat bottomed vessel about 53 feet long, 15 feet wide, and almost 4 feet deep in the center. It is equipped with both sails and oars, designed to carry heavy loads, usually armed with one gun at the bow and two mid-ship.

Hessian: A German mercenary soldier who fought with the British army. Most of the German soldiers came from the kingdom of Hesse-Cassel, hence the name. Other German states that sent soldiers include Brunswick, Hesse-Hanau, Waldeck, Ansbach-Bayreuth, and Anhalt-Zerbst. (See Photos NJ-7, NJ-8.)

Howitzer: A cannon with a short barrel and a bore diameter greater than 30 mm and a maximum elevation of 60 degrees, used for firing shells at a high angle of elevation to reach a target behind cover or in a trench.

Hussars or **Huzzars:** Horse soldiers resembling Hungarian horsemen. They usually wore furred bonnets adorned with a cock's feather, a doublet with a pair of breeches, to which their stockings are fastened, and boots. They were armed with a saber, carbines, and pistols.

Jaeger: A hunter and gamekeeper who fought with the Hessians for the British army. They wore green uniforms, carried rifles, and were expert marksmen (see Photo NJ-8).

Jollyboat: A sailing vessel's small boat, such as a dinghy, usually carried on the stern. "A clincher-built ship's boat, smaller than a cutter, with a bluff bow and very wide transom, usually hoisted at the stern of the vessel, and used chiefly as a hack-boat for small work."[1]

Langrage: A particular kind of shot, formed of bolts, nails, bars, or other pieces of iron tied together, and forming a sort of cylinder, which corresponds with the bore of the cannon.

Letter of marque: A license granted by a monarch authorizing a subject to take reprisals on the subjects of a hostile state for alleged injuries. Later: Legal authority to fit out an armed vessel and use it in the capture of enemy merchant shipping and to commit acts which would otherwise have constituted piracy. See also **Privateer.**

Light infantry: Foot soldiers who carried lightweight weapons and minimal field equipment.

Loophole: Aperture or slot in defenses through which the barrels of small arms or cannon can be directed at an outside enemy. (See Photo NJ-15.)

Loyalist: An American who supported the British during the American Revolution; also called Tory.

Magazine: A structure to store weapons, ammunition, explosives, and other military equipment or supplies.

Man-of-war: A warship (see Photo NJ-27).

Matross: A private in an artillery unit who needed no specialized skills. Matrosses usually hauled cannon and positioned them. They assisted in the loading, firing, and sponging the guns.

Militia: Civilians who are part-time soldiers who take military training and can serve full-time for short periods during emergencies.

Minuteman: Member of a special militia unit, called a Minute Company. A minuteman pledged to be ready to fight at a minute's notice.

Mortar: A cannon with a relatively short and wide barrel, used for firing shells in a high arc over a short distance, particularly behind enemy defenses. They were not mounted on wheeled carriages. (See Photo NJ-9.)

Musket: A firearm with a long barrel, large caliber, and smooth bore. It was used between the 16th and 18th centuries, before rifling was invented.

Open order: A troop formation in which the distance between the individuals is greater than in close order (which is shoulder to shoulder). Also called extended order.

Parapet: Earthen or stone defensive platform on the wall of a fort.

Parley: A talk or negotiation, under a truce, between opposing military forces.

Parole: A promise given by a prisoner of war, either not to escape, or not to take up arms again as a condition of release. Individuals on parole can remain at home and conduct their normal occupations. Breaking parole makes one subject to immediate arrest and often execution. From the French *parole* which means one's word of honor.

Pettiauger or **pettyauger:** 1. A long, narrow canoe hollowed from the trunk of a single tree or from the trunks of two trees fastened together. 2. An open flat-bottomed schooner-rigged vessel or two-masted sailing barge, of a type used in North America and the Caribbean. (See Photo NJ-6.)

Pinnace: 1.A small light vessel, usually having two schooner-rigged (originally square-rigged) masts, often in attendance on a larger vessel and used as a tender or scout, to carry messages, etc. 2. A small boat, originally rowed with eight oars, later with sixteen, forming part of the equipment of a warship or other large vessel. It could also be navigated with a sail. (See Photo NJ-28.)

Polacre: A three-masted vessel with square-rigged sails and pole masts without tops and crosstrees.

Portage: An overland route used to transport a boat or its cargo from one waterway to another; the act of carrying a boat or its cargo from one waterway to another.

Privateer: An armed vessel owned and crewed by private individuals and holding a government commission known as a letter of marque authorizing the capture of merchant shipping belonging to an enemy nation. See **Letter of marque.**

Rampart: An earthen fortification made of an embankment and often topped by a low protective wall.

Ravelin: A small outwork fortification shaped like an arrowhead or a V that points outward in front of a larger defense work to protect the sally port or entrance.

Redoubt: A temporary fortification built to defend a prominent position such as a hilltop.

Regiment: A permanent military unit usually consisting of two or three companies. British regiments generally consisted of 10 companies, one of which was grenadiers. Some German regiments consisted of 2,000 men.

Regular: Belonging to or constituting a full-time professional military or police force as opposed to, for example, the reserves or militia.

Round shot: Spherical ball of cast-iron or steel for firing from smooth-bore cannon, a cannon ball. The shots were referred to by the weight of the ball: a 9-pound shot weighed 9 pounds; a 12-pound shot weighed 12 pounds. Round shot was used principally to batter fortifications. The balls could be heated ("hot shot") and fired at the hulls of ships or buildings to set them on fire. The largest balls (32- and 64-pounders) were sometimes called "big shot." (See Photo NJ-5.)

Sapper: A soldier who specializes in making entrenchments and tunnels for siege operations.

Schooner: A fast sailing ship with at least two masts and with fore and aft sails on all lower masts.

Scow: A flat-bottomed sailboat with a rectangular hull.

Sedan chair: A chair or windowed cabin suitable for a single occupant. It is borne on poles or wooden rails that pass through brackets on the sides of the chair. The two or more porters who bear the chair are called "chairmen." (See Photo NJ-33.)

Shell: An explosive projectile fired from a large-bore gun such as a howitzer or mortar. See also **Bomb, Howitzer,** and **Mortar.** (See Photo NJ-4.)

Ship of the line: A large warship with sufficient armament to enter combat with similar vessels in the line of battle. A ship of the line carried 60 to 100 guns. (See Photo NJ-27.)

Shot: A bullet or projectile fired from a weapon. See also: **Bar shot, Canister shot, Chain shot, Grapeshot, Round shot, Sliding bar shot, Star shot.** (See Photo NJ-5.)

Sliding bar shot: A projectile similar to a bar shot. A sliding bar shot has two interlocked bars that extend almost double the length of a bar shot, thereby increasing the potential damage to a ship's rigging and sails. (See Photo NJ-5.)

Sloop: A small single-masted sailing vessel with sails rigged fore-and-aft and guns on only one deck. In the 18th century, the terms sloop and cutter seem to have been used almost interchangeably.

Sloop of war: A three-masted, square-rigged naval vessel with all her guns mounted on a single uncovered main deck.

Snow: A small sailing-vessel resembling a brig, carrying a main and fore mast and a supplementary trysail mast close behind the mainmast; formerly employed as a warship.

Sons of Liberty: Patriots who belonged to secret organizations to oppose British attempts at taxation after 1765. They often resorted to violence and coercion to achieve their purposes.

Spike [a gun]: To destroy a cannon by hammering a long spike into the touch hole or vent, thereby rendering it useless.

Spontoon: A type of half-pike or halberd carried by infantry officers in the 18th century (from about 1740). (See Photo NJ-14.)

Stand of arms: A complete set of arms (musket, bayonet, cartridge box, and belt) for one soldier.

Star shot: A kind of chain-shot (see Photo NJ-5).

Tory: A Loyalist, also called refugee and Cow-Boy. The Whigs usually used the term in a derogatory manner.

Trunnions: Two pieces of metal sticking out of the sides of an artillery piece. They serve to hold the artillery piece on the carriage and allow it to be raised or lowered. The trunnions are generally as long as the diameter of the cannonball and have the same diameter.

Whig: Somebody who supported independence from Great Britain during the American Revolution. The name comes from the British liberal political party that favored reforms and opposed many of the policies of the King and Parliament related to the American War for Independence.

INDEX

Other titles in the
BATTLEGROUNDS OF FREEDOM series
by Norman Desmarais

Battlegrounds of Freedom: A Historical Guide to the Battlefields of the War of American Independence. 2005. This fascinating travelogue invites readers to re-enact each battle with maps and photos, well-written text, abundant notation of websites, and many other useful references. This comprehensive work covers Maine to Georgia as well as western territories. 260 pages, 19 maps, 109 photos. Paperback. 0-9666196-7-6. $26.95.

The Guide to the Revolutionary War in Canada and New England: Battles, Raids, and Skirmishes. 2009. Follow along as the author retraces every encounter of the Revolutionary War in Canada and New England along geographical lines. 262 pages, 8 maps, 49 photos. Paperback. 978-1-934934-01-2. $21.95.

The Guide to the Revolutionary War in New York: Battles, Raids, and Skirmishes. 2010. Follow along as the author retraces every encounter of the Revolutionary War in New York along geographical lines. 283 pages, 4 maps, 37 photos. Paperback. 978-1-934934-02-9. $22.95.

All titles available at www.buscainc.com or from book vendors everywhere

CPSIA information can be obtained
at www.ICGtesting.com
Printed in the USA
LVHW030737310719
625976LV00001B/262